THE CEMENT OF SOCIETY

STUDIES IN RATIONALITY
AND SOCIAL CHANGE

STUDIES IN RATIONALITY AND SOCIAL CHANGE

Editors: Jon Elster and Michael S. McPherson

Editorial Board:
Fredrik Barth
Amartya Sen
Arthur Stinchcombe
Amos Tversky
Bernard Williams

Jon Elster

THE CEMENT OF SOCIETY

A Study of Social Order

The right of the
University of Cambridge
to print and sell
all manner of books
was granted by
Henry VIII in 1534.
The University has printed
and published continuously
since 1584.

Cambridge University Press

Cambridge

New York   Port Chester   Melbourne   Sydney

Published by the Press Syndicate of the University of Cambridge
The Pitt Building, Trumpington Street, Cambridge CB2 1RP
32 East 57th Street, New York, NY 10022, USA
10 Stamford Road, Oakleigh, Melbourne 3166, Australia

First published 1989

Printed in the United States of America

Library of Congress Cataloging-in-Publication Data
Elster, Jon, 1940–
The cement of society : a study of social order / Jon Elster.
p.   cm. – (Studies in rationality and social change)
Bibliography: p.
Includes index.
ISBN 0-521-37456-1. – ISBN 0-521-37607-6 (pbk.)
1. Collective bargaining – Sweden.   2. Rational expectations
(Economics).   3. Social choice.   4. Social norms.   I. Title.
II. Series.
HD6757.E47 1989   89-30987
305 – dc 19   CIP

British Library Cataloging in Publication Data
Elster, Jon, 1940–
The cement of society : a study of social order. –
(Studies in rationality and social change)
1. Social interactions
I. Title   II. Series
302

ISBN 0-521-37456-1 hard covers
ISBN 0-521-37607-6 paperback

Contents

Preface and acknowledgements

This book has a complicated genesis. For many years, I have been interested in the problem of collective action. Discussions with Brian Barry and Russell Hardin helped me to see roughly where the main problems were located, but I never seemed to get them fully into focus. Concurrently with this preoccupation, and spurred largely by proddings from Amos Tversky and Fredrik Engelstad, I became increasingly puzzled by the relation between rational choice and social norms. I discussed this problem with Pierre Bourdieu, and together we organized a conference on the topic. Once again, I seemed to make progress up to a point, and then confusion descended on me. Clearly, I was going against the grain.

The catalyst for further progress came in 1985, when Nils Elvander of the Swedish Council for Management and Work Life Issues (FA-Rådet) asked me to write a report on bargaining and collective action in the context of their project on collective wage bargaining in Sweden. I accepted in the belief, mistaken as it turned out, that my earlier work on rational-choice theory might help me explain the strategies, stratagems and outcomes of collective bargaining. It soon became clear that the complexity of these bargaining problems defies explicit modelling. My analytical skills, in any case, were not sufficient to reduce the moving, fluid process of collective bargaining to manageable proportions. In the Swedish system of collective bargaining, as I try to explain in Chapters 4 and 6, everything is up for grabs: the identity of the actors, the rules of the game, the set of payoffs, the range of acceptable arguments. The more I understood what was going on, the lower I had to set my sights. The initial aim of explanation was gradually transformed into one of 'thick' phenomenological description. Yet I came to see that here was a set of problems that lent themselves ideally to an exploration of the relation between individual and collective rationality, and between self-interest and social norms. Things that had been out of focus suddenly came together.

More or less simultaneously with this work I completed two other books that complement the present one. Each of them reflects an increasing disillusionment with the power of reason, be it at the level of social actors or at the level of the social scientist who is observing them. In *Solomonic Judgements* I argue that rational-choice theory yields indeterminate prescriptions and predictions in more cases than most social scientists and decision makers would like to think. In *Nuts and Bolts for the Social Sciences*, written for a more general audience, I argue that the basic concept in the social sciences should be that of a *mechanism* rather than of a *theory*. In my opinion, the social sciences are light years away from the stage at which it will be possible to formulate general-law-like regularities about human behaviour. Instead, we should concentrate on specifying small and medium-sized mechanisms for human action and interaction – plausible, frequently observed ways in which things happen. If this sounds vague (and it does), I have to refer the reader to the substance of the three books for proof of the pudding.

The level of discussion may puzzle some readers. It may be too technical for some and insufficiently rigorous for others. Martin Heidegger is reported to have dismissed an argument by saying, 'Nicht tief genug gefragt'. On the other side of the Atlantic or the Channel, dismissal often takes the form of asserting, 'Not clear enough to be wrong'. Many of my arguments will be dismissed on both counts. I can only hope that what is lost in depth and clarity is partially compensated by variety and diversity.

I have benefited greatly from comments I received when presenting parts of this material at the European University Institute (Florence), at the Ecole Normale Supérieure (Paris), at Gary Becker and James Coleman's Rational Choice Seminar at the University of Chicago, at the Philosophy Department of the University of California at San Diego and to the annual meeting of the 'September Group' in London. I am grateful to Jens Andvig, Kenneth Arrow, Lars Calmfors, G. A. Cohen, Michael Dennis, Nils Elvander, Fredrik Engelstad, Aanund Hylland, John Padgett, Philippe van Parijs, Adam Przeworski, Ariel Rubinstein and Michael Wallerstein for comments on earlier drafts of several chapters. Special thanks are due to Stephen Holmes and Cass Sunstein for making detailed written comments on the whole manuscript, to Karl Ove Moene for unfailing patience in teaching me the basics of noncooperative bargaining theory and to Aanund Hylland for doing his best to keep me intellectually honest. Steve Laymon's skilful and imaginative research assistance has been invaluable. A final acknowledgement is owed to Thomas Schelling, whose work on bargaining and collective action serves as a model and inspiration for all who work in this area.

Introduction: the two problems
of social order

Hume wrote, in the abstract to the *Treatise of Human Nature*, that causality is the 'cement of the universe'. What ensures order in the physical world is that events of one type invariably follow upon events of another type. In this book, I discuss the conditions for order in the social world. What is it that glues societies together and prevents them from disintegrating into chaos and war? It is a big problem, second to none in importance. I do not claim to provide a complete answer, nor are the partial answers I offer very deep ones. At the present time, the social sciences cannot aspire to be more than social chemistry: inductive generalizations that stick closely to the phenomena. The time for social physics is not yet here, and may never come.[1]

I shall discuss two concepts of social order: that of stable, regular, predictable patterns of behaviour and that of cooperative behaviour. Correspondingly, there are two concepts of disorder. The first, disorder as lack of predictability, is expressed in *Macbeth*'s vision of life as 'sound and fury, a tale told by an idiot, signifying nothing'.[2] The second, disorder as absence of cooperation, is expressed in Hobbes's vision of life in the state of nature as 'solitary, poor, nasty, brutish, and short'. Instead of referring to predictability and cooperation, economists talk about equilibrium and Pareto optimality. For reasons that will emerge later, I do not adopt this

---

[1] 'Physics is parsimonious. A few basic ideas have a validity that extends across nature from the smallness of the atom to the vastness of the galaxy. Furthermore, these basic ideas capture a variety of factual information in the network of logical connections between them. The person who sees charm and beauty in the ideas of physics may see no enchantment whatsoever in chemistry. Lacking the simple predictive principles that are the stock in trade of physics, chemists are marvelous in their ability to hold in their heads at all times a vast array of information. Physicists, on the other hand, work from a base formed by a few remembered ideas' (Rigden 1987, pp. 36–7).

[2] This kind of disorder may, but need not, imply that the agents are uncertain about what to do. An agent may have a dominant strategy that leaves him in no doubt about what to do, but he may still be ignorant or entertain false beliefs about what others will do. In that case, he may feel *surprise* when the outcome materializes, but never *regret*.

terminology. In Chapter 3 I argue that social norms ensure predictability outside equilibrium and in Chapter 5 that cooperation can lead to Pareto-inferior outcomes.

Disorder as failure to predict is dramatically illustrated by the stock market plunge of October 1987. Even though some analysts could, after the fact, truthfully say, 'I told you so', and even prove that they have put their money where their mouth was, similar Cassandras could probably have been found had the crash occurred six or twelve or twenty-four months earlier. Several writers have suggested[3] that the stock market may be a *chaotic* regime, in the technical sense of a system which is

characterized by three attributes that can have extremely disturbing implications for the use of econometric forecasting procedures: a) Even though a time series is generated entirely deterministically its behavior is statistically very simliar to that of a system subject to severe random shocks; b) chaotic time series may proceed for substantial intervals of time manifesting patterns of behavior which seem extremely orderly, when a totally new pattern appears without warning, only to disappear just as unexpectedly; c) the presence and location of such abrupt transitions are extremely sensitive to parameter values in the underlying model, appearing and disappearing with changes in the third or higher decimal places, which are beyond anything econometrics may be able to aspire to discover.[4]

I am not sure, however, that this is the right direction in which to look for the sources of unpredictability. The nonlinear difference or differential equations that generate chaos rarely have good microfoundational credentials.[5] The fact that the analyst's model implies a chaotic regime is of little interest if there are no prior theoretical reasons to believe in the model in the first place. If, in addition, one implication of the theory is that it cannot be econometrically tested, there are no posterior reasons to take it seriously either.

To understand the problem of unpredictability we should look instead at the structure of social action and interaction.[6] Sometimes people have too little knowledge about others to anticipate what they will do and hence to

---

[3] See the interviews in Gleick (1987).   [4] Baumol and Quandt (1985), p. 3.
[5] This is true, e.g., of the models in Day (1983) and Bhaduri and Harris (1987).
[6] See also Sen (1986).

predict the outcome. Sometimes they have too much knowledge. Sometimes they fail to use the knowledge they have. And sometimes no amount of knowledge, however ingeniously used, can help them. Let me illustrate these four cases, *assuming throughout that people are rational.* In Chapter 3 I discuss how nonrational behaviour may lend stability and regularity to situations that would otherwise be in hopeless flux.

Often, people have seriously incomplete information about each other's rationality, preferences and information. This need not be a destabilizing element. The president of the United States does not know whether the leaders of the Soviet Union would behave rationally in a crisis – for example, whether they would refrain from executing a threat which, at that time, it would not be in their interest to carry out. He does not know the preferences of his Soviet counterparts. (Do they really want world hegemony? Or do they simply want to be left in peace in their own backyard?) And he does not know what their beliefs are concerning his rationality, preferences and information. If, nevertheless, the balance of terror has been fairly stable, it is probably because both parties have made worst-case assumptions about each other, acting on their knowledge about the other party's objective capabilities rather than on any assumptions about subjective states of mind. There is order and predictability in spite of uncertainty and ignorance. (Indeed, more knowledge could make the situation less stable, as explained later.) By contrast, East–West relations have not been known to be orderly in the second sense, that of cooperative behaviour. Although the superpowers have avoided mutual destruction, the agreements on mutually beneficial arms reduction are recent and quite limited in scope.

Often, however, mutual ignorance *is* destabilizing. Consider, for instance, the cobweb cycle generated by people acting on the assumption that current prices will remain in force in the next period. If current prices exceed the equilibrium price, producers will market an above-equilibrium volume in the next period, thus forcing prices down. Assuming that prices will remain low, they will market little in the third period, forcing prices up again, and so on in a cycle that may converge to the equilibrium or diverge from it. Expectations are never fulfilled, and plans never realized. The culprit here is the producer's ignorance about consumers and about other producers. He does not know the full demand schedule. Nor does he know how other producers would react if they knew the schedule, because he does not know what they assume about each other. Under these circum-

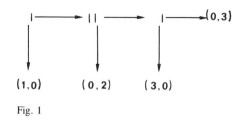

Fig. 1

stances, he might as well assume that prices will remain constant, without being under the illusion that this is any kind of mathematical expectation.[7] The status quo serves as a focal point for belief formation. Like the worst-case hypothesis, assuming perpetuation of the status quo is neither rational nor irrational. It is a maxim for decision making under uncertainty which, in this case, happens to undermine itself when adopted by many people simultaneously.

A surfeit of information can be destabilizing if it is beyond the processing capacities of the agent or organization receiving it. In a complex world, this problem arises frequently and can be quite important from a practical point of view. Theoretically, however, there is not much to say about it. It is more interesting and surprising that apparently simple strategic situations can be indeterminate if the agents are fully informed about each other, yet acquire determinacy if the information falls short of completeness. I shall illustrate this case with an analysis of games in extensive form, the putatively rational outcomes of which are determined by the method of backward induction.[8] Since this method is at the core of the modern approach to iterated games and bargaining, both of which are discussed extensively in later chapters, any doubts about its validity will have important repercussions.

Rather than define backward induction explicitly, I shall illustrate it by means of an example. Consider the game between two players depicted in Fig. 1.[9] There is *common knowledge* that both are rational: both are rational, and know each other to be rational, and know each other to know each other to be rational, and so on. The nature of the game is also common knowledge.

One player moves at a time, beginning with player I. Either he can move down and terminate the game, in which case he gets 1 and player II gets

[7] Keynes (1936), p. 151.
[8] According to Ståhl (1988) this method is due to Zermelo (1912).
[9] The example is taken from Bicchieri (1987).

nothing, or he can decide to continue the game to the second node, leaving the next move to II. She can similarly terminate the game, ensuring 2 for herself and nothing for I, or continue the game to the third node. There, I has a choice between two ways of terminating the game. One ensures 3 to himself and nothing to the other, while the other has the opposite payoffs. It seems clear enough what will happen: I will move down on his first play and the game will end right there. To justify this conclusion, one traditionally invokes the principle of backward induction, reasoning from the last stage of the game back to the first. At the beginning of the game, I contemplates what he would do if he were at the last node of the game tree. He would, obviously, move down rather than across. Knowing that II knows him to be rational, I anticipate that at the second node II will play down, to get 2 rather than 0, which is what she would get if she played across. But that anticipation forces I to move down in the first move, to get 1 rather than 0, which is what he would get if he played across.

This reasoning seems compelling. But it harbours a problem: *why would I contemplate being at the third node?* How could he ever find himself there, if rational players would terminate the game at the first node? The issue turns on the use of counterfactual arguments: under what circumstances can we draw conclusions from premises known to be false? I have argued elsewhere[10] that counterfactuals are assertable when the additional premises used to draw conclusions from the counterfactual antecedent are consistent with that antecedent itself. We cannot, for instance, assert that in the absence of the railroad, economic growth would have been much the same because the automobile would have been invented earlier, if that assertion rests on a theory of technical change that would also allow us to predict the invention of the railroad. Similarly, we cannot assert that I will play down if the third node is reached if that claim is based on an assumption of I's rationality which is inconsistent with that node being reached.

The question, therefore, can be restated as follows. Does there exist a set of assumptions about the players which are strong enough to allow us to infer what the players would do at various nodes in the game while also weak enough to be consistent with these nodes being reached? I have argued that the assumption of rationality and common knowledge is too strong to satisfy the second requirement. Other assumptions may, in special cases, satisfy both requirements.[11]

---

[10] Elster (1978), ch. 6.
[11] The following draws on Binmore (1987a), summarizing the work of Selten, Kreps and Wilson and others. See also Rubinstein (1988a) for perceptive comments.

Fig. 2

1. Player I could assume that the later nodes have been reached as a result of mistakes (the 'trembling hand' assumption). The third node might be reached, that is, if there were some probability that a player might, as it were, push the wrong button. If we consider a game similar to the one in Fig. 1, but extended to a hundred successive moves, this assumption becomes extremely implausible, because it would require each player to make fifty uncorrelated errors before arriving at the final node.

2. A second assumption, therefore, is that the errors are correlated, for example, that II is irrational. From the point of view of player I, asking himself how he might have reached the final mode, it makes more sense to assume that II always moves across (the 'automaton' assumption) and that he has reached the final node by exploiting II's irrationality.

3. Player I might consider a more elaborate possibility, namely that II is either an irrational automaton or a rational player who is deliberately pretending to be irrational in order to induce I to play across rather than down. In the game portrayed in Fig. 1 this assumption has no purchase, but in the game depicted in Fig. 2 it could provide a plausible explanation of why later nodes in the game tree might be reached.

To explain why he might find himself at the third node, I may assign probability p to II being an automaton who always moves across and probability $1 - p$ to II being a rational agent who fakes automatic behaviour in the earlier stages of the game in order to induce I to move across so that she can move down in later stages.

4. We may weaken the assumption that the rationality of the players is common knowledge.[12] In the game portrayed in Fig. 1, we now assume only that I believes that II is rational, that II believes that I is rational and that I believes that II believes that I is rational. When I contemplates being at the third node, he must ask himself whether this assumption is consistent

[12] This argument is due to Bicchieri (1987).

with the belief set. In particular, could II have played across at the second node? To answer this question, he must first explain how she could make sense out of being at the second node. By virtue of the stipulated belief structure, he cannot explain it by assuming that she believes him to be irrational, but he may assume that she believes him to believe her to be irrational, for in that case she might reason that he has played across at the first node in the hope that she might do so at the second. Now, he knows that if the second node is reached, she will in fact play down, as he believes her to believe him to be rational and hence will expect him to play down at the third node. Accordingly, he plays down at the first node. The backward induction argument works, but only because the players' rationality is *not* common knowledge. If the players have less initial knowledge about each other, they can form stable beliefs about each other's behaviour.

Assumptions 1 through 4 differ as follows. Assumption 1 stipulates that I entertains a certain subjective probability that II, while rational, is fallible. Assumption 2 stipulates that I entertains a certain subjective probability that II is an irrational automaton. Assumption 3 stipulates that if, in fact, II is rational she will be aware of I's probability assessment and try to exploit it to her advantage, and that I knows that if II is rational she will be aware of it, and so on. Assumption 4 stipulates that the players are rational and infallible, but that their knowledge about each other's rationality, and knowledge about this knowledge and so on, has an upper limit. Each assumption may, in special cases and under special conditions, provide what we are looking for: a theory which is strong enough to allow us to infer what rational players will do at the various nodes and weak enough to be consistent with their being at those nodes. But none of the assumptions seems to have the simplicity and generality that could support backward induction in a more general context. As a consequence, that principle itself is more vulnerable than appears at first glance.

I suspect that the last word on backward induction has not been said. In later chapters I shall, with some qualms, retain the principle, partly because I am not sure my understanding of these matters is sufficiently deep to allow me to discard it altogether, and partly because the principle may be behaviourally adequate when agents are less than perfectly rational.[13] The fallacy in the backward induction argument, like the fallacies in many

[13] 'My experience suggests that mathematically trained persons recognize the logical validity of the [backward induction] argument, but they refuse to accept it as a guide to practical behavior' (Selten 1978b, p. 133). See also Rubinstein (1988b).

other counterfactual arguments, is so subtle that it may not be perceived by ordinary agents going about their business. The problem awaits further theoretical and empirical clarification. Predictive failures may also occur because people fail to make good use of information which they have. This is irrationality rather than indeterminacy of rationality. In the 1972 presidential campaign, for instance,

> on election eve a large group of the reporters following the McGovern campaign sagely agreed that McGovern could not lose by more than 10 points. These people were wire service reporters, network television reporters, and major newspaper and newsmagazine reporters. They knew that all the major polls had McGovern trailing by 20 points, and they knew that in 24 years not a single major poll had been wrong by more than 3%. However, they had seen with their own eyes wildly enthusiastic crowds of tens of thousands of people acclaim McGovern.[14]

Securities and futures markets also attach excessive importance to current information and insufficient importance to information about the past.[15] A converse fallacy – trying too hard to understand the past – can also lead to predictive failure. For any given set of events in the past, it is usually possible, by looking around for some time, to find some other event set that correlates highly with it. If one requires a 5 per cent significance level, twenty attempts will on the average be sufficient. The chances are, however, that correlations obtained in this way will be spurious and useless for predictive purposes. 'The price that investment analysts pay for overfitting is their long-run failure to predict any better than market averages'.[16]

Finally, some situations are inherently unpredictable. No matter how much or how little information the agents have, and no matter how ingeniously they use it, they will not be able to predict what others will do. I assume that for prediction among and by rational agents to be possible, the predicted outcome must be an equilibrium, that is, a state in which no agent has an incentive to behave differently. Failures of predictability may then occur for three reasons: some situations have no equilibrium; some have multiple equilibria; and some have equilibria which are too unstable to serve as the basis for prediction. The first category is not, perhaps, more than a curiosum,[17] but the other two are quite important.

[14] Nisbett et al. (1982), p. 116. [15] Arrow (1982). [16] Fischhoff (1982), p. 345.
[17] An example is the game in which each person writes down a number and the person who has written down the largest number gains the difference between his number and the

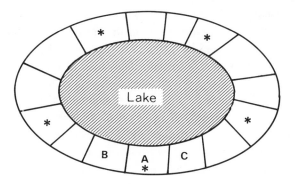

Fig. 3

Games with multiple equilibria that have different winners and losers can be unfathomable. Consider a number of peasant families with plots arranged alongside each other around a lake.[18] The peasants do not have enough cultivated land and would like to fell the trees on their plot, but know that deforestation may bring erosion. Specifically, erosion will occur on any given plot (*A* in Fig. 3) if and only if trees are felled on that plot and on the two adjoining ones (*B* and *C*). Here there are three equilibria, in each of which trees remain standing on every third plot around the lake. One equilibrium, in which trees are felled on the starred plots, is shown in Fig. 3. There is no tacit coordination mechanism, however, by which one of the three equilibria could emerge as the predictable outcome.

Voting – discussed more extensively in Chapter 5 – is another situation with multiple equilibria. The value of voting to the individual depends on how many other people vote. If everybody else votes, the individual has no incentive to do so, since the chance of his being pivotal is negligible. If nobody else votes, he has a strong incentive to do so, since he can decide the outcome by himself. An equilibrium has an intermediate number of voters, each of whom prefers voting to not voting but would prefer not voting to voting if one additional person voted. If there are *n* voters altogether and *m* voters in equilibrium, the number of equilibria equals the number of ways one can select *m* people from a set of *n*. Since *m* is usually small, elections with large electorates will have very many equilibria.

average of all numbers. Decentralized wage bargaining with no holds barred could provide a real-life illustration. Assuming that firms can shift any cost increases onto consumers, workers in each industry or firm have an incentive to ask for higher wage increases than those obtained by other workers. Something like this may happen in hyperinflation.

[18] For a fuller discussion of this example, see Elster (1989b), chs. 9 and 10.

A very general weakness of rational expectation models in economics is that they tend to have multiple equilibria.[19] For an individual, the possibility that there are several predictions he might make, each of which would be self-fulfilling, poses no problem.[20] He can simply make the prediction whose outcome he prefers. A group of individuals who know that if they all act on one set of expectations these will come out true, and if all act on another set these, too, will be verified, are in a more difficult predicament. In special cases they may be able to coordinate their actions. If one set of expectations yields an outcome preferred by everybody, it will be chosen. Also, asymmetries of power can stabilize the situation and ensure coordination around a cooperative equlibrium. The peasants around the lake might achieve coordination through bargaining, if some of them have other plots not threatened by erosion. Because they can survive without their plot by the lake, they can credibly announce that they are felling trees on their land and that others will have to adjust to their actions.[21] But there is no general mechanism for ensuring coordination when there are several equilibria with different winners and losers.[22]

Many games have no equilibrium in pure strategies. Investment in research and development is a plausible example.[23] The only equilibria such games admit consist of mixed strategies, defined as a probability distribution over a subset of the pure strategies. Now, we do not often observe people using lotteries to make decisions in non-zero-sum interactions,[24] and for good reasons. It can be shown that in equilibria with mixed strategies an individual can do no worse for himself — although by definition no better — by using any other probabilistic combination of the pure strategies that enter into his equilibrium strategy, as long as others stick to their equilibrium strategies. The tiniest flicker of uncertainty or ignorance could then induce a shift to his maximin strategy: it will protect him if others

[19] See, e.g., Begg (1982).   [20] Elster (1984), pp. 48, 106.
[21] This principle of 'justice according to Saint Matthew' — to him that hath shall be given — is further discussed in Chapter 2.
[22] Harsanyi and Selten (1988) is a book-length attempt to confront and solve this problem. Yet as observed by Robert Aumann in his foreword to their book, 'Although the theory selects a unique equilibrium, as a theory it need not be unique'. Indeed, their solution concept may be seen as representing one of several *reflective equilibria* in the sense of Rawls (1971). Hence it is not clear that their theory will have much predictive and explanatory power, unless or until it is adopted by economic agents in their decision making.
[23] Dasgupta and Stiglitz (1980).
[24] Elster (1989a), ch. 2, has a survey of the use of lotteries in decision making. See also Rubinstein (1988a) for some further critical comments on the explanatory value of mixed strategies.

deviate from equilibrium (as they will if they reason in the same manner) and it cannot harm him if they do not.[25] We might expect randomization in zero-sum games, in which the equilibrium strategy *is* the maximin strategy, but not in the vastly more important non-zero-sum games. But the agent cannot confidently predict that others will switch to maximin, for then he could exploit that knowledge and choose the strategy that was optimal against the maximin behaviour of others. In that case, however, he would have to contemplate the possibility that others, being in the same situation, would act similarly, thus undoing the premises of his action. The situation is inherently and essentially unpredictable.

Consider now disorder in the second sense, as lack of cooperation. This is the main topic of the present book. Numerous examples will be given later, and various causes of cooperative failures will be distinguished. Here I make some introductory and classificatory remarks, distinguishing among *five main varieties of cooperation:* externalities, helping, conventions, joint ventures and private ordering.

Some forms of cooperation rely on the *externalities* created by individual action. Here it makes sense to talk about individual acts of cooperation: cleaning up litter, curtailing production (as part of a cartel agreement), voting, paying one's taxes, donating blood. People might not want to cooperate in this sense unless they expect others to reciprocate, but reciprocation is not required for cooperative behaviour to be effective. Each act of cooperation brings a small benefit to everybody, including the cooperator. Although the direct benefits to the contributor are too small to motivate him to act, given that there are costs to cooperation, it is better for all if all (or at least some) cooperate than if nobody does. Under universal cooperation, each individual is the target of many small contributions from others, adding up to an amount in excess of the cost of his contribution.

Another category I call *helping behaviour:* assisting a neighbour with the harvest, keeping a promise, telling the truth. On any given occasion, this need not benefit the cooperator at all. Nor are the benefits diffused over a large number of other people. Yet if all help others when they can do so at little cost to themselves, all are better off than they would be if nobody ever helped anyone.[26] As in the first case, cooperation, if undertaken, ben-

---

[25] And even if he is (irrationally) confident that others will stick to the equilibrium, why should he do so? If he is truly indifferent among all probability combinations of the pure strategies, why should he choose the one that realizes equilibrium?

[26] Helping others and keeping promises (repaying loans) are among the examples of the categorical imperative given by Kant in the *Grundlegung*.

efits others whether or not they reciprocate. But it might not be undertaken unless others are expected to return the favour.[27]

A third category is that of *convention equilibria*. As mentioned earlier, in equilibrium no one can improve his outcome by unilaterally deviating from it. An additional feature of a convention equilibrium is that no one would want anyone else to deviate from it either.[28] (Convention equilibria are also characterized by a *strict* preference for one's own and others' conformity to the convention, whereas the ordinary equilibrium concept requires only weak preference.) The rule of driving on the right side of the road generates a convention equilibrium.[29] So does the rule that governs the night life of Brooklyn wiseguys: 'Everybody who had a girl friend took her out on Friday night. Nobody took his wife out on Friday night. The wives went out on Saturday night. That way there were no accidents of running into somebody's wife when they were with their girl friends'.[30]

Often, conventions are equivalent: it is important to have one, but it does not matter which it is. Sometimes, however, one of several possible conventions is Pareto-superior to the others. Although there is no convention that designates the person who should ring up again if a telephone call is accidentally interrupted, it would clearly be useful to have one. It could designate the person who made the call in the first place or the person who received it. Of these, the first is clearly superior, since only the person who made the first call would always know which number to call.

In other, more important cases, different conventions have different winners and losers. Legal systems are usually of this kind. Everybody would rather have some law – virtually any – than no law. Whatever the law is, and assuming that sanctions work properly, everybody would prefer to abide by the law and to have everyone else abide by it.[31] But different groups might have different preferences as to the substance of the law. The weak and the strong, for instance, have a common interest in laws protecting property. The weak prefer a regime that assures them of private property in their own labour power *and* some property rights in external objects

---

[27] See also Popkin (1979); Elster (1985d), sec. 6.2; M. Taylor, ed. (1988); and, of course, Olson (1965).

[28] Lewis (1969). Sugden (1986) proposes a weaker definition.

[29] It is sometimes said that *social norms* are convention equilibria, 'traffic rules of social life'. In Chapter 3 I argue that the similarity is superficial and misleading.

[30] Pileggi (1987), p. 90.

[31] Actually, I do not think that law-abiding behaviour is purely a function of optimally designed legal sanctions. The law is also enforced by social norms. These may in turn be enforced by sanctions, which are not, however, legal. In Chapter 3 I also argue that social norms cannot be wholly reduced to external sanctions.

over a regime that gives them only the former right, but they also prefer that minimal regime over the absence of any regime. The strong prefer the minimal regime, which facilitates the accumulation of wealth, over the more inclusive regime, but they prefer the latter over a lawless state of nature. For the purposes of accumulating wealth, social democracy is more efficient than slavery, even though unfettered capitalism is even better. Unlike the weak, however, the strong would survive in the state of nature. Hence they can impose the minimal regime, since they can credibly threaten to withdraw to the state of nature.

A further category of cooperation is that of *joint ventures,* in which physical collaboration between the parties is required to produce a cooperative surplus. In these cases, unilateral action has literally no impact on the outcome. A paradigm example is the division of labour, as in Adam Smith's pin factory. The collective of workers produce more together than they could do separately, but only on the condition that all make their contribution. If one man is missing, the productivity of all the others falls to zero. Conversely, an extra man makes no difference to the output. In more general production functions there are no strict complementarities, but it remains true that a positive marginal product of a given factor requires a non-zero level of each of the other factors of production.

A wonderful example of division of labour as a joint venture is given by Garrison Keillor in *Lake Wobegon Days,* in which he describes Flag Day in his mythical town. Herman, the organizer of the parade, bought a quantity of blue, red and white caps and distributed them to the townspeople so that they would march through the streets as a Living Flag, while he stood on the roof of the Central Building to take a photograph. Right after the war, people were happy to comply, but later they had second thoughts:

> One cause of resentment was the fact that none of them got to see the Flag they were in; the picture in the paper was black and white. Only Herman and Mr. Hanson got to see the real Flag, and some boys too short to be needed down below. People wanted a chance to go up to the roof and witness the spectacle for themselves.
> 'How can you go up there if you're supposed to be down here?' Herman said.
> 'You go up there to look, you got nothing to look at. Isn't it enough to know that you're doing your part?'
> On Flag Day, 1949, just as Herman said, 'That's it! Hold it now!'

one of the reds made a break for it – dashed up four flights of stairs to the roof and leaned over and had a long look. Even with the hole he left behind, it was a magnificent sight. The Living Flag filled the street below. A perfect Flag! The red so brilliant! He couldn't take his eyes off it. 'Get down here! We need a picture!' Herman yelled up to him. 'How does it look?' people yelled up to him. 'Unbelievable! I can't describe it', he said.

So then everyone had to have a look. 'No!' Herman said, but they took a vote and it was unanimous. One by one, members of the Living Flag went up to the roof and admired it. It was marvelous! It brought tears to the eyes, it made one reflect on this great country and on Lake Wobegon's place in it all. One wanted to stand up there all afternoon and just drink it in. So, as the first hour passed, and only forty of the five hundred had been to the top, the others got more and more restless. 'Hurry up! Quit dawdling! You've seen it! Get down here and give someone else a chance!' Herman sent people up in groups of four, and then ten, but after two hours, the Living Flag became the Sitting Flag and then began to erode, as the members who had had a look thought about heading home to supper, which infuriated the ones who hadn't. 'Ten more minutes!' Herman cried, but ten minutes became twenty and thirty, and people snuck off and the Flag that remained for the last viewer was a Flag shot through by cannon fire.

In 1950, the Sons of Knute took over Flag Day. Herman gave them the boxes of caps. Since then, the Knutes have achieved several good Flags, though most years the attendance was poor. You need at least four hundred to make a good one. Some years the Knutes made a 'no-look' rule, other years they held a lottery. One year they experimented with a large mirror held by two men over the edge of the roof, but when people leaned back and looked up, the flag disappeared, of course.[32]

In joint ventures the parties agree on physical collaboration. *Private orderings* offer mutually beneficial agreements that do not depend on physical collaboration, but only on the voluntary transfer of rights for the purpose of creating a surplus. Bilateral exchange is a simple example. As in the case of joint ventures, private ordering has no place for unilateral co-operation; indeed, the very notion loses its meaning. Private orderings are

[32] Keillor (1986), pp. 123–4.

often the prelude to a joint venture: before the worker mixes his labour power with the capital equipment, there is a contract transferring some of the rights over the labour power to the owner of the equipment.

Very roughly speaking, collective action theory (Chapter 1) deals with the first two kinds of cooperation, while bargaining theory (Chapter 2) deals with the last three. Collective action theory identifies the free-rider problem as the main obstacle to cooperation. Bargaining theory suggests that the main problem is failure to agree on the division of the benefits from cooperation. This is, however, to speak very roughly. A main argument of the book is that *collective action failures often occur because bargaining breaks down.* Often, it would be absurd to ask everybody to contribute equally to a public good. Some need it more than others, or can better afford to contribute. The size of their contributions will then be the topic of bargaining. Sometimes it is pointless or even harmful if everyone makes a contribution. Who shall contribute and who shall be allowed to take a free ride will then be a topic of bargaining. In either case, the collective action will not get off the ground if the potential contributors fail to agree. This common ground between collective action theory and bargaining theory is explored in Chapter 4.

In discussing these problems, I employ two main conceptual tools. The first is *rational-choice theory,* which I have discussed extensively elsewhere.[33] I will not consider it explicitly here, except as a backdrop to the discussion of the other tool: the *theory of social norms.* I have come to believe that social norms provide an important kind of motivation for action that is irreducible to rationality or indeed to any other form of optimizing mechanism. My exposition and defence of this view are given in Chapter 3. In Chapters 5 and 6 I reconsider collective action and bargaining from the additional vantage point of the theory of social norms. The final chapter offers some further considerations and a tentative conclusion.

The reasoning is, as I said, mainly inductive. I rely heavily on examples to illustrate and flesh out the more abstract propositions, which otherwise risk taking on the kind of life of their own which haunts the social sciences like a nightmare. As a result of this inductive strategy, the exposition may at places seem rather loosely integrated. In John Marquand's *Melville Goodwin, U.S.A.* someone remarks about the title character that his stories run around on the floor like rabbits. I would not be surprised if some

[33] Elster (1983a, 1984, 1986, 1989a).

readers thought the same about this book. I have tried, though, to ensure some coherence by using *collective wage bargaining* as the main vehicle of the argument. This problem is examined in some detail in alternate chapters (2, 4 and 6). As explained in the preface, the issue of collective bargaining is actually what I began to study. When it turned out to be too difficult, I switched to the easier task of constructing a framework within which it could be discussed. As a result, wage bargaining and wage formation no longer have the status of explananda, but, more modestly, that of illustrations.

1. Collective action

Introduction

The problem of collective action, also referred to as the problem of free riding or the problem of voluntary provision of public goods, is deep and pervasive. The rational self-interest of individuals may lead them to behave in ways that are collectively disastrous. To get out of this predicament, people may abdicate their power to the state, Hobbes's Leviathan. They may also, however, achieve cooperation by decentralized, uncoerced means. This is the main topic of the present chapter. Decentralized solutions are more fundamental than centralized ones, since compliance with central directives is itself a collective action problem. In this chapter, I state the structure of the collective action problem and discuss how people might rationally want to cooperate rather than take a free ride on others. The analysis is incomplete, since nonrational motives also enter powerfully into the decision to cooperate. These are discussed in Chapter 5.

To motivate the discussion, I begin with a few examples of collective action problems. The formation of a trade union or a price cartel is a collective action problem for the potential members: all benefit if all join, but each benefits more by abstaining. Nonmembers can benefit from wage increases negotiated by the union. Defectors from a cartel can corner the market. Voting presents a problem of collective action in several respects. Those who vote mainly to elect a given candidate face the problem that unless most of the candidate's supporters vote he will lose, whereas any single vote makes literally no difference except in the unlikely event that it is pivotal.[1] Those who vote mainly to express their support of the democratic system face a similar problem, although they at least know that

---

[1] There are exceptions to this statement. Sometimes people vote for a certain winner in order to contribute to a landslide that will give increased legitimacy to his policy; or sometimes they vote for a certain loser in order to contribute to a decent showing. The evidence suggests, however, that this effect is secondary at best.

their vote will not be literally wasted. Cleaning up the environment and abstaining from polluting it are classical collective action problems, as are participation in community work, support of museums or public radio stations, adherence to a revolutionary movement, honesty among taxpayers or among public officials and voluntary donations of blood. The characteristic feature of all these cases is that any individual contribution generates small benefits for many people and large costs for one person – namely the contributor. Although the sum of the benefits typically exceeds the costs, so that there is a collective interest in the contribution, the costs typically exceed the benefit to the contributor, so that there is no individual interest in its being made.

All of these standard examples involve interaction among physical individuals at one point in time. More complex cases involve legal rather than physical agents – for example, trade unions, corporations or states. While each of these may represent the successful overcoming of a collective action problem among the members, their interaction may cause new problems. Sometimes it might have been better for all if the original problems had been left unsolved. In Chapter 4 some cases of this kind are considered in greater detail. Also, we may define collective action problems that involve agents living at different times. The problem of saving, for instance, may to some extent be seen as an intergenerational collective action problem: it is better for all generations if all save something for their successors than if none do, but for each generation it is tempting to live off the capital handed down to it by the past without contributing anything to the future. Most of the discussion here will be directed towards the standard examples, but I shall also consider more complex cases.

The impact of collective action on wage determination illustrates these complexities. In the first place, employees face a collective action problem when facing the employer. Other things being equal, they do better when organized, but each worker can do even better by staying on the sidelines.[2] If they succeed in organizing themselves, however, other things may not remain the same. In particular, employers may be provoked to create formal organizations to protect their collective interests. It is not obvious that the collective of workers facing a collective of employers will do better than individual workers facing individual employers in a competitive market. In the second place, the workers face a temporal problem. If on each

---

[2] Olson (1965).

occasion they extract the maximum from the employers, the firm may invest less and there will be less to extract in the future. A succession of myopic trade union leaderships may cause the workers at all times to do worse for themselves than they would have had the leaders been more farsighted. In the third place, the proliferation of unions may lead to higher-order collective action problems.

Any given union, for instance, need not take account of the inflationary impact of high wage claims since its members spend but a small part of their income on the products of their firm or industry, but all unions may be hurt when all act in this way. In Chapter 4 I consider these problems at some length.

Before turning to the standard collective action problem, I shall consider an important nonstandard case, further discussed in Chapters 3 and 5. This is the *intertemporal, intrapersonal collective action problem* that underlies central cases of weakness of will. Sometimes people voluntarily do things that will be bad for them in the long run, like smoking, drinking or overeating. Or they abstain from doing things that will be good for them in the long run, like saving or exercising. What is preferred at *any* given time has bad effects when done at *all* times. The analogy to the standard collective problem should be clear.

In general, weakness of will means to act against one's better judgement, or to do what one believes that, all things considered, one should not do. The phenomenon, in other words, is characterized by these features. (a) There is a judgement that X is good. (b) There is a judgement that Y is good. (c) There is a judgement that, all things considered, X is better than Y. (d) There is the fact that Y is chosen. A central issue in recent philosophy has been to formulate a correct description of this phenomenon and to find its causal conditions of possibility. Of the contending accounts, I believe that Donald Davidson's analysis comes closest to getting it right.[3] He argues that in weak-willed behaviour the proper causal connections between the agent's desires and beliefs, on the one hand, and his action, on the other, break down. The desires do not cause the behaviour *qua* reasons for it, but in some other way, *qua* sheer psychic turbulence. When the weaker reason wins out, it is because it is in one sense the stronger, not *qua* reason but *qua* emotional excitement or motivational force.

Weakness of will thus defined is a purely formal conception and has

---

[3] Davidson (1980), ch. 2. An alternative account is proposed by Pears (1984).

no substantive implications about the kinds of motives that might be involved. In some contexts X could be a long-term gain and Y a short-term benefit, while in other situations the converse could be true. Also, time need not be involved at all. X could be the benefit to my neighbour and Y some gain to myself, or vice versa. Behaviour guided by social norms can be a form of weakness of will. Even when I know that the total benefit to others of an act of cooperation is smaller than the costs to myself, a norm of fairness might, against my better judgement, compel me to perform it. My norm-generated passion for revenge might get the better of me, against my own better judgement. I return to this problem in Chapters 3 and 5. Here, however, I focus on the special but important case in which Y is short-term and X is long-term benefit.

Note first that a preference for the present over the future is neither a sufficient nor a necessary condition for weakness of will. The non-necessity follows from what was just said. The nonsufficiency is also obvious. A person who lives totally in the present displays no weakness of will, since there is no conflict of interest and hence no possibility for the stronger reason to lose out. And even when there is a conflict, the person may well think that the short-term gain is to be preferred, all things considered. The fact that I know that but not when I shall die makes it rational to weigh the present somewhat heavier than the future. In fact, even when the future is discounted more heavily than what is justified by the consideration of mortality tables, weakness of will need not be involved.

To see this, consider Fig. 1.1. In these diagrams, a person has the choice between an early, small reward A and a larger, delayed reward B.[4] The choice has to be made at the time when A becomes available. The curves represent the present value of A and B at various times before their becoming available. The more distant the future time at which they become available, the lower is their present value. At any given time, the person's preference between these options is derived from a comparison of their present values at that time: he prefers the opinion with the largest present value. Exponentially declining time preferences, as in Fig. 1.1.A, have the following important property. If at one point in time the person prefers the (present value of the) earlier, small reward to the (present value of the) larger, delayed reward, then he does so at all points in time. For reasons that I shall make clear in a moment, I take this to imply that the preference

[4] In the following I assume that all elements of uncertainty have been removed.

Present value

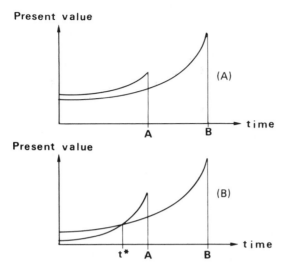

Fig. 1.1

for the smaller reward is his all-things-considered judgement. There is a conflict of values, since the person also feels the attraction of the larger reward, but he decides that on balance he would rather have the smaller one.

If the present value of future rewards declines faster than exponentially, as in Fig. 1.1.B, we have a case of weakness of will, represented by the cross-over point between the curves. Well in advance of the time of choice, the person prefers the larger, delayed reward, but when the moment of choice approaches he comes to prefer the earlier one. It is reasonable to assume that what he thinks ahead of time represents his reflected all-things-considered judgement, and that he simply loses his head when the temptation of the short-term reward becomes imminent. George Ainslie, on whose work I draw heavily here, argues that in human behaviour nonexponential time preferences are the rule rather than the exception.[5]

The cases that concern me here have two important additional features. First, the choice is not between one small early reward and one large delayed reward. If we reflect on cases like smoking or jogging, it is clear that on each occasion the choice is between one early reward and many later rewards. If I skip jogging one morning, I have the immediate benefit of

[5] Ainslie (1975, 1982, 1984, 1986).

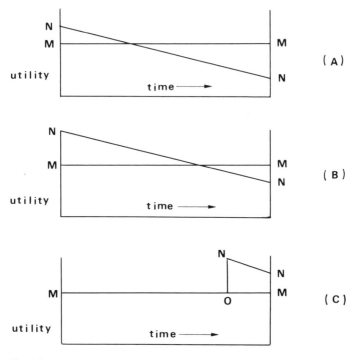

Fig. 1.2

staying in bed. By jogging, I make myself slightly better off at many later times. The (discounted) sum of all the small later rewards can, however, be represented as one large later reward, to which the above reasoning then applies. Second, the choices in question arise over and over again. Each morning I have to decide whether to stay in bed for an extra half hour or go jogging instead. There is, in other words, an extended sequence of choices, each of which has an extended sequence of consequences.

The diagrams in Fig. 1.2 represent the consequences of yielding to temptation (*NN*) and of not doing so (*MM*). Here the utility measured on the vertical scale is instantaneous utility, excluding pleasures of anticipation and memory.[6] The 'prudent' utility profile *MM* serves merely as a reference point, and hence can be drawn as a horizontal line without loss

---

[6] For a fuller discussion of these phenomena and their interaction with time preferences, see Steedman and Krause (1986) and Elster (1985b).

of generality. The profile *NN* has a downward slope for two reasons. In addition to the negative externalities that are my main concern here, the benefits of most noxious activities decrease with repetition.[7] The diagrams cover a certain span of time, which may be seen as roughly coterminous with an adult life.

If weakness of will were strictly analogous to the interpersonal collective action problem, I should be worse off at all times if I always, say, smoked then if I never did so. The asymmetry of time and the finitude of human life destroy this analogy, however. In a group of individuals, each can impose negative externalities on everyone else. In a succession of 'selves', earlier selves cannot be hurt by the later ones. (Remember that I am excluding pleasures and pains derived from anticipation, just as in the similar analysis of interpersonal collective action problem I shall exclude altruistic pleasures.) When I start smoking, I am, for a while, better off than if I had never begun. Beyond the point where the pleasure of current smoking is exactly offset by the cumulative damage done to my body by earlier smoking, I am consistently worse off under the *NN* profile than under the *MM* profile.

What should I do? What will I do? If my only options are always smoking and never smoking, I should compare the area under the curves *MM* and *NN* in Figs. 1.2.A and 1.2.B and choose the profile that encloses the largest area. In Fig. 1.2.A I should never smoke; in Fig. 1.2.B I should always smoke. But this always-or-never framing of the problem is not adequate. I could, for instance, start smoking so late in life that I am always better off by smoking than I would have been by not smoking. This case is illustrated in Fig. 1.2.C. More to the point, as we shall see in Chapter 3, I could try to limit my smoking to, say, five cigarettes a day, getting the exquisite pleasure from a rare cigarette without causing substantial damage to my health. Whatever its shape, there must be some temporal profile of smoking and not smoking that maximizes lifetime utility, keeping other things constant. Assuming I know what that profile is, will I choose it? If I am subject to weakness of will, I will not. Instead, I will yield to temptation on each occasion, thereby making myself worse off at (almost) all times than I would have been had I abstained or chosen the optimal profile.

[7] Solomon and Corbit (1974).

Defining collective action

A collective action problem can be stated as an n-person noncooperative game. This means, crucially, that the players make their choices independently of one another. There are no external mechanisms for enforcing commitments or promises. I will not always assume that the choices are independent in the sense of being made simultaneously. For some collective action problems, like voting, this is a natural assumption to make. For others, such as building a mass movement, it is crucial that contributions can be made at different times, since the efficacy of a contribution and hence its motivating power may depend on the number of contributions already made. Even in sequential choices, however, decisions about whether and when to join are sometimes made simultaneously at the outset. Successive *actions* may reflect simultaneous *decisions*.

Convenient simplifying assumptions (to be questioned later) are the following. Each agent has the choice between two strategies, which will be referred to as Cooperation and Defection. (Randomized strategies are not allowed.) As a result of their choice, a certain outcome is produced. Usually we may think of the outcome as the amount of a certain public good[8] that is made available or, if it is indivisible, the probability that it will be made available. The agents are assumed to be identical and interchangeable. This implies, first, that all that matters for the outcome is the *number* of cooperators, not their specific identity or their place in the social structure[9] and, second, that they have the same preferences over the outcomes. I assume, in other words, that the independent variable is dichotomous – Cooperate or Defect – and that the dependent variable is a continuous function of the number of agents who cooperate. It is often assumed that discontinuous public goods, or 'step goods', offer special analytical problems.[10] Many of these evaporate, however, once it is seen that the *probability* of the step good being provided often varies continuously with the number of cooperators. Thus if a group of citizens face the collective ac-

---

[8] I will not attempt to provide a definition of a 'public good', except to note that for my purposes what matters is defacto nonexcludability. Thus a wage increase is a public good if, for whatever reason, it cannot be restricted to those who struggled to bring it about.

[9] To see how the place of the agents in the social structure could be important, consider the collective action problem that arises for people who are asked to be on the look-out for crime and violence that may take place in their street. The action will be more efficacious if there is someone keeping watch in every third house down the street than if all keep watch in the first third of the houses in the street.

[10] See, e.g., Hardin (1982), pp. 55–61.

tion problem of lobbying to prevent their local school from being closed, each contribution to a campaign can make a (small) difference to the likelihood of that outcome, even though the good itself is an indivisible one.[11] Although the assumption of a dichotomous independent variable – the decision to cooperate – is convenient for many purposes, it is often unrealistic. Often, the problem facing the actor is not *whether* to contribute, but *how much* to contribute. Even when the choice itself is dichotomous, the problem facing the observer is often not *whether* the individual will contribute, but *how likely* it is that he will do so. Explaining tax evasion illustrates the first point. Explaining voting behaviour illustrates the second. Both problems are discussed in Chapter 5.

To *define* the collective action problem, I shall consider only the direct benefits an agent derives from his consumption of the public good. These are what I shall call 'selfish, outcome-oriented benefits.' To *explain* successful collective action we may have to take account of a larger set of benefits, which I postpone for later discussion.

I begin with a survey of various ways of defining a collective action problem:

1. We may define it very broadly, as any binary choice situation in which it is better for all if some make one choice – the cooperative choice – than if all make the other choice, although better for each to make the latter.[12]

2. We may define it more narrowly, as an *n*-person Prisoner's Dilemma in which it is better for all if *all* cooperate than if nobody does so, yet better for each not to do so.

3. We may define it even more narrowly, as an *n*-person Prisoner's Dilemma in which it is *best* for all if all cooperate, yet better for each not to do so.

In Chapter 5 I consider some implications of the first, broader definition. In this chapter, I mainly use the second definition. First, however, I shall briefly discuss how even the broadest definition might be further relaxed.

4. One might weaken the condition that there exists a level of (possibly universal) cooperation that makes *everybody* better off. As an example, consider corruption, further discussed in the concluding chapter. Although

---

[11] I take this example, as well as the idea of using probabilities as the dependent variable, from Oliver, Marwell and Teixeira (1985).
[12] Barry (1985).

a society without corruption is, in an obvious sense, better than a society in which everybody is corrupt, it is usually false that everybody would be better off under the former regime. Powerful individuals benefit so much from corruption that they would, on the whole, lose from its abolition. True, the social product would increase, but their share of it would decline so dramatically that they would be left with less. It is somewhat misleading, therefore, to represent the struggle against corruption as a collective action problem in the standard sense of the term. One might relax the definition by requiring that *almost everybody* be better off under the optimal level of cooperation than under universal noncooperation, or even limit oneself to requiring that *average utility* be higher.[13] But in the latter case we have moved very far away from collective action as traditionally conceived. In particular, the contrast between individual and collective rationality disappears. I will not, therefore, adopt this ultrabroad definition. Average utility will nevertheless play an important role in the reasoning. We may note, in this connection, that the presently discussed definition is the appropriate one for the intrapersonal collective action problem.

5. Next, we could relax the condition that noncooperation be a dominant individual strategy. This condition would not be appropriate, for instance, when only cooperators benefited from cooperation. Consider two problems created by public transportation. The choice between taking the bus and driving one's own car is a standard collective action situation, due to externalities of congestion. The choice between taking the train and driving to work on an uncongested highway could create a different problem. If everyone took the train, fares would fall so much that nobody would want to drive to work. If few took the train, the high fares would induce private driving. Note, however, that as more and more people switched to the train, car drivers would not gain anything since by assumption the road was uncongested even when everybody was driving. It is better for all if all take the train than if none do, but beyond a certain point it is not better for each to drive.[14]

The condition that noncooperation be dominant is also inappropriate when one or more of the actors would be willing to provide the good singlehandedly. A shipowner with many ships might benefit so much from a

---

[13] This amounts (at least roughly) to saying that the winners from cooperation should be able to compensate the losers and still retain a net benefit.
[14] This is an Assurance Game (Sen 1967) with universal driving as one equilibrium and universal train riding as another, Pareto-superior equilibrium.

lighthouse that it would pay him to construct it without any contribution from others, who could then free ride on his effort. There might even be two shipowners each of whom would be willing to build the lighthouse if the other did not.[15] Although it remains true that it is better for all if some cooperate than if none do, it is not unconditionally better for each not to cooperate.

6. Finally, there can be collective action problems even if nobody is made worse off by defection.[16] A Hungarian coffee shop begins to offer high-quality coffee to customers who are willing to pay a bit extra. As the shop has a limited quota of coffee beans, each customer who pays the high price creates an externality for the customers who pay the official price. The official cups of coffee being increasingly diluted, more and more customers are willing to pay the premium. Yet as more and more do so, the quality of black-market coffee approaches the initial quality of the ordinary coffee. In the end, everybody pays the higher price for coffee of ordinary quality. It would appear, therefore, that everybody has lost, in a standard *n*-person Prisoner's Dilemma. The twist to the story is that because of cognitive dissonance reduction, nobody experiences any subjective loss. Since they are paying more for the coffee, it must be better, they tell themselves, than it used to be. Although there are limits to how far perceptions can deviate from reality for the purposes of justifying past effort or expense,[17] this case might well be within the range of psychologically feasible adjustments. The Prisoner's Dilemma yields a Pareto improvement: the shopkeeper gains more and the customers are happy.

The technology of collective action

To make it easier to understand the collective action problem, I shall use, here and in later chapters, the convenient diagrammatic representation introduced by Thomas Schelling.[18] Figure 1.3 indicates how in a group of $n + 1$ individuals the utility payoff to a given individual varies as a function of his own behaviour and that of the others. The behaviour of others is indicated along the horizontal axis, which measures the number of cooperators. If the individual is a cooperator, his utility, measured along the

---

[15] This is a game of Chicken, *n*-person generalizations of which are discussed in Taylor and Ward (1982) and Hampton (1987).

[16] The following draws on Galasi and Kertesi (1987).   [17] Aronson (1984), pp. 151–4.

[18] Schelling (1978), ch. 7.

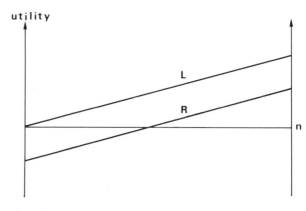

Fig. 1.3

vertical axis, is indicated along the R lines in the diagrams. If he is a noncooperator, his utility is measured along the L lines. We see that the L and R lines intersect the vertical axes in the order which defines the ordinary (two-person) Prisoner's Dilemma: the most highly preferred outcome is unilateral noncooperation (free riding), the next best is universal cooperation, the third best universal noncooperation, while the worst outcome is unilateral cooperation (being exploited). As in the two-person case, noncooperation is a dominant strategy, since the L line is everywhere above the R line.

As we shall see, there is in general no reason why the L and R curves must be parallel, or even straight lines, or even (see Chapter 5) monotonically increasing lines. Figure 1.4 shows two cases in which the L and R functions are nonparallel straight lines.

We can now define *two threshold levels* for collective action, represented by points A and B in the diagrams. Point A is the threshold for self-sustaining cooperation: if there are at least A cooperators, each of them will do at least as well for himself as in the state of universal noncooperation. The noncooperators will, of course, do even better. Point B is the threshold for Pareto improvements. If there are fewer than B cooperators, universal cooperation will improve the outcome for everybody – cooperators and noncooperators. With more than B cooperators, the noncooperators will be better off free riding than they would be under universal cooperation. All states to the right of B are Pareto-optimal.

To each threshold we may associate a particular kind of stability and

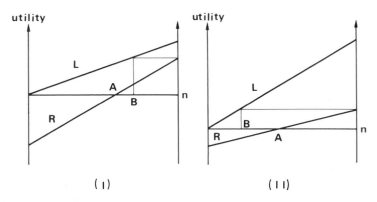

Fig. 1.4

instability. Imagine that a subset of the group has agreed to cooperate, but that they turn out not to be self-sustaining. Even if they are bound to each other with the strongest bonds of loyalty, they will perceive that cooperation is pointless – it is essentially dissipated among the noncooperators – and disband. Imagine next that there are fewer than *B* cooperators. The noncooperators might then perceive the attraction of universal cooperation in a way that they would not if the number of cooperators grew beyond *B*. Conversely, cooperation may be stable to the right of *A* and noncooperation stable to the right of *B*. In Fig. 1.4.I, where *A* is to the left of *B,* we first have a region where both cooperation and noncooperation are unstable, followed by a region with stable cooperation and unstable noncooperation, followed by a region in which both are stable. In Fig. 1.4.II the intermediate region has unstable cooperation and stable noncooperation. Here the term 'stability' is not used in a technical and precise sense, but only to suggest certain dynamic possibilities. Whether these will be realized depends on further motivational considerations, extensively discussed below.

More complicated structures are shown in diagrams D and E in Fig. 1.5 (from Schelling).[19] For the time being I will not question the assumption that the *L* and *R* curves are constrained to be monotonically increasing, that is, that an additional act of cooperation always makes a positive contribution to the public good in question. We must, however, ask what underlies the various shapes of the curves illustrated in diagrams A through

[19] The dotted lines in the diagrams are explained later.

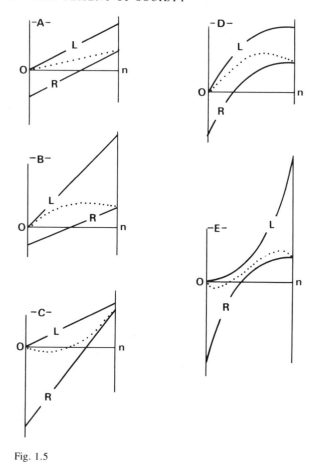

Fig. 1.5

E in Fig. 1.5. For this purpose, we may begin by noting that the L curves indicate the per capita benefit (or expected benefit, if the dependent variable is a probability) of the public good created by the collective action. This benefit is received by cooperators and noncooperators alike. The non-cooperators receive this benefit in its entirety, without any cost to be subtracted. The cooperators, by contrast, receive it net of the costs of cooperating. These costs, therefore, are equal to the distance between the L and R curves.

The Schelling diagrams, while extremely useful, are also somewhat misleading, in suggesting that the L and R curves are the fundamental aspects of the situation. A more accurate procedure would be to derive these curves from the more basic *technology of collective action,* represented by cost and benefit functions.[20] The cost of a contribution to collective action may be an increasing, a constant or a decreasing function of the number of cooperators. Similarly, an additional contribution towards the public good creates an additional per capita benefit which may increase or decrease with the number of contributions already made.[21]

Increasing costs can arise in cases of congestion. When many people join calling-in campaigns to support public television, the line becomes busy and the waiting time to get through increases. Also, if the public good in question is a public bad for other people, they might want to make cooperation more costly as the number of cooperators rises to the point where their activities become dangerous. One could imagine the police in an authoritarian regime tolerating a few isolated dissenters, but cracking down hard on them when they began amounting to an organized opposition. Constant costs are illustrated by abstention from littering: the cost to me of not throwing my cigarette on the sidewalk does not depend on what others do. Decreasing costs can derive from the strategy of 'swamping the appetite of predators'.[22] When a given police force has to spread itself more thinly over an increasing number of revolutionaries, the cost to each of the latter goes down.[23]

We must distinguish between two senses of 'costs of contribution'. First, there are the costs to the contributor; second, there is the sum total of costs created by an additional contributor. If the costs of contribution are nonconstant, an additional contributor can increase the costs for everyone else – or decrease them. In the selfishly individual calculus the latter possibility is irrelevant, but for moral purposes it might be important. In later discus-

---

[20] Here I rely again on Oliver, Marwell and Teixeira (1985). The term 'technology' must be taken in an extended sense, which includes both the physical production function and the utilities of inputs and outputs. A given physical input (a certain number of contributions) gives rise to a certain physical output (or a certain level of probability of the public good) which in turn gives rise to a certain level of utility (or expected utility) for the individual. Hence the utility is a function of a function of physical input. Similarly, the cost of contributing can be measured in physical units (time or money), which must then be assessed in utility terms so as to make comparisons with benefits possible.

[21] Constant marginal benefits are an unlikely case, since they would require both production functions and utility functions to be linear or, if nonlinear, to offset each other exactly to give a linear end result.

[22] Elster (1984), pp. 22–3.

[23] The official task of the police is, of course, to increase the costs of *non*cooperation. See the later discussion of selective incentives.

sions I usually, but not invariably, assume that costs are constant, so that these two definitions give the same result. In this connection a word should also be said about opportunity costs of contributions to collective action. Even when a person, by making a contribution, makes others better off than if he had done nothing or, in the limit, if he had not existed, it could happen that he would have benefited them even more by doing something else. Instead of joining the protest march he could have stayed in his café and comforted the tired marchers by selling them hot chocolate. By joining the march, he adds to the costs of others.

Increasing marginal benefits can be illustrated by the cleaning of litter from a beach: the last bottle that is removed makes a greater aesthetic difference than the penultimate one. As a second example consider the creation of a community center: 'Hours and dollars have to be spent buying the land and materials and building the structure before the last few hours of painting it and furnishing it produce big payoffs in having a place to meet'.[24] Decreasing marginal benefits are frequent. 'A simple substantive example . . . might be calling city hall about a pothole in a middle-class urban area: the first person who takes the time to call makes the probability .4 that the hole will be fixed, the second raises it to .7, the third to .8, the fourth to .85, the fifth to .88', and so on.[25] In general, the benefit function can be expected to be S-shaped, with marginal benefits first rising and then decreasing. The benefits may even become negative – acts of cooperation may actually harm others or deprive them of benefits which the cooperators would otherwise have provided. Examples are given in Chapter 5.

The most frequent type of collective action problem is probably that in which costs are constant and benefits first rise slowly, then more rapidly and then more slowly again.[26] The net benefits – and average benefits per group member – first decline, then rise and then decline again. Figure 1.6 shows gross total benefits, total costs and net total benefits of cooperation as a function of the number of cooperators. Total (and average) net benefits are maximized when the marginal benefit of an extra act of cooperation is equal to the (constant) marginal cost, that is, where a parallel to the cost line is tangential to the gross benefit curve.

The dotted lines in Fig. 1.5 also represent average net benefit to all group members – cooperators and noncooperators – as a function of the number of cooperators. By definition, these are constrained to be overall

---

[24] Oliver, Marwell and Teixeira (1985), p. 527.   [25] Ibid., p. 526.   [26] Ibid.

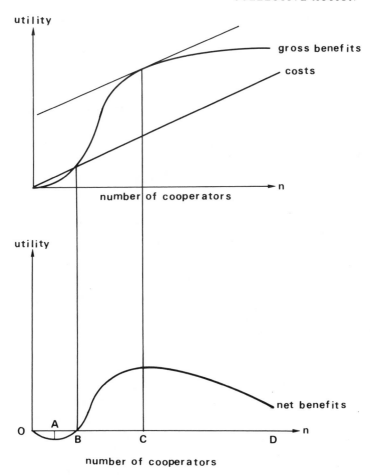

Fig. 1.6

increasing: they begin at the point of universal noncooperation and end at the point of universal cooperation. Unlike the L and R curves, the average-benefit curves need not be monotonically increasing, but can contain declining stretches. The diagrams show cases in which a small number of cooperators actually reduce the average benefit to below the level of universal noncooperation and cases in which the last people to join the collective action have a similarly negative impact. These phenomena arise because the costs to the cooperator are so high that they not only offset the benefit to the cooperator himself (this is always the case in collective action problems), but even exceed the sum total benefits generated by his contribution. Isolated acts of protest, for example, are often very costly to the individual and have little impact on the probability that the relevant public good – be it a wage increase or freedom of speech – will be provided. They may be pointless not only from a selfishly rational point of view, but even from the utilitarian point of view which is guided by total or average benefit. As I said, we shall also find cases in which the L and R curves themselves have declining stretches, either with few cooperators or with nearby universal cooperation.

This concludes my statement of the collective action problem. I now discuss possible solutions to the problem, by which I mean possible explanations of the fact that successful collective action sometimes does occur. They are not, or only marginally, recipes for engineering collective action.

Rational cooperation

Any explanation must rest on an analysis of the beliefs and motivations of individual agents. The explanandum, properly stated, is *individual participation* in collective action, that is, individual choice of the cooperative rather than the noncooperative strategy. One must emphatically not try to explain successful collective action in terms of the benefit it brings to the group. Even though by assumption it is better for all if all cooperate than if none do, it is also true by assumption that it is even better for the individual – at least in terms of the restricted set of benefits we have been discussing so far – to abstain from cooperating. Hence 'group rationality' is of no avail in explaining collective action. These gestures in the direction of methodological individualism will have to suffice for the present purposes.[27]

I snall focus on the analysis of individual motivations, whereas beliefs will be relegated to second place. The importance of beliefs for the explanation of collective action is twofold. First, each potential cooperator must have some idea of the technology of collective action – the benefits and costs of contributing at various levels of cooperation. Second, he must form an estimate of what that level is likely to be – an estimate, that is, of the expected number of other cooperators. Each of these beliefs is heavily shrouded in uncertainty and subject to cognitive and motivational biases.

[27] See also Popkin (1979); Elster (1985d), sec. 6.2; M. Taylor, ed. (1988); and, of course, Olson (1965).

To the extent that people have any idea of the technology of collective action, it probably amounts to no more than an estimate of the difference between universal cooperation and universal noncooperation, as well as a notion that individual cooperation is pointless at or close to either extreme. To the extent that potential contributors are at all influenced by the expected number of other contributors, their beliefs may be parametric or strategic. Voters, for instance, may assume that turn-out will be the same as in the last election.[28] Or they may expect turn-out to be low if one candidate is predicted to be a certain winner. Either belief may also be shaped by wishful thinking: a worker may have excessively optimistic beliefs about the wage concessions that a united collective may wrest from the employers or about the number of other workers that are likely to join him in the strike. I will not offer a general account of belief formation, but touch on the issue when necessary.

I shall propose a typology of individual motivations that rests on a number of heuristic distinctions. First, I distinguish between rationality and social norms as motives for cooperating. I need not spell out at length what I mean by rationality, but only indicate that I use a minimalist notion of rationality, as consistent, future-oriented and instrumentally efficient behaviour. Second, I distinguish between selfish and nonselfish motivations. Within the former we may further distinguish between outcome-oriented and process-oriented motivations. Within the latter, I distinguish between positive and negative orientations towards others – between altruism, on the one hand, and envy and spite, on the other. The main categories are set out in Fig. 1.7.[29] In theory, there might also be a category for rational, nonselfish, process-oriented motivations, based on altruism or envy. A person might join collective action to promote or obstruct the process benefits of other people. These phenomena may occur, but probably too infrequently to merit separate consideration.

With one exception, the first member of each dichotomy has a certain methodological primacy over the second. (a) We have learned from Don-

---

[28] Cf. the remarks on the cobweb cycle in the Introduction.

[29] In Elster (1985a) I wrongly assimilated process benefits and social norms under the common heading of 'non-outcome-oriented motivations'. In Chapter 3 I argue that social norms are, in fact, not outcome-oriented, but in a sense different from that in which process benefits are not outcome-oriented. People who join collective action to reap the pleasures of participating are oriented by that goal, although they may not care about the further goal of consuming the public good. To the extent that people are motivated by social norms they do not care about either goal, or indeed about any goal at all.

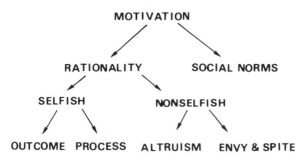

Fig. 1.7

ald Davison that local irrationality can be imputed only on a broad background of rationality.[30] It is logically consistent to imagine that everyone always acts rationally, but not that everyone always acts irrationally. (b) Similarly, it is possible to imagine a world in which everyone always acts exclusively for his own selfish benefits, whereas a world in which everyone always acts exclusively for the sake of others is an incoherent notion. The second-order values of altruism and morality are parasitic on the existence of some first-order benefits; for instance, the second-order pleasure from giving presupposes an expected first-order pleasure of the recipient. (c) Later I also argue that process values are, in a somewhat different sense, parasitic on outcome values. (d) By contrast, altruism and envy are on a par, neither having a logical primacy over the other.

The primacy of selfish and outcome-oriented motivations is a purely methodological one, with no implications for the empirical frequency of the various types of motivation.[31] It might conceivably be the case, for instance, that almost all individuals in a given society got their happiness from contemplating the first-order pleasures of a single individual in their midst (and the higher-order pleasures thus generated).[32] Also, the process benefits of action might be much larger than the outcome benefits and in

---

[30] Davidson (1980).

[31] The first argument is an exception: for irrational behaviour to be a meaningful notion, people must act rationally almost all the time.

[32] Imagine a group of individuals in a room with hedonometers attached to their heads. Initially, all the hedonometers are dimmed. Then one individual picks up an apple and begins eating it, whereupon his hedonometer starts glowing. When the others notice this effect, their hedonometers light up too. Moreover, when they look around at each other, the spectacle of many lights makes the hedonometers glow even more strongly, and so on.

that sense 'more important', although the latter are 'more important' in the sense of being logically primary.

Hence when trying to explain individual participation in collective action, one should begin with the logically most simple type of motivation: rational, selfish, outcome-oriented behaviour. If this proves insufficient to explain the phenomena we observe, we must introduce more complex types, singly or in combination. In this chapter I consider only *rational motivations*, based on self-interest or altruism. The discussion of nonrational motives is postponed until Chapters 3 and 5. In Chapter 5 I also address the important and neglected issue of *mixed motivations*, by which I mean cases in which successful collective action is made possible by the interaction of individuals who participate for very different reasons. The discussion of envy is postponed until Chapter 6 and, especially, the concluding chapter.

Rational, selfish, outcome-oriented motivation

It might seem as if individuals with this type of motivation would never cooperate, since by assumption they would have defection as a dominant strategy. In the collective action literature, however, there are several attempts to argue that under certain conditions these individuals might find cooperation to be in their interest. Some of these attempts amount to changing the nature of the decision problem, whereas others argue more subtly, that even in the unadulterated Prisoner's Dilemma, cooperation might emerge as being in the long-term interest of the agents. I shall discuss these in turn.

In his classic discussion of the problem, Mancur Olson argued that collective action might come about in two ways. Either one of the agents would have a sufficiently large interest in the public good to provide it single-handedly, even though he would then be exploited by the others. Or some subset of the agents might be able to force or induce the others to cooperate, by providing them with negative or positive selective incentives. These are incentives which are contingent upon the behaviour of the agent, unlike the public good, which is available to everyone if it is provided at all. Negative incentives or punishments are linked to noncooperative behaviour, whereas positive incentives or rewards are linked to cooperative choices. In trade union formation, negative incentives have varied from social ostracism to the use of violence against strikebreakers or un-

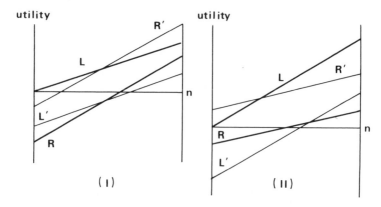

Fig. 1.8

organized workers.[33] More recently, unions have been able to demand a 'collective bargaining fee' from nonmembers who benefit from negotiated wage increases, thus effectively eliminating the free-rider option.[34] Positive incentives can take the form of favourable insurance schemes available only to union members, pension plans, access to union leisure centers and the like.[35]

The use of selective incentives could have strong or weak effects, by which I mean that it could make cooperation either a dominant strategy or, more weakly, an equilibrium strategy. Consider Fig. 1.8.I.

A small negative incentive or a small positive incentive would have the effect of shifting the L and R curves towards each other, so that universal cooperation would now be preferred to unilateral defection, but universal defection would remain preferred to unilateral cooperation. Hence universal cooperation would, in addition to universal defection, become a new equilibrium point.[36] We can well imagine that in early stages of unionization the costs of cooperation imposed on the worker by his employer were larger than the punishment for noncooperation imposed on him by his fel-

---

[33] Chen (1986) offers an account of the Chinese revolution that strongly emphasizes the Communist leaders' use of negative selective incentives in recruiting peasants to the movement.

[34] The 'right-to-work' laws that have been passed in many American states amount to a license for free riding. See Eissinger (1975) and Haggard (1980).

[35] In contrast to Chen (1986), Popkin (1979) strongly emphasizes the use of positive incentives by the Vietnamese Communist leaders in recruiting the peasants.

[36] The incentives would have to be stronger for cooperation to become a dominant strategy, since this would require the R curve to lie about the L curve everywhere.

low workers, whereas with growing unionization the reverse inequality holds. Figure 1.8.II illustrates the converse possibility. Here, small selective incentives might induce a few cooperators but cease to be efficacious when dominated by the steeply rising costs of cooperation. If rural evolutionaries try to recruit the peasantry by selective incentives, they may succeed initially but soon discover that the authorities are able to impose far higher costs on cooperation.

In the presence of selective incentives Fig. 1.8.I has one all-cooperative and one all-defecting equilibrium.[37] Figure 1.8.II has neither. Both have a number of mixed equilibria, in each of which the number of cooperators is defined by the intersection between L and R' or between L' and R. Note that in Fig. 1.8.I the partially cooperative equilibrium induced by punishment (the intersection between L' and R) is *worse for all* than universal unpunished noncooperation. The mixed equilibria are unstable in Fig. 1.8.I, but stable in Fig. 1.8.II. Let us characterize cooperation as *individually accessible* if it is in the interest of an individual in a noncooperative state to take the first step towards it and as *individually stable* if it is not in any individual's interest to take the first step away from it. In Fig. 1.8.II partial cooperation is individually accessible and individually stable. In Fig. 1.8.I full cooperation is individually stable but not individually accessible. To get there on a purely voluntary basis, individuals must be able to anticipate that others will cooperate. To do so, something like common knowledge about their situation is required – a condition that is rarely satisfied in social life. In the collective action problem without selective incentives, coordination is of course neither individually stable nor individually accessible.

Consider corruption in the light of these distinctions. There is a striking variety in the extent of corruption in different countries. In some it is almost absent, in others it is rampant and in intermediate cases it is frequent but not cripplingly so. To explain the variation, economists typically look for differences in opportunities, institutions and incentive structures, while sociologists are likely to search for differences in norms, values and traditions. The intermediate cases provide perhaps the strongest argument for the sociological explanation: people in a given society face the same institutions but may have different values. The preceding discussion suggests a third possibility: people may have similar values, within and across so-

---

[37] Formally, it represents an *n*-person Assurance Game (Sen 1967).

cieties, and similar institutional structures and yet, for accidental reasons, end up in different equilibria.[38] The intermediate cases provide a valuable methodological lesson: even when people face identical external opportunities, we should not infer that differences in behaviour must reflect different preferences. Frequency-dependent equilibria are quite possible.[39] I shall have more to say about corruption in the concluding chapter.

The choice between rewards and punishments as selective incentives depends on the technology of the collective action. If it is important to have nearly universal participation (i.e., if the average-benefit curve does not flatten out before almost everybody has joined), reliance on rewards can be very costly since they actually have to be paid out. There is little point in collective action if the gains are wiped out by the costs of inducing people to participate. It may then be more efficient to rely on punishment, which works mainly by deterrence and only secondarily by actual administration. Punishment is cheaper than reward, because anticipation replaces implementation.[40] Conversely, when there are large benefits from the first contributions and then rapidly decreasing marginal benefits, reliance on rewards may be more attractive – if it is technically and morally possible to withhold them from some of the would-be cooperators. A dilemma can arise if withholding is impossible. One might then have to induce universal participation by punishing noncooperators, even if the optimal number of cooperators is a substantially smaller subset.

The provision of selective incentives cannot be the general solution to the collective action problem. To assume that there is a central authority offering incentives often requires another collective action problem to have been solved already. Before a union can force or induce workers to join, it must have overcome a free-rider problem in the first place. To assume that

[38] Although the diagrams in Fig. 1.8 do not show a case with a noncooperative equilibrium, a cooperative equilibrium and a stable mixed equilibrium, this could happen under more complex technologies of collective action. Andvig and Moene (1988) offer an insightful discussion of such cases.

[39] See Frank (1988) for a similar argument about altruistic behaviour.

[40] I assume here that promises to reward and threats to punish are credible. As further explained in the concluding chapter, this assumption is quite fragile in many cases. Once the revolution has succeeded, it is not clear that it will be in the interest of the leaders to keep their promises to place their followers in positions of authority or to carry out threats to execute nonfollowers. Realizing this, people might hesitate to join in the first place, unless the leaders could find a way to add credibility to their statements of intention. Popkin (1979), p. 261, argues that the Vietnamese leaders demonstrated their credibility by choosing an austere life style that signalled their lack of opportunism. Alternatively, if the administration of rewards and punishments is a continuous process rather than a one-shot event, the leaders can rely on 'Tit-for-Tat' tactics (as discussed later).

the incentives are offered in a decentralized way, by mutual monitoring, gives rise to a second-order free-rider problem.[41] Why, for instance, should a rational, selfish worker ostracize or otherwise punish those who do not join the union? What is in it for him? True, it may be better for all members if all punish nonmembers than if none do, but for each member it may be even better to remain passive. Punishment almost invariably is costly to the punisher, while the benefits from punishment are diffusely distributed over all members. It is, in fact, a public good. To provide it, one would need second-order selective incentives, which would, however, run into a third-order free-rider problem. We shall encounter a similar problem in Chapter 3, when discussing the enforcement of social norms.

These objections to the selective-incentive argument, while important, are not always decisive. If the technology of providing incentives differs sufficiently from the technology of the original problem, decentralized monitoring can be selfishly rational. Consider, for instance, a small workers' cooperative based on equal revenue sharing. The workers face a collective action problem in which the cooperative option is to work hard and the noncooperative one is to shirk. The second-order problem created by mutual monitoring involves a much smaller free-rider gain, if there is one at all. 'Some activities allow individuals to work and to observe one another's performance simultaneously, for example, so that output and monitoring are joint products'.[42] If monitoring is costless for the worker, it will have a positive net value since it always offers some benefits ($1/n$ of the productivity increase caused by his monitoring).[43] Also, the workers might deliberately organize the work process so as to minimize the costs of monitoring. Finally, minimal altruism or weak social norms, although insufficient to solve the first-order free-rider problem, might solve the second-order problem if the costs of cooperation are substantially smaller at this level, as they tend to be.

There can be little doubt about the importance of selective incentives in collective action. In particular, social disapproval of noncooperators is often

[41] Frohlich and Oppenheimer (1970). See also Oliver (1980), on which the following discussion draws heavily.

[42] Putterman (1986), p. 315.

[43] Actually, this view may be too rosy. Williamson (1975), pp. 37–9, refers to the negative 'atmosphere effects' caused by vertical monitoring. Horizontal monitoring is vulnerable to the same problem. J. S. Mill (1976), p. 790, cites an example from a French cooperative, in which 'the tailors complained that [the wage system] caused incessant disputes and quarrels, through the interest which each had in making his neighbours work. Their mutual watchfulness degenerated into a real slavery; nobody had the free control of his time and actions'.

invoked to explain low levels of defection. What is more controversial is whether the expression of disapproval, when it occurs, is always and everywhere a selfishly rational action. As just argued, it may sometimes be so. I argue in Chapter 3 that it need not always be so. More generally, those who provide selective incentives for people who would join only for selfishly rational motives need not themselves be guided solely by this motivation.

Collective action problems can also be transformed if contributions are made conditional upon each other.[44] The 'money-back' method stipulates that promises to contribute will be enforced only if a sufficient number of others promise to do the same. The advantage of this method, which is frequently used in fund-raising campaigns, is that nobody risks being taken advantage of. Some might, however, successfully free-ride on others. By contrast, the 'fair-share' method stipulates that if sufficiently many cooperate, others have to do so too. This eliminates the possibility of free riding but not the risk of being taken advantage of. American unionization rules provide an example. Workers in a plant decide by majority vote whether they want to be represented by a union. If the decision is positive, even those who voted against unionization are compelled by law to pay union dues.[45] It is not clear under what conditions such transformations of the game will induce collective action.[46] They are in any case vulnerable to the objection raised earlier against selective incentives as a general solution to collective action: they presuppose the presence of a centralized agent with coercive authority.

A more intriguing proposal is that cooperation could be selfishly rational even when the payoffs remain those of the Prisoner's Dilemma. Although

---

[44]   The following summarizes Dawes et al. (1986).

[45]   The example is not perfect, because the costs to the worker of voting for unionization are negligible if the majority is against it. Another example is presented by 'efforts of apartment dwellers to resist developers who wish to convert their apartment building into a condominium. The developers offer to sell the units at a reduced rate to anyone wishing to vote for conversion prior to a specified deadline. One "contributes" to the apartment dwellers' effort, then, by withstanding the offer. If the effort fails and the conversion proceeds, those who withstood the offer are out of pocket to the extent of the reduced offer: they have to pay the higher rate. However, it is not possible for an apartment dweller to free ride on the restraint of others because if a sufficient number withstand the offer, the conversion won' (Dawes et al. 1986, p. 1171). This example is not perfect either, since accepting the offer is not an individually dominant strategy.

[46]   In their experiment Dawes et al. (1986) found that the fair-share method was much more effective than the money-back method.

there have been attempts to demonstrate this even for the one-shot Prisoner's Dilemma,[47] most arguments rest on the difference between one-shot games and repeated games. Intuitively, the idea is simple. When the same people interact over and over again, they may choose to cooperate out of fear of retaliation, hope of reciprocation or both.

There is an important distinction between the finitely repeated Prisoner's Dilemma and the open-ended, indefinitely repeated one. As mentioned in the Introduction, it is not quite clear what rationality demands of us in the finitely repeated game. Pending a resolution of the problem of backward induction, we should be hesitant about accepting the nearly unanimously held view[48] that defection is the rational strategy in such games. Most actual situations are, however, open-ended. The same people meet over and over again, without a predetermined terminal date.[49] In the indefinitely iterated two-person Prisoner's Dilemma, which has been studied in some detail,[50] each player can choose among various reaction functions, each of which tells him what to do in any given game as a function of the history of choices of both players. One such function is the rule 'Always defect'. Another is conditional cooperation, 'Tit for Tat', defined as follows. 'Always cooperate in the first game. In each subsequent game, cooperate if and only if the other player cooperated in the previous game.' It can be shown that under certain conditions, the use of Tit for Tat by both players is an equilibrium of the game. One of these conditions is that the rate of time discounting not be too high.[51] If a player does not care much about future payoffs, he will be tempted to defect in the first game to reap the higher reward. Tit for Tat is not a dominant strategy: against consistent defection, it does worse than consistent defection.

---

[47] The early attempt by Howard (1971) is generally viewed as unsuccessful. See, e.g., Taylor (1987), pp. 180–4. A recent attempt is that of Gauthier (1986). It fails, in my opinion, to argue successfully for its two crucial premises that (a) persons can *decide* to adopt a disposition to cooperate and (b) others are able to detect this disposition. A different argument for the rationality of cooperating in one-shot games in Sen (1987), pp. 81–9, is too opaque to be readily comprehended.

[48] Hardin (1982) is an exception.

[49] For a possible real-life example of defections induced by backward induction in a finitely repeated game, see Bowman (1989), p. 200.

[50] See notably Axelrod (1984); M. Taylor (1987); Sugden (1986), ch. 6.

[51] 'Too high', that is, relative to the reward parameters. If the gains from unilateral defection are very high and those from mutual cooperation comparatively small, even low rates of time discounting may induce defection. In the final chapter I argue that in iterated bargaining games the reward parameters are themselves influenced by the rate of time discounting.

The iterated two-person Prisoner's Dilemma is not, however, very relevant to the problem of collective action.[52] For this, we need an understanding of the iterated n-person Prisoner's Dilemma. The formal results for this case are neither numerous nor robust.[53] They seem to indicate that cooperative behaviour is most likely to come about if all players use the following strategy. 'Always cooperate in the first game. In each subsequent game, cooperate if and only if all other players have cooperated in all previous games'. Here cooperation is maintained by the shared knowledge that it will be permanently unravelled by a single defection. If all players adopt the 'trigger strategy' of cooperating if and only if all cooperated in the previous game, cooperation may be selfishly rational, always assuming that the rate of time discounting is not too high. Cooperation among international bankers is to some extent achieved in this way.[54] Trigger strategies may also be important in keeping sectoral labour unions together in a central bargaining unit.[55]

Intuitively, the requirement of unanimity may appear too strong. Could not cooperation be sustained if a large proportion of the members followed the strategy of cooperating if and only if a large proportion cooperated in the previous game? I do indeed believe this to be a plausible mechanism, but it must be stated more carefully. As a game-theoretic equilibrium with selfishly rational individuals, it is highly precarious. It requires that there be some number m of individuals such that each of them cooperates if and only if *exactly* $m - 1$ other individuals cooperated in the previous game.[56] This degree of fine-tuning is psychologically implausible. More plausibly, and more robustly, conditional cooperation of this kind can be sustained by a *norm of fairness,* to be discussed in Chapter 5. With the exception of trigger strategies the explanation of cooperation as selfishly rational behaviour in an iterated n-person Prisoner's Dilemma is not very promising.

Rational, selfish, process-oriented motivations

Could not participation in collective action be viewed as a benefit rather than as a cost to the individual? This way of turning the problem on its

---

[52] As I argue in later chapters, the iterated Prisoner's Dilemma, or similar iterated games, are highly relevant to bargaining problems in which the two bargainers meet each other over and over again.

[53] See Taylor (1987), ch. 4, and Friedman (1986), sec. 3.3.

[54] Lipson (1986), pp. 215–17.   [55] Holden and Raaum (1988).

[56] Taylor (1987), pp. 89–92. I have simplified his analysis by assuming that those who do not cooperate conditionally are unconditional noncooperators.

head might appear to be quite liberating. An analogy could be the change in development economics that took place when it was realized that at some stages of economic development, the alternative of consumption versus investment was a misleading one. Increasing consumption is also the best investment in the future, via the impact on health and productivity.[57] Similarly, as Albert Hirschman put it, 'The benefit of collective action for an individual [may not be] the difference between the hoped-for result and the effort furnished by him or her, but the *sum* of these two magnitudes'.[58]

There are two distinct ways in which this idea may be spelled out. First, participation in collective action can be quite enjoyable. Social and political demonstrations can assume the aspect of a festival and attract participants by virtue of the food, drink or music that is offered. Although these are usually presented as rewards offered to people who have joined the demonstration for other, outcome-oriented reasons, they are sometimes intended to induce participation which would otherwise not be forthcoming. This is, obviously, a special case of inducing collective action by offering selective incentives. It differs from the examples cited earlier in two respects. (a) The incentives offered to the participants are not intended to offset the costs of participation: rather they are intended to make participation costless, indeed pleasurable. (b) People who join for the sake of these benefits are parasitic on people who do so for other reasons. The organizers of a demonstration would hardly be motivated by the prospect of the free drinks or music provided by themselves.

Second, people may join collective action to achieve self-realization, consciousness raising, self-respect and the like. There is no doubt that sustained work for a worthwhile goal has desirable effects of this kind. What is more questionable is whether people can coherently join a movement *solely* for this motive. As I have argued elsewhere, self-respect and self-realization belong to the class of 'states that are essentially by-products'.[59] They can arise only as side effects of actions undertaken for other, outcome-oriented purposes. Only if the participants believe in the goal of the movement will they approach it with the seriousness of purpose that is a necessary condition for self-realization. The point can be stated in Hirschman's algebraic language. Denote the benefit of collective action for an individual by z, the expected value of the outcome of (his contribution

[57] See Dasgupta and Ray (1986, 1987) for a version of this view.
[58] Hirschman (1982), p. 82.
[59] Elster (1983a, sec. II.9; 1988).

to) collective by x, and the expected value of the participation itself by y. To Hirschman's statement that $z = y + x$, I would add that y is itself a function $f(x)$ of x, constrained by $f(0) = 0$.[60] At least this would hold for rational actors. I am not denying that people sometimes try to achieve self-realization by joining a movement without believing in its goals or possible success, any more than I would deny that people sometimes make an effort to behave spontaneously or to acquire a belief in which they have no faith but which would have instrumentally useful consequences. I do deny, however, that these are rational, coherent plans.

People who participate in collective action for the sake of process benefits are in a sense free riders on the movement. To the extent that the efficacy of collective action depends on the sheer number of participants,[61] these individuals can be useful. If, however, dedication and long-term planning are needed, those who are involved in collective action just for the kick it provides will not contribute much to success and may well detract from it. Successful collective action often requires the ability to wait – to delay action rather than seize upon any occasion to act. The self-defeating character of activism, or left-wing opportunism, is a well-known theme in the history of social movements.[62] Activism may appear to be a highly motivated form of cooperation, but in a temporal perspective it can well represent a noncooperative strategy. As mentioned earlier, collective action problems may arise over time as well as across individuals.

Rational, nonselfish, outcome-oriented motivations

These motivations can take many forms. Here I shall consider only those that derive from the concern to maximize a (possibly weighted) sum of the welfare of all members of the group. Maximizing an unweighted sum amounts to utilitarian ethics. Altruism, as I shall use the term, involves maximizing a weighted sum. The weights are assumed to be non-negative, and weights assigned to others to be strictly smaller than that attached by

---

[60] Note that this is fully consistent with $f(x) > x$ for all positive x. In that sense the process values can be 'more important' than the outcome values. The sense in which the latter are more important is given by the condition $f(0) = 0$.

[61] For two recent formalizations of this idea see Roemer (1985a) and DeNardo (1985). Both treatments lack microfoundations, since they focus on the effects rather than the causes of mass behaviour.

[62] See especially the fascinating study by Meisner (1967), showing the influence of Bergson's philosophy of the Now on Chinese activism and populism.

the individual to his own welfare. Altruism, on this conception, denotes a purely psychological inclination, not a moral attitude.[63] I may just find myself deriving pleasure from other people's pleasure, even when there is no obligation or indeed no occasion to act for the sake of promoting their pleasure. To be sure, for altruism to have much bite, it must imply that there are some occasions on which I would increase someone else's first-order pleasure rather than my own.[64] But there is no need to assume that such behaviour always derives from a feeling of moral obligation. Altruism need not be anything more lofty than the converse of spite – I take pleasure not only when things go badly for X, but also when they go well with Y.

Formally, the most natural way to model altruism is as an externality in the utility function, so that my utility depends both on my consumption and on that of other people.[65] Simple models[66] represent the utility function of the altruist agent as a weighted sum of the consumption of the various members of the group, himself included. Here the weights may differ across individuals. In particular, the consumption of most other people may be assigned zero weight, with positive weights being reserved for the agent himself and his close associates. To this one may object, however, that utility cannot be assumed to be a linear function of consumption. The altruist can be expected to experience decreasing marginal utility from other people's consumption as well as from his own. To overcome this difficulty, it is natural to assume that what matters for the altruist agent is a weighted sum of his own and other people's *utility* rather than consumption. To overcome the apparent circularity of this definition, we may distinguish between exclusive and inclusive utility: the first refers to the first-order pleasures of doing and consuming, while the latter also takes account of the higher-order pleasures derived from other people's pleasure. The

---

[63] For a good analysis of the differences between selfishness, altruism and morality see Feinberg (1984), pp. 70–9. Scheffler (1982) defends a conception that one might call *moral altruism*, as distinct from psychological altruism. On this view, assigning different weights to other people's welfare allows one to take account of a frequently made objection to utilitarianism (see notably Williams 1973), namely that the impersonal benevolence it requires is inconsistent with personal integrity.

[64] Even lexicographically secondary altruism, which takes account of other people's welfare only in the choice among options that are indifferent from the point of view of the agent's own welfare, can have valuable results. My 'zone of indifference' may be quite large, and the options within it can be evaluated quite differently by other people.

[65] This kind of interdependence must be distinguished from that which makes my *consumption* dependent on that of other people. For the latter, see Pollak (1976).

[66] See M. Taylor (1987), ch. 5, and Marwell (1982).

inclusive utility function of the altruist agent can then be defined as a weighted sum of exclusive utility functions.[67]

Utilitarianism tells an agent to cooperate if and only if his contribution will bring about an increase in the average benefit. For most practical purposes, this means that he should cooperate if and only if he expects to be on an increasing stretch in the dotted lines of the diagrams of Fig. 1.5. In Fig. 1.5.A, the average-benefit curve is monotonically increasing, so that a utilitarian would have cooperation as a dominant strategy. In the other cases in Fig. 1.5, the choice of strategy depends on expectations about other people's behaviour, a topic further pursued in Chapter 5. To be on an increasing stretch means to cause, by one's contribution, the production of an additional amount of the public good such that the total gain in welfare exceeds the private costs of contributing. In principle, however, the utilitarian should be concerned not only about the direct or first-order welfare gains he causes, but also about the indirect, second-order gains he causes to be caused by other people. Even when his contribution taken by itself has a negative impact on the average net benefit, it may make it worth while for other utilitarians to contribute. Under conditions of increasing benefits or decreasing costs, the gains he causes to be caused may well exceed the first-order losses, in which case he ought to cooperate. If, however, there are decreasing costs to cooperation, he may not see why *he,* rather than some other utilitarian, should set the snowball rolling.

Utilitarianism has a peculiar feature which is responsible for some of its curious implications for the problem of collective action. This is the strict egalitarianism of the welfare calculus, in which each is to count for one and nobody for more than one. In particular, the agent is to count his own gains and losses exactly on a par with those of other people. Hence if the costs *to him* of cooperating exceed the total benefits from his contribution, he should not make it. Utilitarianism is not an other-regarding doctrine: it is self-and-other-regarding. Sometimes this makes good sense, but it can

---

[67] More generally, we could stipulate that the arguments in the inclusive utility function of the altruist agent are his own exclusive utility and the inclusive utility of everyone else. If some of the others also have altruist motivations, it might seem as though we run into an infinite regress, as suggested by M. Taylor (1987), pp. 118–19. Under reasonable assumptions, however, the sum of the successive increments of utility converges to a finite level, as shown by Becker (1976), p. 270, n. 30. Aanund Hylland (personal communication) has shown that even if the weight I attach to the inclusive utility of other people is less than the weight I attach to my own exclusive utility, the weight I attach to their exclusive utility could be larger than the weight I attach to my own.

also encourage self-indulgence, self-deception and the like.[68] For most people, acting morally is always strenuous, and it is easy to exaggerate the costs to oneself of cooperating. Knowing this, a utilitarian who is sufficiently rational to know his own propensities for irrational behaviour might be well advised to discount these costs in the calculus. He would then cooperate if and only if he expected to increase the *gross* benefits from cooperation, that is, if and only if he expected to be on a rising part of the L and R curves. Although I have assumed these to be monotonically increasing, Chapter 5 discusses some cases in which they are not.

The treatment of altruism parallels that of selective incentives. For the altruist, the weighted sum of utility increments which his contribution generates for others *is* a selective reward.[69] With linear production functions, this reward is independent of the level of contribution, and the reasoning based on Fig. 1.8 applies directly. With nonlinear production functions, the size of the reward depends on the number of contributors.

This chapter has been no more than an introduction to the problem of collective action. Several crucial aspects remain to be discussed. The assumption that the actors are homogeneous and interchangeable, while useful for expositional purposes, is clearly unrealistic. In Chapter 4 I consider the complexities that arise when the interests and resources of the agents differ. Also, the survey of motivations behind cooperation has been deliberately limited to rational outcome-oriented motives. After a general discussion of social norms in Chapter 3, I discuss their relevance to collective action in Chapter 5. There I also consider how various kinds of motivations can come together and build upon each other to produce collective action. There is no privileged motivation for cooperative behaviour across all situations. Nor, for any given situation, can we expect to find one type of motivation to provide the main explanation of successful collective action. I shall argue that mixed motivations are essential for cooperation. Certain motivations act as catalysts for others, while the latter act as multiplicators for the former.

[68] Often, utilitarians accuse others of moral self-indulgence. See, e.g., Williams (1981), ch. 3, who makes an attempt to refute a utilitarian charge of this kind. But the self- and other-regarding aspect of utilitarianism makes it vulnerable to a similar objection.

[69] Others can, in fact, benefit in two capacities: *qua* consumers of the public good and *qua* fellow altruists. If (as assumed in the text) the cooperator does not take account of the latter aspect, there could be a collective action problem among the altruists.

2. Bargaining

Introduction

Bargaining occurs when there are several cooperative arrangements and the parties have conflicting preferences over them. By a cooperative arrangement I mean any outcome (a) that is better for everybody than the state of anarchy, (b) in which there are no exploiters, defined as noncooperators whose cooperation would cost them less than it would benefit them and others, and (c) in which nobody ends up being exploited, that is, as a cooperator whose cooperation costs him more than it benefits himself and others.[1] By anarchy I mean, following the typology of cooperation set out in the Introduction, the absence of any of the following: actions with positive externalities,[2] helping, a convention equilibrium, a feasible joint venture or a private ordering.

The parties are assumed, that is, to have a common interest in arriving at some agreement but a conflict of interest over which agreement that is to be. The central problem of bargaining, in theory and practice, is that *the very plurality of cooperative arrangements may prevent any of them from coming about*. Bargaining differs from the narrowly defined collective action problem, in which there is typically a unique cooperative arrangement: that in which *everybody* participates *equally*. It also differs from cases in which there are several cooperative arrangements, but no conflict of interest, either because all are indifferent among the arrangements or because one of them is better for everybody than the others.

Bargaining must be distinguished from attempts to reach agreement by rational *discussion*.[3] One way of characterizing the latter is as bargaining in which strategic misrepresentation and other forms of jockeying for position are not allowed. Although this may capture part of the idea of ra-

---

[1] Or, more briefly, Pareto optimality without exploitation.
[2] A notion that can be extended to include the presence of negative externalities.
[3] For the latter, see, e.g., Midgaard (1980) and Habermast (1982).

tional discussion, it gives too much weight to the bargaining power of the parties. In rational discussion, the only thing supposed to count is the 'power of the better argument', including arguments that are radically dissociated from the bargaining power of the parties. Arguments from behind the 'veil of ignorance' stipulate, for example, that certain actual features of the parties are irrelevant, be it their wealth (meritocratic theories), wealth and skills (Ronald Dworkin)[4] or wealth, skill and preferences (Rawls). Bargaining, by contrast, takes account of all actual features of the parties. This is why, for instance, no bargaining process, however untainted by strategic elements, would leave the severely handicapped with anything.[5] Since they make no contribution to the net social product, they have no bargaining power. Similarly, the interests of future generations cannot be represented in a process of bargaining.[6] It follows that justice cannot be based on bargaining if one believes, as I do, that any theory of justice is constrained by an intuition that the handicapped and the future generations should not be left to their own devices.

In this chapter I discuss mainly a narrow range of bargaining problems, those, namely, that arise in joint ventures and private orderings. Bargaining problems arising out of externalities are postponed until Chapter 4. As a paradigm case of a joint venture I use cooperation between labour and capital in production, giving rise to negotiations over the division of gains from cooperation. As a paradigm case of private ordering I use bargaining over financial custody and financial settlement in the aftermath of divorce.[7]

These examples are convenient in that they involve two parties only, since theories of bargaining have been developed mainly with the two-person case in mind. Although they can be extended to the general n-person case, this extension is often artificial. n-Person bargaining theory rests on the assumption that cooperation is either total or totally absent. More precisely, the only coalition that can form is the grand coalition involving all agents, agreeing to coordinate their actions for mutual benefit. If that coalition does not form, no cooperation occurs. Sometimes this conception is empirically adequate and the general conclusions of two-person theory

[4] Dworkin (1981).

[5] It is no counterargument to say that their welfare might enter as an argument into the utility functions of other bargainers. The welfare of the handicapped should not rest on this fragile and contingent basis.

[6] For the same reason, it is no counterargument to say that the welfare of future generations may enter into the utility functions of the currently living, by concern for one's children, for example.

[7] This example is discussed at some length in Elster (1989a), ch. 3.

apply. Cartel formation, for instance, is often pointless unless all firms participate, since a single outsider might corner the market.[8] In joint ventures that require the participation of all partners, smaller coalitions are pointless. Usually no single member of a firm has the power to bring production to a complete halt, but the members may always be partitioned into groups in such a way that each group is indispensable. If the workers are organized in different unions that correspond to one such partition, n-party bargaining will be the rule.[9]

If, however, the unions that organize the firm's workers cut across functional divisions, so that two workers doing similar work could belong to different unions, bargaining that allows for coalitions of any size will tend to occur. This is also true if unions are organized along functional lines, but not in such a way that each corresponds to an indispensable group of workers. In these cases, management will try to ally itself with one union against the other. Each union has the choice between forming a united front and allying itself with the management. In such cases, n-person bargaining theory is of little help in predicting the outcome. Although there are many theories of coalition formation, I think it is fair to say that none of them is very satisfactory. Indeed, the very fact that there are so many suggests that none of them is very useful.

I shall consider three ways of approaching bargaining phenomena. First, we can try to *predict* the outcome of bargaining from the assumption that people's behaviour is guided by specific principles. In this chapter, I assume throughout that bargainers are rational. In Chapter 6 the idea that they are guided by social norms is introduced as an alternative hypothesis. Next, we can try to *describe* the pattern of outcomes that are realized in actual (experimental and real-life) bargaining. Finally, we may lay down normative principles to *evaluate* the outcomes of bargaining, by comparing them with the outcome that ought to be reached. These principles might, for instance, guide an arbitrator. I refer to these as the analytical, behavioural and normative aspects of bargaining. The main problems in the literature can then be formulated as follows. Will rational bargaining lead to a normatively acceptable outcome? Are the predictions of rational bargaining theory confirmed by behavioural evidence? If not, is there an alternative theory that performs better in this respect? If so, are the outcomes predicted by this theory normatively acceptable?

---

[8] Olson (1965), pp. 40–1.   [9] Horn and Wolinsky (1988).

From the pioneering work of John Nash,[10] bargaining has been considered mainly as a cooperative game. In this approach, the problem is not to predict whether a Pareto-optimal agreement will be reached, but to determine which settlement the parties will agree on. Failures to realize gains from cooperation are excluded by definition. (Somewhat paradoxically, the possibility of disagreement nevertheless plays a role in determining what the agreement will be.) The next section states the basic assumptions and results of this approach, which remains a fundamental tool for understanding bargaining processes.

Beginning with Nash himself, many writers have felt, however, that the cooperative theory of bargaining is an unsatisfactory description of behaviour. Pareto optimality should be derived as a theorem from individualistic premises, not stipulated as an axiom. If bargaining is understood in a normative sense, as (costless) arbitration rather than as a process of proposals and counterproposals, the stipulation that the gains from cooperation be fully realized is more acceptable, but in analytical and behavioural context the possibility of bargaining failure cannot be excluded *a priori*. There are two ways to handle this issue. One is to search for microfoundations for collective rationality, to argue that individually rational players will avoid bargaining failure. Another is to offer a positive theory of disagreement in bargaining, distinguishing between the conditions under which agreement will be reached and those in which failure may be expected. In particular, if the parties have less than full information about each other's preferences and information, bargaining may break down as each party forms unrealistic expectations about the concessions the other is willing to make.

The present chapter surveys a variety of theories and models, without displaying great faith in any of them. The reader might well wonder about the point of the exercise. The justification for my procedure is that by working through and reflecting upon these models, we enhance our understanding of the underlying issues. By seeing why and where a particular model goes wrong, we become aware of features of bargaining that otherwise would have gone unnoticed or been taken for granted. Also, each of the models probably has substantial explanatory power in special cases. In rational or 'norm-free' bargaining with full information, for instance, the standard economic models probably perform quite well. If the assumptions of rationality and full information are violated, the process of bargaining

---

[10] Nash (1950, 1953).

becomes more opaque, yet nonstandard models may at least suggest in which direction the outcome will differ from that predicted by the standard model.

Cooperative models of bargaining

Bargaining can occur over divisible or indivisible objects. Let us first assume that the objects are continuously divisible and that the point of contention is how to divide them among the parties. The objects may be one-dimensional or many-dimensional. Labour and management negotiate simultaneously over working conditions, salary, employment, the contract period and the like. Any given proposal or counterproposal is a multidimensional package. It is often convenient, however, to represent the package in terms of the utilities which the bargainers assign to it. The set of feasible bargains is represented by, or reduced to, the set of feasible utility pairs. As a result, much information about the physical features of the bargaining situation is discarded. Within a given bargaining situation, two physically different proposals may be indistinguishable in terms of the utilities assigned to them by the bargainers. Two bargaining situations which represent totally different physical problems may be represented by the same set of feasible utility pairs.

The source of utility may be one's own consumption of the object of bargaining, or someone else's consumption, possibly even that of the other bargainer, which may have positive or negative weight in one's own utility function. There is no need to assume that bargainers are selfish. Even a society of altruists would have to bargain over the allocation of goods among them. If I derive utility from your consumption of a good and you from mine, each of us will want to shift consumption towards the other. The conflict will be resolved by a sequence of offers and counteroffers that is formally indistinguishable from, say, the process of labour–management bargaining described later. The basic source of bargaining problems is scarcity of resources, not selfish motivations. Note also that because the parties are bargaining over utilities, it makes no sense to suggest that malevolent bargainers, who derive pleasure from each other's noncomsumption, have an incentive to let bargaining break down. The suggestion would involve double counting, since any externalities in the utility function would already be incorporated into the representation of the feasible utility pairs.

For analytical purposes, the representation of the situation as bargaining over utility is often quite acceptable. If the task is to predict the outcome of bargaining among rational individuals, it is not implausible to assume that they are interested only in the utilities they derive from the outcomes, and not in the physical carriers of these utilities. If, however, one suspects that bargainers are not always fully rational, the simplification may be less defencible. If they are subject to cognitive bias and distortion, they may be distracted by irrelevant physical aspects of the situation.[11] Attempts to predict the outcome that do not take account of such psychological tendencies are then likely to fail. Also, in the absence of full information about preferences, salient features of the physical situation may be important determinants of the outcome. Equal or proportional physical diversion are obvious focal points when utilities are unknown.[12] Moreover, for normative purposes the physical aspects of the situation may be directly relevant. It has been shown experimentally that the problem of distributing a given number of avocados and grapefruit between two people yields very different ethical intuitions when we are told that these fruits are valued for their taste and when we are told that they are valued for their content of vitamin C, even if the utility functions are identical in both cases.[13]

Assuming, then, a situation in which two parties are bargaining over divisible objects represented by their utilities, we can state the cooperative approach in terms of a diagram (Fig. 2.1). The *bargaining situation* is fully described by a set of feasible utility pairs (derived from the set of feasible physical bargains) and a disagreement point which specifies the utility of the outcome that will be produced if the parties fail to reach agreement. (The role of the disagreement point is controversial, and discussed later.) We assume that the set of feasible utility pairs includes all points in the area circumscribed by *OPABTO* and that *d* is the disagreement point. The feasible set is assumed to be convex, meaning that all points on a line between two feasible points are also feasible. If, for instance, the bargaining is over the division of a sum of money, the decreasing utility of money will ensure the convexity of the feasible set. The question is which if any of the feasible points will be chosen as the outcome or the 'solution' to the

---

[11] See notably Bazerman and Carroll (1987).   [12] Schelling (1963).

[13] Yaari and Bar-Hillel (1984). They also show, more disturbingly perhaps, that intuitions differ in situations that have identical representations in utility space *and* rest on similar evaluations.

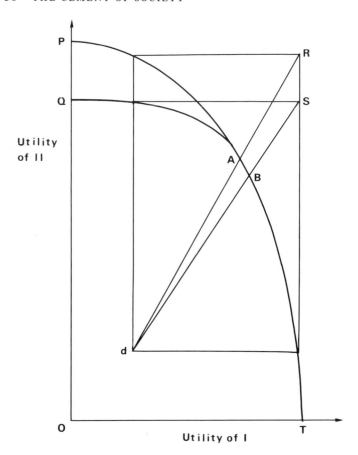

Fig. 2.1

bargaining problem. A *theory of bargaining* – analytical or normative – can be summarized by a function f which for any bargaining problem – any convex set S and any disagreement point d – picks an element in S as the outcome that will be reached or ought to be reached.

The construction of such a function is a nontrivial task. Nash did it by laying down conditions which one would expect any pair of rational bargainers (or any fair arbitrator) to respect and showing that there was only one function satisfying all of them. Specifically, he stipulated four conditions:

1. *Pareto optimality.* It should not be possible to improve the outcome for one party without loss for the other. The solution should be on the Pareto frontier, *PABT* in the diagram.
2. *Invariance.* The solution should be invariant with respect to positive linear utility transformations. This condition is explained later.
3. *Symmetry.* If the feasible set is symmetrical around the 45° line, with the disagreement point on that line, the solution should also be on that line.
4. *Independence of irrelevant alternatives.* If we have two bargaining problems (*S, d*) and (*T, d*) with *S* included in *T* and if the solution to (*T, d*) is a member of *S*, it should also be the solution to (*S, d*). Or more simply, if the solution in a larger game remains feasible in a smaller game, it should also be the solution in the latter.

Nash proved that these conditions, together with the assumption that the set of feasible utility pairs is convex, uniquely define a solution concept: the outcome of bargaining is constrained to be the point in the feasible set which *maximizes the product of the utility gains* of the parties, compared with the disagreement point. In the game (*OPABTO, d*) this is the point *A*. From a normative point of view, this solution concept has no special appeal, apart from the axioms which jointly imply it. Indeed, it might appear positively unattractive, because of the following property. If we assume that a poor man and a rich man are bargaining over the way to divide some amount of money large enough to be very important to the poor man, the Nash solution will assign most of it to the rich man, because he can more credibly make a proposal favourable to himself and say, 'Take it or leave it'.[14] This is the 'Matthew effect' in bargaining.

The Nash solution often corresponds well to institutions about the way people actually behave in bargaining situations, but one might argue that it ought not to be chosen by an arbitrator who tries to reach a fair decision. Other solutions might appear more attractive, such as the point which maximizes the sum of the utility gains of the parties, the point on the Pareto-frontier point that equalizes their utility gains or, more strongly, some point that implies a larger utility gain to the poor man than to the rich. These proposals, however, violate the invariance condition (about which more later). And in any case one might argue that even from an arbitration

[14] Luce and Raiffa (1957), pp. 129–32.

point of view, the task is not necessarily to find the abstractly just outcome, but one that is *appropriate* given the bargaining power of the parties.[15]

Before I discuss the axioms, it is time to meet an obvious objection: How does bargaining theory handle situations in which there is only a small number of feasible outcomes? Does it single out one of them as the solution? In that case, how does it handle symmetrical cases in which each of two nondisagreement outcomes gives everything to one party and nothing to the other? We can use Solomon's judgement to illustrate the problem. Before he knew anything about the preferences of the parties, he had to treat them as identical. There was no reason for preferring one woman over the other. The set of feasible outcomes not being convex, the symmetrical solution prescribed by the Nash axioms is not available. Solomon's first proposal, cutting the child in half, effectively amounted to an arbitration impasse. The reactions of the women to that proposal enabled him to form a better impression of their preferences and, indeed, to make a better decision. But what if both women had reacted as the true mother did, the false one hoping that her willingness to give the child to the other would stop Solomon from doing so? In that case, what should he have done?

Let us consider a similar problem that arises between spouses in child custody bargaining, conceived as private ordering and not as arbitration. I shall assume that there are two children, a boy and a girl, with four possible custody arrangements (with respective utility assignments) corresponding to the vertices of Fig. 2.2.

In most divorces, bargaining over custody takes place simultaneously with bargaining over the financial settlement. The two negotiations tend to be coupled, so that the parents try to extract financial advantages by offering custody and vice versa. Let us suppose that the vertices represent the parties' utility for the various custody arrangements together with one particular financial settlement, namely that which the court will make if the parties cannot reach agreement by themselves.[16] Intermediate outcomes can then be generated by allowing the parties to transfer money to each other, if necessary by borrowing. These outcomes will *not* correspond to the straight lines between the vertices. Because the parties have decreasing marginal utility of money and because the utility of money interacts with

[15] Selten (1987), pp. 46–7.
[16] Courts, unlike bargaining spouses, dissociate financial settlements from custody settlements.

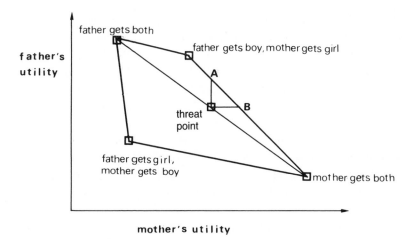

Fig. 2.2

that of custody, the relation will be more complex. But the set of intermediate outcomes will be convex, as required by bargaining theory, so
that a solution can be derived.

Side payments are not always feasible. Perhaps one of the parents has
no money and is unable to get a loan. Or perhaps the situation is such that
side payments are thought to be ethically unacceptable. The parents might
agree, for instance, to make the financial settlement before the custody
decision, because it will hurt the children to think that they are convertible
into money. Another, more general way of generating intermediate outcomes is then available, at least in principle. Solomon could have flipped
a coin to decide between the women. The parents can use a lottery in which
the various allocations are assigned definite probabilities, adding up to 1.
To each such lottery corresponds a point within the quadrangle defined by
the four allocations. The utility of a lottery is simply the sum of the utilities
of the allocations weighted by their probability. (This is explained later.)
Thus the points on a line between two vertices correspond to lotteries in
which the allocations underlying these vertices are assigned probabilities p
and $1 - p$, with p taking on all values between 0 and 1. In this way, the set
of feasible outcomes is rendered convex, so that bargaining theory can be
applied.

To predict the outcome of the bargaining, we must first make an assumption about the threat point. We can stipulate, as in Fig. 2.2, that the

parents believe that in a legal dispute each of them has a 50 per cent chance of getting custody of both children. This belief could be brought about in several ways. If the legal rule is to give custody according to what is in the best interests of the child, the parents might well believe that there is no detectable difference in fitness between them, so that, for all they know, each has as good a chance as the other of getting custody. Or the legal rule might actually be to use a fair coin to settle the issue.[17] Whatever the grounds for the fifty–fifty expectation, it follows that the expected utility of the parents in the case of a legal dispute is midway on the line between the vertices corresponding to maternal custody of both children and paternal custody of both. Both parents know that by going to court they can achieve at least this level of expected utility; hence they will reject any proposed solution which offers them less. (For simplicity, I ignore the costs of litigation.) If, moreover, we assume that they will not accept any solution which is worse for both than some other feasible outcome, we see that if they reach an agreement, it will be somewhere on the line AB. Each point on AB assigns a probability p that the mother gets custody of both children and a probability $1 - p$ that the father gets the boy and the mother gets the girl. By inspecting Fig. 2.2 we can see that p ranges between .22 and .45 (approximate values).

When parents bargain over custody, they will rarely if ever choose a point on AB. Indeed, I think lotteries are virtually never used to settle private, nontrivial disputes. I have no systematic empirical evidence to back this claim, only casual observation, together with some general arguments. First, of course, the conditions under which lotteries or probabilistic compromises are superior to physical compromises may not often be realized. In particular, when side payments are available and acceptable, they provide a much more robust form of compromise. Second, even when a lottery seems to be called for, lack of enforceability might prevent it from being used. Each party might agree to a lottery in the hope that the outcome will be his or her preferred alternative, and then renege if it turns our differently. The knowledge that this may happen could easily prevent a lottery from being attempted in the first place.[18] And as far as I know, no country has a public official or public institution with the power to carry

[17] I discuss this proposal in Elster (1989a), sec. 3.5.

[18] Lotteries in private bargaining without a third-party enforcer will be used only if the parties are moved by 'self-interest without guile', as explained in the concluding chapter.

out and enforce lotteries privately agreed upon by the parties. Hence I shall not consider lotteries as a serious way of resolving bargaining impasses.

Let us, then, limit our attention to bargaining over divisible objects and to bargaining over indivisible objects in which side payments are possible. With convexity thus ensured, the plausibility of the Nash solution depends on the plausibility of the four axioms. I have already discussed the condition of Pareto optimality, and I shall have more to say about it later. First, however, I discuss the other Nash conditions one by one.

Invariance has the effect of imposing a special kind of utility function on the bargaining situation. At one extreme, one can show that with purely ordinal utility functions the bargaining problem cannot be defined.[19] At the other extreme, one may argue that well-known problems associated with interpersonal comparison of utilities prevent us from defining such solution concepts as 'maximize the sum of the utility gains' or 'equalize the utility gains'. An intermediate category, represented by the invariance condition, is that of a von Neumann–Morgenstern utility function, in which utility is uniquely given up to an arbitrary positive multiplicative constant and an arbitrary additive constant.[20] The relation between any two utility functions which represent the preferences of a given individual is like the relation of Celsius to Fahrenheit temperature scales. Statements such as 'The sum of temperatures in New York and Chicago is larger than the sum of temperatures in London and Paris' are not meaningful, since they do not always retain their truth value when we go from Celsius to Fahrenheit. By contrast, the statement 'The difference in temperature between New York and Chicago is larger than that between London and Paris' is meaningful, since its truth value does not depend on the choice of temperature scale. Analogously, interpersonal comparisons of utility levels are meaningless with von Neumann–Morgenstern utility functions, but some interpersonal comparisons of intrapersonal differences are feasible. In particular, statements comparing the rate of change of the marginal utility of money and commodities are meaningful. In the bargaining problem between the rich man and the poor man, the latter is at a disadvantage because for him the marginal utility of money decreases rapidly while for the rich man it is approximately constant.

The invariance condition is, however, implausible, on analytical, be-

---

[19] Shubik (1982), pp. 92–8.
[20] For a lucid exposition, see Luce and Raiffa (1957), ch. 2.

havioural and normative grounds. To see why, consider two bargaining problems A and B, both involving the same bargainers I and II.[21] In both problems the bargainers are assumed to be indistinguishable, in the sense that any utility function that represents I's preferences can also represent those of II. In both games, the object of the bargaining is to agree on two numbers p and q between 0 and 1 and summing to 1 or less. If they agree, I has probability p of winning the prize in a certain lottery and II probability q of winning the prize *in another lottery*. If they cannot agree, neither gets anything. In bargaining problem A both lotteries involve similar prizes, namely two bicycles. By symmetry and Pareto optimality, the outcome of the bargaining must be $p = q = .5$. In bargaining problem B everything is unchanged, except that the prize in I's lottery now is a Rolls Royce. Assuming invariance, it is easy to see that the solution must be the same, that is, $p = q = .5$. Consider, namely, the utility to I of any outcome (p, q) in II. Writing u for the utility to him of the Rolls Royce and v for the utility to him of the bicycle, the utility of (p, q) to him is $p \cdot u = p[u/v]v = [u/v]pv$. In other words, the utility he derives from any given probability in the second bargaining problem equals the utility he derives from the same probability in the first problem, multiplied by a positive constant u/v. But this means that the second bargaining problem can be derived from the first by a positive linear transformation, so that the solution must be the same.

This result is analytically implausible. In problem B, II would certainly be able to demand $q > .5$. He could say, credibly, that since I's desire for a Rolls Royce was much stronger than his own desire for a bicycle, I must accept $p < .5$: 'Take it or leave it'. To be sure, this involves interpersonal comparison of utilities, but not a very difficult one since the prizes are so different, assuming that I and II are reasonably similar persons.[22] From a normative point of view it is also arbitrary that I should get a 50 per cent chance of a very valuable object and II a 50 per cent chance of a much less

[21] The following draws upon Kalai (1985) and Roth (1987).

[22] For an argument that interpersonal comparisons of utility are not only possible but inevitable see Davidson (1986). A method for constructing interpersonal comparisons from intrapersonal comparisons is proposed by Ortuño-Ortin and Roemer (1987). It is clear that sometimes we have no difficulty carrying out such comparisons. It would be tempting to conclude that with more progress in psychology an increasing number of cases should lend themselves to comparison. This presupposes, however, that utility (or happiness, welfare or well-being) is a one-dimensional concept. If, however, utility is many-dimensional (as suggested in Sen 1980–1), we may never be able to do better than a partial ordering of welfare levels.

valuable one. Surely, in the absence of further information about them[23] the reasonable solution would be to choose p and q so as to equalize expected monetary reward – not to equalize the chances of getting two very different rewards. When we throw away information not only about the physical nature of the problem, but also about interpersonal utility information, we lose an essential aspect of the bargaining process. In fact, our intuitions about the bargaining problem between the rich man and the poor man probably derive as much from interpersonal comparisons of utility as from the fact that the poor man's marginal utility decreases more rapidly. To a poor man, an extra dollar simply means much more than it does to the rich, who has, therefore, much less to lose if no bargain is struck.[24]

Alvin Roth and his collaborators conducted extensive behavioural studies of the invariance condition.[25] They found that with different prizes the outcome of bargaining was not a fifty–fifty allocation of the chances. On average, the outcomes favoured the party with a smaller prize. They did not find, however, that the outcomes clustered around the allocation that would give equal expected monetary value. Rather the distribution was bimodal and tended to 'cluster around two "focal points": the equal probability agreement and the "equal expected value" agreement that gives each bargainer the same expected value'.[26] This finding suggests that to have an equal division of *something* is more important than the nature of the dividendum. This idea, which is also supported by studies from non-bargaining contexts,[27] is explored in Chapter 6.

Symmetry is intended to capture the idea that when the parties have the same bargaining power, the outcome should in some sense reflect that equality. Given invariance, 'bargaining power' cannot here refer to absolute levels of utility. It has to be understood in terms of features which remain invariant under positive linear transformations. If we think again in terms of an underlying monetary bargain, one such feature could be the rate of decrease of the marginal utility of money. The notion of bargaining power is discussed separately later.

---

[23] It could be, of course, that A is so inept at transforming goods into utility that he requires a Rolls Royce to achieve the same utility level for which B needs only a bicycle. But surely the burden of proof will then be on A to produce evidence about this unlikely state of affairs.

[24] I am grateful to Luc Bovens for helping me see more clearly the relation between intrapersonal and interpersonal comparisons of utility in such cases.

[25] Summarized in Roth (1987).

[26] Ibid., p. 21.   [27] Harris and Joyce (1980).

Independence of irrelevant alternatives implies, in terms of Fig. 2.1, that when the feasible set is restricted from *OPABTO* to *OQABTO*, the solution should remain at *A* since this point remains feasible. One might want to object to this condition. It would appear that the bargaining strength of II is weakened when the part of the feasible set which is most favourable to him is eliminated. Hence if outcomes reflect bargaining strength, II should fare worse in the smaller bargaining problem than in the larger. At the very least, he should not be able to improve his position when the odds change against him. To capture this intuition Ehud Kalai and Meir Smorodinsky have proposed an alternative condition, to be substituted for the Nash independence condition.[28] This *axiom of monotonicity*, like the independence condition, is stated as a comparison between two bargaining problems. It says that if, for every utility level that player I may demand, the maximum feasible utility level for player II is at least as large in the second game as in the first, then the utility level assigned to player II according to the solution should not be less in the second game than in the first. Or, more briefly, no one should suffer from the feasible set expanding in his favour.

Kalai and Smorodinsky proved that this condition, together with Pareto optimality, invariance and symmetry, implies the following solution concept. The utility gains should be proportional to the maximum feasible gains which the parties could achieve. In Fig. 2.1, the (nonfeasible) combination of the maximal feasible gains for the problem *OPABTO* is represented by the point *R*.[29] The solution occurs at the intersection between the Pareto frontier *PABT* and the line from *R* to the disagreement point *d*. In this case, the Nash solution and the Kalai–Smorodinsky solution happen to coincide. If, however, we restrict the feasible set to *OQABTO* the Nash solution remains at *A* while the Kalai–Smorodinsky solution is moved to *B*.

This solution concept is arguably more plausible than that of Nash, both on behavioural and on normative grounds. 'Intuitions about "bargaining power" and "fairness" might include the notion that if A *could* win a lot in a bargaining situation, he or she is "entitled" to more than if he or she could only, in the best of circumstances, win a little'.[30] Although the ex-

---

[28]   Kalai and Smorodinsky (1975).
[29]   The maximum feasible gains are constrained by the disagreement point. What I can get in the event that II gets less than his disagreement payoff cannot be relevant to the outcome.
[30]   McDonald and Solow (1981), pp. 905–6.

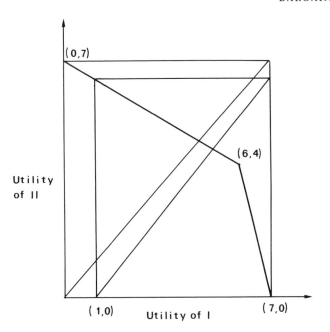

Fig. 2.3

perimental evidence is ambiguous,[31] one would expect wage bargaining, for instance, to be sensitive to the maximal feasible gain. Higher unemployment benefits, which increase the workers' reservation wage and hence reduce the maximal feasible profit, should strengthen the bargaining power of the workers. Under the Kalai–Smorodinsky solution this will always happen. In the cooperative Nash model, it may or may not happen. (We shall later see that in noncooperative models it essentially never happens.) Thus in Fig. 2.3, define S as the set spanned by $(0, 0)$, $(0, 7)$, $(6, 4)$ and $(7, 0)$ and compare the two bargaining games with disagreement points $d = (0, 0)$ and $d' = (1, 0)$. We may think of the second game as defined by an increase in the reservation wage for the workers (player I). We observe that under the Kalai–Smorodinsky solution, the outcome is shifted

[31] In their experiments, Nydegger and Owen (1975) found that the Nash solution was a better predictor than the Kalai–Smorodinsky solution. So did Roth and Malouf (1979). In support of their view, however, Kalai and Smorodinsky cite Crott (1971). The results reported by Nydegger and Owen are dominated by their subjects' massive preference for equality. A better test would involve a problem with an asymmetrical Nash solution.

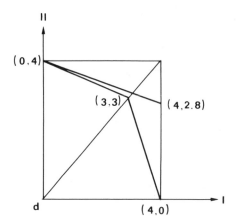

Fig. 2.4

in favour of the workers, whereas under Nash it can easily be shown to be the same in both cases, namely (6, 4).

Normatively, the monotonicity axiom seems more plausible than the independence axiom. It would seem perverse to accept a solution concept which entailed that one person could get less as a result of the feasible set expanding in his favour. Figure 2.4 (from Kalai–Smorodinsky) shows how this might happen. There are two games, both with disagreement point (0, 0) and spanned by [(0, 0), (0, 4), (3, 3) and (4, 0)] and [(0, 0), (0, 4), (4, 2.8) and (4, 0)], respectively. The Kalai–Smorodinsky solutions are found at the intersections between the diagonal and the bargaining frontiers: (3, 3) in the smaller game and (40/13, 40/13) in the larger. The Nash solutions are at the corners in both games. In the second game II is more highly favoured than in the first game,[32] and yet under Nash he ends up with less in the second.

If we try to assess the two conditions from an analytical point of view, to determine which, if any, would be respected by rational players, intuition can easily lead us astray. Both conditions have analogues in the theory of individual choice, where they are plausible and perfectly consistent with each other. Here the independence condition says that choices should not change when the feasible set contracts to exclude an item that was not chosen in the first place. If the menu offers beef, chicken and salmon and

---

[32] Actually, both parties are more highly favoured. However, I gains under both solution concepts when the feasible set is expanded in his favour.

the customer has chosen chicken, he should not, barring special circumstances,[33] switch to beef upon hearing that the restaurant is out of salmon. The monotonicity condition for individual choice simply says that less is never preferred to more. Barring special cases,[34] this condition also seems innocent and compelling.

When we go from one-person choice to two-person bargaining, however, the conditions are far from compelling. This is partially reflected in the fact that they cannot be satisfied simultaneously, given the other Nash axioms, but since those axioms themselves are far from unquestionable we should not place too much weight on the inconsistency. One should just be wary in general of thinking that the constraints on the outcome of individual choice carry over to the outcome of bargaining.[35] The conditions must be justified directly as conditions *on bargaining,* not by analogy from individual choice.[36]

Both the independence condition and the monotonicity conditions are stated in terms of a comparison between two bargaining situations. There is no reason for these to involve the same persons, or the same bargaining objects. All that matters is that the feasible utility sets and the disagreement points are related in certain ways. Yet the conditions should also apply to the special case when the same individuals are bargaining under different circumstances. When interpreted in this way, Nash's independence condition appears implausible. Consider, for instance, wage bargaining under full employment, before and after protectionist measures have been passed for the industry in question. Michael Wallerstein has shown[37] that (a close relative of) the Kalai–Smorodinsky solution ensures that both workers and management benefit when protectionism is introduced in a situation of full employment. The workers get higher wages, the management higher prof-

---

[33] He might rationally do so, however, if he believes that restaurants which make good chicken always make a point of being well stocked with salmon. Levi (1986) shows that similar behaviour might also occur as a by-product of a rational way of coping with value conflicts. Less rational ways in which the feasible set can affect preferences are discussed in Elster (1983a), ch. 3.

[34] A restaurant customer might prefer less to more if he believes that the quality of each item is inversely proportional to the number of items from which he can choose. A rational individual who knows his own propensity to overeat might want to have less food in the house rather than more. Elster (1984), ch. 2, offers a survey of such cases.

[35] Crawford (1984), p. 378.

[36] An attempt to provide strategic foundations for the independence condition is that of Binmore (1987b). The argument is less compelling, however, than the corresponding argument for the irrelevance of outside options, further discussed later.

[37] Wallerstein (1987).

its. Under the Nash solution, however, the workers do not benefit at all from the larger earning power of their firm.[38] By contrast, in a situation of unemployment workers do benefit from protectionism under both solution concepts. Hence Wallerstein concludes, 'Unions, according to the Nash solution, are foul-weather allies in protectionist coalitions'. While the Nash solution, like any bargaining solution, specifies that both parties benefit from cooperating, it does not always imply that both parties gain from an increase in the gains from cooperation. Intuitively, this makes no sense. Surely, the workers would insist on a share in the increased earnings made possible by protectionism.[39] If the Nash solution predicts otherwise, this goes only to show how implausible it is.

This observation can be generalized. All varieties of formal bargaining theory, when applied to wage negotiations, imply that the primary thing to be explained is the wage level. Wage increases, by contrast, are secondary – to be derived by subtracting one wage level from another. There is no analytical difference between wage differences and wage increases. It makes no difference whether (S, d) and (S', d') are two bargaining games that take place on two different planets or two games that take place between the same management and the same union in two successive years. In actual wage bargaining, of course, these two cases differ vastly, since the workers remember what they got last time. The baseline for bargaining is given not only by what they would get in the absence of any cooperation, but also by what they got in the previous round of negotiations. If (S, d) and (S', d') took place on two different planets, the outcome might conceivably be the same even though the first occurred in a nonprotectionist and the second in a protectionist context. It is *not* conceivable, however, that a union would accept an unchanged wage when the firm suddenly benefited from protectionist measures. One cannot assume that wage increases can simply be derived from wage levels. Sometimes a separate analytical apparatus may be needed to explain wage increases. I return to these matters in Chapter 6.

Noncooperative bargaining theory

Usually, we think of competition and bargaining as intensely interactive and conflictual processes, involving winners and losers, failures as well as

---

[38] The result presupposes a production function of the Cobb–Douglas kind. With other functions, the counterintuitive conclusion does not follow.

[39] I am indebted to Fredrik Engelstad for forcing this point on me.

successes. Mainstream economic theory has taken the bite out of both, representing them by the equilibrium features of their outcomes rather than by their internal dynamics. Reactions to the aseptic and sanitized notion of competition have come mainly from the Austrian school of economics, including contemporary followers of Joseph Schumpeter.[40] By and large, the mainstream remains unaffected by the criticism. Although the objections are often telling, their target is well and alive, protected by the fact that you cannot beat something with nothing. Where the alternative writers pride themselves on the realism of their models, the mainstream economist sees only ad hoc assumptions in stark contrast to the simplicity and power of equilibrium theory.[41]

Attempts to desanitize bargaining theory have proved more successful, but only after several false starts. The features of bargaining that must be incorporated into a dynamic model with rational players include the following. First, bargaining is a *process* that can be broken down into successive offers and counteroffers. A bargaining solution must be defined as the outcome of a process of bargaining or, more subtly, as driven by the anticipation of this process, which need not actually take place. Second, bargaining is *costly*. For one thing, players who care more about the present than the future always suffer from a delay. A fifty–fifty split of a dollar between you and me tomorrow is worth less to each of us than the same division today. 'If it did not matter when people agreed, it would not matter whether or not they agreed at all'.[42] Other costs of bargaining are discussed later. Third, threats made in the course of bargaining must be *credible*. A rational bargainer with no access to precommitment devices will not be taken seriously if he makes a threat which it will not be in his interest to carry out when the time to do so arrives. A father might say, for instance, that if the mother gets custody he will not exercise his visitation rights, thus harming the child and, through the child, the mother. But if the mother knows that the father is too rational to cut off his nose to spite his face, she will not take the threat seriously. Management cannot credibly threaten with lock-out if the workers know that the ensuing loss of customers would cripple the firm.

An early attempt to provide noncooperative foundations for cooperative bargaining theory was made by John Harsanyi.[43] He showed in 1956 that a model of stepwise bargaining, governed by a concession rule proposed

---

[40] Nelson and Winter (1982) offer the most fully developed version of this view.

[41] For elaborations of this argument, see Elster (1983c, 1986).

[42] Cross (1965), p. 196.   [43] Harsanyi (1956), more fully set out in Harsanyi (1977a).

by Fredric Zeuthen some twenty-five years earlier, converges to Nash's solution of bargaining as a cooperative game. One problem with Harsanyi's argument is that there is far from full agreement that the concession rule is rational. A deeper problem stems from the fact that although bargaining in his model takes place in real time, so that the sequence of proposals and counterproposals actually has to be gone through, it is assumed to be costless. He neglects the fact that in a temporally extended sequence of proposals and counterproposals the parties are in effect bargaining over a shrinking pie. An agreement may finally be reached, but in the meantime much of the gain from cooperation has been squandered.

Harsanyi's model satisfies only the first requirement, that the model of bargaining be process-oriented. Other models, which also satisfy the second requirement, rest on artificial assumptions about motivation and expectations.[44] Ariel Rubinstein's path-breaking 1982 article provided the first model in which all three requirements are satisfied.[45] To explain the workings of the model, I shall proceed in three steps. First, I shall explain the idea of a *perfect equilibrium,* which is central to these noncooperative models of bargaining. Next, I shall illustrate the idea with respect to a particular bargaining problem. Finally, I shall use an ingenious technique invented by A. Shaked and J. Sutton to derive the solution to a simple, although representative, bargaining game.

The traditional equilibrium concept in noncooperative game theory is, like the best-known solution concept in cooperative bargaining theory, associated with John Nash.[46] As explained in the Introduction, an equilibrium (or Nash equilibrium, as it is usually called) is a set of strategies that are best replies to each other. In equilibrium, nobody can improve his outcome by unilateral deviation. In games with several equilibria, game theory often has no way of determining which will in fact be chosen.[47] In such cases, it was usually assumed that one equilibrium is as likely to be realized as any other, until Reinhard Selten demonstrated that only perfect

---

[44] Cross (1965); Coddington (1968).

[45] Rubinstein (1982). An early forerunner of Rubinstein's model is found in Ståhl (1972). The relation between the two models is explained in Ståhl (1988).

[46] Nash (1951).

[47] Harsanyi and Selten (1988), who offer a 'general theory for equilibrium selection', point out (p. 366) that 'Rubinstein's approach provides an interesting alternative in many cases to our own theory for selecting a unique solution to sequential games. But in its present form it seems that it cannot be extended to games involving simultaneous moves by the players'. My concern here is with sequential games, for which Rubinstein provides a simple and tractable analysis.

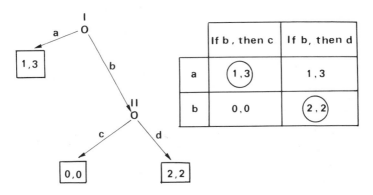

Fig. 2.5

equilibria – to be defined in a moment – will in fact be chosen.[48] Nash equilibria that are not perfect, such as equilibria that rest on noncredible threats, will never be realized.

Figure 2.5 offers two representations of the same game.[49] The left-hand representation shows the game in *extensive form,* as a sequence of moves and countermoves. Player I moves first. If he chooses *a,* the game is over. If he chooses *b,* player II chooses between *c* and *d.* Numbers at the end nodes represent payoffs to the players, the first number being the payoff to I. The right-hand representation has reduced the game to the *normal form,* which states the relations between strategies and outcomes in a compact way. In fact, the normal-form representation is too compact, since vital information is lost. In the normal form there are two equilibria, (1, 3) and (2, 2). For all we know, either might be realized. The extensive form makes it clear, however, that the outcome (1, 3) will never be reached, unless II can precommit himself to use *c* in case I plays *b.* The threat to use *c* is not credible, since it will not be in II's interest to execute the threat if the second node should be reached. If we assume that precommitment is unfeasible, I will play *b.*[50]

I shall now extend this reasoning to sequential bargaining games, in which the parties take turns making proposals and counterproposals. The game comes to an end when one party makes an offer that is accepted by the other. For simplicity, assume that the parties are bargaining over the

---

[48] Selten (1975).   [49] The example is taken from Harsanyi (1977b).

[50] In the next chapter and in the concluding chapter I discuss how *social norms* could lend credibility to I's threat.

Fig. 2.6

division of a dollar. A *strategy* in sequential bargaining is a response function that for any sequence of offers and counteroffers up to a given point defines a unique behaviour: either acceptance of the previous offer or, if that is rejected, a new offer. An *insistent offer* is a response function that always makes the same demand and accepts only if the same proposal is made by the other party. Clearly, any Pareto-optimal pair of insistent offers is an equilibrium. If one party insists on getting $1 - x$ and the other insists on x, we are in equilibrium, for any x between 0 and 1. But are all these equilibria perfect? Is the threat to hold out credible?

Consider the game depicted in Fig. 2.6.[51] Players I and II are to divide a dollar. We assume that the parties incur costs in each bargaining period – for instance, because of the need to pay lawyers. (Time discounting is *not* assumed here.) The utility to I of getting s at t is $s - 0.1t$. The utility to II of getting s at t is $s - 0.2t$. Clearly, II is at a disadvantage, since his lawyer is twice as expensive as I's.[52] Suppose that II has decided to hold out for 0.5 and that at time t I makes an offer of $(0.6, 0.4)$. Can II credibly hold out? If II accepts, she gets $0.4 - 0.2t$. If she holds out for 0.5, she can *at most* get $0.5 - (t + 1)0.2 = 0.3 - 0.2t$. But that is less than she could get by accepting the offer; hence the threat to hold out is not credible. Note that the credibility of threats is intimately linked to the costs of bargaining.

Consider next a worker and a firm bargaining over a dollar, with the cost of bargaining represented by the fact that future payoffs are discounted to present value by a factor d, the same for both parties. This is the only cost of bargaining. Offers are made and accepted or rejected in the same time period. But a new offer has to be made in a new period. In other words, to refuse an offer always involves a costly delay, which may or may not be offset by the prospect of getting a better deal. The firm makes the first offer. Then consider the subsequence shown in Fig. 2.7.

[51] From Rubinstein (1982).
[52] This difference might reflect superior bargaining abilities of II's lawyer. But there is no way in which this element can be incorporated into this model.

Fig. 2.7

Considered from $t = 0$, the discounted value of what the firm and the worker will have to divide at $t = 2$ is d^2. Let us look (still from the point of $t = 0$) at the subgame that begins at $t = 2$. Suppose that M cents is the maximum the firm can get in any perfect equilibrium of this subgame. We do not know what this maximum is, except that it is determined by the feasible set and by the *bargaining power* (explained later) of the parties. In this case, the only source of asymmetrical bargaining power derives from the fact that the firm moves first. Discounted to $t = 0$, the value of this maximum is $d^2 \cdot M$. Consider now, still from the point of view of $t = 0$, what the worker should do at $t = 1$. He does not have to offer the firm more than $d^2 \cdot M$, because the firm cannot credibly hold out for more. If the firm rejects the offer, it has to go into a new period, in which it can get at most $d^2 \cdot M$. At $t = 1$, the total value of the dividendum is d. Thus the worker gets at least $d - d^2 \cdot M$. Consider now the offer made by the firm in the first period. Any offer it makes has to leave the worker with at least $d - d^2 \cdot M$. Hence the maximum of what the firm can get is $1 - (d - d^2 \cdot M)$. But the game at $t = 0$ is identical to the game at $t = 2$. In both cases, the two players look down the same infinite path of offers and counteroffers. Hence the maximal amounts the firm can get in these two games must be the same.

From $M = 1 - (d - d^2 \cdot M)$ we derive $M = 1/(1 + d)$. This also turns out to be the minimum of what the firm can get, since the game argument can be repeated, minima and maxima being interchanged throughout. Since M is both the maximum and the minimum of what the firm will get, it defines the outcome of the bargaining game. The worker's share is $d/(1 + d)$. The agreement will be reached in the first bargaining round, since neither party can gain from holding out. Assume that $d = 0.9$, so that both are quite patient. Then the firm gets 0.53 and the worker gets 0.47. Assume that $d = 0.5$, so that both are quite impatient. Then the firm gets two-thirds and the firm gets one-third. In other words, the heavier the parties discount the future, the larger the advantage of being the first player.

This argument relies heavily on backward induction and hence is vulnerable to the objections stated in the Introduction. On the one hand, the argument is supposed to show that the firm and the worker will reach agreement instantaneously, agreeing to share the dollar as just stated. On the other hand, what forces agreement is the prospect of offers and counteroffers in later bargaining rounds. *But the assumption that there will be later bargaining rounds is inconsistent with the conclusion derived from that assumption.* When the firm contemplates the idea of being at $t = 2$, it should know that this can occur only if something goes wrong, since if both are rational they will never get that far down the path. Perhaps the reason they are at $t = 2$ is that the worker is irrational. But in that case, he might be so stubborn as to hold out for something he should know he cannot get. Faced with a potentially irrational opponent, the firm might have to concede more than it would otherwise have done. The worker, of course, has to go through similar reasoning. The outcome is essentially indeterminate. As I said in the Introduction, I suspect that the last word on the matter has not been said.

By now, a variety of noncooperative bargaining models have been proposed, differing mainly in the determinants of the costs of bargaining.[53] First, there are time-preference models similar to the one just discussed, but allowing for the possibility that the parties may have different rates of time discounting. Second, there are fixed-cost models of the kind mentioned earlier, with, for instance, the need to pay lawyers being the main cost of bargaining. Third, there are models that stipulate an exogenously given probability that bargaining might break down – for instance, because the opportunity for a joint venture ceases to be present. A firm and an inventor bargaining over a contract run the risk, for instance, that if negotiations drag out another firm might preempt the idea. Some models relax the assumption of alternate offers and counteroffers by stipulating that after the proposal and rejection of an offer there is a positive probability that the same party will make the next offer.[54]

Bargaining power

Both cooperative and noncooperative models of bargaining try to capture the notion of bargaining power. Focusing on the simple case of dividing a sum of money, deviation from equal division can be explained only by

[53] For surveys, see Sutton (1986) and Binmore, Rubinstein and Wolinsky (1986).
[54] See, e.g., Moene (1988b).

This demonstration does not automatically provide microfoundations for the Nash solution as traditionally conceived. For one thing, when the bargaining interval is incompressible – perhaps because the union leader has to go back to his constituency to discuss the offer – the Nash solution will not obtain. More important, the disagreement point in the noncooperative version of the Nash solution differs from the traditional conception of the status quo in bargaining. Because the point is fundamental, it should be discussed at some length.

Using wage bargaining as an example, we can ask what happens if management and the union fail to reach agreement. There are two ways of looking at the matter. One is to assume that the parties fall back on their *outside options*, that is, on the state which would obtain if the joint venture were definitely dismantled. The workers may find a job in another firm or live on unemployment benefits. Assuming that managers act only as representatives of the owners, they may sell off the physical assets of the firm and redeploy the capital elsewhere. In child custody bargaining, the outside option of the parties is represented by the expected legal decision. An alternative is to assume that the joint venture is only temporarily dismantled until agreement is reached. In that case the parties must do with their *inside options*, that is, what they can get during the conflict. The workers might have to rely on their strike funds. The firm might get support from the employers' association. One of the parents usually has temporary custody until they agree on a final settlement or refer the matter to the court.

It seems clear that both inside and outside options are relevant to the outcome of bargaining.[57] Noncooperative theorists argue, however, that they matter in fundamentally different ways.[58] Outside options *constrain* the outcome but do not influence it in any other way. Inside options affect

[57] A good example is provided by inside subcontracting in Hungarian enterprises (Szirá-czki 1989). In this system, skilled workers in the firm are allowed to set up work partnerships that 'have authority and legal status as semi-autonomous economic units to enter into contracts [usually with the mother enterprise] to produce goods and services during free hours, using factory equipment'. The outside options in firm–partnership bargaining are, for the firm, the price of outside labour (often Polish workers or workers hired from cooperatives) and, for the workers, normal overtime pay. Inside options also affect the outcome, since workers 'frequently use their tacit knowledge of the economic difficulties of firms to bargain for better rates for their partnerships'. Sabel and Stark (1982), p. 458, make the opposite argument: 'The existence of such a secondary economy clearly augments the bargaining power of workers in the primary plants'. To the extent that these secondary jobs are in inside subcontracting, the argument seems incorrect. Since only workers who already hold a regular job in the firm are allowed to enter work partnerships, they cannot credibly threaten to leave the firm and work full time in the second economy.

[58] See especially Sutton, Shaked and Binmore (1986).

unequal bargaining power. Here I consider mainly bargaining power derived from the material preferences and resources of the parties as well as from the temporal structure of the bargaining process. In Chapter 6 I also discuss *social norms* as a determinant of the outcome of bargaining.

In some models, bargaining power is simply taken as a parameter to be estimated. The *generalized Nash solution* is often used for this purpose. Whereas the simple Nash solution states that the outcome of bargaining will be the utility pair (u_i, u_{ii}) which maximizes the product $u_i \cdot u_{ii}$, the generalized solution defines it as the pair which maximizes the product $u_i^a \cdot u_{ii}^{1-a}$, with $0 < a < 1$. [I assume that the disagreement point is $(0, 0)$.] Here a is a parameter that is supposed to capture all determinants of relative bargaining power: bargaining ability, resources to hold out during a conflict, support in public opinion or anything else that might be relevant, including normative considerations. Econometric work can then be carried out to estimate the parameter. In addition, by stipulating that bargaining power is a linear function of variables like unemployment and cost of living, one can estimate the importance of each determinant of bargaining power in shaping the outcome.[55] I will not comment on this approach, except to say that it is vitiated by its lack of microfoundations and the mechanical character of the assumptions.

There have been attempts, however, to provide noncooperative foundations for the generalized Nash solution.[56] In models with an exogenously given probability of break-down, the outcome favours the party whose estimate of this event is lower. In models with different rates of time preference, the outcome favours the less impatient party who can say, credibly, that he does not mind waiting. In both models, it can be shown that as the length of the bargaining intervals goes to zero, the outcome of the bargaining game converges to a generalized Nash solution. In the first model, the bargaining parameter is a function of the rates of time preference and in the second a function of the subjective probabilities assigned to a breakdown. With positive intervals between the offers, the party who makes the first proposal has an advantage, but in the limit it does not matter who moves first. In the special case where the parties have the same time preferences or the same beliefs, the noncooperative outcome converges to the simple Nash solution.

[55] Svejnar (1986) is an example of this procedure.
[56] The following draws on Binmore, Rubinstein and Wolinsky (1986).

the outcome via the bargaining power the parties can derive from them. Specifically, *inside options determine whether threats are credible*. Hence the noncooperative version of the generalized Nash solution says that the agreement will maximize the weighted product of the utility gains of the parties compared with their inside options. In cooperative models, by contrast, it has been tacitly assumed, albeit with some confusion,[59] that what is maximized is the weighted product of the utility gains compared with the outside options.

Here is a numerical illustration. Suppose that workers in the firm are currently earning $8 per hour. They know that they could get a job in another firm at $6. Their strike fund will ensure them an income equivalent to $4 per hour. Under these conditions, assume that the outcome of bargaining is $9. Assume now that the reservation wage increases from $6 to $7, while everything else remains constant. The noncooperative theory then predicts that the change will not affect the bargaining outcome. If, however, the strike fund swells to ensure the workers $5 per hour, the workers might well be able to get $10 instead of $9. Outside options serve as floors on what the workers will get but have no role beyond that. The workers can credibly threaten to leave the firm if they are offered less than what they could get elsewhere, but they cannot credibly threaten to leave the firm if the alternative wage is below the management's offer. And it makes no difference to the credibility whether the alternative wage is well below that offer or only a little below. By contrast, the credibility of a strike threat is affected by *any* change in the value of the inside option.

The point can be brought home by a comparison of two varieties of noncooperative models.[60] In both, there are costs of bargaining from discounting. One case is defined by the feature that if a random event occurs (with known probability), the party whose turn it is to make an offer can either decide to quit the game, in which case both players receive fixed payoffs, or decide to stay in with a new proposal. The other case is defined by the feature that if the random event occurs, the game is over and the players receive their fixed payoffs. In the former case, the fixed payoffs

---

[59] McDonald and Solow (1981) seem to confuse inside and outside options. Using the cooperative framework, they write that the disagreement outcome for the workers is an outside option, determined by such elements as unemployment benefits, the value of leisure, the value of working around the house, net gains from illegal activities and the expected value of alternative employment opportunities (p. 899). For the firm, the disagreement is an inside option: zero profits or even negative profits if there are fixed costs that have to be paid (p. 905). The same confusion is found in Svejnar (1986), p. 1057.

[60] Sutton (1986).

serve as outside options. They constrain the outcome of the game but do not otherwise affect it. In the second case, however, it can be shown that the fixed payoffs do affect the outcome over and above the constraining effect. The intuition behind this result is that 'small options, if chosen voluntarily, have no effect; the "exogenous intervention" mechanism serves to make (even small) threats credible'.[61]

Let me summarize. When agreement is forced by the risk of bargaining breaking down, the classical Nash model gives the right result. The outcome maximizes the product of the gains relative to 'fall-back' outside options, but *only because these options cannot be freely chosen*. The outside options shape the outcome because they are, as it were, part of the inside options. By contrast, when agreement is forced by time discounting, outside options have no effect beyond that of constraining the outcome. Within the constraints, the solution is determined by the inside options.

The argument about 'the irrelevance of outside options' is related in spirit to the condition that the outcome be independent of irrelevant alternatives. Changes in options that would not be realized anyway should not affect the outcome. Whether these options are inside the bargaining range or fall-back options in case bargaining fails, they can have no effect on the outcome beyond constraining it. The alternative view – that changes in options far from the outcome might nevertheless affect it – would involve a social analogue to action at a distance. Within the paradigm of 'norm-free' bargaining, these arguments are compelling. Rational players would not take account of changes that have no impact on the bargaining power of the parties.

Behaviourally, however, there is no doubt that irrelevant alternatives and outside options do make a difference. Figure 2.8 represents a symmetrical bargaining game *OCD* with outside options at the origin and the solution at *B*. Consider now a truncation of the feasible set that excludes all alternatives above *AB*. If we believe in the independence of irrelevant alternatives, the solution in the modified game *OABC* should remain at *B*. Common sense suggests that it will not: player I will not accept that II will get his best possible payoff whereas I will have to be content with something well below his maximum. A trade union leader, for instance, could never make his constituents accept an outcome whereby he had to make all the concessions and management none. The Kalai–Smorodinsky solu-

[61]   Ibid., p. 715.

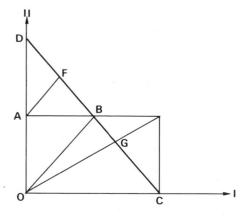

Fig. 2.8

tion, which suggests that the outcome in the modified game will be at G, is more plausible.

Consider now a different truncation of the game, from OCD to ABD, resulting from a change in the outside option of II.[62] Within the noncooperative framework, this should not make any difference: the solution should remain at B. Once again, however, this is behaviourally implausible. We may imagine that I and II are bargaining over the division of a sum of money, for example, $200. In the original game, they get nothing if they fail to agree. In the modified game, II is sure to get $100 if they fail to reach agreement. This game can be plausibly described as if I and II were bargaining over $100, in which case we would expect the solution to yield an equal division at F rather than remain at B. The noncooperative theory of rational bargaining tells us that all three games should have the same solution at B. Common sense tells us that they will have three different solutions. The discrepancy between theory and common sense may be due to a faulty conception of rationality, as suggested by the comments on backward induction. Or, assuming that conception to be correct, common sense may induce deviations from rational behaviour. The latter position is unstable, however, since ultimately the raw material for any theory of rational behaviour is our intuitions about what it makes sense to do in particular cases.

These deviations from what the theory tells rational players to do are

---

[62] I am indebted to Michael Wallerstein for this example.

frequently found in real-life bargaining. I have already argued that 'irrelevant' alternatives are relevant to capital–labour bargaining. Similarly, outside options affected the outcome, over and above their constraining effect. Workers look at the wage rate in other firms, to preserve existing wage differentials. The norms of fairness that govern capital–labour and labour–labour relations form the topic of Chapter 6.

The main determinants of bargaining power are time preferences, risk aversion and inside options. The more impatient, the more risk averse and the lower one's disagreement utility, the weaker is one's bargaining position. These subjective elements are often highly correlated with one another and with the objective wealth of the parties. Under standard conditions the less wealthy are more impatient, are more risk averse, and have a lower level of disagreement utility.

The relation between the objective and the subjective elements in bargaining is complicated. In principle, only subjective elements matter, yet in practice only the objective ones are observable. If psychology were essentially similar across people, all subjective differences would be caused by objective differences. Just as one person has different time preferences and risk attitudes at different levels of wealth, subjective differences across persons can be induced by objective differences. But subjective differences cannot be fully reduced to objective ones. The parties' external circumstances may be identical and yet their personalities or temperaments may differ.[63]

Some people are content because they have much, others because they have learned to be content with little. In either case, their bargaining power is enhanced: by caring less about what they get, they get more.[64] Attitudes towards risk can similarly arise in two ways. First, there is the wealth-induced effect: a rich man will be more willing to take risks than a poor man. Second, people differ intrinsically in their subjective attitudes towards

[63] For a striking example, consider a play once planned by Jean-Paul Sartre. 'Colette Audri, with whom Sartre once discussed this play, tells us that the play was to be called *The Wager* (after Pascal's wager), and would concern a child who is not wanted by his father. The mother, however, does not let herself be pressed into abortion, although a horrible life has been prophesied for the child: severe trials and reverses, poverty, and finally death at the stake. The child is born, grows up, and everything takes place as prophesied. "In fact he changes nothing material in his existence", Sartre says, "and his life ends, as foretold, at the stake. But thanks to his personal contribution, his choice and his understanding of freedom, he transforms this horrible life into a magnificent life" ' (Føllesdal 1981, pp. 403–4).

[64] Could this provide an incentive for strategic character planning? Gandhian techniques of nonviolence suggest that the question is not wholly absurd.

risk taking, independently of their external circumstances. Some people are naturally cautious, others are daring or even reckless. In von Neumann–Morgenstern utility functions these two mechanisms are inextricably intertwined, but in principle they can and should be distinguished.[65] Whatever the source of risk aversion, it usually is a handicap in bargaining.[66] Time preferences, finally, also arise in two ways. First, again, there is a wealth-induced effect: a rich man can better afford to wait. Second, people may differ intrinsically in their subjective rates of time preference, independently of their external circumstances.

The upshot of these remarks is the following. Bargainers can enhance their bargaining power to the extent that they can credibly communicate low utility gains, low risk aversion and low time discounting. To the extent that these follow naturally from their external situation, no special evidence is needed for these claims to be credible. To the extent that they go against what one might expect from the external situation, special evidence *is* necessary. The evidence must not be related to the bargaining situation, because if it is, the adversary will assume that it has been produced for the special purpose of gaining an advantage in bargaining. A union that incurs the costs of a strike in order to prove that it is less impatient and risk averse than would otherwise be assumed might end up having the worst of both worlds. It loses in the current round without gaining the credibility that would get it more the next time around.

Temporal asymmetries in the bargaining process can also influence the bargaining power of the parties. I have already mentioned that the party who moves first has an advantage. In addition, a party that needs more time to respond to a proposal by the other party has an edge in the bargaining process. The more the bargaining pie shrinks during the period when the union considers an offer by the employers, the more the latter have to lose by not giving in to the union's claim and hence the more likely they are to do so.[67] The internal weakness and lack of integration of many

[65] For attempts to construct cardinal utility functions without any element of intrinsic attitudes to risk see Shubik (1982), pp. 421–4 (reporting a result of L. Shapley) and Sen (1977), p. 339. Unfortunately, both proposals rest on shaky psychological foundations, in that they require subjects to make comparisons whose subjective meaningfulness is highly doubtful.

[66] In special cases, risk aversion may enhance one's bargaining power. Thus 'for bargaining games in which potential agreements involve lotteries which have a positive probability of leaving one of the players worse off than if a disagreement had occurred, the more risk averse a player, the better the terms of the agreement which he must be offered in order to induce him to reach an agreement and to compensate him for the risk involved' (Roth and Rothblum 1982).

[67] Barth (1988). See also de Geer (1986), p. 353.

unions may, paradoxically, enhance their bargaining power because they can claim, *credibly,* that it will take them a long time to respond to the management's offer. Conversely, the management of a subsidiary of a multinational firm may gain bargaining power by pointing out that any counterproposal by the union will have to be sent back to headquarters.

Uncertainty, manipulation, inefficiency

The noncooperative models of bargaining discussed earlier capture part of what goes on in real-life bargaining, but far from all. While emphasizing the role of threats, they ignore the haggling, bluffing, posturing and jockeying for position which are part and parcel of any negotiation in the real world. No actual haggling takes place in these models, only virtual haggling, as a result of which agreement is reached in the first moves of the game.[68] There are no elements of uncertainty, nor any possibility for strategic prebargaining moves. The remainder of this chapter is devoted to these issues.

I shall discuss three closely related questions. First, what is the role of information and uncertainty in bargaining? Second, what is the scope for strategic manipulation in bargaining? Third, how many of the benefits from cooperation are realized in actual bargaining? The first and the second questions are related because uncertainty creates an incentive for strategic misrepresentation of preferences and other factual matters (such as wage statistics). The first and the third are related because uncertainty, with or without misrepresentation, may lead to the break-down of bargaining. The second and third are related because attempts to influence the feasible set or the disagreement point can lead to waste of resources, through failure to reach agreement or for other reasons. The central argument, linking all three questions, is easily summarized: *to increase their distributive shares, bargainers engage in tactics that either decrease the probability of reaching agreement or decrease the size of the total to be shared.* In both cases, social losses result.

Uncertainty and the role of information

Uncertainty is massively important in bargaining. Because the buyer and seller of a house do not know each other's reservation prices, they often

---

[68] Binmore (1987a), p. 179, has a quote from Hobbes that is also appropriate here: 'For the Schooles find . . . no actuall Motion at all; but because some Motion they must acknowledge, they call it Metaphoricall Motion, which is but an absurd speech'.

go through an intricate dance of soliciting and misrepresenting informa-tion.[69] Also, the buyer knows that the seller knows more about the house than he can find out from brief or even from extensive inspection. If he buys in the summer, he has largely to take the seller's word for what it will be like in the winter. The example suggests that the distribution of information is doubly asymmetrical. First, on each side there are subjective items that only that side knows, such as that party's preferences and infor-mation. Second, there can be information about objective items which in principle is available to both parties but in practice to only one of them.

Uncertainty about preferences has several aspects. In all bargaining, risk attitudes and time preferences are central. In bargaining over multidimen-sional packages, the parties' subjective trade-offs among the components can be very important. Interpersonal comparisons of utility can have a massive impact. Bargainers who meet each other over and over again usu-ally end up learning a great deal about each other's preferences, but one-off bargains are obviously very different. Even bargainers who know each other intimately may nevertheless be able to exploit third-party uncer-tainty, if unresolved conflicts are to be arbitrated.[70] In court a husband may be able to present himself as a caring and competent father, although it is common knowledge between his wife and himself that he would neglect the child were he to get custody. In private ordering between the parties, the wife may therefore have to accept a bad financial settlement in order to get custody.[71]

Uncertainty about objective items, although a less fundamental problem, is also widespread. The seller of an oriental carpet can be assumed to know more about its quality than do most prospective buyers. Under conditions of asymmetrical information buyers may be subject to the 'winner's curse': if their offer is accepted, they will suspect that they could have gotten a better deal. There may not even be *any* offer such that, if it is accepted, it should have been made.[72] There may be *no* club willing to accept them as members which they would want to join. To see this, consider two parties bargaining over a piece of land on which there may or may not be oil. Both parties know that the owner of the land knows the exact value to him of

---

[69] Raiffa (1982), ch. 3, uses bargaining over a house as the introductory example in his splendid account. See also Scheppele (1988) for the question of legal redress for misrepre-sentation.

[70] For this distinction between 'common knowledge' and 'public knowledge' see the edi-torial introduction to Binmore and Dasgupta, eds. (1987), p. 19.

[71] I am assuming that it is also common knowledge that the father desires custody, since otherwise his threat to go to court would not be credible.

[72] Samuelson (1985); Samuelson and Bazerman (1985); Thaler (1988).

the oil, but that the prospective buyer knows only that the value to the seller is somewhere between 0 and $100 million, with any value in this range being equally likely. They also know that whatever the value is to the seller, it is half again as large for the prospective buyer, perhaps because he owns adjacent land that will make it easier to refine the oil. Assume now that the buyer makes an offer of X, which the seller accepts. From this the buyer can infer that the land is worth at most X to the buyer. More precisely, he knows that the value to the buyer is somewhere between 0 and X, with any value in this range being equally likely. From the buyer's point of view, the expected value of the land to the seller is, therefore, $X/2$, and its expected value to him is half again as large, that is, $3X/4$. But this is less than what he offered to pay. Realizing that *any* offer he could make that would be accepted by the buyer would be likely to buy him a piece of land worth less to him than he paid for it, he will decide not to make any offer at all. Although there is room for a mutually beneficial deal, none will be struck.

Management usually knows more than unions about the firm's ability to pay. The firm's duty to disclose this information is often severely limited. In Britain, the Employment Protection Act of 1975 obliges the employer to disclose to trade unions 'information without which the trade union representatives would to a material extent be impeded in carrying out . . . collective bargaining', subject, however, to numerous qualifications and exceptions.[73] The employer is not obliged to disclose information unless the amount of work and expenditure it would require is 'proportionate to the value of the information'. Since 'it is extremely difficult to define *ex ante* what the value of the information in collective bargaining will be',[74] employers can do more or less as they want to. In deciding how much to disclose, they will be guided both by efficiency and by distributive shares, knowing that disclosure may facilitate agreement, but also skew agreement in the union's favour.[75]

There are theories of bargaining under incomplete information,[76] but I do not think they are very useful. They rest on the assumption that although the bargainers are not certain about each other's preferences or about the

---

[73] Here I draw upon Foley and Maunders (1977).   [74] Ibid., p. 18.   [75] Ibid., p. 106.

[76] See, e.g., Myerson (1984, 1985) and Rubinstein (1985a). I do not claim to have fully mastered these highly technical papers. Their results, however, cannot be more robust than their premises, and it is the latter which I criticize in the text. I am not implying that these authors are unaware of the frailty of their premises.

quality of the object of bargaining, they have well-defined subjective prob-ability distributions over these variables. One model, for instance, assumes that the values of the object to the parties 'are independent random vari-ables and that each is uniformly distributed over the interval from 0 to 1 (in some monetary scale)'.[77] The obvious question is: why the uniform distribution? Perhaps the assumption is supposed to be justified by the principle of insufficient reason. That principle, however, is highly dubious[78] and in any case rarely appropriate in bargaining situations. A bargainer usually has enough information to entertain a subjective distribution of the *ordinal* probability of the values. He may, for instance, have a notion of the most probable value of the object to the other party, but no idea of how fast the probability of other values tapers off as we go to the extremes. In that case, should he assume that the distribution is normal? Lognormal? Or simply that it is a member of a family of distributions with known properties?[79] In my opinion, Bayesian theories of bargaining suffer from a fundamental lack of realism, as do the closely related theories of incentive compatibility. Their results are achieved at the cost of assumptions that are not merely heroic, but close to the supernatural.[80]

This being said, I have no alternative theory to offer about the behaviour of rational bargainers in situations of uncertainty. Most likely, no such theory will ever be forthcoming. I do not mind: rational-choice theory cannot explain everything. In fact, the first task of rational-choice theory must be to circumscribe its own limits.[81] This is not to say that the outcome of bargaining is indeterminate, only that a particular theory of bargaining fails to yield determinate results.[82] To achieve or approach predictive de-terminacy, we then have to consider other theories. Herbert Simon's theory of bounded rationality suggests that bargainers set themselves a target and give in as soon as it is reached. Thomas Schelling's theory of focal points suggests that psychological salience and prominence are important. The theory of social norms – set out in Chapter 3 and applied to bargaining in Chapter 6 – suggests that notions of fairness matter. All of these theories

[77] Myerson (1985), p. 116.   [78] See, e.g., Luce and Raiffa (1957), pp. 284–5.

[79] See Hey (1981) for a devastating critique of optimal-search rules that are similarly based on the assumption that people have well-defined subjective probability distributions.

[80] Elster (1989a), ch. 2, argues, in fact, that Bayesian decision theory is to modern deci-sion making as astrology was to decision making in earlier times.

[81] This is the central argument in Elster (1989a).

[82] See Pen (1959), p. 91, for comments on the 'pathetic fallacy' of projecting our igno-rance of the outcome of bilateral monopoly onto the situation itself.

are closer, perhaps, to description than to explanation. Again, this is fine in my book, since I believe that at the present time the social sciences cannot aspire to be much more than a phenomenological study of mechanisms.[83]

Strategic manipulation of bargaining parameters

The standard bargaining models ignore the possibility of strategic misrepresentation. To see how this problem arises, we may note that a bargaining process can be broken down into the following parts. (a) There is an underlying physical bargaining environment consisting of the physically feasible outcomes and the disagreement outcome. (b) There are the preferences of the players over the physical environment.[84] (c) Combining (a) and (b), we can define the bargaining problems in utility terms (S and d). (d) Assuming a given theory of rational bargaining, we can determine the solution to the bargaining problem (S, d). (e) The parties choose agents to implement the solution. Of these (c) is merely a mathematical transformation; (d) is assumed to be exogenously given and not subject to strategic manipulation. The remaining elements, however, do lend themselves to such manipulation.

Consider first strategic distortion of preferences. For a given physical environment, a given solution concept and a given implementation, the outcome is a function of the preferences. If the real preferences are unknown, the function might instead take reported preferences as its arguments. In that case, the parties face a noncooperative game in which they have to choose which preferences to report. It has been shown that when the parties bargain over a single good, the dominant strategy is to report linear (risk-neutral) utilities, leading to equal division of the good.[85] Here strategic distortion of utility at most affects distribution, not efficiency. In bargaining over many goods, misrepresentation can also generate inefficient outcomes.[86]

Consider next strategic action related to the implementation of the solution. If rational bargainers can be expected to reach a conclusion that favours one party, that party may try to turn the tables on the other by

---

[83]   For a defence of this view, see Elster (1989b), ch. 1 and passim.

[84]   For simplicity, I assume that both parties have full knowledge about the physical aspects of bargaining, so that there is no room for strategic misrepresentation on factual matters.

[85]   Crawford and Varian (1979).   [86]   Sobel (1981).

sending an irrational substitute to the bargaining table.[87] A person who is too stupid to understand the weakness of his bargaining position may refuse to yield where a rational bargainer would back down. Or one might delegate the bargaining to a person who can be counted on to carry out a threat even if it will not be in his interest to do so when the time to execute it arrives. Some societies foster codes of honour that add credibility to threats that otherwise would not be believable. It might make sense to hire a mafioso to represent one at the bargaining table (unless, of course, the other party does the same). I have more to say about this in the next chapter.

Consider, finally, strategic moves that take place before the parties sit down at the bargaining table. Let us assume that the parties know that the actual bargaining will take place according to a specific deterministic model.[88] The outcome, then, depends wholly on the feasible set S and the disagreement point d. With known preferences over the physical environment, the solution is a function of the latter. *The bargainers will then try to manipulate the physical environment in a direction that skews the outcome in their favour.*[89] In two-party bargaining, each party has an interest in manipulating the parameters to its advantage. If both parties engage in such maneuvering, both may lose. I discuss such failures of collective rationality in Chapter 4.

In addition to the parties directly involved, third parties may have an interest in shaping the parameters. The distinction is not sharp, since the parties might try to achieve their goal by influencing a third party with the power to shape these parameters. Unions and employers lobby for laws that, if passed, would enhance their bargaining power. Unions want laws requiring formal training and licensing for certain types of work. This affects d, by preventing employers from threatening to use unskilled labour.

---

[87] Schelling (1963) remains the best study of such bargaining ploys.

[88] Actually, what follows also applies, if more loosely, to the case in which uncertainty prevents the bargaining from being fully deterministic.

[89] This principle can be used to determine whether a given attempt to reach agreement is a case of bargaining or of, say, rational discussion. Was the Constitutional Convention of 1787 a case of bargaining or of rational discussion? Many aspects of the Constitution, such as the rule whereby a slave was to be counted as three-fifths of a free person for the purpose of representation in Congress, certainly seem like the kind of compromise typically found in bargaining. If the process was purely one of bargaining we would also expect, however, the states to have made strategic moves before the convention for the purpose of strengthening their bargaining position. Minimally, we would expect them to have drummed up public opinion in a way that would make it more difficult for them to make concessions. Without evidence of such strategic behavior, we should be wary of applying the bargaining model.

Employers lobby against minimum wage legislation. If they are successful, this affects S, by expanding the set of feasible outcomes.

Consider first how the government can use its legislative powers to shape the disagreement point. If the law determines the outcome when private bargaining fails, it serves as a disagreement point for the latter. The decision that would be made in a court or by an arbitrator, as well as the cost of legal fees, will have to be taken into account by the parties in their private bargaining. In divorce bargaining, the financial settlement will be influenced by the law regulating custody disputes. A maternal presumption rule, for instance, enhances the financial bargaining power of women. The shift to the principle that custody should follow the best interests of the child reduces their power correspondingly.[90] In labour–management bargaining, the government has an incentive to facilitate speedy agreement and to avoid costly strikes. To achieve this goal it may act on the disagreement point, by preventing strikes or lock-outs of indefinite duration. Although the intention may simply be to avoid loss of production, there will be distributional side effects. If management can afford to hold out longer than the union, an upper limit on the duration of strikes and lock-outs will favour the latter.

Third parties can also act on the feasible set – for example, by outlawing certain outcomes. Often, some possible contracts are forbidden because legislators believe (a) that they are inherently undesirable and (b) that they would otherwise be potential outcomes of private bargaining. 'It is well known, for instance, that courts will invalidate contracts by which people would sell themselves into slavery or bind themselves to perform immoral acts. . . . It is less well known that courts will refuse to enforce agreements by which people would waive the right to marry, to divorce, to sue for relief under the bankruptcy laws, to alienate labour freely, or to require a landlord to provide an apartment that meets minimum standards of habitability.'[91] In all cases, the reason is that in the absence of regulation there would be a real danger that such contracts would be made.[92] In particular, there may be a collective action problem that is overcome by banning certain contracts. If workers bargain individually with their employer, they

---

[90] Weizman (1985); Elster (1989a), ch. 3.   [91] Coleman and Silver (1986), p. 109.

[92] An alternative procedure would be to act on the disagreement point, e.g., to alter the initial endowments of the parties so that such bargains would not be expected to be struck (except under circumstances that would in themselves be grounds for invalidation). Yet if the point is to ensure that, say, contracts to sell oneself into slavery are *never* made, outright bans are necessary.

may all agree to work long hours even though all would be better off if all worked short hours.[93] Each worker may have to accept long hours since the employer may, credibly, point to the existence of other workers who are willing to do so. Unionization is one way out of this collective action problem. Legislation is another.[94]

Minimum-wage legislation and legislation on working conditions, including the length of the working day, affect the bargaining power of the parties. The extent of the impact depends on one's view of the bargaining process. Suppose that if the union and management had bargained over wage and length of the working day without any legal limitation on either, they would have agreed on $6 per hour and a forty-hour week. If legislation sets the minimum wage to $5 and the maximum length of the week to forty-two hours, will the outcome be different?[95] Under the Nash solution, the condition of independence of irrelevant alternatives says that the outcome should not differ. The Kalai–Smorodinsky solution, by contrast, implies that legislation matters *even if the outlawed outcome would never have been the outcome of bargaining unconstrained by legislation.* Suppose that legislation had set the minimum wage at exactly $6 or the maximum working week at exactly forty hours. In modern societies, it is surely implausible that the union would not achieve any gains over and above what the law ensured them. In societies less extensively permeated by norms of fair division it is perhaps more plausible that the outcome would be unaffected by irrelevant alternatives.[96]

From third-party manipulation I now turn to manipulation by the parties themselves. Consider first strategic action on the feasible set. In addition to the lobbying efforts discussed earlier, the parties have a powerful incentive to manipulate public opinion and the mass media. If a union leader,

[93] Hardin (1988), pp. 92–4.

[94] For an argument in favour of the latter solution see Fried (1984).

[95] As earlier, the question can be understood in two ways: as a question in comparative statics or as a question about what will happen following a transition from one regime to the other. Under the second, intuition strongly suggests that the laws will make a difference. The first supports the same intuition, albeit less strongly.

[96] Intuitively, the following account seems to make sense. Each party possesses a certain amount of bargaining power. If it does not have to spend bargaining power on one issue, because the law ensures that it will get what it wants without bargaining, it has more power to spend on other issues. Similarly, if the law ensures that it can get most of what it wants without bargaining, less expenditure of bargaining power on that issue is necessary than it would be were there no legal constraints. Anyone who has engaged in bargaining will, I believe, recognize that there is something to this intuition, often expressed in phrases like 'I do not want to spend my bargaining chips on this issue'. I do not know, however, how to transform the intuition into a formal theory of bargaining.

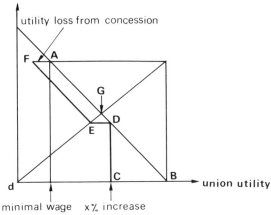

Fig. 2.9

for instance, publicly states that he will resign unless his members get a wage increase of at least x per cent, the announcement amounts to a change of the feasible set of outcomes. To see this, consider Fig. 2.9.

Here, AB is the Pareto frontier in the absence of any public announcements. If the union makes an announcement, this amounts to imposing a cost $ED = FA$ on the union if it accepts a wage increase short of x per cent. The frontier shifts to $CDEF$.[97] The Nash solution will then shift in the union's favour, as suggested by intuition. The Kalai–Smorodinsky solution shifts from G to E, to the detriment of both parties, as we might expect from the monotonicity argument underlying that solution. Here the Kalai–Smorodinsky solution concept is less adequate intuitively than the Nash solution. An arbitrator might, however, announce that he will impose the Kalai–Smorodinsky solution, to prevent wasteful jockeying for position.

Consider next manipulation of the disagreement point and, more specifically, of the inside options.[98] This is, I believe, by far the most important

---

[97] After the announcement, the feasible set is no longer convex. Strictly speaking, this does not allow us to apply the Nash and Kalai–Smorodinsky solution concepts. It is easy to verify, however, that the reasoning in the text also applies to the convex hull of $CEDF$, obtained by substituting a straight line from D to F for DEF.

[98] Outside options do not lend themselves to strategic manipulation. The workers in one firm have little influence over what workers earn in other firms to which they could credibly threaten to move. The management may, however, use blacklisting to prevent workers from exiting.

target of strategic action by the parties. Workers may try to build up strike funds to support themselves in case of a disagreement. These funds represent unproductive expenditures. Employers' associations may build up the equivalent of strike funds to support their member firms during strikes.[99] Management may build up large inventories, 'both to reduce the costs of strikes when they occur and to enhance their bargaining position by reducing their vulnerability to strike threats'.[100] Stockpiling also, however, involves obvious dead-weight losses. Resources that would otherwise be used for productive purposes may be spent on warehouses. Management may deliberately refrain from hiring young productive workers, preferring instead older, married workers with high mortgage payments that make it difficult for them to hold out during a strike. Although older workers produce less, their presence ensures that there will be more time in which to produce.

Moreover, the management may deliberately refrain from investing in capital-intensive technology which would make the firm more vulnerable to pressure by workers.[101] The decline of the U.S. steel industry since 1959 has, in particular, been explained as the result of fear of investing in 'hostage capital'.[102] Suboptimal investment induced by fear of worker militancy may doubly harm the workers, not only by the loss of an important bargaining chip, but also by the reduction of the total to be shared, since the use of suboptimal technology reduces the income of the firm.

It would be in the interest of management *and* workers if the latter could promise not to engage in costly strikes, because this would induce management to invest in more productive technology.[103] Making credible promises involves problems, however, which mirror those of credible threats. In theory, both problems can be solved by the method of side bets:[104] one lodges a sum with a third party, which is forfeited if the threat is not carried out or the promise not kept. In practice, no societies to my knowledge

---

[99] Conflict funds involve a waste of resources because they have to be kept in fairly liquid form, earning a lower interest than in their most productive use. De Geer (1986), pp. 53–4, shows how the Swedish Employers' Association was able to overcome this problem through an agreement with the banks that allowed them to borrow against their nonliquid assets.

[100] Crawford (1985), p. 376. Empirical evidence on the importance of inventories for bargaining strength is found in Holden (1987a).

[101] For a discussion of this issue, see Baldwin (1983), Grout (1984), van der Ploeg (1987) and Moene (1988a).

[102] Baldwin (1983).

[103] For extensive discussion of these issues, see also Williamson (1985), chs. 7 and 8.

[104] Schelling (1963).

have evolved institutions that make and enforce side bets of this kind. Because of the losses that would occur if both sides of a conflict used them to make binding threats, the absence of these institutions might, on balance, be a good thing. An alternative solution might emerge if the union and firm knew that they would have to bargain again on later occasions. 'If the game between the union and the firm is played over and over again, it is possible to sustain the inconsistent (Pareto-superior) outcome as long as the discount rate is small enough and/or the length of the punishment interval is long enough, even though explicit binding contracts are unavailable'.[105] I return to this issue in the concluding chapter.

I have cited cases in which inside options are affected by the directly involved in a conflict. They can also be shaped, however, by the associations to which the parties belong or by legislative action. From the bargainers' point of view, in other words, inside options can be either strategic weapons or institutionally given constraints. The latter case has been studied by Karl Ove Moene in a noncooperative model of labour–management bargaining.[106] By varying the threats at the disposal of labour and management, he shows that bargaining environments differ systematically in their impact on wages, profit and employment.

Moene assumes that the union's objective function is set by majority voting among the workers and that layoffs occur in inverse order of seniority.[107] If the workers know that layoffs will never concern as much as half of the work force, the union's only interest will be to maximize wages. It will not care about employment. (From the social point of view, needless to say, employment matters.) Hence the firm can set employment unilaterally, taking account of the wage effects of its decision. Wages are set by bargaining with the union. The inside options shaping the outcome could be any of the following: go-slow, work-to-rule, official strikes or illegal wildcat strikes. The first two can be reduced to a common formula: the workers reduce their work effort somewhat and receive some fraction of the going wage. In go-slow actions the fraction is strictly smaller than 1; in work-to-rule it equals unity. The last two can also be reduced to a common formula: no work is done, workers receive some income during the strike, whereas the firm receives some support from the employers' association to which it belongs. The difference between the two forms of in-

[105] van der Ploeg (1987), p. 1488.   [106] Moene (1988b).   [107] Oswald (1985, 1986).

dustrial action is that wildcat strikes have a smaller strike fund (and that unions may have to pay a fine).

Moene shows that from the point of view of maximizing employment, wages and profits, these bargaining environments can be ranked in the following order:

Employment	Wages	Profits
1. Wild-cat strikes	1. Work-to-rule	1. Wild-cat strikes
2. Official strikes	2. Go-slow	2. Official strikes
3. Go-slow	3. Official strikes	3. Go-slow
4. Work-to-rule	4. Wild-cat strikes	4. Work-to-rule

Workers want high wages, firms want high profits and the government wants high employment. We observe that the interests of government and employers coincide fully, both being opposed to the interests of the workers. These conclusions rest on two assumptions. First, the workers' income during a go-slow action is at least as high as their strike support during a legal strike. Second, the support to firms during a strike is at least as high as the net profit during a go-slow action. The second assumption is empirically vulnerable, since in most countries firms receive no strike support from central funds. In these countries, the assumption holds only when the firm is totally crippled by a go-slow action. But then the first assumption is not very plausible.

Assume instead, therefore, that firms receive no central support and that go-slow income is the same percentage of the going wage as go-slow output is of normal output. If we also assume that support during a legal strike equals go-slow income, the above conditions are violated and the conclusions do not hold. Under these new and more realistic assumptions, Moene shows that a movement from a go-slow regime to one with legal strikes leads to higher profits, higher employment *and* higher wages. If the firm faces a downward-sloping demand curve, this implies lower output prices as well, benefiting consumers. All is for the best in the best of all possible worlds. Needless to say, this is a special case with few implications about actual bargaining. The argument nevertheless is important, because it shows that the effects of the bargaining environment can be subtle and not immediately detected by intuition. It is clear enough that workers do better for themselves when there are some legal forms of industrial action than when all actions are illegal. It is less obvious which form of legal action they should prefer and what the consequences are for other parties.

The inefficiency of bargaining

One of the main points of bargaining is to make joint ventures possible, by enabling the parties to agree on the division of the gains to be made from cooperation. If they cannot agree on how to share the gains, there may be no gains to share. Bargaining, however, has costs of its own. In the words of the late Leif Johansen, *'Bargaining has an inherent tendency to elimi-nate the potential gain which is the object of the bargaining'*.[108] The reasons he cites for this tendency can be paraphrased as follows. (a) Because of uncertainty about the range of realistic proposals, the parties may begin with excessive claims and never be able to meet half-way. (b) There is a pervasive tendency to bias the presentation of information in one's favour, so that even unbiased information is not believed, leading to inefficiency. (c) To make information credible, mere words are not enough: one must put one's money where one's mouth is and actually expend resources on credibility. (d) Similarly, threats may not be credible unless one carries them out, with a socially undesirable waste of resources. (e) In particular, parties may carry out a threat to establish a reputation for being tough negotiators. (f) The strategy of precommitting oneself to a particular claim can be disastrous if both parties follow it. (g) In particular, if the parties are organizations that try to mobilize their members, they may end up playing the sorcerer's apprentice.[109]

Most of these problems, as well as some not included in Johansen's list, were discussed earlier in this chapter. To supplement the list, I shall propose another typology of bargaining costs and bargaining failures, drawing on the typology of cooperative problems set out in the Introduction.

The cost of bargaining failures. If people fail to reach agreement in a joint venture, the production forgone can be a substantial loss. To quote one example at random, 'There began in the UK during 1979 some 1080 stop-pages of work due to industrial disputes, involving 4.548 million workers and resulting in 29.474 million working days lost'.[110] Failure to agree on

---

[108] Johansen (1979), p. 520. Italics in original.   [109] Ibid., pp. 518–19.
[110] Sapsford (1982), p. 3.

a private ordering can block Pareto-efficient outcomes. The 'winner's curse', for instance, may prevent mutually beneficial deals from being struck. Failure to capture positive externalities can be serious, as when OPEC countries fail to agree on an allocation of quotas. Failure to agree on the terms of mutual helping can occur between neighbours, if there is disagreement over what constitutes fair reciprocation. Failure to agree on a convention equilibrium can yield large inefficiencies, as in the coexistence of VHS and Beta videocassette recorders or, more importantly, of different systems of weights and measures. The causes of these failures include uncertainty and the various forms of strategic manipulation mentioned earlier and further discussed in Chapter 4. In Chapter 6 I argue that the appeal to norms of equity and equality can also lead to bargaining failures. Finally, theory[111] and experiments[112] indicate that the probability of disagreement increases when the potential gains from agreement increase, contrary to what intuition might suggest.

The costs of preparing for bargaining. These costs derive from strategic manipulation of the bargaining environment. Investments in improving one's bargaining position are a dead-weight loss for society, although they may increase the share and the final outcome of the investor.[113] When all parties deploy such strategies, everybody may end up being worse off than if nobody had prepared for bargaining. I do not know of any empirical studies of the magnitude of these effects, but I suspect they might be non-negligible.

The costs of conducting bargaining. The main task of unions is to prepare for and conduct wage bargaining. Workers pay substantial membership dues, which have to be counted among the costs of bargaining. The magnitude of these costs is indicated by the fact that if workers instead used these funds to buy shares in their firm, most firms would be worker-owned after a few decades.[114] There are similar costs on the employer's side, and in maintaining the arbitration system.

The costs of decentralized bargaining. As I further discuss in Chapter 4, local and sectoral wage bargaining give rise to collective action problems.

---

[111] Crawford (1982).   [112] Malouf and Roth (1981).

[113] When they increase the share without improving the final outcome, such strategies are individually irrational.

[114] Moene and Ognedal (1987).

Separate bargaining creates externalities that can make everybody worse off than if a single, encompassing union had negotiated on behalf of all.[115] There are exceptions to this statement. Sometimes all are better off by virtue of not being able to present a united front. By and large, however, unity makes for moderation and collective gains.

[115] This is a major theme in Olson (1982).

3. Social norms

Introduction

One of the most persisting cleavages in the social sciences is the opposition between two lines of thought conveniently associated with Adam Smith and Emile Durkheim, between *homo economicus* and *homo sociologicus.* Of these, the former is supposed to be guided by instrumental rationality, while the behaviour of the latter is dictated by social norms. The former is 'pulled' by the prospect of future rewards, whereas the latter is 'pushed' from behind by quasi-inertial forces.[1] The former adapts to changing circumstances, always on the lookout for improvements. The latter is insensitive to circumstances, sticking to the prescribed behaviour even if new and apparently better options become available.[2] The former is easily caricatured as a self-contained, asocial atom, and the latter as the mindless plaything of social forces or the passive executor of inherited standards. In this chapter I attempt to characterize this contrast more fully. I also argue that while social norms are extremely important for solving the first problem of social order, their contribution to the second problem is more ambiguous. Social norms do coordinate expectations. They may or may not help people to achieve cooperation.

Generally speaking, three solutions have been proposed to resolve the opposition between the two paradigms. First, there is the eclectic argument that some forms of behaviour are best explained on the assumption that people act rationally, whereas others can be explained by something like the theory of social norms. Alternatively, the eclectic view could be that both rationality and social norms are among the determinants of most actions. By and large, I shall adopt one or the other of these eclectic views.

---

[1] For a useful exploration of this contrast, see Gambetta (1987).

[2] The theory of social norms must be supplemented by a theory of what happens if the prescribed behaviour ceases to be feasible. Durkheim's theory of anomie was in part intended to answer this question (Besnard 1987).

Second, one might argue that what seems to be norm-oriented action is, in reality, a form of rational or, more generally, optimizing behaviour. I shall argue against this view. Third, there is the converse reductionist strategy of trying to reduce rationality to one social norm among others. One might argue, for instance, that the modern Western emphasis on instrumental rationality is not present in all cultures. We adopt it because we are socialized into thinking in this manner, even when it is actually counterproductive in its own instrumental terms. I will not comment further on this view, which to my knowledge has not been clearly articulated by anyone.[3]

Rational action is concerned with outcomes. Rationality says, 'If you want to achieve Y, do X'. By contrast, I define social norms by the feature that they are *not outcome-oriented*.[4] The simplest social norms are of the type 'Do X', or 'Don't do X'. More complex norms say, 'If you do Y, then do X', or 'If others do Y, then do X'. Still more complex norms might say, 'Do X if it would be good if everyone did X'. Rationality is essentially conditional and future-oriented. Its imperatives are hypothetical, that is, conditional on future outcomes one wants to realize. The imperatives[5] expressed in social norms either are unconditional, or, if conditional, are not future-oriented. In the latter case, norms make the action dependent on past events or (more rarely) on hypothetical outcomes. Rational actors follow the principle of letting bygones be bygones, cutting one's losses and

---

[3]   See, however, Neurath (1913) and Elster (1989a) for discussions of 'pseudorationalism' or 'hyperrationality', i.e., the obsessional desire to have decisive reasons for acting, even in cases in which reasons are unavailable or prohibitively expensive. This tendency could, perhaps, be stated as a social norm: never act unless you have sufficient reason. For a discussion of a different set of cases in which instrumental behaviour can be instrumentally counterproductive, see Elster (1983a), ch. 2. Other works that would seem relevant to the view that rationality is but one norm among others are those of Hollis and Lukes, eds. (1982) and MacIntyre (1988). I have not succeeded, however, in extracting from these writings a clear and refutable theory. In my view, the task is doomed to failure, for reasons stated by Davidson (1980). There can be no society in which people *as a rule* knowingly refuse to choose the best means to realize their goals. If we observe people asserting that their goal is A and that they believe B to be the best means of realizing A, yet observe them doing C instead, we do not in general conclude that they fail to follow our standards of rationality. Rather we tend to conclude by imputing other goals or beliefs to them. Verbal behaviour is only one type of, and by no means privileged, evidence for imputing goals and beliefs to other people. Much of the time we impute goals and beliefs on the basis of actions, together with an assumption that people are, by and large, rational. Davidson argues, and I agree, that there is simply no other way to make sense of other people.

[4]   A related distinction between 'terminal values' and 'adjectival values' is made by Lovejoy (1968), pp. 79–81. Terminal values are outcomes of actions, whereas adjectival values inhere in the actions themselves.

[5]   I am disregarding the purely descriptive sense of norms, the adjectival correspondence of which is 'normal' rather than 'normative' (Stroll 1987).

ignoring sunk costs. In the operation of social norms, by contrast, the past plays an essential role. The notion of cutting one's losses is foreign, for instance, to the relentless pursuer of revenge or to the trade union leader who would rather fight and lose than not fight at all.[6]

For norms to be *social*, they must be (a) shared by other people and (b) partly sustained by their approval and disapproval.[7] Some norms, like norms against cannibalism or incest, are shared by all members of society. Other norms are more group-specific. Managers and workers, or workers of different skill levels, do not have the same idea of fair distribution. One might ask whether there could be a stable frequency-dependent polymorphism of norms, analogous to what one finds in many areas of animal behaviour.[8] Or perhaps there might be a stable, frequency-dependent coexistence of norm-guided behaviour and rational, self-interested behaviour.[9] The problem with these suggestions is the lack of a plausible mechanism that could explain how norms appear and disappear according to the expected payoffs associated with them.[10] From the fact that honesty sometimes pays, one cannot infer that honesty will appear if and only if it pays.

The other respect in which these norms are *social* is that other people are important for enforcing them, by expressing their approval and, especially, disapproval. These sanctions can be very strong. In societies with a strong code of honour, the ostracism suffered by a person who fails to avenge an offence can be crippling. One might ask whether the existence of sanctions does not make it rational to follow the norm, thus undermining the contrast between rational behaviour and norm-guided behaviour. A partial answer is provided in the next paragraph. A fuller discussion is provided later.

In addition to being supported by the attitudes of other people, norms are sustained by the feelings of embarrassment, anxiety, guilt and shame that a person suffers at the prospect of violating them, or at least at the

---

[6] See Golden (1988) for examples of trade union leaders who knowingly seek defeat.

[7] By and large, I shall limit myself here to expressions of disapproval. Approval is usually sought for actions that go out of the ordinary and excel in some way, not for actions that conform to a given standard. For a discussion of the relation between love of praise and fear of blame as mainsprings of human motivation, see Lovejoy (1968), p. 133 and passim. See also the comments in the concluding chapter on the relation between envy-avoidance and envy-provocation.

[8] See, e.g., Maynard-Smith (1982).   [9] Frank (1987, 1988).

[10] The most plausible case is that in which the strategies have associated with them differential rates of survival, rather than simply different degrees of economic success. The discussion of *furbi* and *fessi* in the concluding chapter might provide an example, although I doubt it.

prospect of being caught violating them.[11] Social norms have a *grip on the mind* that is due to the strong emotions their violations can trigger. I believe that the emotive aspect of norms is a more fundamental feature than the more frequently cited cognitive aspects. If norms can coordinate expectations, it is only because the violation of norms is known to trigger strong negative emotions, in the violator himself and in other people.

Most social norms are simple to obey and to follow, compared with the canons of rationality which often require us to make difficult and uncertain calculations. The operation of norms is to a large extent blind, compulsive, mechanical or even unconscious. This statement somewhat exaggerates the unreflective character of norm-guided behaviour.[12] Later, it will become abundantly clear that social norms offer considerable scope for skill, choice, interpretation and manipulation. In some contexts, following the lodestar of outcome-oriented rationality is easy compared with finding one's way in a jungle of social norms. In Chapter 6 I argue, for instance, that the plurality of social norms regulating collective bargaining can obstruct rather than facilitate agreement, whereas negotiation from threat advantage would force immediate settlement. I still want to retain the basic contrast between rationality and social norms, however. The force of norms – the feature that makes manipulation and interpretation worth while – is that they do have a grip on the mind; otherwise, there would be nothing to manipulate. I shall return to this point.

One might question whether this conception of social norms corresponds to what earlier writers have meant by that phrase. I am quite confident that there is substantive extensional agreement, in that most of the examples of social norms cited in the next section would also be given that name by most of those who have written on the topic. The degree of intensional agreement is less clear, and I am not sure it matters much. Some writers have defined social norms by what they do – their consequences for social life – rather than by what they are. Others have defined them by their causes, that is, by the social and psychological mechanisms that sustain them. I have chosen to define norms mainly by their intrinsic nature rather than by their causes or effects.

Social norms must be distinguished from a number of other, related

[11] Edelman (1987) offers a systematic discussion of the nature, causes and consequences of embarrassment in social life. The stronger emotions of guilt and shame are brilliantly discussed in Levy (1973), ch. 10 and passim.
[12] I am grateful to John Padgett for pressing this point on me, although I am sure he will not think I have drawn the full implications from it.

phenomena. First, social norms differ from moral norms. To bring out the difference, let us distinguish between obligation, permission and interdiction (the moral analogues of necessity, possibility and impossibility). Social norms consist of nonconsequentialist obligations and interdictions, from which permissions can be derived. Some moral theories, like utilitarianism, rest on consequentialist obligations and interdictions. These are different in a straightforward way from social norms. Other theories, like libertarianism, rest on nonconsequentialist permissions, from which certain interdictions can be derived. The basic notion of these theories is an assignment of rights to individuals, together with an injunction to others not to violate them. Rights assignments bear some resemblance to social norms. The principle 'finders keepers', for instance, could be variously interpreted as a right or a social norm.[13] (It could also be justified, however, by rule-utilitarian incentive-effect arguments.) Still further theories, like Kant's moral philosophy, rest on nonconsequentialist obligations. These have an even greater similarity to social norms. In fact, later in this chapter and in Chapter 5 I classify 'everyday Kantianism' as a social rather than a moral norm. I am not claiming that this bears a very close relation to Kant's own theory, however.

Second, social norms differ from legal norms.[14] For one thing, obedience to the law is often rational on purely outcome-oriented grounds. Although most people do not consider punishment to be merely the price tag attached to a crime, laws are often designed as if this were the case, so that legal sanctions will suffice to deter people from breaking the law. The law does not rest on informal sanctions and the voice of conscience, but provides formal punishment. More important, it is individually rational for law enforcers to apply these sanctions: they will lose their jobs if they do not. By contrast, or so I shall argue, the enforcement of social norms is not in general individually rational.

Third, norms are not convention equilibria. Consider the social norms that have the greatest similarity to conventions, such as norms of dress, etiquette and manners. One might argue that such norms are traffic rules of social life: it does not matter which set of rules one adopts, as long as

[13] Sugden (1986), ch. 5, argues that the rule is a convention (in his sense, not mine). In ch. 8 he also argues that conventions tend to harden into social norms or rights, a point that is explored in Chapter 6.

[14] An intermediate case of considerable interest are professional norms, such as the norms regulating lawyer–client or doctor–doctor relations. Abbott (1983) offers a good survey with many valuable observations.

there is agreement on one set. As in convention equilibria, one not only would want to follow the norm itself but would want others to follow it. The analogy is, however, misleading. If I violate a traffic rule, two bad things can happen to me. I can have an accident, and I may be blamed by bystanders, because bad things can happen to them if I drive recklessly. If I pick up the wrong fork at the dinner table, the only bad thing that can happen to me is that others will blame me for my bad manners. Convention equilibria are guided by outcomes in a substantive sense, not just in the formal sense that people want to avoid disapproval. I return to this distinction later.

Fourth, social norms differ from private norms, the self-imposed rules that people construct to overcome weakness of will.[15] As explained in Chapter 1, people often face what amounts to an intrapersonal collective action problem. They would be better off if they never smoked, never drank, never took a second helping of dessert than they would if they always engaged in these practices. They would be better off if they engaged in a regular practice of exercising, saving or educating themselves than they would if they never did any of these things. Yet at any given moment the activity which has bad long-term consequences may seem more attractive. To overcome temptation, people may *bunch their choices* by asking the perennial question, 'If not now, when?' In doing so, they set up a domino effect in which failure now predicts failure in the indefinite future. By raising the stakes, they make it easier to resist temptation.[16] The price they have to pay is rigid adherence to the rule. In William James's phrase: 'Never suffer a single exception.'

In this respect, private norms are just as mechanical as social norms. They dispense with the need to consider consequences, since the proscribed action is laid down by an unambiguous rule: *don't do it*. To show that the rule has its price, recall that in a collective action problem universal cooperation is not always the optimum. Similarly, it is not clear that my life on the whole will go better for me if I *never* drink, *never* smoke or *never* eat ice cream or that I should jog *every* day, save a little bit *every* month or read a good novel *every* week. It would be better if I gave myself an occasional break. At the very least, as I enter old age, dissaving will

---

[15] The following draws heavily on Ainslie (1975, 1982, 1984, 1986).
[16] Ainslie shows that this is a formal implication of a specific model of weakness of will in terms of nonexponential time preferences. But the idea is also intuitively plausible. I return to the problem in Chapter 5.

make more sense than saving, and there is no reason why I should not take up smoking if I want to. But even in the midst of life the pleasure gained from occasional indulgences exceeds the sum total of the many small harms they do to my future selves, pleasures being both more keen and less harmful the rarer they are.[17] Yet the person who has made the unbreakable rule for himself is incapable of fine-tuning resistance to temptation. The anxiety he feels at the very thought of yielding deters him from doing so even when he can see that it might be a good idea.[18]

Private norms, like social norms, are non-outcome-oriented and sustained by feelings of anxiety and guilt. They are not, however, sustained by the approval and disapproval of others since they are not, or not necessarily, shared with others. I may feel a need to protect myself against an addiction to watching television sports on Sunday simply because there are other things I want to do more, not because my friends would frown on me were they to learn about it. In fact, most of my friends may be happily and guiltlessly addicted to the practice. To be sure, many cases are ambiguous. There are social norms against smoking, drinking and overeating. Or consider the following comment on Tahitian religion:

> [An] expressed motive for the involvement in religion is 'protection from one's own impulses to bad behavior'. Teiva, for example, says that all villagers are religious (although not enough to save themselves from hell) because they remember the savage pagan behavior of their ancestors, the wars and cannibalism (matters which missionary teachings constantly emphasized when they portrayed the salvation from savagery brought by religion), and being afraid of backsliding, use religion to protect themselves from doing evil.[19]

Here a socially inculcated practice is voluntarily accepted as a means to impulse control.[20] Borderline cases notwithstanding, the distinction between private and social norms is fairly clear. The superego, to use Freud-

---

[17] I am not here considering addictive effects that might remove the intermediate strategies from the feasible set.

[18] *Not* yielding to temptation can, therefore, also be a form of weakness of will. Davidson (1980), p. 30, uses the example of the compulsive toothbrusher to bring out this point. As I remarked in Chapter 1, compliance with social norms can also be a form of weakness of will.

[19] Levy (1973), pp. 184–5.

[20] Stephen Holmes (personal communication) asks whether this practice is at all intelligible: can one intentionally 'decide to believe' in religion *just* to keep from backsliding?

ian terms, may be a private construct or a social one, originating either in the individual himself or in his environment.

Fifth, norm-guided behaviour must be sharply distinguished from habits and compulsive neuroses. Although similar in their mechanical character and lack of concern for consequences, they differ in several respects.[21] Unlike social norms, habits are private. Unlike private norms, their violation does not generate blame or guilt.[22] Unlike neuroses and private norms, habits are not compulsive. The habit of washing one's hands after dinner is not like the neurotic's need to wash his hands ten or fifty times every day. Nor is it like the private norm of *always* washing one's hands after dinner, regardless of the degree of inconvenience and need. Habits begin as intentional behaviour which later, as a result of repetition, loses its conscious, deliberate character. Compulsive neuroses are more complex and not well understood.[23]

Sixth, I would distinguish social norms from tradition. The distinction is tenuous, but I think it can be made. *Tradition* I understand as mindlessly repeating or imitating today what one's ancestors did yesteryear. The subject matter of tradition, thus understood, is how to build a house, when to sow and when to harvest, how to dress when going to church on Sunday and so on. Traditions are subject to drift, by the cumulative result of many imperfect imitations, unless external forces keep them from deviating[24] or the activity in question varies discretely rather than continuously.[25] By contrast, *traditionalism* – the deliberate imitation of some original model – is not subject to drift.[26] If the traditionalist makes a mistake in copying the model, the mistake will not be passed to the next generation, which will go back to the original rather than to the previous copy. Tradition has

[21] We may note, however, the claim by Fenichel (1945, p. 586), that 'many forms of reaction which today are designated as compulsion neuroses are normal and institutionalized in other civilizations'.

[22] Durkheim wrote that 'a rule . . . is not only a habitual means of action, it is, above all, an obligatory means of acting' (cited after Camic 1986).

[23] 'For reasons no one understands, the compulsions are expressed in behaviors such as hand washing, which correlates with the obsession of contamination, and counting and checking, which is associated with being obsessed with doubt' (Gazzaniga 1988, p. 125). Nor do we know much about the etiology of compulsion, except that it is likely to have a strong biological component (ibid., p. 130).

[24] Elster (1983b), pp. 135–8, reports Eilert Sundt's analysis of boat construction in northern Norway as an example of tradition constrained by seaworthiness.

[25] Like the Norwegian tradition of ending the Christmas holidays on the twentieth day following Christmas Eve.

[26] See, e.g., the analysis of traditionalism in Chinese painting in Levenson (1968), vol. 1, pp. 26–32.

a short memory, traditionalism a long memory. Traditionalism is usually supported by social norms. Tradition may be supported by a norm (as in deciding how to dress for church), but need not be so. A person who deviates from tradition in technical matters, for example, may be regarded by his neighbours as stupid or eccentric but not as a transgressor of a norm.

Finally, we must distinguish social norms from various cognitive phenomena to which they bear some resemblance. It follows from my definition of social norms that they have the effect of focusing and coordinating expectations. They help to solve what I referred to in the Introduction as the first problem of social order. If the norm to do X is shared within a community, each will expect others to do X. An alternative means of focusing expectations is by psychological salience or prominence.[27] One option may stand out, by virtue of simplicity, symmetry, temporal or alphabetical priority or some other feature. Maxims for allocating resources often correspond to such focal points: divide equally, divide proportionally, do as we did last year, flip a coin. Sometimes salience is unambiguously different from norms. When we lose each other in a foreign city, there is no norm to meet at the hotel: it is simply the obvious thing to do. In other cases the distinction is harder to draw. In particular, the importance of norms of equality may be related to their salience.

I conclude these introductory comments with three methodological remarks. The first is that the distinction between rationality and social norms does not coincide, as is often taken for granted, with the distinction between methodological individualism and a more holist approach. Although these two distinctions go together in Durkheim and many others, I believe one can define, discuss and defend a theory of social norms within a wholly individualist framework.[28] A norm, in this perspective, is *the propensity to feel shame and to anticipate sanctions by others at the thought of behaving in a certain, forbidden way*. As explained earlier, this propensity becomes a *social* norm when and to the extent that it is shared with other people. As will be explained, the social character of the norm is also manifest in the existence of higher-order norms that enjoin us to punish violators of the first-order norm. To repeat, this conception of a network of shared beliefs and common emotional reactions does not commit us to

---

[27] Schelling (1963).
[28] Sperber (1984) provides a useful starting point for an individualistic analysis of culture, although for my purposes I would give more emphasis to emotions and less to cognitive representations.

thinking of norms as supraindividual entities that somehow exist independently of their supports.

Second, social norms can exist on an unconscious or barely conscious
level. Consider the culture-specific norms that dictate the minimal permis-
sible distance I must keep from another person while talking to him in an
unconstrained situation. If I move closer to him than, say, thirty centime-
ters, he will move away and look at me in a strange way, as if wondering
whether I am drunk, aggressive, inappropriately amorous or just uncouth.
Noticing his behaviour, I will feel embarrassed, blush and escape from his
company as soon as possible. In many people, this norm of distance is so
ingrained that they never violate it. Some may move in circles in which it
is never violated. They have never had the occasion to think of it and
formulate it consciously as a norm of behaviour. They will instantly recognize a violation, yet may be unable to formulate the norm that has been
violated. Nor will the violators themselves always understand exactly where
they went wrong. These norms require a somewhat more complex analysis
than the phrase I italicized in the preceding paragraph, but can be handled
on basically similar lines, as propensities to act and to react, resting on an
involuntary reinforcement mechanism rather than on conscious inculca-
tion.

Third, I want to repeat that the contrast between norms and self-interest
need not generate a distinction among different kinds of action. Both types
of motivation may enter into a single action. Often, norms and self-interest
coexist in a parallelogram of forces that jointly determine behaviour. When
the norms require me to do X and self-interest tells me to do Y, I may end
up with a compromise. If I know I should kill to avenge an offence but
fear that I will be killed in return, I may swallow my pride and limit myself
to a demand for blood money.[29] Alternatively, self-interest may act as a
constraint on norms: I do X provided that the costs – the direct costs of
doing X and the opportunity costs of not doing Y – are below a certain level.
I regularly carry out my civic duty of voting, unless the weather is so bad
that I will be drenched going to the election locale or so glorious that I
would rather go on a picnic. Conversely, norms may constrain and limit
self-interest. Cutthroat competitiveness in bargaining may coexist with
trustworthiness in respecting the agreement that is reached ('self-interest
without guile'). In this chapter I usually ignore this kind of interaction

---

[29] Boehm (1984), ch. 8, emphasizes this aspect of revenge decisions.

between norms and self-interest. By contrast, I have quite a bit to say about another mode of interaction, namely the extent to which norms are shaped by self-interest. In Chapters 5 and 6, both forms of interaction are considered.

Examples

To fix our ideas, it is necessary to offer some examples of social norms. For convenience, and without any claim of completeness, I have grouped them in ten major categories. Some of them are very general and apply across a variety of arenas. Others are more arena-specific. It may well be possible to subsume them, too, under more general norms, but I will not try to do that. I do not claim that these are all the important norms there are. Many, such as norms regulating marriage and kinship, are neglected. My task here is not to offer a full analysis of norms – their varieties and hierarchies – but to argue for their reality, importance and autonomy.

Consumption norms

Simple, paradigmatic cases of social norms are those regulating manners of dress, manners of table and the like. *Le côté de Guermantes* shows that these norms, while utterly trivial in themselves, may be the object of obsessive interest and form the major criterion by which people are judged, accepted and rejected. In *La distinction* Pierre Bourdieu has extended the notion of consumption norms to cultural behaviour: Which syntax, vocabulary and pronunciation do you adopt? Which movies do you see? Which books do you read? Which sports do you practise? What kind of furniture do you buy?[30] There is a subtle blend, in such cases, of individual preference and social norms. At one extreme, manners of table – such as the rule to begin with the outermost fork – have no element of personal taste. At the other extreme, many choices of books or leisure activities are wholly personal. What one does in the privacy of one's home is, by and large, not the target of social approval and disapproval, nor of internalized norms and feelings of guilt. This is not to say that these choices are uncaused or uncorrelated with one's social background and environment. The point is simply that these social forces do not serve as a homeostatic mechanism keeping deviants in line.

[30] Bourdieu (1979).

In between are the ambiguous and seemingly overdetermined cases that form the target of social satirists. The snob follows the social norm, while believing that he simply has superior taste. When the norm changes, his preferences change with it. It is not that he has a taste for conformity, only that his tastes conform to those of others. The behaviour of others is the cause of his utility function, not an argument in it.[31] This may lead him into trouble. All tourists know the feeling that one would be perfectly happy were it not for the other tourists, not recognizing that a common force has lead them all to converge on the same place. Moreover, the snob does not hesitate to condemn those who do not conform to the norm, further undermining his claim to a personal preference.

More than other norms, cultural norms and consumption norms have strong elements of innocent play and not-so-innocent gamesmanship.[32] While some are norm followers, others, like the Duchesse de Guermantes, are norm setters. Some are in the grips of norms, while others are normative virtuosi who delight in calculated transgressions and creative refinements. 'Is there any keener joy for a writer rigorously trained in artistic discipline, or for a borderline Protestant like Gide or Eliot, than becoming reverently conscious of strict rules which he may some day delight in breaking?'[33] Sometimes norms are deliberately violated to put in their place those who believe they can get a foothold in an upper class by going by the book, while amused tolerance is reserved for those who violate the norms because they do not know any better.

Norms against behaviour 'contrary to nature'

Rules against incest and cannibalism exist in most societies. 'Unnatural' sexual acts, such as homosexuality or sodomy, are often frowned upon. There is often much hypocrisy surrounding these practices. In a case described by Colin Turnbull, a young man was severely punished for having committed incest with his cousin. 'Yet it was plain that everyone had known about the incest for months. Incest with one's cousin was wrong – the Mbuti seemed unanimous about this – but it was not until the incest be-

---

[31] Both cases must be distinguished from that discussed in Chapter 1, in which the *utility* of other people is an argument in one's utility function.

[32] As I argue in Elster (1981), the main flaw in the argument of Bourdieu (1979) is the assumption that all play is ultimately a form of gamesmanship.

[33] Peyre (1967), p. 227.

came indiscreet that it required action'.[34] Until recently, the same was true about attitudes towards homosexuality in Western societies. Public knowledge that someone was homosexual in private was much less offending than homosexual behaviour in public. Members of the Bloomsbury circle got away with it, while Alan Turing was faced with the choice between going to jail and having hormonal treatment.

Let me digress to expand this point, which is of quite general importance: to violate a norm in public shows a disdain for public opinion that is often more severely disapproved of than the norm violation itself.[35] Conversely, by hiding the violation, one respects and upholds the norm. In the limit, the norm may be respected even though everybody knows that nobody pays more than lip service to it. This seems, for instance, to characterize many norms of socialist behaviour in China and in the USSR. 'One attitude toward study and criticism is: well, we have to go along, even though we hate it; we know everyone is lying, but we have to go along so we don't leave a bad impression. . . . The situation is an embarrassing one: everyone is aware of the ridiculous and undignified role he plays in this charade; its seriousness is ensured by the foreman, silent and attentive, but always very much in evidence'.[36] This psychologically baffling *culture of hypocrisy* is sustained by a feeling of guilt from complicity: since everybody is both victim and perpetrator of these practices, nobody can denounce them.[37]

The norm against cannibalism allows for exceptions in case of *force majeure*. When the survivors of a 1972 aircrash in the Andes ate the flesh of the dead, they were not condemned but forgiven, absolved and even turned into celebrities of heroic stature.[38] It may even be acceptable for a group to kill and eat some among themselves, provided the victims are selected in a proper way. The custom of the sea in such cases has been to use a lottery,[39] and it is hard to think of any other procedure that would be found acceptable.[40]

Again, this can serve as a point of digression. Whenever there is a norm, there are often a set of adjunct norms defining legitimate exceptions. Often,

[34] Edgerton (1985), p. 136, summarizing Turnbull (1961).

[35] Abbott (1983), pp. 859–60, finds that 'enforcement of [professional] ethics . . . is a function largely of the visibility of the offence'.

[36] From two reports from the People's Republic of China, cited in Walder (1986), pp. 156, 157.

[37] Kolakowski (1978), vol. 3, pp. 83–91.   [38] Edgerton (1985), p. 51.

[39] Simpson (1984), p. 140.

[40] See Elster (1989a), ch. 2, for a general discussion of selection by lot.

these are less explicit than the main norm and rely heavily on judgement and discretion. They form, as it were, a penumbra around the main norm, a grey area that leaves room for maneuvering. Robert Edgerton has shown that there are large variations in norm enforcement. Some societies enforce their norms more strictly than do others.[41] Some norms are enforced more strictly than others.[42] Some individuals are treated more leniently than others.[43] And some circumstances are more extenuating than others.[44]

Norms regulating the use of money

Money can be perceived as essentially good or essentially bad. Both Marx and Simmel, for instance, insisted on the liberating effects of money.[45] Others have been deeply critical of the effects of money on social relations. Partly this is because money can turn into an end in itself, as in speculation and interest bearing, thus diverting energy from productive purposes.[46] Partly it is because money can be used improperly, to buy things that money should not be able to buy. Thus there have been norms or laws against buying salvation, votes, public office, spouses and exemption from military service, to cite but some examples.[47] I shall discuss two cases not regulated by law but nevertheless subject to social norms.

Consider a suburban community where all houses have small lawns of the same size.[48] Suppose a houseowner is willing to pay is neighbour's son ten dollars to mow his lawn, but not more. He would rather spend half an hour mowing the lawn himself than pay eleven dollars to have someone else do it. Imagine now that the same person is offered twenty dollars to mow the lawn of another neighbour. It is easy to imagine that he would refuse, probably with some indignation. But this has an appearance of irrationality. By turning down the offer of having his neighbour's son mow his lawn for eleven dollars, he implies that half an hour of his time is worth at most eleven dollars. By turning down the offer to mow the other neighbour's lawn for twenty dollars, he implies that it is worth at least twenty

---

[41] Edgerton (1986), chs. 8 and 9.   [42] Ibid., ch. 11.   [43] Ibid., ch. 4.
[44] Ibid., chs. 3, 5, 6.
[45] Simmel (1978), ch. 4; Marx (1865), p. 1033. (Needless to say, this statement does not fully summarize Marx's attitude towards money.)
[46] See, e.g., Kuran (1983).
[47] For fuller lists, see Simmel (1978), ch. 5, and Walzer (1983), pp. 100–3. To their examples one could add the widespread norm against the sale of land (Stone 1972, p. 73; Finley 1981, ch. 4).
[48] I am indebted to Amos Tversky for suggesting this to me as an example of social norms.

dollars. But it cannot both be worth less than eleven and more than twenty dollars.

As an explanation, it has been suggested[49] that people evaluate losses and gains forgone differently. Credit card companies exploit this difference when they insist that stores advertise cash discounts rather than credit card surcharges. The credit card holder is affected to a lesser extent by the lost chance of getting the cash discount than by the extra cost of paying with the card. Similarly, the houseowner is affected to a greater extent by the out-of-pocket expenses that he would incur by paying someone to mow his lawn than by the loss of a windfall income. But this cannot be the full story, because it does not explain why the houseowner should be indignant at the proposal. Part of the explanation must be that he does not think of himself as the kind of person who mows other people's lawns for money. It *isn't done,* to use a revealing phrase that often accompanies social norms. One may argue that the norm serves an ulterior purpose. Social relations among neighbours would be disturbed if wealth differences were too blatantly displayed and if some treated others as salaried employees. Yet on any given occasion, that would usually not be the reason or motive for refusing the offer, or for not making it. It simply isn't done.

Next, there seems to be a social norm against walking up to a person in a cinema queue and asking to buy his place. Note that nobody would be harmed if someone did this. Other people in the queue would not lose their place. The person asked to sell his place would be free to refuse. If he accepted, he and the buyer would both gain by the exchange. The norm against buying places in a queue may be related to the finding that people consider queuing a more equitable way of allocating surplus tickets to a baseball game than either a lottery or an auction.[50] Although a totally wasteful activity, queuing seems to create a special entitlement to scarce goods.

Norms of reciprocity

These norms enjoin us to return favours done to us by others.[51] The potlatch system among the American Indians is a well-known instance. According to one (contested) interpretation the potlatch was something of a poisoned gift: 'The property received by a man in a potlatch was no free

---

[49] Thaler (1980), p. 43.
[50] The finding was reported in an earlier version of Kahneman, Knetsch and Thaler (1986a).
[51] Gouldner (1960).

and wanton gift. He was not at liberty to refuse it, even though accepting it obligated him to make a return at another potlatch not only of the original amount but of twice as much'.[52] An extreme example of such ambiguous altruism is found in Colin Turnbull's description of gift and sacrifice in this society among the miserable Ik of Uganda:

> These are not expressions of the foolish belief that altruism is both possible and desirable: they are weapons, sharp and aggressive, which can be put to divers uses. But the purpose for which the gift is designed can be thwarted by the nonacceptance of it, and much Icien ingenuity goes into thwarting the would-be thwarter. The object, of course, is to build up a whole series of obligations so that in times of crisis you have a number of debts you can recall, and with luck one of them may be repaid. To this end, in the circumstances of Ik life, considerable sacrifice would be justified, to the very limits of the minimal survival level. But a sacrifice that can be rejected is useless, and so you have the odd phenomenon of these otherwise singularly self-interested people going out of their way to 'help' each other. In point of fact they are helping themselves and their help may very well be resented in the extreme, but it is done in such a way that it cannot be refused, for it has already been given. Someone, quite unasked, may hoe another's field in his absence, or rebuild his stockade, or join in the building of a house that could easily be done by the man and his wife alone. At one time I have seen so many men thatching a roof that the whole roof was in serious danger of collapsing, and the protests of the owner were of no avail. The work done was a debt incurred. It was another good reason for being wary of one's neighbours. Lokeléa always made himself unpopular by accepting such help and by paying for it on the spot with food (which the cunning old fox knew they could not resist), which immediately negated the debt.[53]

These transactions, like the potlatch, involve repeated prestations and counterprestations among the same individuals. A more intriguing form of

---

[52] Helen Codere, cited after Piddocke (1965).

[53] Turnbull (1972), p. 146. These strategies are universally employed. As I was completing this book, I came across a passage in a crime novel (Engel 1986, p. 155) making the same point: 'I decided to make a fast getaway. I had done Pete a favour and it didn't pay to let him thank me for doing it. It was more negotiable the other way. I heard him calling after me but I kept going'.

reciprocity is that which Eilert Sundt found on the Norwegian West Coast.[54] Here wedding guests were expected to give a certain amount of money to the bridal couple, who in turn were expected to do the same when they were invited to a wedding. Presumably most of the guests were already married and hence could not hope for a later counterprestation. Intergenerational reciprocity is also found between parents and children. Assuming that parents cannot disinherit their children, the latter have no incentive to take care of their parents in old age, except perhaps to make sure that they do not squander the inheritance by going into expensive old-age homes. Yet most societies have a norm that you should help your parents, in return for what they did for you when you were at a similarly helpless stage.

Reciprocity is not the combination of two unconditional norms: X should do A and Y should do B. It is a conditional norm: if X does A, Y should do B. It often goes together with another conditional norm: if X does A, X should also do B. There is, let us assume, an unconditional norm that I should give a Christmas gift to my children.[55] There may be a conditional norm that if I give something to a friend for Christmas, he has an obligation to reciprocate. Suppose the friend is wealthy and there is a norm that wealthier people should give more in absolute terms (although allowed to give less in relative terms). I can then exploit the situation to my advantage by making the initial gift. Finally, there is the less explicit but powerful norm that if I begin offering gifts to someone at Christmas, I am expected to go on doing so in the future. Not wanting to incur the obligation, I might hesitate to take the first step.

The Chinese notion of *guanxi,* a kind of instrumental friendship,[56] illustrates the same point.[57] At one extreme of the spectrum of *guanxi* are situations in which preexisting affective ties are the basis for mutual help. At the other extreme are relations that differ little from sheer bribery. In between are situations in which the tie is created by unilateral donations by one party for the purpose of inducing some unspecified reciprocation at some unspecified date. Doctors who can dispense certificates of illness or superiors who can allocate scarce consumption items are frequent targets

---

[54] Sundt (1974–8), vol. 3, p. 183.

[55] Caplow (1984) studies mainly unconditional norms of Christmas gift giving. They regulate partly the recipients and partly the value and nature of the gifts. When there are unconditional norms for A to give to B and for B to give to A, each will expect reciprocation, but the obligation is to give, not to reciprocate.

[56] The term is from Wolf (1966).

[57] The following draws on Walder (1986), pp. 179–86; see also Hwang (1987).

of such instrumental giving. It is clear from the following description that the practice has a normative component that goes beyond a simple exchange of favours:

> This is a very deliberate thing. You have to make it seem like it isn't a bribe. It is a very subtle art. You can say, 'I don't need this anymore, just let me leave it in your office for a while'. It's really a gift, but on the surface it doesn't look like it. It's a delicate and complicated matter. . . . It's like a down payment that obliges the person to do you a favor later on, or lose face. . . . Of course many people think it's wrong, but it still goes on.[58]

Medical ethics

In their professional training doctors are inculcated with certain norms of proper treatment which turn out to subvert more rational, outcome-oriented criteria. Examples include the norm that more serious cases should be treated before less serious cases and the norm that each patient should be given the fullest possible treatment. I shall have more to say about the first norm, but first a few words about the second. It is easy to see how this norm can subvert efficiency if, as is plausible, treatment has decreasing marginal efficacy. When medical treatment is a scarce resource, the goal of saving lives or of promoting health dictates that it should be spread thinly across many patients rather than concentrated on a smaller number. Yet this principle goes against a deeply ingrained tendency in the medical profession to help each patient as much as possible.

Napoleon's chief medical officer, Baron Larrey, and the first to set up norms for medical 'triage', insisted on treating the most serious cases first. 'Those who are dangerously wounded must be tended first, *entirely without regard to rank or distinction*. Those less severely injured must wait until the gravely wounded have been operated on and dressed'.[59] Larrey may have believed that this was also the most efficient principle, assuming that the worst cases were also the ones that could most benefit from treatment. Yet a second's reflection shows that the relationship is much more likely to be as depicted in Fig. 3.1.

In this diagram, the expected benefit from treatment is represented by

---

[58] Walder (1986), p. 185.   [59] Cited after Winslow (1982), p. 2.

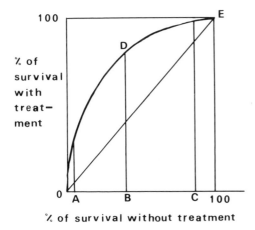

Fig. 3.1

the distance between the 45° line and the curve *ODE*. The worst cases, who are almost certain to die without treatment, are also unlikely to benefit much if treated. Conversely, the best cases, who are almost certain to get well spontaneously, do not benefit much from treatment. The largest benefits come in the intermediate cases. To select patients for treatment when not all can be treated, one might use one of three criteria. (a) Choose the patients who will benefit most from treatment, that is, those with a prior survival chance about *B* in Fig. 3.1. (b) Choose the patients with the smallest prior survival chance, that is, about *A*. (c) Choose the patients having the largest chance of surviving without treatment, that is, those about *C*. By and large, the first, utilitarian criterion is the one that is adopted by health authorities in most countries. By contrast, practising doctors often follow the second criterion, which corresponds more closely to the norms of their profession. In one study of admission to intensive care units the authors found that 'physicians appeared to be reluctant to conserve resources by withdrawing care from acutely ill patients even when the anticipated benefit of that care was vanishingly small'.[60] The third criterion is in clear violation of both social efficiency[61] and medical norms. Yet there

[60] Singer et al. (1983), p. 1159.
[61] At least when the social goal is that of saving the maximum number of lives. If the goal is that of treating soldiers to get them ready for combat, it may make sense to treat the least seriously wounded before the moderately serious cases, as has indeed become the practice in modern warfare (Winslow 1982, pp. 6–11).

is some evidence that mental health professionals allocate their attention in this way – that 'large numbers of highly trained provider groups are being well paid mostly to talk about personal matters to people with mild emotional problems' while people with severe mental disorders go untreated.[62] In Norway, private hospitals systematically select patients by the third criterion, leaving the more serious cases for treatment in public hospitals.

Hence we see that efficiency in the pursuit of health is threatened from two sides. On the one hand, the preference of doctors for profit or for a quiet life may lead them to select the least serious cases, which require fewer efforts and make their statistics look good. While a fully rational practice in the light of these desires, it thwarts the effort of the public health system. On the other hand, efficiency is undermined by doctors' professional norms, which lead them to concentrate on critically ill patients even when the very acuteness of their condition makes treatment unlikely to succeed. Those norms are not outcome-oriented, at least not in the relevant sense of enjoining the doctor to compare the outcomes of alternative actions. Rather, they tell the doctor to compare the outcomes of alternative *in*actions: who is most likely to die if not given treatment?

Codes of honour

This term might be used as a synonym for social norms in general, since norm violation is usually thought of as dishonourable. I use it in a more restricted sense, however, to designate codes that regulate *the life of the proud man,* in the sense of the classical moralists. Usually, codes of honour come as a package that has both positive and negative components. On the positive side, they tell people to act courageously, to return favours, to honour commitments and to tell the truth. On the negative side, they enjoin people to insult others, to carry out any threats they might have made and to retaliate if others try to take advantage of them.[63] Crucially, they tell people to act in these ways even when it would appear to be in their self-interest to behave otherwise. A further analysis of codes of honour is postponed until the next section and the concluding chapter. Here I shall adduce a few examples, beginning with the Roman concept of *dignitas:*

---

[62]   Knesper, Pagnucco and Wheller (1985), p. 1367.

[63]   Codes of honour include, therefore, norms of reciprocity and norms of retribution. But these norms can also exist separately, thus justifying the separate discussion in the text.

Much light can be shed on the nature of power in this world through considering the usages of the word *dignitas*. It might well be applied to those various moments and attributes, displaying high position . . . : the parade of wealth, the shouting herald who went first in the street, the showy costume and large retinue, the holding of oneself apart, and the limitation of familiar address. All this might be called the substance of *dignitas*. But the term had a darker side, too. As used by Cicero, Caesar, or Pliny, it meant the ability to defend one's display by force if need be; to strike back at anyone who offended one or hurt or offended one's dependents; to avenge oneself and others, and to be perceived as capable of such baneful, alarming conduct. In both Greek and Latin authors. . . . revenge was approved and a man was called good who could deliver a hard blow as well as extend a kindly gesture.[64]

Similarly, the unwritten laws of Albania between the wars had two sides.[65] On the one hand, there was an absolute obligation to be truthful in oath telling, which was widely used to regulate contested property cases. 'A man detected in a false oath became an outcast, despised and condemned by all his fellows, and was never again invited into any house in the tribe'.[66] On the other hand, there was an equally absolute obligation to seek revenge for an offence. 'A man slow to kill his enemy was thought "disgraced" and was described as "low-class" and "bad". Among the Highlanders he risked finding that other men had contemptuously come to sleep with his wife, his daughter could not marry into a "good family" and his son must marry a "bad" girl'.[67] Similarly, the Montenegrin code of honour tells people not only to take revenge under appropriate circumstances, but also not to lie and steal within the tribe.[68]

Sometimes the positive part of the code seems more prominent. James Coleman, summarizing Joseph Wechsberg's *The Merchant Bankers*, describes the practices of diamond dealers and bankers as follows:

In both of these close communities, verbal agreement will suffice because (a) the reputation for trustworthiness is of central importance in

---

[64] MacMullen (1988), p. 69. He does not assert, however, that truth telling and promise keeping were required by *dignitas*. My conjecture is that they were not.
[65] The following draws on Hasluck (1954).   [66] Ibid., p. 193.   [67] Ibid., pp. 231–2.
[68] Boehm (1984), p. 77.

both businesses; and (b) that reputation is shared and quickly commu-
nicated among all those on whom the trustee depends for his future
business – i.e., for future placement of trust. The concern with integrity,
trustworthiness, reputation is almost an obsession among merchant bankers
in the City of London. Wechsberg quotes: '. . . if a man has been an
old customer and friend we'll do anything for him. Even when money
is tight, we won't take advantage of him. We are very jealous of our
name.' . . . '[Merchant banking is] a sense of commercial honor, an
absolute fairness in all dealings, willingness to suffer pecuniary loss, if
need be rather than tarnish by one unworthy act the good name of the
firm'.[69]

Conversely, some codes appear to be mainly negative. The picture which
emerges of mafiosi or wiseguys, for instance, is the following.[70] Their
code of honour does not allow them to make empty threats, to accept
others' breaking of their promises or to suffer threats without retaliating.
It does not require them to honour their own promises. In dealing with
ordinary citizens this allows them to use either force or guile, whichever
is the most appropriate. When dealing with other wiseguys they must be
more careful. Opportunism (not honour) then dictates that promises be kept
or, as an alternative, that the promisee be killed. Similarly, threats are
never made among wiseguys; they simply take each other out without
prior warning. There is no honesty among thieves.

Norms of retribution

Some societies have had norms of strict liability for harm, regardless of
intent or circumstances. Edgerton reports that the Jalé of New Guinea have
extreme and rigid rules of liability. 'For example, should a man's wife die
in childbirth, the husband was liable for her death; had he not impregnated
her, the Jalé said, she would not have died'.[71] Even more dramatically:

Kevel was cutting down a large branch of a tree that grew close to a path
when the woman approached. Disregarding both the markings that Kevel

---

[69] Coleman (1982), pp. 286–7.
[70] The following is based on Pileggi (1987), on Smart (1983), and possibly on the reading
of too many crime novels. Gambetta (1988a,b), while allowing for a role of codes of honour
in mafia operations, emphasizes explanations based on rational self-interest.
[71] Edgerton (1985), p. 161.

had placed across the path to warn people of danger and his furious shouts, she hurried on. As the woman passed the tree, the branch broke and killed her and a child she was carrying on her shoulders. My informants insisted that Kevel had to indemnify the woman's relatives because 'the branch fell down by his hands', even though the accident occurred through the woman's own fault.[72]

More generally, retributive systems can (a) require both intent and success as conditions for liability or, more weakly, regard the lack of either as an extenuating circumstance; they can (b) accept lack of intent, but not lack of success, as an excuse or (c) vice versa; or they may (d) accept no excuses whatsoever. By targeting action rather than the outcome of action, social norms can sanction people for acting in a way that *may* have a bad outcome, regardless of whether it actually occurred or was foreseen. One might argue that such norms *are* ultimately guided by outcomes and hence do not fall under my definition. Yet although outcomes may enter into the definition of the target action or be part of the explanation of why certain actions are targeted, application of the norm need not be outcome-oriented.[73] One might counter that norms of strict liability have good outcomes on the whole, even if on particular occasions they may appear absurd. This is manifestly false, however: no good incentive effects are created by a social norm that makes people responsible for all actions in which they are causally involved. Rather, the effect is to make people excessively cautious, to the point of paralysing any initiative. As we shall see later, many social norms have this effect.

A widespread form of retribution is the vendetta or feud. Whether highly organized as in the Mediterranean countries[74] or among the Yanomanö Indians of Amazonas,[75] or more loosely structured as in the southern Appalachians in the late nineteenth century,[76] the feud rests on powerful conditional norms. Although there may be some leeway as to whether an ini-

---

[72] Koch (1974), p. 88, cited after Edgerton (1985), p. 162.

[73] As I make clear below, a similar observation applies to norms of cooperation.

[74] Busquet (1920) contains much information about Corsican vendettas. Black-Michaud (1975) is useful, but marred by a high ratio of functionalist speculation to facts and mechanisms. Hasluck (1954), chs. 22–5, contains extremely detailed descriptions of the norms regulating blood feuds in Albania. The most valuable book on Mediterranean vendettas is perhaps Boehm (1984), if once again we disregard the dubious functional explanations.

[75] Chagnon (1988).

[76] Rice (1982) is a blow-by-blow account of the most famous of these feuds.

tial offence is serious enough to exact retribution,[77] the first act of revenge almost inexorably leads to others. Vendettas are 'nonrealistic' conflicts in Lewis Coser's sense. They differ from, say, raids in that they are 'not oriented towards the attainment of specific results'[78] like the acquisition of cattle or money. They involve strong group pressures and strong feelings of honour and shame. Referring to his childhood in Montenegro, Milhovan Djilas writes that

> revenge is an overpowering and consuming fire. It flares upon and burns away every other thought and emotion. Only it remains, over and above everything else. . . . Vengeance – this is the breath of life one shares from the cradle with one's fellow clansmen, in both good fortune and bad, vengeance from eternity. . . . It was our clan, and Uncle Mirko – his love and suffering and the years of unfulfilled desire for revenge and for life. Vengeance is not hatred, but the wildest and sweetest kind of drunkenness, both for those who must wreak vengeance and for those who wish to be avenged.[79]

The other side of the coin is the sufferings of the man who fails to take revenge when the norms of vengeance tell him to do so. In Corsica, he is constantly exposed to the *rimbecco,* an insult reserved for those who have failed to revenge an offence:

> The life of the individual who is exposed every day to the *rimbecco* is hell. . . . 'Whoever hesitates to revenge himself, said Gregorovius in 1854, is the target of the whisperings of his relatives and the insults of strangers, who reproach him publicly for his cowardice.' . . . 'In Corsica, the man who has not avenged his father, an assassinated relative

---

[77] For instance, a young Corsican girl is compromised if a man tries to take off her head covering, but an insistent look from a man who meets her on the street can also be sufficient (Busquet 1920, p. 355). In Kohistani Thull, offence was taken at men who 'stare at wife or daughter, reflect light from a snuff box mirror on a wife or daughter, propose intimacy with a wife or daughter, look through a camera at a wife or daughter, flee or attempt to flee the community with a wife or daughter, or have illicit sexual relations with a wife or daughter' (Lincoln-Keiser 1986, pp. 500–1). Clearly, some of these are easier to ignore than others, should one want to do so. (They are also easier to impute without justification, should one want to do so.) Boehm (1984), pp. 145–9, argues that in a feud two decisions are largely discretionary: the decision to go out of one's way to insult somebody and the decision by the insulted party to retaliate by homicide. Later decisions are more automatic, although, he argues, not fully so.

[78] Coser (1986), p. 49.   [79] Cited after Lincoln-Keiser (1986), p. 491.

or a deceived daughter *can no longer appear in public*. Nobody speaks to him; he has to remain silent. If he raises his voice to emit an opinion, people will say to him: avenge yourself first, and then you can state your point of view'. The *rimbecco* can occur at any moment and under any guise. It does not even need to express itself in words: an ironical smile, a contemptuous turning away of the head, a certain condescending look – there are a thousand small insults which at all times of the day remind the unhappy victim of how much he has fallen in the esteem of his compatriots.[80]

Acts of vengeance are paradigmatic examples of norm-guided action. 'Who sees not that vengeance, from the force alone of passion, may be so eagerly pursued as to make us knowingly neglect every consideration of ease, interest, or safety?'[81] Because of the high stakes involved, these norms are at the opposite extreme from the no less paradigmatic norms of etiquette. The challenge to any theory of social norms is to account for both.

Work norms

The work place is a hotbed of norm-guided action. In Chapter 6 I discuss the role of social norms in collective wage bargaining. Here I give three other examples of work-related norms. The first two are targeted directly at work and work performance, while the third concerns wage differentials within the firm.

There is a social norm against living off other people and a corresponding normative pressure to earn one's income from work. This norm can explain why workers in ailing industries sometimes refuse wage subsidies. They may, however, accept much more expensive subsidies to the firms that employ them. In Norway, workers in the textile industry are envious of the workers in the aluminium industry, who can demand energy subsidies rather than outright wage subventions. Similarly, the fishermen in northern Norway prefer state support to shipowners to direct wage subsidies. In all cases, however, the main goal and effect of the subsidies is to ensure employment.[82] A rose by another name may smell more sweet. One

---

[80] Busquet (1920), pp. 357–8. I have already quoted a similar description by Hasluck (1954), pp. 231–2. See also Bourdieu (1966) for a subtle discussion of the predicament of the man who fails to avenge an offence.
[81] Hume (1751), app. 2.   [82] Elster (1988).

norm may apply to the glass that is half full and another to the one that is half empty. Norms, like preferences, are defined over actions or outcomes *as described in a specific way*.[83]

At the work place one often finds informal norms among the workers that regulate their work effort. Typically, these set lower as well as upper limits on what is perceived to be a proper effort. The Hawthorne study of Western Electric quotes workers as saying, 'You should not turn out too much work. If you do, you are a ratebuster', and 'You should not turn out too little work. If you do, you are a "chiseler" '.[84] It has been argued that the norm against rate busting is due to sheer conformism[85] or to envy.[86] The obvious alternative explanation – that the norm is a rational response to the constant pressure of management to change piece rates – will concern us later.

George Akerlof – one of the rare economists to take social norms seriously – has proposed 'a theory of social custom, of which unemployment may be one consequence'.[87] He argues that the persistence of 'fair' rather than market-clearing wages can be explained by assuming that employed workers have a 'code of honour' that forbids them to train new workers who are hired to do the same job for lower wages.[88] Because new workers require on-the-job training to learn their job, the refusal of old workers to train them deters the employer from hiring them, thus generating involuntary employment. Although one can think of more plausible explanations for worker and employer reluctance to two-tiered wage systems,[89] Akerlof's proposal is at least worth considering. An objection to his argument is discussed and refuted later.

---

[83] See Tversky and Kahneman (1981) for a discussion of framing of preferences.

[84] Roethlisberger and Dickson (1939), p. 522.

[85] Jones (1984).   [86] Schoeck (1987), pp. 31, 310.   [87] Akerlof (1980).

[88] His article was written before the introduction of two-tiered wage systems in several American airlines.

[89] Employers might oppose the system if they fear that the newly hired will strike for higher wages once they are hired or that their lower status will be bad for their morale and, hence, for their productivity. Workers might oppose it because of the potential it creates for divide-and-rule tactics on the part of the employers (Bowles 1986). Or they might oppose it simply because of the psychological uneasiness created by face-to-face interaction among unequals, a mechanism that may also be at work when affluent industrial countries limit the number of immigrants. The old workers will neither take a cut in wages nor work side by side with workers paid less than themselves. The average Norwegian will neither subsidize immigrant workers nor accept the existence of second-rate citizens, in spite of the fact that many potential immigrants would vastly prefer being second-rate citizens of Norway to their current situation.

Norms of cooperation

In Chapter 1 I surveyed outcome-oriented maxims of cooperation. A utilitarian, for instance, would cooperate if and only if his contribution increased the average utility of the members in the group. There are also, however, non-outcome-oriented norms of cooperation. A full discussion is postponed until Chapter 5, but brief definitions are in order here.

On the one hand, there is what I call 'everyday Kantianism': cooperate if and only if it would be better for all if all cooperated than if nobody did. In one sense, this norm is outcome-oriented since it refers to the outcome that would be realized if everybody acted in a certain way. In another sense – the sense that is relevant here – the norm disregards outcomes, since it does not enjoin an individual to consider the outcome of *his* action. The norm is conditional upon hypothetical outcomes, not actual ones.

On the other hand, there is what I call 'the norm of fairness': cooperate if and only if most other people cooperate. This norm is conditional upon the past behaviour of others. Clearly, these others cannot all be motivated by the norm of fairness. They might, for instance, be utilitarians or Kantians. In Chapter 5 I try to bring out how these motivations can build upon each other in various ways to produce collective action.

Norms of distribution

The definition just given of the norm of fairness may seem too restrictive. When people talk about 'norms of fairness', what they usually have in mind is fairness of distribution rather than fairness of contribution. These norms include norms of equality, norms of equity, reference-point norms and more complex norms such as the one embodied in the Kalai–Smorodinsky solution to bargaining problems. I refer to Chapter 6 for a more extensive discussion of norms of distribution. Here I make only a few general remarks.

Democratic societies, according to Tocqueville, are characterized by a pervasive norm of equality. At certain times, 'the passion for equality seeps into every corner of the human heart, expands and fills the whole. It is no use telling them that by this blind surrender to an exclusive passion they are compromising their dearest interests; they are deaf'.[90] Norms of distri-

---

[90] Tocqueville (1969), p. 505.

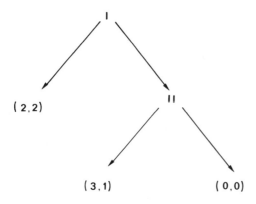

Fig. 3.2

bution, like other social norms, have a grip on the mind and an emotional appeal that is largely independent of their contribution, if any, to individual or social welfare. Norms of equality may imply, for instance, that if there is not enough of an indivisible good to go around, it is better that it be destroyed than that only some should receive it. Or they may imply that scarce water should, like grace, fall impartially on barren and on fertile ground. Or, more radically, they may enforce equality even if everybody would be better off if some inequality were allowed.

One might object that norms of distribution are not social norms as I have defined them, since they refer to what people shall *get*, not to what they shall *do*. Norms of behaviour can, however, be derived from norms of distribution. For any norm of distribution defining the fair outcome as *X*, there is a norm of behaviour telling people not to accept less than *X*. Often, people will refuse to share on what they perceive to be unfair terms, preferring to break off negotiations and take a loss rather than accept what they would get according to their threat-based bargaining power. In doing so, they may (or may not) end up better off than they would have had they bargained solely from threats. Figure 3.2, which may be usefully contrasted with Fig. 2.5, provides an illustration.

Here we assume that II believes so strongly in egalitarian norms of distribution that he is willing to accept (0, 0) rather than (1, 3). Knowing this, I can do no better than to bring about (2, 2). There is good experimental evidence that people behave in this way.[91] I argue in Chapter 6 that

---

[91] Güth, Schmittberger and Schwarze (1982); Kahneman, Knetsch and Thaler (1986b).

labour–labour wage bargaining displays similar features. Note, however, that II may be thwarted if I strongly believes in some other norm, for example, a norm of equity, that would justify the distribution (3, 1). In that case, the bargaining impasse (0, 0) might be the outcome.

The reality and autonomy of norms

I shall argue for the reality of norms and for their autonomy. By the reality of norms I mean their independent motivating power. Norms are not merely ex post rationalizations of self-interest, although they can certainly be that sometimes. They are capable of being ex ante sources of action. By the autonomy of norms I mean their irreducibility to optimization. There is no single end – genetic, individual or collective – that all norms serve and that explains why there are norms. Nor, for any given norm, is there always any end that it serves and that explains why it exists. Although these claims do not amount to the absurd view that norms are uncaused, I cannot offer a positive explanation of norms. I do not know why human beings have a propensity to construct and follow norms, nor how specific norms come into being and change.[92] The problem is closely linked with that of explaining emotions, another poorly understood area of human life.

A fundamental problem that arises in the analysis of social norms is the extent to which they have real, independent efficacy and the extent to which they are merely rationalizations of self-interest.[93] Is it true, as argued by early generations of anthropologists and sociologists, that norms are in the saddle and people merely their supports? Or is it true, as argued by more recent generations, that rules and norms are just the raw material for strategic manipulation or, perhaps, for unconscious rationalization and dissonance reduction?[94]

Sometimes people invoke a social norm to rationalize self-interest. Sup-

[92] See, however, the concluding chapter for some speculative remarks about norm change.
[93] There is a third position, advocated by Cancian (1975). She argues that norms as defined by Parsons and others have no relation whatsoever to behaviour, neither as ex ante generators of action nor as ex post justifications of action. Among her subjects in a Mayan community, she found no correlation between norm clusters elicited by comparison questions and choices in three sets of alternative actions: (a) whether an individual farmed nearby or took advantage of the new road and farmed far away; (b) whether he sent his children to school; and (c) whether he used Western doctors in addition to native curers. She also provides a subtle and thoughtful discussion of an alternative conception of norms, with emphasis on norms as rules for validation of one's social identity by others.
[94] For a brief history and clear statement of this distinction, see Edgerton (1985), ch. 1.

pose my wife and I are having a dinner party for eight, and that four persons have already been invited. We discuss whether to invite a particular couple for the last two places and find ourselves in disagreement, for somewhat murky reasons. I like the woman of the couple, and my wife does not like the fact that I like her. But we do not want to state these reasons. (Perhaps there is a social norm against doing so.) Instead we appeal to social norms. I invoke the norm of reciprocity, saying that 'since they had us over for dinner, it is our turn to invite them now'. My wife invokes another norm: 'since we have already invited two single men, we must invite two women, to create a balance'.

In wage negotiations, sheer bargaining power counts for much. Appeal to accepted social norms can also have some efficacy, however. To justify wage increases, workers can refer to the earning power of the firm, the wage level in other firms or occupations, the per cent wage increase in other firms or occupations, and the absolute wage increases in other firms or occupations. When changes are being compared, they can choose the reference year so as to make their own case as strong as possible. Employers use similar arguments to resist claims for wage increases. Each argument can be supported by a norm of fair wages. There is a norm of fair division of the surplus between capital and labour. Employers will appeal to this norm when the firm does badly, workers when it does well. There is a norm of equal pay for equal work. Workers will appeal to this norm when they earn less than workers in similar firms, but not when they earn more. The norm of preservation of status, or wage differences, can also be exploited for bargaining purposes. I discuss these matters at greater length in Chapter 6.

Social psychologists have studied norms of distribution to see whether there is any correlation between who subscribes to a norm and who benefits from it. Some findings point to the existence of a 'norm of modesty': high achievers prefer the norm of equity (i.e., reward proportional to achievement).[95] More widespread, however, are findings which suggest that people prefer the distributive norms which favour them.[96] This corresponds to a pattern frequently observed in wage discussions. Low-income groups invoke a norm of equality, whereas high-income groups advocate pay according to productivity. I return to these issues, too, in Chapter 6.

[95] Mikula (1972); Mikula and Uray (1973); Kahn, Lamm and Nelson (1977). The findings in Yaari and Bar-Hillel (1987) on the whole also support this view.

[96] Deutsch (1985), ch. 11; Messick and Sentis (1983).

Conditional norms lend themselves easily to manipulation. I have cited the example of gift giving, but there are many other cases. There is, for instance, a general norm that whoever first proposes that something be done has a special responsibility for making sure that it is carried out. This can prevent the proposal from ever being made, even if all would benefit from it. A couple may share the desire to have a child and yet neither may want to be the first to suggest the idea, fearing that he or she will then get special childcaring responsibility.[97] The member of a seminar who suggests a possible topic for discussion is often saddled with the task of introducing it. The person in a courtship who first proposes a date is at a disadvantage.[98] The fine art of inducing others to make the first move, and of resisting such inducements, provides instances of instrumentally rational exploitation of a social norm.

Even the codes of honour underlying the vendetta lend themselves to manipulation and exploitation. In eighteenth-century Corsica, for instance, a young woman lost her honour if a man came up to her in a public place and touched her or removed the scarf covering her hair.[99] Nobody would then want to marry her, except the offender – who might well commit the dishonouring act for that very reason. He might even be in connivance with the girl if her parents were against their marriage. The strategy, however, was risky. Sometimes the parents would feel that only the death of the offender could remove the offence.

Even when there is only one relevant norm, it can be interpreted so as to coincide with self-interest. If the action targeted by the norm is appropriately redescribed, it may no longer fall under it. Hence the norm holder has an incentive to frame the situation so that the norm tells him to do what he would like to do anyway.[100] Norms of cooperation, for example, easily lend themselves to reinterpretation. Abstaining from voting or from paying union dues seems like a paradigm case of noncooperative behaviour. Yet the lazy voter or the miserly worker may tell himself that in a larger perspective his abstention is a form of cooperation. By not voting he signals that the spectrum of candidates is too narrow and that reform of the nominating procedure is required. Staying outside the union is a noncooperative act if the reference group comprises the other workers in the firm. By focusing on the costs of bargaining and by extending the reference group

---

[97] I am indebted to Ottar Brox for this example.   [98] Waller (1937).
[99] Busquet (1920), p. 112.
[100] See Fischhof (1983) for a discussion of 'hedonic framing' of preferences.

to society as a whole, refusal to join the union can be seen as an act of cooperation.[101]

Some have said that this is all there is to norms: they are tools of manipulation, used to dress up self-interest in more acceptable garb. But this cannot be true. Some norms, like the norm of vengeance, obviously override self-interest. A more general argument against the cynical view of norms is that it is self-defeating. 'Unless rules were considered important and were taken seriously and followed, it would make no sense to manipulate them for personal benefit. If many people did not believe that rules were legitimate and compelling, how could anyone use these rules for personal advantage?'[102] Or again, 'if the justice arguments are such transparent frauds, why are they advanced in the first place and why are they given serious attention?'[103] The ambiguous altruism of the Ik illustrates both the reality of norms and their manipulability. If some people successfully exploit norms for self-interested purposes, it can only be because others are willing to let norms take precedence over self-interest. Moreover, even those who appeal to the norm usually believe in it, or else the appeal might not have much power.[104] The power of norms derives from the emotional tonality that gives them a grip on the mind.

The would-be manipulator of norms is also constrained by the need to be consistent. Even if the norm has no grip on his mind, he must act as if it had. Having invoked the norm of reciprocity on one occasion, I cannot just dismiss it when my wife appeals to it another time. An employer may successfully appeal to the workers and get them to share the burdens in a bad year. The cost he pays is that in a good year he may also have to share the benefits. By making the earlier appeal, he committed himself to the norm of a fair division of the surplus. Finally, the manipulator is constrained by the fact that the repertoire of norms on which he can draw is, after all, limited. Even if unconstrained by earlier appeals to norms, there may not be any norm available that coincides neatly with his self-interest.

---

[101] A telling example of how a norm may be turned around by changing the reference group is found in Astrid Lindgren's (1985) novel *Brothers Lionheart*. It takes place in a mythical country governed by a cruel tyrant, to whom an underground opposition emerges. The leader of the opposition – one of the brothers of the title – refuses to use violent means to overthrow the tyrant. His frustrated followers ask him, 'What if everyone acted like you?' To which he replies, 'If everyone acted like me, there would be no problem, would there?' implicitly extending the reference group to supporters of the regime.

[102] Edgerton (1985), p. 3.   [103] Zajac (1985), p. 120.

[104] This is the central argument in Veyne (1976).

When I say that manipulation of social norms presupposes that they have some kind of grip on the mind since otherwise there would be nothing to manipulate, I am not suggesting that society is made up of two sorts of people: those who believe in norms and those who manipulate the believers. Rather I believe that most norms are shared by most people – manipulators as well as manipulated. Rather than manipulation in a direct sense, we are dealing here with an amalgam of belief, deception and self-deception. At any given time we believe in many different norms, which may have contradictory implications for the situation at hand. A norm that happens to coincide with narrowly defined self-interest easily acquires special salience.[105] If there is no norm handy to rationalize self-interest, or if I have invoked a different norm in the recent past, or if there is another norm which overrides it, I may have to act against my self-interest. My self-image as someone who is bound by the norms of society does not allow me to pick and choose indiscriminately from the large menu of norms to justify my actions, since I have to justify them to myself no less than to others. At the very least, norms are soft constraints on action.[106]

Often, norms have a much more direct impact on action. Norms of revenge, for instance, create obligations, not options. In all but the upper reaches of the Guermantes circle or in the world of the middle class described by Bourdieu, norms of etiquette have the force of commands. Their inhabitants are constantly worried about doing too much or too little, too early or too late, on the wrong occasions or to the wrong people. The fact that some norms are somewhat mysterious and inscrutable does not imply that people can interpret them at will, in conformity with their self-interest. Rather a correct interpretation is supposed to exist, one that is known to (indeed, usually laid down by) the high priests and priestesses of fashion. Similarly, a study of Montenegrin blood feuds refers to 'the compulsive or obligatory nature of taking vengeance' and to vengeance as a 'culturally patterned psychological compulsion'.[107] Milhovan Djilas's description of

---

[105] Similarly, when there exists several theories of the economy, the one that makes my self-interest coincide with the general interest naturally acquires special salience. Through wishful thinking I am caused to believe, quite sincerely, that I advocate the policy because it corresponds to the good for all.

[106] For a similar argument see Føllesdal (1981).

[107] Boehm (1984), pp. 57, 143. More than most other writers on the vendetta, however, he emphasizes the latitude of interpretation of the norm of revenge and the frequency with which it is overridden by the desire for self-preservation.

vengeance as 'the wildest and sweetest kind of drunkenness' is similarly hard to square with the view that norms are merely the carriers of self-interest.

A final comment on this topic is in order. Sometimes it is assumed that adherence to social norms is a matter of psychic costs that have to be traded off against other interests. In this perspective, the strength of a norm can be measured by how much you must bribe people to violate it.[108] More generally, the costs of adhering to the social norm might simply be prohibitively high, even in the face of external pressures and internal anguish. I return to this point in Chapter 5, when discussing norms of cooperation and the costs of adhering to them. While valid, this approach is incomplete. The grip of a norm on the mind also depends on its resistance to rival norms. Sometimes all one has to offer people is an alternative norm or an alternative description of the targeted action. Political entrepreneurs trade on this possibility. It may be easier to seduce a Communist or a Christian than to bribe him. Strength of conviction, as measured by the resistance to bribery or the willingness for sacrifice, should not be confused with depth of conviction, as measured by resistance to change.[109]

Turning now to the autonomy of norms, I shall discuss and reject four arguments to the effect that norms are really optimizing mechanisms in disguise. The first argument is that norms can be directly reduced to individual rationality: people have an incentive to avoid the sanctions reserved for violators. The second is that norms can be indirectly reduced to individual rationality: they help us economize on costs of decision, overcome weakness of will, enhance the credibility of threats and promises and the like. The third is that norms are collectively rational: they emerge to prevent market failures. The final argument is that norms promote genetic fitness. I shall concentrate on the first and third arguments, which probably command more agreement than the others.

When people obey norms, they often have a particular outcome in mind: they want to avoid the disapproval – ranging from raised eyebrows to social ostracism – of other people. Suppose I face the choice between taking revenge for the murder of my cousin and not doing anything. The cost of revenge is that I may be the target of countervengeance. This event

---

[108] North (1981), ch. 5, especially p. 47.

[109] According to Tocqueville (1969, p. 187) strong but not deeply held convictions characterize times of revolution, whereas postrevolutionary eras are times of 'universal doubt and distrust'. In the latter, 'people are not so ready to die for their opinions, but they do not change them; and there are to be found both fewer martyrs and fewer apostats'.

is not a certainty, since the opposing family, clan or tribe may pick on another member of mine, but there is a distinct possibility that at some point I will be targeted for retaliation. At worst, the cost of not doing anything is that my family and friends will desert me, leaving me on my own, defencelessly exposed to predators. At best, I will lose their esteem and my ability to act as an autonomous agent among them. A cost–benefit analysis is likely to tell me that revenge (or exile) is the rational choice. More generally, norm-guided behavior is supported by the threat of social sanctions that make it rational to obey the norms.[110]

In response to this argument, we can first observe that norms do not need external sanctions to be effective. When norms are internalized, they are followed even when violation would be unobserved and not exposed to sanctions. Shame, or anticipation of it, is a sufficient internal sanction. I do not pick my nose when I can be observed by people on a train passing by, even if I am confident that they are all perfect strangers whom I shall never see again and who have no power to impose sanctions on me. I do not throw litter in the park, even when there is nobody around to observe me. If punishment were merely the price of crime, nobody would feel shame when caught. People have an internal gyroscope that keeps them adhering steadily to norms, independently of the current reactions of others.

It is useful to separate internalization of (noninstrumental) norms from internalization of (instrumental) values. Consider, for instance, Elliott Aronson's distinction between three kinds of response to social influence:

[Any] specific action may be due to either compliance, identification, or internalization. For example, let us look at a simple piece of behavior: obedience of the laws pertaining to fast driving. Society employs highway patrol officers to enforce these laws, and, as we all know, people tend to drive within the speed limits if they are forewarned that a certain stretch of highway is being carefully scrutinized by these officers. This is compliance. It is a clear case of people obeying the law in order to avoid paying a penalty. Suppose you were to remove the highway patrol. As soon as people found out about it, many would increase their speed. But some people might continue to obey the speed limit; a person

---

[110] Akerlof (1976) argues, along these lines, that in India it is rational to adhere to the caste system, even assuming that 'tastes' are neutral, i.e., that nobody has a positive preference for discrimination.

might continue to obey because Dad (or Uncle Charlie) always obeyed speed limits or always stressed the importance of obeying traffic laws. This, of course, is identification. Finally, people might conform to the speed limit because they are convinced that speed laws are good, that obeying such laws helps to prevent accidents, and that driving at moderate speed is a sane and reasonable form of behavior. This is internalization. And with internalization you would observe more flexibility in the behavior. For example, under certain conditions – at 6:00 A.M., say, on a clear day with perfect visibility and with no traffic for miles around – the individual might exceed the speed limit. The compliant individual, however, might fear a radar trap, and the identifying individual might be identifying with a very rigid model – thus, both would be less responsive to important changes in the environment.[111]

Compliance corresponds to the public aspect of norms. Identification is one major mechanism whereby norms are internalized. What Aronson calls internalization I would refer to as internalization of a moral norm. The *social norm* of driving below the speed limit is not outcome-oriented. The *moral norm* of driving in a way that creates no risk to other drivers is, by contrast, defined in instrumental terms. It allows me to exceed the speed limit when doing so has no bad effects. The example illustrates the distinction between two kinds of consequences of norm violations. On the one hand, there are the consequences to the agent if he is caught violating the norm. On the other hand, there are the consequences to others if the violation of the norm harms them. Compliance rests exclusively on consideration of the first kind of consequence. Internalization of values rests on both. Identification does not rest on any kind of outcome-oriented calculations. It would allow me to drive fast neither when it was safe to do so nor when lives might be saved by doing so.[112]

The internalization of social norms provides one answer to the claim that people obey norms because of the sanctions attached to norm violations. Another answer emerges if we ask why people would sanction others for violating norms. What is in it for them?[113] One reply could be that if

---

[111] Aronson (1984), p. 35.

[112] Imagine an everyday Kantian who arrives at the scene of a traffic accident caused by fast driving and then drives away to get an ambulance. Although the lives of the surviving passengers are at stake, he refuses to exceed the speed limit, justifying his behaviour by saying, 'If everybody behaved like me, there would be no traffic accidents'. See also Astrid Lindgren's story cited earlier.

[113] This question is related to the second-order free-rider problem discussed in Chapter 1.

they do not express their disapproval of the violation, they will themselves be the target of disapproval by third parties. When there is a norm to do X, there is usually a higher-order norm to sanction people who fail to do X, perhaps even a norm to sanction people who fail to sanction people who fail to do X.[114] As long as the cost of expressing disapproval is less than the cost of receiving disapproval for not expressing it, it is in one's rational self-interest to express it. Now, expressing disapproval is always costly, whatever the target behaviour. At the very least it requires energy and attention that might be used for other purposes. One may alienate or provoke the target individual, at some cost or risk to oneself. However, when one moves upwards in the chain of actions, beginning with the original violation, the cost of receiving disapproval falls rapidly to zero. People do not frown upon others when they fail to sanction people who fail to sanction people who fail to sanction people who fail to sanction a norm violation. Consequently, some sanctions must be performed for motives other than the fear of being sanctioned. I argued in the preceding paragraphs that sometimes there is an unmoved mover at the very beginning of the chain. Here I have argued that every chain must have one.

I now turn to the relation between social norms and individual, collective or genetic optimization. If it could be demonstrated that norms exist because they maximize individual utility, collective welfare or genetic fitness, their autonomy would be threatened. Nonconsequentialist norms could still, if the preceding arguments are accepted, be the proximate motivation of behaviour, but the ultimate explanation would be consequentialist. Norms would exist because they have good consequences for individuals, societies or genes. I shall argue against each of these optimality explanations. I have no robust alternative account to offer of people's propensity to follow norms and the emergence of particular norms in particular societies. At various places in this chapter and in Chapter 5 I suggest, in a somewhat speculative vein, some psychological mechanisms that might contribute to an explanation.

I do not know of anyone who has explicitly and systematically argued that compliance with social norms has individually valuable consequences, over and above the avoidance of sanctions, and that, moreover, norms owe their existence to these consequences. I believe, however, that for many economists the instinctive reaction to the claim that people are motivated by irrational norms would be that on closer inspection the norms turn out

---

[114] See Axelrod (1986) for this conception of 'metanorms'.

to be disguised, ultrasubtle expressions of self-interest.[115] But even if it turns out that I am arguing against a strawman, I hope that the following discussion may be independently useful in further clarifying the nature of normative behaviour.

I have already said that some social norms can be individually useful, such as the norm against drinking or overeating. If people are reduced to choosing between corner solutions, because they are unable to live moderate and temperate lives, it makes sense for them to follow a simple unbreakable rule of total abstention. Moreover, these private norms can take on a social aspect, if people with similar problems join one another for mutual sanctioning, each in effect asking the others to punish him if he deviates. Alcoholics Anonymous provides the best-known example. 'Each recovering alcoholic member of Alcoholics Anonymous is kept constantly aware, at every meeting, that he has *both* something to give *and* something to receive from his fellow alcoholics'.[116] Another writer, emphasizing the second aspect, says that 'primacy is always given to maintaining one's own sobriety, even as a prior condition to helping others. This kind of enlightened selfishness naturally benefits everyone in the long run'.[117]

It might also be argued that social norms are individually useful in that they help people to economize on decision costs. A simple mechanical decision rule may, on the whole and in the long run, have better consequences for the individual than a fine-tuned search for the optimal decision. This argument, however, confuses social norms and habits. Habits certainly are useful in the respect just mentioned, but they are not enforced by other people, nor does their violation give rise to feelings of guilt or anxiety.

A further argument for the view that it is individually rational to follow norms is that they lend credibility to threats or promises that otherwise would not be believable. Vendettas are not guided by the prospect of future gain but triggered by an earlier offence. Although the propensity to take revenge is not guided by consequences, it can have good consequences. If other people believe that I invariably take revenge for an offence, even at

---

[115] Becker (1976), pp. 5, 14, argues, for example, that the 'combined assumptions of maximizing behavior, market equilibrium and stable preferences, used relentlessly and unflinchingly . . . provides a valuable unified framework for understanding *all* human behavior'. In the course of a discussion of norms of equity, Zajac (1985) conjectures that 'many, perhaps all of the Propositions can be formulated as models of rational economic agents acting to achieve self-interest'.

[116] Kurtz (1979), p. 215.   [117] Royce (1981), p. 248.

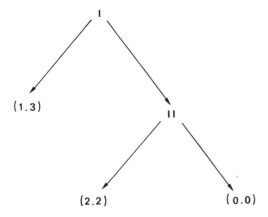

Fig. 3.3

great risk to myself, they will take care not to offend me. If they believe that I will react to offence only when it is in my interest to react, they need not be as careful. From the rational point of view, a threat is not credible unless it will be in the interest of the threatener to carry it out when the time comes. The threat to kill oneself, for instance, is not rationally credible. Threats backed by a code of honour are very effective, since they will be executed even if it is in the interest of the threatener not to do so.

Consider Fig. 3.3, reproducing part of Fig. 2.5. Here II's threat to move right if I moves right might be credible if II is known to be of Sicilian origin. Knowing that II is willing to act against his own interest to carry out his threat, I will rationally move left. So it might appear as if adhering to the code is individually rational, although the person abiding by it is not motivated by rational considerations.[118]

This observation, while true, does not amount to an explanation of the norm of vengeance. When a person guided by a code of honour has a quarrel with one who is exclusively motivated by rational considerations, the first will often have his way.[119] But in a quarrel between two persons guided by the code, both may do worse than if they had agreed to let the legal system or the council of elders resolve their conflict. If I is moved by a code of honour that forbids him to be taken advantage of, he will move right and take a loss rather than yield to II's threat. For this reason, mafiosi

[118] Schelling (1963) remains the *locus classicus* for this line of argument.
[119] Ibid., p. 27.

seem to do better for themselves in the United States, where they can exploit the rationality of ordinary people (or of other criminals), than in Sicily, where they meet people who share their values. Since we are talking about codes of honour that are shared social norms, the latter case is the typical one. The rationality of following the code then reduces to the desire to avoid sanctions, discussed earlier. Moreover, one cannot rationally decide to behave irrationally, even when one knows that it would be in one's interest to do so. One can try to appear to be irrational without really being irrational, but in practice the real thing is usually more convincing.[120]

Let us consider, against this background, Napoleon Chagnon's analysis of blood revenge among the Yanomanö. 'At first glance, raids motivated by revenge seem counterproductive. Raiders may inflict deaths on their enemies, but by so doing make themselves and kin prime targets for retaliation. But ethnographic evidence suggests that revenge has an underlying rationality: swift retaliation serves as a deterrence in the long run'.[121] As he describes them, most fights begin over sexual issues, but once begun take on a momentum of their own. Hence the effect of vengeance must be to reduce the levels of infidelity, rape, seduction and breach of promise to below what they would otherwise have been.[122] It is clear from his account, however, that many of the sexual affronts are directed towards those who have shown themselves to be cowardly in retaliation. The system may create as much sexual aggression as it prevents. Moreover, the extraordinarily high rate of death by violence (30 per cent of the deaths among adult males) suggests that the deterrence is not very effective. Although an individual in this society who does not comply with the norms of vengeance is likely to have a miserable life, I have argued that this fact does not prove that the practice of revenge is based entirely on rational considerations, for

[120] 'It has been said that Richard Nixon deliberately cultivated the image of someone who was capable and liable to act irrationally in a crisis, so as to dissuade the Russians from creating one. More plausibly, perhaps, his advisors did not mind him exhibiting his erratic and unpredictable ways, and may well have encouraged them. In any case faking unpredictability is too demanding, since it involves acting arbitrarily in innumerable small ways, not just grand-standing on occasion' (Elster 1983a, p. 74). On the superiority of the real thing, see also Schelling (1963), pp. 36, 38. The reputation-effect argument developed by Kreps and Wilson (1982) rests, as they recognize, on ad hoc assumptions that may limit its predictive and explanatory power.

[121] Chagnon (1988), p. 986.

[122] Ultimately, Chagnon argues in terms of inclusive genetic fitness rather than in terms of individual rationality. For the present purposes, however, it does not matter whether the concern for close relatives has a genetic basis.

why should others rationally make it their business to make him miserable?

James Coleman similarly argues that commercial honour 'is not a matter of abstract morals but pure self-interest: a merchant banker would be never trusted, i.e. nevermore be allowed to participate in the flow of credit, if his integrity in keeping agreements was not trusted, and his business would rapidly decline if his investment judgement was not trusted'.[123] To evaluate this argument, we may first note that trustworthiness in promising differs from credibility in threatening. The ability to make credible threats is useful if and only if others do not have it. The ability to make credible promises is useful if and only if others have it too.[124] Hence the norm of keeping promises, unlike the norm of carrying out threats, can be both individually rational and a social norm. Usually, however, these two aspects of codes of honour go together. If British merchant bankers have no tendency to engage in irrational revenge behaviour, Coleman may well be right. If, as I suspect, they would be willing to suffer a loss rather than continue to deal with someone who had once betrayed their trust, he might be wrong.[125] In the latter case, we must evaluate the individual rationality of the whole package rather than that of the positive side only. I return to this issue in the concluding chapter.

The distinction between the usefulness of norms and their rationality can also be brought out by considering Akerlof's explanation of workers' refusal to train new workers who are hired at lower wages. In an analysis of wage rigidity, Assar Lindbeck and Dennis Snower argue that the explanation is to be sought in the self-interest of the employed workers. By keeping potential entrants out, they can capture a greater portion of the benefits of monopoly power. The weapons at their disposal for keeping the unemployed at bay include the following:

> First, by being unfriendly and uncooperative to the entrants, the insiders are able to make the entrants' work more unpleasant than it otherwise

---

[123] Coleman (1982), p. 287.

[124] An exception to this statement occurs in two-step sequential interaction, where it is sufficient that the last party to move can be trusted by the first. An example is given in the concluding chapter.

[125] It is important to see that the bankers have three options, not just two. (a) They can continue to deal with the traitor on a basis of trust. (b) They can refuse to deal with him. (c) They can deal with him but insist on bringing their lawyer along. If they refuse to exercise the third option even when it would be in their interest to do so, they are cutting off their nose to spite their face. If they refuse to exercise the first option, they may simply be playing Tit for Tat.

would have been and thereby raise the wage at which the latter are willing to work. In practice, outsiders are commonly wary of underbidding the insiders. This behaviour pattern is often given an *ad hoc* sociological explanation: 'social mores' keep outsiders from 'stealing' the jobs from their employed comrades. Our line of argument, however, suggests that these mores may be traced to the entrants' anticipation of hostile insider reaction and that this reaction may follow from optimisation behaviour of insiders. Second, insiders are usually responsible for training the entrants and thereby influence their productivity. Thus insiders may be able to raise their wage demands by threatening to conduct the firm's training programs inefficiently or even to disrupt them. . . . In sum, to raise his wage, an insider may find it worthwhile to threaten to become a thoroughly disagreeable creature.[126]

The insider may, to be sure, make this threat, *but is it credible?* If an outsider *is* hired, would it then still be in the insider's interest to be unfriendly and uncooperative? Since Lindbeck and Snower believe that 'harassment activities are disagreeable to the harassers',[127] they ought also to assume that outsiders will recognize this fact and, in consequence, will not be deterred by fear of harassment. I believe Akerlof is right in arguing that it takes something like a social norm to sustain this behaviour.

Among economists, those who do not subscribe to the individual rationality of norms will mostly argue for their collective rationality, claiming that social norms have collectively good consequences for those who live by them[128] and that, moreover, these consequences explain why the norms exist. For the view to have predictive and explanatory power, the term 'socially useful' must be clarified. It could mean that a society with the norm is at least as good for almost everybody and substantially better for many than a society in which the norm is lacking. (Compare the discussion of various definitions of collective action problems in Chapter 1.) Or it could mean that the norm is one that would be chosen by a rule-utilitarian to maximize the total utility of society. Most writers on the topic probably use it in the first sense, perhaps with an implied clause that no other norm could bring further Pareto improvements.

[126] Lindbeck and Snower (1986), p. 108.   [127] Lindbeck and Snower (1988), p. 171.
[128] As will be clear from examples given below, there is no reason to expect that a norm will always have good consequences for those to whom it does not apply.

Among those who have argued for the collective optimality of norms, Kenneth Arrow is perhaps the most articulate and explicit:

> It is a mistake to limit collective action to state action. . . . I want to [call] attention to a less visible form of social action: norms of social behavior, including ethical and moral codes. I suggest as one possible interpretation that they are reactions of society to compensate for market failure. It is useful for individuals to have some trust in each other's word. In the absence of trust, it would become very costly to arrange for alternative sanctions and guarantees, and many opportunities for mutually beneficial cooperation would have to be forgone. Banfield has argued that the lack of trust is indeed one of the causes of economic underdevelopment.
>
> It is difficult to conceive of buying trust in any direct way (though it can happen indirectly, e.g. a trusted employee will be paid more as being more valuable); indeed, there seems to be some inconsistency in the very concept. Non-market action might take the form of a mutual agreement. But the arrangement of these agreements and especially their continued extension to new individuals entering the social fabric can be costly. As an alternative, society may proceed by internalization of these norms to the achievement of the desired agreement on an unconscious level.
>
> There is a whole set of customs and norms which might be similarly interpreted as agreements to improve the efficiency of the economic system (in the broad sense of satisfaction of individual values) by providing commodities to which the price system is inapplicable.[129]

I shall adduce three arguments against this view. First, not all norms are Pareto improvements. Some norms make everybody *worse* off,[130] or, at the very least, they do not make almost everybody better off.[131] Second,

---

[129] Arrow (1971), p. 22. See also Ullmann-Margalit (1977), p. 60.

[130] In the sense that almost nobody does better and many do substantially worse than if the norm had not existed.

[131] As observed by James Coleman (forthcoming), many norms have the effect of shifting the distribution of benefits along the Pareto frontier rather than of moving to or towards the frontier. The functionalist argument considered here might be extended to this case, by arguing that the norm is explained by the benefits it brings to those whom it makes better off. The question of a mechanism then becomes decisive. For reasons set out elsewhere (Elster 1983a, ch. 2), I do not believe that intentional, manipulative imposition of the norm by those whom it makes better off is a plausible mechanism.

some norms that would make everybody better off are not in fact observed. Third, even if a norm does make everybody better off, this does not explain why it exists, unless we are also shown the feedback mechanism that specifies how the good consequences of the norm contribute to its maintenance. Of these arguments, the second by itself is not very strong. It serves, however, to refute a possible objection to the third argument.

To support my first argument it is useful to go through, once again, the norms enumerated above.

Consumption norms

These norms do not appear to have any useful consequences. If anything, norms of etiquette seem to make everybody worse off, by requiring wasteful investments in pointless behaviours. Let me, nevertheless, mention three possible arguments for the social usefulness of these norms, together with corresponding objections.

First, there is the argument that norms of etiquette serve the useful function of confirming one's identity or membership in a social group. Since the notion of social identity is rather elusive, the argument is hard to evaluate. A weakness is that it does not explain why these rules are as complicated as they often are. To signal or confirm one's membership in a group one sign should be sufficient, like wearing a badge or a tie. Instead, there is often vast redundancy. An Oxford-educated person's manner of speaking differs from standard spoken English in many more ways than what is required to single him out as an Oxford graduate.

Second, there is the argument that the complexity of the rules serves an additional function, that of keeping outsiders out and upstarts down.[132] It is easy to imitate one particular behaviour, but hard to learn a thousand subtly different rules. But that argument flounders on the fact that working-class life is no less norm-regulated than that of the upper classes. Whereas many middle-class persons would like to pass themselves off as members of the upper class, few try to pass themselves off as workers.

Third, one might combine the first and second positions and argue that norms simultaneously serve functions of inclusion and exclusion. Evans-Pritchard's classical argument about the Nuer can help us here. 'A man of

---

[132] Bourdieu (1979) carries this argument to absurd lengths. It is critically examined in Elster (1981).

one tribe sees the people of another tribe as an undifferentiated group to whom he has an undifferentiated pattern of behaviour, while he sees himself as a member of a segment of his own group'.[133] Fine-tuned distinction and gamesmanship within a group is consistent with 'negative solidarity' towards outsiders. This view is more plausible, but it does not really point to any social benefits of norm following. It is not clear why the working class as a whole would benefit from the fact that it contains an infinite variety of local subcultures, all of them recognizably working class and yet subtly different from one another in ways that only insiders can understand. Nor is it clear that the local varieties provide collective benefits to members of the subculture. To say (as many do) that norms 'confirm one's identity' as a member of the group is, I believe, misleading, since by and large people do not adopt the self-conscious attitude implicit in this phrase. Statements about identity tend to conflate the observer's and the actor's point of view. Norms *constitute* the identity of the group whose members obey the norm, but this does not imply that they derive the benefit of their identity being confirmed when they follow the norm.[134]

Norms against behaviour 'contrary to nature'

Norms against cannibalism and incest are good candidates for collectively beneficial norms. Everybody benefits from a norm that forces people to look elsewhere than to other people for food. Norms against incest may well be optimal from any perspective: individual, collective or genetic. (In some societies the norm may overshoot a little, by banning sexual relations with not-so-close kin, so that the norm is not, strictly speaking, Pareto-optimal.) Norms against sodomy, by contrast, involve harmful restrictions of freedom and no benefits. They make everybody worse off. Norms against homosexuality might also, under conditions of overpopulation, make everybody worse off.

---

[133] Evans-Pritchard (1940), p. 120.

[134] One might say, perhaps, that norms are useful in limiting the number of potential interaction partners to a small and manageable subset, thus making for greater focus and consistency in social life. As in many other cases, too much freedom of choice reduces the value of freedom (Elster 1983a, pp. 78–80). A community of norms would then be a bit like a convention equilibrium, since it is important that one's partners limit *their* partners by the same device. This explanation, however, fails to account for the emotional tonality of norms and for their capacity to induce self-destructive behaviour.

Norms regulating the use of money

It is far from obvious that the norm against buying places in a cinema queue has useful consequences. It may well be a pointless prohibition of potential Pareto improvements. If the forbidden practice were allowed, it is not clear that anybody would lose, and some would certainly gain, namely those who could earn an income standing in line for others. Although competition might drive the gains down to zero for the marginal place seller, the inframarginal sellers would benefit. This in itself shows that the norm does not create a Pareto improvement. A general-equilibrium proof, well beyond my competence, would be needed to show that it does in fact create a Pareto-inferior state.[135]

When discussing this problem, I have met the argument that the norm is a special case of a more general norm against flaunting one's wealth – a norm that on the whole has beneficial consequences. I have two counterarguments. First, the norm against flaunting one's wealth operates within a community of people who know one another, not among strangers waiting in line. There is no norm against standing in line with expensive furs or jewelry, although this, too, is a way of flaunting one's wealth. Second, the norm against flaunting one's wealth is beneficial only against a background of envy. Would it not be even better if there were a norm against expressing envy? I return to this point in the next paragraph and then again in the concluding chapter.

The norm that prevents us from accepting or making offers to mow other people's lawns for money seems more promising. If I am hard up I may be tempted to accept or solicit an offer, thinking, correctly, that one transaction cannot matter. But an unintended consequence of many monetary deals among neighbours could be the loss of the spontaneous mutual-help behaviour that is a main benefit of living in a community. By preventing deals, the norm preserves the community. The norm could also have a more disreputable aspect, however. It is true that if I offer my neighbour money to mow my lawn, I flaunt my wealth in a way that is disruptive of community. But the norm against flaunting one's wealth may just be a special case of a higher-order norm: *Don't stick your neck out.* 'Don't think you are better than we are, and above all don't behave in ways that make us

---

[135] Perhaps the proof would be easier if one considered the problem of buying a place in a bus queue, since it is even less likely that the absence of a norm against this practice would create a group of people who tried to earn an income by selling their places.

think that you think you are better than we are'. This norm, which prevails in many small communities, can have very bad consequences. It can discourage the gifted from using their talents and may lead to their being branded as witches if they nevertheless go ahead and use them.

Norms of reciprocity

It is plausible – although hard to prove rigourously – that these norms do, on the whole, have good consequences. To the extent that the norms are the object of strategic manipulation, they can lead to a waste of resources, as in the potlatch or Turnbull's roof-thatching example. Also, norms of reciprocation are part and parcel of vendetta norms, thus ensuring that killings go on indefinitely rather than slowly petering out. More frequently, however, they are invoked to ask for help when one needs it strongly and others can provide it at low cost to themselves.

Medical ethics

The norms that treatment should be as thorough as possible and that more serious cases should be treated before less serious ones seem, on their face, to be collectively undesirable. More people would get well if each patient were treated less thoroughly and if intermediate cases had priority over extreme ones. One might argue, perhaps, that these perfectionist norms have desirable side effects that offset whatever inefficiency they might appear to have when seen in isolation. It might be impossible to sustain the dedication and compassion of doctors were they constantly called upon to make comparisons and cost–benefit calculations. A remote analogy might be the desirable side effects of the somewhat pointless perfectionism of the postal services in some countries, especially in the past. By imposing the principle of next-day delivery for all letters, no matter how remote the destination, costs were incurred that would also appear excessive if taken in isolation. Yet the unbreakable principle, together with the heroic tales spun around its strict implementation, may have contributed to an occupational pride and motivation that led to better service than any commercial system could ever realize at the same cost.[136] I do not know how to evaluate this argument. It should not be dismissed out of hand, but neither does it provide hard evidence for the optimality of norms.

[136] For a related argument, see Sjölund (1987), p. 63.

Codes of honour

One set of effects of codes of honour is to enhance the credibility of threats and promises. I postpone this issue until the concluding chapter. Another set of effects is to reinforce norms of reciprocity and norms of retribution. In both cases, the net effects are indeterminate.

Norms of retribution

The Jalé norm of strict liability is, as I said, likely to produce socially harmful passivity and excessive caution. Norms of vengeance lead to violence in quarrels that otherwise would have been resolved peacefully. One could argue, however, that there will be fewer quarrels in societies with strong norms of vengeance, since everybody knows that they can have disastrous consequences. But it is not clear that this would be a good thing. One could probably get rid of almost all criminal behaviour if all crimes carried the death penalty, but the costs of creating this terror regime would be prohibitive. It could be argued, however, that life in a vendetta-ridden society would be better than the state of nature, in which there is no regulation of conflicts. But this difference cuts both ways. In the state of nature, people are supposed to be rational. They do not engage in pointless acts of revenge. People would initiate more aggression, but react less aggressively to it. 'The question remains . . . whether feuds created more disruption than they controlled'.[137] I return to this issue in the concluding chapter.

Other alleged collective benefits of vendettas include the catch-all benefit of social cohesion,[138] an argument which is too speculative to merit further consideration, and the benefit of maintaining population at a constant level.[139] The latter argument, in Christopher Boehm's exposition, goes like this. Excess population creates land hunger. Land hunger leads to quarrels over pastures. Such quarrels lead to feuding. Intertribal feuding easily escalates into warfare. Warfare reduces population 'through the killing of male warriors, through losses of noncombatants who were captured and sold into slavery, and also through the famines and epidemics that followed serious defeats'.[140]

All of this may well be true. Boehm goes on to argue, however, that feuding also had another collectively beneficial effect: it 'helped to keep

[137] Boehm (1984), p. 183.   [138] Black-Michaud (1975).   [139] Boehm (1984), ch. 10.
[140] Ibid., p. 176.

the Montenegrin tribes divided among themselves so that they never posed enough of a threat to be more than a nuisance to [the Turkish] empire. . . . Feuding . . . kept the segmentary system from unifying to a degree that might invite extinction at the hands of the Turks'.[141] At the same time, he argues, feuding never escalated to the point of undermining the ability of the tribes to put up a fight against Turkish invaders. Feuding took place at exactly the right level: there was enough of it to reduce the strength of the tribes to the point where they did not pose a threat to the Turks, but not so much that they would lose strength and provide an easy prey to the Turks. All of this may well be true. We should be suspicious, however, of an explanation that imputes so many ecological benefits to feuding, especially since Boehm himself admits that he has little or no empirical evidence for these assertions. In any case, of course, it remains to be shown that these benefits, taken individually or in conjunction, provide an *explanation* of feuding.

Norms of work

The obligation to work is clearly socially useful. The norm against two-tiered wage systems does not seem to benefit employed workers, while harming both employers and the unemployed, who have a common interest in such systems. At least this is true if we accept Akerlof's (somewhat implausible) tale. If employed workers have good reasons to think that new workers will drive their wages down, the code of honour makes good collective sense, at least with respect to the short-run interests of the local group of workers. Society as a whole might, however, suffer. In that case, codes of honour would embody solutions to local collective action problems while also creating a higher-order problem.

Somewhat similar arguments apply to the norm against rate busting. In a well-known case, it has been argued that the norm is pointless and wasteful, since 'changes in piece rates at the Western Electric Company . . . are not based upon the earnings of the worker. The company's policy is that piece rates will not be changed unless there is a change in the manufacturing process'.[142] The last clause of this policy statement appears in a different light, however, when we read the report of a knowledgeable engineer: 'I was visiting the Western Electric Company, which had a reputation of never cutting a piece rate. It never did; if some manufacturing

---

[141] Ibid., p. 185.   [142] Roethlisberger and Dickson (1939), p. 534.

process was found to pay more than seemed right for the class of labor employed on it – if, in other words, the rate-setters had misjudged – that particular part was referred to the engineers for redesign, and then a new rate was set for the new part'.[143]

There is no doubt that workers often express the view that any increase in effort will induce management to reduce rates.[144] It remains to be shown, however, that this argument against rate busting is more than rationalization of envy.[145] In the words of one notorious rate buster: 'There are three classes of men: (1) Those who can and will; (2) those who can't and are envious; (3) those who can and won't – they're nuts!'[146] (Those in the third category, presumably, are moved by solidarity and feelings of justice.) The question cannot be treated separately from the behaviour of management. On the one hand, management has a clear incentive to make it clear that they will never cut rates as a result of increased efforts, nor engage in the subterfuges described by the engineer who visited Western Electric. On the other hand, *how can management make this promise credible?* They cannot commit themselves to never introducing new methods of production, nor easily prove that a new method is not just a subterfuge for changing rates. Knowing this, workers have good reasons to be sceptical.

Three conclusions emerge. First, both management and workers would benefit if a way were found to distinguish justified from opportunistic changes in piece rates. Second, the worker collective as a whole may well benefit from the norm against rate busting, since management cannot credibly commit itself to maintaining rates. Third, however, the norm may work against the interest of society as a whole, including the working class as a whole, if the loss of productivity caused by the norm is sufficiently serious.[147] Even granting that the norm represents the successful solution of a collective action problem within the enterprise, it might create a new problem among enterprises.

Norms of cooperation and distribution

The norms of cooperation are, on the whole, socially useful, although in exceptional cases they, too, can make everybody worse off, as will be

---

[143] Mills (1946, p. 9), cited after Roy (1952), p. 43. See also Burawoy (1979), p. 165.
[144] The readings in Lupton, ed. (1972) provide ample evidence on this point.
[145] Roy (1952), p. 43.   [146] Reported in Dalton (1948), p. 74.
[147] As participant-observer in a machine shop Roy (1952) found substantial losses due to deliberately suboptimal efforts.

shown in Chapter 5. The effect of norms of distribution was briefly mentioned earlier and is further discussed in Chapter 6.

At the very least, I believe that I have demonstrated that the social usefulness of social norms cannot be taken for granted. In fact, I think I have shown more than that. I am sure that each of my claims about nonoptimality could be contested. The social sciences being what they are, the facts can be represented and explained in different ways. I think, however, that the cumulative impact of the claims is harder to refute. Some norms do not make everybody better off: they make everybody worse off, or they shift the balance of benefits to favour some people at the expense of others.

Many norms that would be socially useful are in fact not found to exist. If public transportation were widely chosen over private driving, the roads would be less congested and everyone would spend so much less time commuting that the loss of comfort would be offset. Yet there is no social norm to use public transportation in crowded cities. In many developing countries private insurance motives create an incentive to have large families, although the aggregate effect is overpopulation and pressure on resources. Yet there is no social norm against having many children. If American citizens had followed the norm 'Buy American', they would all have been better off. But there is no such norm. (Note that if all countries inculcated similar norms in their citizens, all would be worse off.) The small Italian village described by Edward Banfield would certainly have benefited from a social norm against corruption. Instead, it had what appears to have been a norm against public-spirited behaviour. Nobody would associate with a person stupid enough not to violate the law when he could get away with it.[148] Criminals could benefit from a minimum of solidarity among themselves; yet, as I said, there is no honesty among thieves. The reader can certainly think of other examples. Such examples do not in themselves refute the view that norms exist because they are collectively beneficial. But they refute a possible defence of that view against the objection I now proceed to state.

Even assuming that a given norm appears to yield a Pareto improvement, we are still left with the question of explaining why it exists. To assume that the collective benefits of the norm automatically provide an explanation is to fall victim to a widespread functionalist fallacy.[149] In the absence of a mechanism linking the benefits to the emergence or perpetuation of the norm we cannot know if they obtain by accident. We should be

---

[148] Banfield (1958), p. 95.   [149] Elster (1982; 1983b, ch. 3; 1985d, ch. 1).

suspicious of theories of society that deny the possibility of accidental benefits.[150] Moreover, and perhaps more important, the beneficial or optimal nature of the norm is often controversial. It is only a slight exaggeration to say that any economist worth his salt could tell a story – produce a model, that is, resting on various simplifying assumptions – which proves the individual or collective benefits derived from the norm. The very ease with which such 'just-so stories' can be told suggests that we should be sceptical about them. We would be much more confident about the benefits if a mechanism could be demonstrated.

There are not many plausible candidates for a feedback mechanism. Reinforcement could not work here, since the benefits are collective rather than individual. Chance variation and social selection might seem a better alternative.[151] On this account, social norms arise by accident. Societies which happen to have useful norms thrive, flourish and expand; those which do not disappear or imitate the norms of their more successful competitors. Whether the successful societies proceed by military conquest or economic competition, the end result is the same. The argument is popular, but feeble. The norms of the strong are not as a rule taken over by the weak, nor do the weak always disappear in competition with the strong. Greece was conquered by Rome, but Rome assimilated more Greek norms than the other way around.[152] When China was conquered by the barbarians, the latter ended up assimilating and defending the culture they had conquered. Today, few developing countries are taking over the norms and work habits that were a precondition for Western economic growth, nor is there any sign of these countries going out of existence.

One might, however, deny the need to demonstrate a mechanism. If it could be shown that all potentially useful norms are in fact realized, we would surely be entitled to infer that the norms are due to their usefulness even if we have no idea about a mechanism.[153] Similarly, Newton had no idea of the mechanism of gravitation and yet the observed correlations were so strong that he did not hesitate to infer a causal relationship.[154] More controversially, the universal fact of biological adaptation entitled

---

[150] Elster (1983a), sec. 3.10.

[151] Faia (1986) presents a good discussion of the (severely limited) range of cases in which social selection arguments make good sense.

[152] Veyne (1979).

[153] This view is brilliantly defended by G. A. Cohen (1978). For comments, see Elster (1980, 1985d).

[154] This analogy was suggested to me by Kenneth Arrow.

Lamarck to infer that the structure and behaviour of organisms can be explained by the adaptive benefits they bring.[155] By comparison, the fact that his guess about a mechanism was wrong is of secondary importance.[156] I have been concerned to show, however, that the case of social norms is different and that there are many counterexamples to the claim that all potentially useful norms are realized.

This does not add up to a strong claim that the social usefulness of norms is irrelevant to their explanation. I find it as hard as the next person to believe that the existence of norms of reciprocity and cooperation has *nothing* to do with the fact that without them civilization as we know it would not exist. Yet it is at least a useful intellectual exercise to take the more austere view and to entertain the idea that civilization owes its existence to a fortunate coincidence. On this view, social norms spring from psychological propensities and dispositions that, taken separately, cannot be presumed to be useful, yet happen to interact in such a way that useful effects are produced. I return to this perspective in Chapter 5.

The final argument against the autonomy of norms is that they owe their existence to their contribution to genetic fitness. Once again I do not know of explicit statements of this view. Several writers, however, have taken this position on the closely related issue of the emotions of guilt and shame that sustain norm-guided behaviour.[157] I know too little about evolutionary biology to evaluate these claims. I would like, nevertheless, to record my scepticism and make a few general remarks.[158]

Evolutionary explanations do not take the narrow form 'Feature X exists because it maximizes the genetic fitness of the organism'. Rather their general form is 'X exists because it is part of a package solution that at some time maximized the genetic fitness of the organism'. The latter form allows for two facts that the former excludes. First, there is the omnipresent phenomenon of *pleiotropy*. A tendency to conform to a social norm might detract from genetic fitness and yet be retained by natural selection

---

[155] Actually, of course, Lamarck at most showed that all features of organisms are adaptive, not that all potentially adaptive features are realized.

[156] This analogy is used by G. A. Cohen (1978), ch. 8. I think it is of dubious value, since Lamarck also got the facts wrong about adaptation. He thought that adaptation meant ecological fitness, as measured by expected life span, whereas Darwin showed that it meant reproductive fitness, measured by the number of offspring. The example supports the claim made in the text, that without knowledge of a mechanism we should be wary of imputing optimality.

[157] Trivers (1971); Hirschleifer (1987); Frank (1988).

[158] Inspired largely by Kitcher (1985).

if it is the by-product of a gene whose main product is highly beneficial. Second, the general form allows for *time lags*.[159] A social norm may be maladaptive today and yet have been adaptive at the stage in history when the human genome evolved and, for practical purposes, was fixed. When I said that norms might owe their existence to 'psychological propensities and dispositions', a natural reply would have been that these in turn must be explicable in terms of genetic fitness. Let me concede the point,[160] provided that the explanation is allowed to take this general form. Advocates of evolutionary explanations, however, usually have the narrower form in mind. I am not saying that in doing so they are always wrong, only that they cannot take it for granted that an explanation of the narrow form always exists. What is true is that a plausible story of the narrow form can almost always be told. Again, however, the very ease with which just-so stories are forthcoming should make us wary of them. Imputations of optimality require hard work, not just armchair speculation.[161]

The basic question I have been discussing in this chapter concerns the interaction between norms and consequentialist motivations, notably self-interested ones. An analogy may help us understand the nature and the difficulty of the problem. Rational-choice theory stipulates that action is determined by subjective preferences and objective opportunities. Psychological theory suggests that preferences are in part shaped by opportunities, because people often limit their aspirations to what they can achieve. But preferences are not fully reducible to opportunities, at least not by this particular mechanism. The unknown residual is a brute fact, at least for the time being. Similarly, people's motives are determined by self-interest and by the norms to which they subscribe. Norms, in turn, are partly shaped by self-interest, because people often adhere to the norms that favour them. But norms are not fully reducible to self-interest, at least not by this particular mechanism. The unknown residual is a brute fact, at least for the time being.

---

[159] Similarly Arrow (1971) writes that 'the social conventions may be adaptive in their origins, but they can become retrogressive. An agreement is costly to reach and costly to modify; and the costs of modification may be especially large for unconscious agreements'. North (1981), p. 49, makes a similar suggestion. This stratagem may be seen as strengthening the view that norms can be explained in terms of collective optimality (by suggesting a general answer to counterexamples) or as weakening it (by making it more difficult to falsify). In my view it does nothing to strengthen the case, since – unlike the biological analogue – there is no general theory that suggests a mechanism by which useful norms come to evolve.

[160] But see Kitcher (1985), pp. 214–18.

[161] This might seem like a nasty, unsubstantiated slur. I refer to Kitcher (1985) for massive documentation.

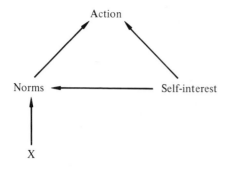

Fig. 3.4

Actions, on this view, are shaped jointly by norms and self-interest (or, more generally, consequentialist motivations). The fact that the agent is swayed by one norm rather than by another is, in turn, partly but not wholly explained by self-interest. I have been discussing various proposals for the residual explanation (X in Fig. 3.4) and found them wanting. Unfortunately, I have little to offer instead. Later chapters contain some speculations and conjectures, which, however, are far from adding up to a theory.

4. Bargaining and collective action

Introduction

Bargaining and collective action interact in three main ways. First, bargaining may fail because of collective action problems that arise in the course of negotiations. To get an edge in wage bargaining, labour and management may use tactics that are individually rational but collectively disastrous. Second, decentralized bargaining may create collective action problems because the parties involved in one bargaining process fail to take account of the externalities their agreement imposes on those involved in other, simultaneously occurring processes. The members of any given union are but marginally hurt by the price increases induced by their wage demands, but an across-the-board increase harms members of all unions. Third, collective action problems may require bargaining to allocate the burdens and benefits from cooperation. If unions agree on centralized bargaining, there will be bargaining over the wage profile to present to employers. In this chapter I discuss how these problems arise in interactions between employers and unions *(capital–labour bargaining)*, among employers *(capital–capital bargaining)* and among unions *(labour–labour bargaining)*. Since my main examples, here and in Chapter 6, will be taken from Swedish collective bargaining, I also offer a brief description of that system.

First, however, I want to make some general comments on the third problem – the bargaining problems embedded in collective action. Chapter 1 proposed a simplified analysis of collective action problems, in which I assumed that the actors were homogeneous and interchangeable. Although heterogeneity is the main source of bargaining in such problems, the need to negotiate can also arise in the homogeneous case with binary choices.[1]

---

[1] If the size of contributions varies continuously, the problem will be solved by everybody contributing $1/n$ of the optimal total contribution.

Assume, namely, that the collective action problem is such that universal cooperation is not the optimal outcome. In Chapter 1 we saw how this could happen if the costs of cooperation increase rapidly (or the benefits from cooperation decrease rapidly) with the number of cooperators. In that case, the cost to the last cooperators of contributing may exceed the sum total of all the small increments they add to the welfare of the group members. The average benefit of the group would be maximized if some members were allowed to take a free ride. In the next chapter I argue that sometimes universal cooperation is worse *for everybody* (not just on the average) than partial or limited cooperation. In such cases the argument for allowing free riding is even stronger, since the last cooperators would actually harm others, not just benefit them too little for their contribution to be worth while. In such cases there is an *internal optimum,* which is superior to each of the corner solutions (universal cooperation and universal noncooperation). If, as could also happen (see Chapter 5), universal cooperation is actually worse for all than universal noncooperation, finding an internal solution is essential and not just a matter of fine-tuning.

To select the noncooperators in a group of homogeneous individuals one may use individual lotteries or joint lotteries. In either case one might supplement the lottery with a system of side payments, so as to ensure equality ex post, not merely ex ante. In repeated interactions, equality ex post may also be ensured by having a new lottery for each occasion. Suppose the group has n members and that the optimal number of cooperators is m. If each individual uses a lottery that assigns him an m/n chance of cooperating, the law of large numbers will ensure that approximately m people will in fact end up cooperating. Assume, for instance, that all members of a suburban community would prefer driving to work over taking the bus if and only if congestion were less than what would be created by one-third of them driving. The optimum would be achieved when all tossed a die and drove if either a 2 or a 5 came up. An alternative solution would be to select some by lottery to be allowed to drive. In either case, the drivers might or might not compensate the nondrivers. If the lotteries occurred daily, there would be no need for a compensation scheme. On the other hand, daily lotteries would be inefficient, since they would force people to have a car which they used only one day out of three. The best solution might be to have a once-and-for-all joint lottery with side payments.

Individual lotteries are an implausible allocation mechanism. Joint lotteries without side payments were observed in an experimental situation set up so as to exclude compensation schemes.[2] Here seven people were told that they would get a public good if and only if a subset (three or five) made a voluntary contribution. In a few cases too many people contributed. In no case was the minimum level not reached. The subjects, who were allowed to communicate with each other, used three methods to select the contributors: volunteering, lottery and (in one case) assessment of needs.[3] It is likely that they would have used side payments had that option been open to them.

In real-life situations, there are practical and moral obstacles to the use of side payments.[4] On the one hand, the group must not be so large as to make the bargaining costs prohibitive. Voting is probably a collective action problem with an internal optimum, but in any except the smallest assemblies it would not be worth while to bargain over who should be exempt from voting. On the other hand, the collective action situation must be ethically consistent with side payments. In voluntary community work, for instance, there is often little point in each and every family turning out to work on the children's playground. They might end up tripping over each other's feet. Side payments, while feasible, would not be acceptable, given the norms regulating the use of money in communities (Chapter 3).[5] Side payments, therefore, can be used only in small groups whose members stand at arm's length from one another. These two conditions point in opposite directions, making it unlikely that they will often be jointly satisfied. In practice, it is much more probable that we shall observe one of the two corner solutions. Cartels – competition among the few – might appear to be an exception. Yet, as Schelling observes, if the fact of compensation would be evidence of illegal collusion, side payments might not be acceptable in this case either.[6]

The case of heterogeneous actors is more interesting. In any collective action problem with asymmetries among the actors,[7] bargaining may be required to allocate the costs and benefits of cooperation. Since virtually

---

[2] Van de Kragt, Orbell and Dawes (1983).

[3] Similarly, Griffin (1985) suggests lotteries, rotation and differential needs as methods for allocating the right to take a free ride in cases where universal cooperation is pointless.

[4] The following comments apply to side payments generally, including cases in which universal participation *is* desirable.

[5] Side payments in kind would, however, be acceptable. ('Could you look after my kids while I work on the playground?')

[6] Schelling (1963), p. 31.

[7] See Hardin (1982), ch. 5, for a survey of asymmetries in collective action.

any real-world collective action problem is asymmetrical, the importance of this problem can hardly be exaggerated. I believe, in fact, that the pure free-rider problem is a much less serious obstacle to collective action than is usually argued. Because of internalized norms of cooperation (Chapter 5) more people are reluctant to act as free riders. Rather cooperation breaks down because people fail to agree on a reasonable or equitable distribution of the costs and benefits involved. Uncertainty about preferences, and the possibility of misrepresenting them, is one reason. Another is that even with full information about preferences, people might fail to agree on an allocative criterion. They might look beyond sheer bargaining strength for some social norm to guide the allocation. If, as is usually the case, different norms favour different groups, a bargaining impasse may result. These problems of bargaining among heterogeneous actors are more fully discussed later in this chapter and again in Chapter 6.

Collective bargaining in Sweden

In this section, I briefly characterize the Swedish system[8] of collective bargaining that has been in place over the past decade. First, however, I shall say a few words about how the system came into being.[9]

From the beginning of the century, collective bargaining in Sweden developed in six stages. Until recently, it was characterized by increasing degrees of centralization, as measured both by the emergence of encompassing organizations and by their increasing coercive powers over members. (a) Around the turn of the century, national unions came into being in the various industries, supporting local strikes by assessing nonstriking members around the country. In this way, they were able to take on the employers one by one, using the 'whipsaw tactics' of the 'rolling strike'. (b) 'Employers responded by amassing their own central strike insurance funds, and calling massive industry-wide lockout of union members, which had the effect of pulling the plug out of union strike funds and quickly bringing unions to their knees'.[10] (c) 'The effect of these tactics was then, naturally, to force union executives to secure an ever tighter hold on the tactics and resources of the organization, preventing autonomous locals from setting unsupportable strikes in motion'.[11] The upshot was central

[8] The following draws heavily on Elvander (1988). I have also benefited from de Geer (1986), Sjölund (1987), Nilsson (1987) and Calmfors and Forslund (1988).

[9] This historical overview relies on Swenson (1987, 1989).

[10] Swenson (1987).   [11] Ibid.

bargaining at the industry level. (d) In the 1930s, interunion conflicts created the conditions for increased power to LO, the central blue-collar organization. As high wages in the construction industry created dissatisfaction among the metal workers, they demanded and got LO intervention to
stop a strike of the building workers. (e) Between 1941 and 1956, central
bargaining at the supraindustrial level emerged, and remained in force until
1982. (f) The central employers' association, SAF, wishing to avoid inflationary wage rivalry, was an important driving force behind centralization.
In the 1980s, as we shall see, employers became increasingly conscious of
the disadvantages of central bargaining, which became linked to solidaristic wage policies that came into conflict with the employers' desire for
wage differentiation.

The current Swedish bargaining system is defined by three cross-cutting
distinctions. First, there is a division between three economy-wide unions
that organize, respectively, blue-collar workers, lower functionaries and
higher functionaries. The blue-collar union LO is the best known and traditionally the most powerful, although with the increasing number of functionaries the balance of power has shifted. Of the three unions, the first
two are further divided along sectoral lines, the last along occupational
lines. Second, there is a distinction between private and public employees.
Third, within the latter category there is a distinction between state employees and municipal employees. All lower functionaries belong to one
union and all higher functionaries to another, but there is not a one-to-one
correspondence between unions and bargaining cartels. One cartel bargains
on behalf of (lower and higher) private functionaries, whereas no less than
four bargain on behalf of public functionaries. In addition there are two
cartels that bargain on behalf of blue-collar workers in the public sector.
In Fig. 4.1, links between unions and their bargaining cartels are represented by heavy lines. Links between employers and unions (or their cartels) are represented by thin lines.

Instead of central bargaining, the private sector can choose to conduct
sectoral (industry-level) bargaining. Even when there is central bargaining,
sectoral negotiations implement (and occasionally distort)[12] the central

---

[12] Bargainers at the central level are more interested in overall wage equality, e.g., equalization across individuals in the same firm. Bargainers at the sectoral level are more interested
in wage equity, i.e., equal pay for equal work across firms. Because the latter have some
discretion in implementing the central agreement, they sometimes use it to promote their own
distributive concerns (Nilsson 1987, p. 30).

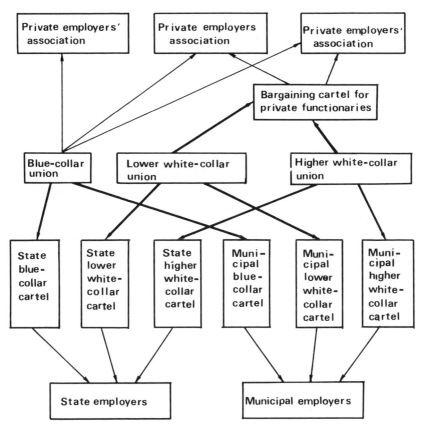

Fig. 4.1

agreements. In addition, there is always local (plant-level) bargaining. Negotiations at the central or sectoral level set the tariff wage, and plant-level bargaining then determines the wage drift. The latter is quite important, amounting on the average to about half the total wage increase in the industrial sector. In most bargaining rounds since the Second World War central bargaining has been the rule and sectoral bargaining the exception. Sectoral bargaining, which prevailed before 1956, recurred for the first time in 1982 and then again in 1983–4 and 1988.[13]

---

[13] Here and elsewhere dates refer to the period in which the bargaining actually occurred, not to the period that was the object of the bargaining. These can overlap, since wage increases are often given retroactive force.

As one can easily imagine, a bargaining process involving all these parties and levels is very complex. Although the bottom line, here as elsewhere, is bargaining over wages and working conditions, much time is spent bargaining over the formal framework for bargaining. At the central level, the fundamental feature of collective wage bargaining is *the absence of a constitution* that could provide a predictable and nonmanipulable framework for bargaining.[14] At the expiration of a contract period, everything is up for grabs: the level of bargaining, the length of the next contract period and the issues to be negotiated. The outcome of central bargaining is not simply a wage rate or a wage profile. It can also include guidelines for local-level bargaining and escalator clauses that trigger wage increases or renegotiations if inflation or wages of other workers exceed a certain level. In addition, work-time reductions, the modalities of sickness pay and issues of security of employment may (or may not) come on the agenda. Often, the compromise that is reached contains exquisitely ambiguous phrases that dump unresolved problems onto the future or to the local level. The issues are clouded in wage statistics that are nearly incomprehensible to anyone but a few experts, and in any case not open to public inspection and discussion.

There have been proposals to introduce some constitutional measures in central bargaining, similar to the Danish 'time table' that specifies when offers must be made, responses given and an agreement reached (if no agreement is reached mediation takes place).[15] A time table would, for instance, prevent the parties from adopting various tactics of brinksmanship, such as the practice of stretching out negotiations in the hope that the other side will lose its nerve. Also, it would prevent the jockeying for position that ensues because each union (in decentralized bargaining) or bargaining cartel wants to be the last one out. Swedish employers have been quite willing to entertain such constitutional thoughts, on the condition that the coordination include both the private and the public sector. Unions have been less enthusiastic, probably because they have more to lose from a more constrained time table.[16] For one thing, members of SAF's bargaining delegation are often top managers who may be willing

---

[14] For an analogy one may look to fourteenth-century Florence, described in Najemy (1982), which in turn is briefly summarized in Elster (1989a), pp. 81–5.

[15] The following draws on Arbetsmarknadsdepartementet (1988).

[16] The following draws on de Geer (1986), pp. 363–4.

to make concessions just to get back to their main job. For another, delay in reaching an agreement will often lead to retroactive wage raises that are more difficult to pass on to consumers.

Bargaining at the local level *is* constrained by a constitution that specifies legal modes of conflict. In Chapter 2 I discussed how these modalities – work-to-rule, go-slow, strikes – affect the outcome of local bargaining. In addition, local bargaining is to some extent constrained by decisions taken at the central level. Some constraints are quite soft, as when central bargaining includes a suggestion that average drift should not exceed a specified level. Others are more specific. Thus in the 1985 bargaining round the two-year agreement in the blue-collar private sector contained a clause that half the difference between expected and realized wage drift in the first year should be deducted from the agreed-upon increase in the tariff wage for the second year. The policy did not succeed, perhaps because it created an incentive to demand very high local increases in the first year. When the value of each dollar in wage drift over and above the expected level is reduced to fifty cents, it makes sense to insist on more.

Bargaining within and between unions or bargaining cartels is an essential part of the overall bargaining system. Sometimes the internal bargaining is resolved before the external confrontation, but they can also take place in parallel, right up to the last minute. Some unions or cartels have a highly heterogeneous clientele. The cartel representing private functionaries, for instance, represents the interests of lower functionaries who earn less than their public counterparts, as well as those of higher functionaries who earn more. Similarly the metal workers' union represents all workers in the mechanical industries, not just the highly skilled elite. On the one hand, this union must pay considerable attention to the latter, who might otherwise defect to the functionaries' union. On the other hand, it must pay attention to the solidaristic wage policy that has been a constant goal of LO. In a phrase that resonates with the theme of the present work, Peter Swenson writes that LO's emerging egalitarianism 'provided the cement for a potentially unstable balance of power among the LO unions'.[17]

Across unions or cartels the differences are also considerable. The metal workers' unions and the typographical union have traditionally been strong unions that have accepted the solidaristic wage policy with reluctance and,

[17] Swenson (1989), p. 55.

on several occasions, supported the move to decentralized bargaining. Industrial workers and private functionaries have sometimes been able to work in tandem but have often been split by alliances with private employers. In recent years, employers and workers were pitted against functionaries in 1981, employers and functionaries against workers in 1983 and workers and functionaries against employers in 1986. The four cartels (the 'Gang of Four') representing lower public functionaries and public blue-collar workers have at times been able to coordinate their efforts. At other times, their alliance has split because the blue-collar workers, traditionally close to the Labour party, were more willing to listen to the socialist government's demand for wage moderation.

In most of the postwar period, the issue of central versus decentralized bargaining has been on the agenda. Even in the long period – from 1956 to 1982 – when central bargaining prevailed, it had to be chosen anew on each round of negotiations.[18] For the employers the main argument for central bargaining was that it would induce worker moderation, yielding lower wage increases and fewer strikes. In addition, SAF found that total lock-out was easier to deploy and to justify than partial lock-outs (as discussed later). For the unions there were two main arguments: justice and efficiency. Central bargaining would enable LO to impose 'solidaristic wage policies', and to internalize the effects of various parts of the labour market on each other.

For the employers, however, the arguments against central bargaining became increasingly important. For one thing, the solidaristic wage policy made wage differentiation, which the employers believed to be necessary to attract skilled workers, more costly. Because unskilled workers secured large increases in the central part of the bargaining process, skilled workers had to be offered more in the subsequent local bargaining.[19] For another, the moderating effects of central bargaining became less valuable as an ever-larger proportion of the workers became organized outside LO. This development also weakened the efficiency argument for central bargaining in the eyes of the workers and undermined their resistance to the employer-initiated move to decentralized bargaining.

The process that led to the break-down of central bargaining in 1983 was initiated by employers in the mechanical industries, spearheaded by the powerful Volvo industries, which, directly or indirectly, make up about

---

[18] The following draws on de Geer (1986), pp. 323–9.   [19] Nilsson (1987), pp. 32–3.

10 per cent of the Swedish industrial production and 12 per cent of exports. By bargaining separately with the metal workers they hoped to achieve a more differentiated wage policy. The central association of employers shared the substantive goal of wage differentiation, but feared that separate bargaining might obstruct the strategic goal of maintaining their organization intact. Yet they did not mind a split in the united front of workers, especially since this might make it even more difficult to achieve the unification of workers and functionaries that was a long-standing goal of LO and a long-standing fear of the employers. By contrast, LO was opposed to decentralization both on substantive and on strategic grounds.

In their bargaining with the other branches of the employers' association, the employers in the mechanical industries decided to build up a separate fund out of which they could support their member firms in case of a conflict. This conflict fund served, in effect, as a bargaining chip in two distinct negotiations. Against other employers it added credibility to their threat to leave the central association unless its statutes were changed so as to allow separate bargaining with the metal workers. In addition, of course, it served the normal purpose of adding credibility in the latter bargaining itself. The metal workers' union accepted separate negotiations, against the wishes and the pressure of LO, because it hoped to get (and in fact did get) concessions on several long-standing grievances.

In addition, the metal workers got concessions on relative wages. The employers in the mechanical industries were also negotiating with the private functionaries in a similarly decentralized fashion. This was the year in which, at the central level, there was an alliance between private employers and functionaries against the industrial workers. Within the mechanical industry, however, a different coalition formed – between employers and workers against the functionaries. To achieve the support of the workers for separate bargaining it was important to keep the wage increases of the functionaries at a moderate level, and in the first year (1983) these did in fact receive less than other private functionaries.

In the 1983–4 bargaining over decentralized bargaining, there were three propositions on the table: full centralization, full decentralization and voluntary centralization among the sectors that so desired. LO ranked the alternatives in this order, whereas the employers ranked them in exactly the opposite order. In the ensuing compromise, each party got its second-best alternative, full decentralization. It is not clear why LO would rank the alternatives in this order. It is possible that it actually preferred partial decentralization, but expressed a different preference to force employers to accept full centralization, wrongly believing that they would prefer this over full decentralization. And the employers might well have had this preference, if their desire to keep the organization together had been stronger than the need to accommodate the mechanical industries.

Bargaining over the contract period has several aspects. First, there is a general tendency for employers to want longer and unions to want shorter periods. Employers need a long planning horizon, partly to prevent unions from taking advantage of high investment levels (Chapter 2).[20] The difference may also be related to different attitudes towards risk. In a rapidly and unpredictably changing environment, ability to renegotiate the contract is more important for risk-averse employees than for more nearly risk-neutral employers. This problem, however, can be finessed by the inclusion of automatic compensation for inflation in the contract. Second, there is a conflict of interest over the synchronization of the contract periods in different sectors. LO traditionally wants full synchronization for workers and functionaries, as part of its general desire for fully unified bargaining. The employers and functionaries have the opposite preference. Also, one union may want its contract period to expire soon after that of another union, so as to be able to renegotiate if the latter gets a good settlement. Nobody wants to be the wage leader whose results serve as a floor on the demands of the unions whose contracts expire later. Again the problem can be finessed by contract clauses granting automatic compensation for higher wages achieved by other unions.

Even if negotiations are separate and synchronized, they may still be interdependent. Since the bargaining process is time-consuming and can rarely be kept fully secret, the unions will make more or less well founded guesses about each other's claims. Thus in the 1984 bargaining round, the metal workers' union and the public functionaries negotiated simultaneously, each of them believing (or claiming to believe) that the other demanded and was likely to get large increases. Whether or not the beliefs were true in the first place, they became self-fulfilling: both got more than they would otherwise have achieved. With separate and successive negotiations, the union who is first out knows that its result will set a trend for the later agreements. In principle, it thus has an incentive to moderate its claims: little is gained by a large increase if it triggers large increases

[20] See also van der Ploeg (1987), p. 1466, and de Geer (1986), p. 212.

Table 4.1. *Wage contracts for blue-collar workers*

Year	Contract
1960–1	Two-year central agreement
1962–3	Two-year central agreement
1964–5	Two-year central agreement
1966–8	Three-year central agreement; earnings development guarantee
1969–70	Two-year central agreement; earnings development guarantee
1971–3	Three-year central agreement; earnings development guarantee
1974	One-year central agreement; earnings development guarantee; agreement on wage restraint in exchange for elimination of fiscal drag and increased payroll taxes
1975–6	Two-year central agreement; earnings development guarantee; agreement on wage restraint in exchange for elimination of fiscal drag and increased payroll taxes
1977	One-year central agreement; automatic compensation of consumer price inflation above threshold; earnings development guarantee
1978–9	Two-year central agreement; right to new negotiations without peace obligation if consumer price inflation above thresholds; earnings development guarantee
1980	One-year central agreement; earnings development guarantee; price freeze to facilitate wage negotiations; failed attempt on part of government to exchange tax reductions for negotiated wage increases
1981–2	Two-year central agreement; earnings development guarantee; automatic compensation if consumer price inflation above threshold
1983	One-year central agreement on general frame; central agreement did not encompass the engineering industry; industry negotiations without peace obligation; earnings development guarantee
1984	No central agreement; industry bargaining; engineering and steel industries key sectors; most contracts of one-year duration; earning development guarantees; tax scale adjustment and temporary freezing of profits to meet union demands; temporary price freeze
1985	One-year central agreement on frame; industry negotiations without peace obligation; earnings development guarantee; tax rebate to facilitate central agreement; freezing of profits in 'renewal funds'; price freeze to affect negotiations in engineering industry
1986–8	Two-year central agreement; earnings development guarantee; right to new negotiations without peace obligation if consumer price inflation above threshold; temporary price freeze when unions abstained from demanding compensation for price increases
	No central agreement; industry bargaining; engineering industry key sector

ing. Before the parties can bargain, however, they have to solve
collective action problem, namely how to organize themselves.
ffe and Helmut Wiesenthal argue that there is an asymmetry be-
rkers and captialists in their ability to organize, partly because of

---

across the board and hence high inflation that offsets the wage gains. In practice, unions do not seem to take account of these effects, probably because the rank and file will accept moderate demands only when the bargaining is centralized so that everyone can see that others are not getting more.

In addition to definite settlements, many contracts contain conditional clauses, stipulating that if event X occurs then Y will automatically also happen. The triggering event X can be a certain level of inflation, a certain level of negotiated wage increase or wage drift for workers in other unions, changes in the income tax or some more complex construction. Thus in the 1983 bargaining round, private functionaries and their employers agreed that if the wage increases obtained by other unions contributed to an inflation in excess of the government's goal of 4 per cent, either party could call for renegotiation. In a striking display of the art of having it both ways, the functionaries also demanded and got the right to renegotiate if other workers were to get an increase in their real wage as a result of an inflation rate *below* 4 per cent. 'The agreement contained protecting clauses for almost any conceivable change in the environment'.[21] The event Y that is triggered off can be a straightforward wage increase or, as in these examples, a right to renegotiate the agreement.

Often, agreements dump problems onto the future. The conditional clauses that trigger renegotiating rather than any specific outcome are one example. A constant headache are the so-called overhangs, agreed-upon wage increases that do not take effect until after the expiration of the contract period. In the next bargaining round the parties then have to decide whether the negotiated wage increase will come on top of the overhang from the preceding period or whether the overhang will be counted as part of the increase. If the employers do not concede to a claim made by the union, the latter can save face by obtaining a promise to pursue the matter in later negotiations. When a framework for wage drift is decided centrally, the implementation is left to plant-level bargaining. The framework being a guideline rather than a set of explicit instructions, it will, in fact, not bind the local bargaining. In practice, the suggested average turns into a floor. If agreements are silent, vague or ambiguous on such points, they are so deliberately, not by accident. Ambiguity is intentionally used to achieve agreement.

[21] Elvander (1988), p. 105.

The government enters multiply into the collective bargaining process. First, governments of various political persuasions have tried to achieve 'combined settlements', by offering tax rebates in return for moderate wage claims.[22] Second, Labour governments have a special relationship with LO that, depending on circumstances, can make it easier or more difficult to impose moderation. On the one hand, there is the 'Nixon–China' effect. Only a politician with unimpeachable hard-line credentials could 'give up' Taiwan. Similarly, a socialist government that asks for moderation in the national interest is less suspect of being the extended arm of business. On the other hand, of course, the socialist party depends on the vote and support of blue-collar workers. Third, the government plays an important role as employer in the public sector. This can also affect bargaining in the private sector, if unions anticipate that unemployment caused by high wage claims will be absorbed by the public sector.[23] Finally, the government can enter into the final stage of bargaining as mediator and arbitrator. Arbitration occurs only at the demand of the parties. In theory, the arbitrators will only try to find a compromise between the parties, and not take account of the wider economic interests of the country. In practice, the government is rarely able to pull its punches and abstain from using the arbitration mechanism to further these interests. Needless to say, this danger of role confusion is especially large in the public sector.[24]

The political system affects bargaining in still another way, since unions often have a choice between collective bargaining and legislation to promote their claims. In the 1964 bargaining round, the union claims included, in addition to wage demands, measures concerning layoffs, dismissals and reemployment. 'The bargaining over the security measures was conducted under the threat that LO might turn to legislative measures. This might give a less favourable solution, and also reduce the value of these issues as bargaining chips in the wage negotiations'.[25] The value of this threat depends, obviously, on the cost to LO of using its political clout. In principle, the 'Swedish model' is defined by a hands-off attitude of the political authorities. Labour and capital are supposed to solve their problems without interference by the state.[26] In practice, the close links between LO and the Social Democratic governments have ensured unions a

---

privileged access to the political arena. Nevertheless, even socialist politicians are reluctant to be seen as too closely linked with the unions; also, they do not want to be responsible for excessively costly measures. Two years later, SAF decided to call LO's bluff in a similar situation, when LO demanded better conditions for sickness pay and added that a proposal for legislation had already been written up. SAF assessed, however, that politicians might be less than enthusiastic over the reform, which promised to be quite costly.

The final element in this thumb-nail description of the Swedish system concerns the offensive and defensive weapons at the disposal of the parties.[27] On the offensive side, the threat of legislation has just been mentioned. The key offensive weapons, however, are strikes and lock-outs. Strikes are not legal in local bargaining, nor, as a rule, in the sector negotiations that implement central agreements. Other things being equal, each party naturally prefers to use its weapons in a way that hurts the other party maximally and itself as little as possible. The refusal to work overtime, for instance, hurts workers relatively little but is often very costly to firms. When unions in the public sector pick a subset of workers to strike, they choose strategically important groups such as doctors or customs officers. When public-sector employers declare lock-outs, they choose teachers as the target, presumably because the short-term harm caused by the closing of schools is deemed small. In fact, they may even benefit, through lower wage payments. On the defensive side, strike funds of both parties are an important determinant of staying power, as is membership size on the union side. Strike funds affect the credibility of threats, while the size of the membership affects its effectiveness. A brief summary of the LO–SAF negotiations over the last thirty years is presented in Table 4.1.[28]

Labour–capital bargaining

The topic of this section is bargaining between organized labour and organized capital and the problems of collective action

---

[22] Contrary to a claim that is sometimes made, the government does not use welfare policy as a carrot for the unions. There may be an overall correlation between wage moderation and a highly developed welfare state, but the causal mechanism is not that of a simple quid pro quo.

[23] Flanagan (1987), pp. 160–1.   [24] Sjölund (1987), pp. 22–3.

[25] de Geer (1986), p. 190.   [26] Elvander (1988), ch. 1, and passim.

[27] The discussion of 'normative' weapons is postponed until
[28] From Calmfors and Forslund (1988). A similar, more collective bargaining from 1961 through 1986 is found in (1988), pp. 182–201. The Norwegian and Swedish collective ilar in most respects, also differ in some features. The role instance, much greater in Norway. A comparative study valuable insights into which institutional features affect they do so).

the difference in their goals and partly because of the difference in their abilities. On both counts, workers are at a disadvantage. Hence, they conclude, successful collective action by the working class requires a paradoxical bootstrapping act, to be described in a moment.

First, let us look at the alleged asymmetries. On the one hand, Offe and Wiesenthal argue, the collective action problem facing workers is much more difficult to solve than that facing firms. The latter have essentially one interest – profit – while the former have to agree on a trade-off between wages, working conditions and other interests. In the light of the empirical findings discussed later, this claim is dubious. The heterogeneity of firms and industries as an obstacle to collective action seems equally serious as the plurality of workers' needs.[29]

On the other hand, Offe and Wiesenthal claim that in the struggle between capital and labour, capital has an edge because of the weapons at its disposal. In particular, 'by introducing (labour-saving) technical change, capital can release itself partially from its dependence upon the supply of labour, thereby depressing the wage rate'.[30] It is not clear whether this argument is supposed to apply to the individual firm or to an association of firms; in any case, it is invalid on both readings. At the level of the enterprise, we saw in Chapter 2 that the firm is made *more* vulnerable, not less, by the introduction of labour-saving machinery. At the level of the association, we run into a free-rider problem: while it may be good for all firms if all bias their search for new techniques in a labour-saving direction, no individual firm has an interest in doing so.[31]

Be this as it may, Offe and Wiesenthal argue that workers, because of their disadvantaged position, have no hope of winning within the rules of the game. To achieve their goals, they must transcend the game. They must

employ a form of collective strategy of conflict which not only aggregates the individual resources of the members of the association in order to meet the common interests of these individuals, but which also *overcomes the individuality* of those resources and interests as well as the

[29] Workers might also, of course, differ in the ways they trade off needs against one another. Wages might be more important for one worker, job satisfaction for another. In that sense, workers face a twofold coordination problem, whereas capitalists face only one. I still believe firms have the more serious problem, because of the much greater magnitude of the free-rider gains that can be made by a defecting firm.
[30] Offe and Wiesenthal (1980), pp. 75–6.   [31] Elster (1983b), pp. 102–3.

obstacles to effective organization by defining a *collective identity* on the basis of which the chance to change existing power relations is no longer *exclusively* determined by those power relations themselves. That is to say that those in the inferior power position can increase their potential for change only by overcoming the comparatively higher costs of collective action by *changing the standards according to which these costs are subjectively estimated* within their own collectivity. . . . workers' organizations in capitalist systems always find themselves forced to rely upon nonutilitarian forms of collective actions, which are based on the redefinition of collective organizations – *even if the organization does not have any intention of serving anything but the members' individual utilitarian interests, for example, higher wages.* . . . [The] working class . . . is, so to speak, in constant search for those modes of collective action that allow for a more 'reliable', less distorted conception of interest.[32]

The 'paradox that *interests can only be met to the extent that they are partly redefined*'[33] would not really be a paradox were it simply stated as a sufficient condition. It can happen that as a result of changed preferences an individual or a group undertakes actions that satisfy the earlier preferences to a greater extent than actions taken on the basis of those earlier preferences themselves. Unless the change of preferences is the result of a highly improbable process of planned self-transformation or a slightly less improbable process of reinforcement,[34] this would just be an accident of no larger significance. It is neither likely nor desirable that it should occur. In general, this is also true if the change of preferences is a necessary condition for realizing the earlier desires. In the special case in which the old preferences are retained along with the new ones, the change may, in fact, be desirable, but is still not likely to occur. This is the case discussed by Offe and Wiesenthal. If workers, retaining their utilitarian interests in higher wages, develop a collective identity that *also* includes an interest in solidarity and discipline, their utilitarian interests are more likely to be satisfied. My claim is that contrary to what they argue, this fact does not set up any pressure towards or 'search for' this collective identity. In any case, I remain sceptical about the explanatory value of the concept of collective identity.

[32] Offe and Wiesenthal (1980), pp. 78–9, 96.   [33] Ibid., p. 79.
[34] As in Cohen and Axelrod (1984).

Assuming that both sides of the conflict are organized, what are their goals? Private employers strive to maximize profits or, more generally, the discounted present value of expected future earnings. From this basic fact we may deduce secondary objectives, such as the desire to pay low wages unless high wages are necessary to attract or retain skilled workers. The objectives of public employers are more difficult to ascertain. In theory, their goal is to carry out political decisions as efficiently as possible. In practice, public agencies have interests of their own, such as maximizing the number of employees.[35] They may prefer to hire many functionaries at lower wages, even when it would be more efficient to hire a smaller number of skilled specialists at higher wages.

The objective function of labour unions is a much-disputed matter. As mentioned in Chapter 2, if layoffs occur by seniority and union policy is decided by majority voting, the union will be interested only in wages and not care about employment.[36] If layoffs occur randomly and workers decide by majority voting, the union will take account of employment as well as of wages. The objective function in this case is expected income of the workers, that is, a weighted sum of wages and unemployment benefits, the weights being the probabilities of retaining the job or losing it. If unions are run dictatorially and leaders want to maximize union income (perhaps because they retain a fixed percentage for themselves), their goal will also be a function of wages and employment, but not the same function as in the previous case. If unions are run dictatorially and leaders want to maximize their following, they will care only about employment and not about wages. Finally, the union demands may be modelled as the outcome of bargaining between union leaders and members.[37] I will not take a stand on this issue, but indicate how various assumptions about union goals suggest different kinds of collective action problems.

The interest in wages can be further differentiated. First, workers have an interest in future as well as in present wages. More precisely, they seek to maximize the present value of a future wage stream. Next, workers have an interest both in nominal and in real wages. Here I limit myself to real

---

[35] This can also be a political goal, if the public sector is supposed to absorb unemployment.

[36] This will not be true if there is a serious chance that more than half the work force will be laid off, as could happen if the union successfully makes confiscatory wage demands so that the firm has to close down. But the union is not likely to make such claims; nor, if made, are they likely to be granted.

[37] Pemberton (1988).

wages, postponing a discussion of nominal wages until Chapter 6. More-over, they have an interest in relative as well as absolute wages. The discussion here is restricted to absolute wages, relative wages being also postponed until Chapter 6. Finally, workers have an interest in before-tax as well as after-tax wages. Impressionistic evidence suggests that in Swedish collective bargaining, workers maximize some function (perhaps a weighted sum) of relative and absolute wages in the next contract period, with wages measured in terms of after-tax purchasing power. As before, I need not take a stand on the issue, since I limit myself to pointing out the collective action problems that can arise on various assumptions.

Two-party bargaining can lead to collective action problems when both parties try to influence the bargaining situation to their advantage, by precommitment to certain demands or by investments in their inside options. In Chapter 2 I argued that when both parties invest in bargaining power to increase their share of the total, the latter may shrink so much that both get less than what they would have received under 'naive' bargaining. Here I shall discuss inefficiencies generated by precommitment.

Consider first a problem of bargaining under certainty, illustrated in Fig. 4.2, and assume that the Nash solution will be implemented. The set of feasible outcomes is the area spanned by (0, 7), (4, 6), (6, 4) and (7, 0). The disagreement point is (0, 0). By symmetry and Pareto optimality, the solution must be at A, that is, (5, 5). Assume now that player I has some-how precommitted himself in a way that eliminates the option (4, 6).[38] Within the smaller feasible set, spanned by (0, 7), (6, 4) and (7, 0), the Nash solution will now be (6, 4). Conversely, if player II eliminates (6, 4), the solution will be (4, 6). Clearly, each player has an incentive to carry out the respective eliminations, assuming that the other does not do so. If both of them do so, however, the outcome will be at C, that is, (3.5, 3.5) – which is worse for both than the original outcome (5, 5). This noncoop-erative game, in which each player has the choice between 'precommit' and 'not precommit', has the form of 'Chicken'. It pays each player to precommit if and only if the other does not. If we change (0, 7) and (7, 0) to (0, 9) and (9, 0), respectively, a party that achieves unilateral precommitment gets 5.4 and the other 4.5. The result of mutual precommitment is now B(4.5, 4.5). If II precommits, I obtains the same utility (4.5) by precommitting and by not precommitting. If II does not precommit, I's

---

[38] He may have achieved this by laying his reputation on the line, as explained in Chapter 2, or by burning his bridges in one of the other ways discussed by Schelling (1963).

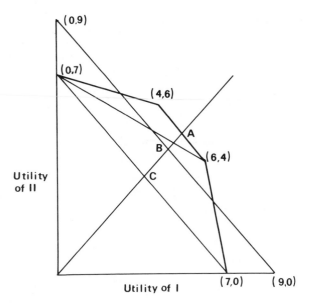

Fig. 4.2

utility by precommitting is 5.4 and by not precommitting 5. As a (weakly) dominant strategy precommitment will be chosen, yet the outcome is worse for both if both precommit than if neither does. This game of precommitment, in other words, is (almost) a Prisoner's Dilemma.

Vince Crawford has constructed a model of bargaining under uncertainty in which precommitment also is the dominant strategy in a Prisoner's Dilemma.[39] The rules of the game are as follows. If neither precommits himself, a Pareto-optimal compromise is achieved; if one party precommits himself, he gets what he demands; if both precommit themselves and their claims are compatible, they get at least what they asked for; if they precommit themselves to incompatible claims, they get the disagreement outcome. The bargainers have two choices: whether or not to precommit themselves and, if they do precommit themselves, whether or not to back down. More specifically:

bargaining is viewed as a two-stage process, in which bargainers are perfectly informed about everything except their costs of backing down.

[39] Crawford (1982). He asserts that with precommitments under certainty, 'questions of timing take on primary importance', implying that the game of precommitment then has the form of Chicken. The example in the text shows that this is not always the case.

In the first stage, bargainers simultaneously decide whether or not to attempt commitment. An attempt, if one is made, consists of the announcement of a demand (in utility terms) and a draw from a probability distribution, whose realization is the cost (again in utility terms) that must be borne if the bargainer in question later decides to accept anything less than his demand. In the second stage, each bargainer learns his own, but not his opponent's, costs of backing down (the outcome of his draw); whether or not his opponent attempted commitment, and what demand, if any, he made. He then decides, taking into account this information, whether or not to retreat from his demand. . . . The second-stage part of his strategy takes the form of a rule that relates his action to the situation in which he finds himself.[40]

Crawford shows that 'the Nash equilbrium of the commitment game has the usual property of the noncooperative equilibria of the Prisoner's Dilemma games – in spite of its clear individual rationality, it leads to an outcome that is collectively "irrational" because the positive probability of impasse that results implies that its distribution of outcomes is not ex ante Pareto-efficient'.[41] When the bargaining parties agree to negotiate privately rather than make their claims public, this can be understood as a move to prevent such mutually disastrous attempts to precommit themselves. Since the promise cannot be made binding, however, defections often occur. If the bargainers expect to meet again and gain in the future, long-term self-interest may make them stick to the agreement, in a 'Tit-for-Tat' equilibrium. But *since collective wage bargaining lacks a constitution,* so that one never knows who will bargain with whom in the future, self-interest dictates a shorter time horizon.

Inefficiencies can also arise in the actual bargaining itself, without uncertainty or precommitment. W. Leontief showed in 1946 that labour–capital bargaining may yield outcomes that are worse for both parties than some other feasible result.[42]

In Fig. 4.3 we assume that the wage w is set first and that the firm then sets employment L unilaterally so as to maximize profits. Then $L(w)$ shows the combinations of wages and employment that may arise. The union is

[40] Ibid., pp. 127–8.
[41] Ibid., p. 143. The result is proved under two sets of assumptions. He first assumes that the parties know the distribution from which the draw is taken. Since he recognizes the fragility of this assumption (see Chapter 2), he later replaces it with the assumption that the parties use rough expectational heuristics.
[42] Leontief (1946).

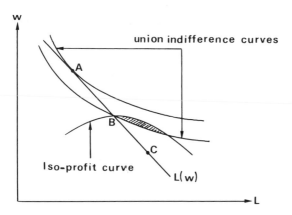

Fig. 4.3

supposed to care about both wages and employment, as indicated by the shape of the indifference curves. If the union has the power to set the wage unilaterally, the outcome will be at A. C is the outcome that will be reached under perfect competition, with no union power. Here the wage is set by the labour market, and the firm simply adjusts to it. With genuine wage bargaining the outcome will be some point B between these extremes. The union would prefer any point above the indifference curve passing through B. Similarly, the firm would prefer any point below the iso-profit curve passing through B.[43] As shown in Fig. 4.3, the points in the hatched area are preferable to both the union and the firm, compared with the outcome B that will be reached through collective bargaining. The reason for the inefficiency is that if the workers agreed on a wage corresponding to a wage–employment combination in this hatched area, the firm would have no incentive to stick to the agreement which, by construction, does not maximize profits. If wages are set by bargaining before the firm unilaterally set employment, and if the firm has no means of credibly committing itself to a nonoptimal level of employment, inefficient bargains will be struck.

Capital–capital bargaining

Firms in an industry or members of an employers' association have an interest in a common policy towards consumers or workers. By agreeing

---

[43] To see that iso-profit curves must have this shape, it is sufficient to observe that by definition their maximum must lie on $L(w)$.

on a common price or a common wage they can do better for themselves than they would if they competed for customers or workers. Because firms and industries tend to be heterogeneous in a number of respects, this collective action problem typically requires extensive bargaining over the distribution of costs and benefits. Inability to agree on this distribution is usually a much bigger problem for cartel stability than is the more frequently discussed free-rider problem.

The coordination problems of cartels are well known. Oil companies and later the OPEC countries have had formidable difficulties in maintaining a common policy.[44] The international oil companies used a double system. On the one hand, they allocated market shares proportionally to sales in a given reference year (the 'As Is' rule).[45] On the other hand, c.i.f. prices were set equal to the price posted in the Mexican gulf plus what it would cost to transport the oil from the gulf, regardless of its actual origin (the 'Gulf Plus' rule). The system worked reasonably well, partly because the major companies were prepared (up to a point) to bear some costs of free riding and partly because some consumer countries had an interest in high oil prices, 'to protect nuclear power, coal, natural gas and high-cost oil firms'.[46] The OPEC countries did reasonably well as long as they delegated the actual extraction to private companies. By stipulating a posted price for oil and taxing the companies 50 per cent of that price, they created a range 'below which individual oil companies would spontaneously begin to curtail production rather than sell at lower prices'.[47] When the OPEC countries went into production and sale for themselves, the cartel did not hold. The first production quotas were set in 1980, but in general were nor respected.

The oil cartels illustrate the 'exploitation of the great by the small'.[48] In a heterogeneous group, some actors may be large enough to provide a public good single-handedly, without any contribution from others, who may then take a free ride. However, large firms can force small firms to cooperate, by underselling them or by pressuring their banks, customers and suppliers. On balance, the large *are* more powerful than the small. They can afford to wait it out and are often better able to survive without cooperation. Sometimes there are several actors each of whom would pro-

---

[44] The following draws on Moran (1987).

[45] As observed by Müllensiefen (1963), the allocation of quotas must use verifiable quantities like sales, not unverifiable ones like capacities. However, the use of sales to set quotas will, if anticipated, create an incentive to expand sales wastefully just before cartellization.

[46] Moran (1987), pp. 595–6.   [47] Ibid., pp. 596–7.   [48] Olson (1965), p. 29.

vide the good single-handedly were he sure that the others would not. Each of two large firms in an industry could be willing to invest in nonpatentable basic research, yet abstain in the hope that the other will do it. Although a game of Chicken rather than a Prisoner's Dilemma, it is a collective action problem in the sense that it is better for both if one of them invests than if neither does. Bargaining over side payments may or may not ensure agreement, depending on the ploys of misrepresentation and precommitment utilized by the parties.

In the oil industry, the 'As Is' rule provided a stable focal point for agreement. In a rapidly changing environment, the past may not help the parties coordinate in the present. Members of the American railroad cartels in the late nineteenth century had 'great difficulty in determining what each considered an equitable allocation of either freight or revenue. In time of rapidly growing traffic, percentage shares agreed upon at the start of the year were outmoded by the end of the year. The more efficient roads, like the Pennsylvania, which increased their share of the traffic actually carried, resented having to pay large sums into the pool at the end of each accounting period'.[49] Because of the cartel instability, the railroads sought to become self-sufficient, by expanding their network of lines instead of having to cooperate with other roads. This 'system building proved costly to individual roads and to some extent to the national economy as well. The great growth of the individual enterprises often led to a redundancy of facilities'.[50] In Chicken-like situations, the result may be oversupply as well as undersupply of public goods.

John Bowman's work on cartellization and unionization in the bituminous coal industry in the United States is a study of heterogeneity.[51] Coal is produced and transported under widely differing conditions, inducing very different cost structures. The need of different mines for cooperation varies correspondingly, as shown by the Schelling diagrams illustrated in Fig. 4.4. The diagrams show the profit of a low-cost firm (A), a medium-cost firm (B) and a high-cost firm (C) as a function of the firm's choice to cooperate or not to cooperate and of the number of other cooperators. The horizontal line represents zero profits, so that firms below that line are in danger of bankruptcy. Low-cost firms can survive under full competition; medium-cost firms can survive with some cooperation; and high-cost firms can survive only by free riding. High-cost and medium-cost firms have a

[49] Chandler (1977), pp. 142–3.   [50] Ibid., p. 147.   [51] Bowman (1989).

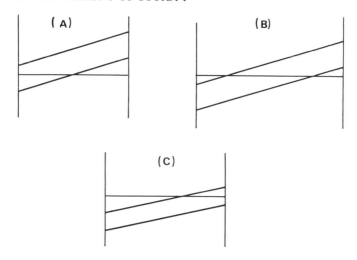

Fig. 4.4

strong incentive to create a cartel. They are, however, in a very weak bargaining position since, unlike low-cost firms, they need the cartel strongly. Low-cost firms can impose a quota allocation or a price structure that just allows medium-cost and high-cost firms to survive, since they can say, credibly, 'Take it or leave it'. As we saw in Chapter 2, this 'Matthew effect' obtains quite generally.

Bowman shows that the coal operators around the turn of the century invented a particularly ingenious strategy to maintain their cartel. The main noncooperative strategy in the coal industry was wage and price cutting. There were other ways of cutting costs, but reducing wages was the most effective method. To stop the price cutting, a collective wage agreement with the unions was essential. 'The joint conference of 1898 between the mine workers and operators from Ohio, Pennsylvania, Illinois, and Indiana . . . established the union-enforced organization of the coal industry which endured with greater or less success for the next twenty-five years'.[52] Side payment to high-cost operators took the form of a differentiated wage scale. Not surprisingly, this turned out to be the Achilles heel of the system. 'The system of differentials that was supposed to preserve ''competitive equality'' operated in an extremely haphazard way that was a function more of the relative strength of different groups of miners and operators than of any

[52] Ibid., p. 107.

rational calculations of relative production costs. . . . The competition among operators which had formerly been carried out through unilateral wage reductions was now carried out in the arena of wage negotiations.'[53]

The history of the Swedish employers' association (SAF)[54] similarly shows that employers in the member industries were far from united in their struggle with the workers. Usually, the problem was heterogeneity or selectivity rather than the simple free-rider temptation, as will be shown by some examples.

In the early years of the association, the textile industries thought it unfair that they should pay as much as others to the common strike funds, given the low strike proneness of textile workers. For the years 1911–26, their association had paid 5 362 000 kronor to the strike funds of the central association, whereas they had received only 275 000 kronor in strike compensation. A solution was found that allowed the textile manufacturers to remain in SAF. In 1932, the association had severe difficulties in forming a sympathy lock-out in support of the paper industries, which were engaged in protracted industrial conflict. Before the effort finally succeeded, many firms in the paper industries had given notice that they would be leaving SAF. That there were even greater problems in the following year suggests that concerted employer action may be especially difficult in recessions and depressions, when every penny counts and contributions to the common good are more likely to be seen as sacrifices. 'The strong, centralized Swedish employers' association had, because of internal differences of opinion, failed to exploit one of the deepest depressions of the century to achieve a general reduction in wages'.[55] A more recent example of strong internal division on the employers' side occurred in 1962, when there was a regular revolt by a 'camarilla' of strong member associations, mainly in the export industries, who accused the leadership of being soft on the demands of the workers. Yet the camarilla itself had internal fissures that were cleverly exploited by the SAF leadership, who eventually came out on top. More recently, the cement of the employers' common interests proved too weak to keep the engineering industries from breaking out in 1983.

Selectivity, that is, the realization of an internal optimum to the collective action problem, has also proved to be a difficulty. Sometimes, SAF would have preferred limited forms of industrial action – for example, to

<hr />

[53] Ibid., p. 116.   [54] de Geer (1986).   [55] Ibid., pp. 102–3.

single out a few industries for partial lock-out rather than branding the weapon of total conflict. Yet for reasons of internal cohesion these selective tactics were unfeasible: it had to be 'all or none'.[56] Although SAF might try to justify selective tactics by offering side payments or by arguing that industries must take turns in bearing the brunt of conflict, the disruption wrought by work stoppage is potentially so profound, intangible and incalculable as to make an agreement on fair terms impossible.

Labour–labour bargaining

In this section I consider the problems of collective action that arise from decentralized bargaining in which many unions negotiate separately with many employers' associations. Consider first the problem of plant-level union formation as a collective action problem across (as opposed to within) groups of workers. Because of an 'implied threat effect', nonunionized firms have an incentive to invest in keeping their workers from organizing.[57] If the wage level below which unorganized workers would unionize is a, the level in unionized firms is b and union member dues amount to c, then it is in the firm's interest to pay them a. If $c > b - a$, unorganized workers are actually better off than their organized counterparts. If $c < b - a$, as is usually the case, why would not the nonunionized workers organize themselves? In addition to the usual free-rider problem, the answer[58] lies in the high start-up costs of union formation. Needless to say, management tries to make these costs as high as possible.[59] The obstacles to union formation include not only free riding within the group, but also the possibility of free riding on other unions and deliberate obstruction by the management.

Consider next the collective action problems created by decentralized unions in a fully unionized economy. I shall discuss *eight problems* of this kind. First, there is the collective action problem created by the relative-wage component in the wage demands. I return to this issue in Chapter 6.

Second, there is the problem created by unions raiding each other for members. In countries with a high degree of unionization, competition for members is constant sum. For the unions taken as a whole, there is no net

---

[56] Ibid., pp. 127, 328–9, 377.

[57] For a discussion of this threat effect see Oswald (1981).

[58] See also Elster (1985d), sec. 7.1.4, for a closely related analysis of how landowners might act strategically to induce *capitalist* nonorganization.

[59] Freeman and Medoff (1984), ch. 15.

gain, while the losses may be considerable. In Sweden, a municipal union actually used the strike weapon to prevent the loss of members to another LO union following a reorganization. In theory, unions resorting to such tactics can be expelled. In this case, the internal bargaining power of the municipal workers, who have 28 per cent of the LO members, prevented this from happening.

Third, decentralized unions invite divide-and-rule tactics. When the employers can ally themselves now with one union, now with another, they can do better for themselves not only compared with centralized bargaining but also compared with decentralized bargaining without alliance formation. The scope for such tactics depends on the partitioning of the workers into unions. If competing unions organize the workers in a given industry, as in the relation between the French CFDT and CGT, firms can gain by playing one union off against another. When capital is indispensable but neither group of workers is, divide and rule works well.[60] When each group of organized workers is indispensable, as in the relation between blue-collar and white-collar unions, the situation is more fluid.

The remaining five problems arise out of externalities. The outcome of bargaining in one sector or firm may have a negative impact on workers in other sectors and firms, through the effect on prices, employment, investment, public goods and trade. Central bargaining, which internalizes these effects, can then make all workers better off. I shall focus on externalities of sectoral bargaining, but first comment briefly on plant-level bargaining. It is widely believed[61] that wage drift created by local bargaining aggravates inflation (and unemployment), thus making everybody worse off than they would have been had all shown moderation. It is not clear, however, that this has to be the case. 'To the extent that wage drift is anticipated by central negotiators, it may be just one institutional form for centrally determined wage increases'.[62] In one model that incorporates this idea,[63] bargaining takes place in three stages. First, the central labour union sets the tariff wage unilaterally. Next, firms set employment levels. Finally, firms and local unions bargain over the wage drift. The outcome is derived by working backwards in the chain. Firms set employment levels, anticipating the outcome of wage bargaining.[64] The central union sets the tariff

[60] Shapley and Shubik (1967).   [61] Schwerin (1980, 1982).
[62] Calmfors (1987a), p. 179.   [63] Holden (1987b).
[64] This part of the model builds on Moene (1988), presented in Chapter 2 of the present volume.

wage, anticipating the effect on employment and wages. Under the assumptions of the model, employment is always higher under a mixed regime with central and local bargaining than in a system with central bargaining only. Wages may or may not be higher. 'This is in sharp contrast with the usual argument that bargaining on two levels increases wages and reduces employment'.[65]

Most models that allow us to compare sectoral and central bargaining assume (mainly, I suspect, for reasons of mathematical convenience) that unions set wages unilaterally, anticipating the effect on employment.[66] Strictly speaking, therefore, these are not models of *bargaining*, but of union monopoly power. It is hard to tell which, if any, of the results surveyed here would survive in an explicit (cooperative or noncooperative) model of bargaining. This being said, I proceed to a brief review of externalities generated by sectoral bargaining with unions as wage setters.

Consider first the effect of decentralized bargaining on prices and employment.[67] Assuming that union utility is a function of nominal wages, the price level and employment, what happens when unions negotiate separately over nominal wages? A wage increase for a union in sector A affects its members in three ways. First, other things being equal, it amounts to an increase in purchasing power. Second, however, to the extent that wage increases are passed along to consumers in the form of higher costs and union members are among the consumers of their own products, their purchasing power will be somewhat reduced by the wage increase. Third, higher wages will somewhat reduce the demand for their labour and hence the level of employment. Taking account of all three effects, unions choose the wage level that maximizes their utility. In general, they accept hurting themselves somewhat *qua* consumers and seekers of employment in return for higher wages.

In addition, the union affects the welfare of other unions, in two ways. First, members of other unions suffer *qua* consumers of the products of sector A. Call this the *price effect*. Second, higher wages for workers in A may affect the demand for other workers. Call this the *employment effect*. If labour of type A and type B are complements, an increase in A's wage rate that reduces the demand for A labour will also reduce the demand for

[65] Holden (1987).

[66] An exception is Höglund (1987), who presents a stylized model in which an employer is simultaneously engaged in Chicken games with two unions, which as a result find themselves placed in a Prisoner's Dilemma with respect to each other.

[67] The following draws upon Hersoug (1984), Calmfors (1986) and Oswald (1979).

B labour. Blue-collar work and white-collar work, for instance, tend to be complements. When these groups bargain separately, as they do in Sweden, both end up with lower employment and higher wages than under the optimal arrangement that could have been achieved by central bargaining. They are made worse off by the price effect and by the employment effect. If, however, A and B types of labour are substitutes, an increase in A's wage will shift the demand curve for B's labour to the right. B workers will take the increase in demand partly in higher wages, partly in higher employment. The employment effect, in this case, is indeterminate. The price effect remains negative, of course. The net outcome of the price and employment effects may be quite small, however, if the two types of labour are substitutes for each other.

If unions are monopoly wage setters, they should prefer centralized to decentralized bargaining, since any wage profile that would result from decentralized bargaining can also be imposed by central bargaining. While true as a statement about the utility of the *unions,* this may be false as a statement about the utility of the *workers* or the welfare of *taxpayers.* If unions care only about wages, they have no incentive to take account of the impact of their wage claims on employment. And even if they care about employment, they have no incentive to take full account of the fact that unemployment benefits and retraining programs are funded out of payroll taxes or, more generally, of the fact that unemployment means loss of production and ultimately less to share. If, therefore, decentralized bargaining leads to higher employment than would be observed under central bargaining, the former may be socially preferable *in this respect.* In other respects, of course, decentralized bargaining may have bad effects that more than offset this advantage, when it exists.

Decentralized bargaining also creates externalities for investment. Assuming that workers care about future as well as present income, the working class as a whole has an interest in moderating its wage claims so as to create room for investment by firms. The workers in any particular union, however, have a much weaker incentive to moderate its claims when bargaining separately with the employers. The 'firms' investment decisions depend partly on workers outside the union, perhaps because firms employ members of multiple unions or because the cost of inputs depends on wages paid to other unions in other industries'.[68] In addition, the wage benefits

---

[68] Przeworski and Wallerstein (1987), p. 11.

from investment will not wholly accrue to the current workers in the firm, since employment must also be expected to expand. 'Thus, existing employees must sacrifice some share of pie today in order to make a bigger pie tomorrow – but then there will be a proportionately larger number of colleagues wanting to share it'.[69] Since future union members have no vote, their wage and employment interest will not be part of the union's utility function. For these two investment-related reasons, the long-term interests of the worker collective as a whole are best served with central bargaining.[70]

A further collective action problem arises when unions maximize after-tax rather than before-tax income. Union members, needless to say, benefit from the public goods and welfare policies that are financed by taxation. Yet members of any individual union receive only a small portion of the benefits financed by the taxes they pay. A central union, by contrast, would be in a better position to make a rational trade-off between its members' desires for private and public goods. Even a centralized union would not, however, internalize all the benefits financed by the taxes paid by its members. Since the benefits are diffused throughout the population at large, including people who have left the labour market or have not entered it, central unions will not ensure an optimal provision of public goods.

Decentralized bargaining tends to create tighter vertical bonds between employers and workers in a given industry at the expense of horizontal bonds among workers in different industries. As a result, protectionism that is contrary to the general interest may be pushed through.[71] Unions and firms in industries that produce for the home market and do not depend on imported inputs have a common interest in protectionism. If they successfully lobby for tariffs, there is a risk that other countries may retaliate, thus hurting unions and firms in other industries that depend on exporting their products or importing inputs. Ultimately this will also affect workers in the protected industries, but not necessarily so much that they would have abstained from lobbying if they had anticipated the chain reaction it would trigger. Although not a Prisoner's Dilemma, it is a collective action problem in a loose sense of the term: it is better for almost everybody if no

---

[69] Aoki (1984), p. 69.

[70] Lancaster (1973), argued, however, that even when capital and labour confront each other as unified actors, the equilibrium time profile of wages and investment may be such that both parties are worse off than if they had coordinated their policies.

[71] The following draws on Wallerstein (1985).

unions lobby for protectionism. A centralized union would not support policies that would harm a majority of the members.

As the last example shows, coordinating union policy is not simply a matter of making everyone better off. Sometimes there will be losers from centralization and coordination. More important, even when everybody can be made better off it remains to agree on one particular agreement. *The task of coordinating separate bargaining processes is itself a bargaining problem.* Consider the problem facing a central union that is about to set a wage profile for its members. An obvious possibility is to choose a profile that preserves the relative wages that would have been obtained by decentralized bargaining. Under reasonable conditions, everybody can be made better off by a coordinated profile that respects wage differentials.[72] But workers in low-wage industries will protest. They will argue that a coordinated wage policy must do two things. In addition to eliminating externalities it must create a more egalitarian wage structure. But now workers in high-wage industries will protest, since under the more egalitarian structure they may not do much better than they would in a decentralized system. Clearly, the outcome will depend on the strength of the norm of equality invoked by the low-income groups. I return to that issue in Chapter 6.

In the preceding paragraph I focused on heterogeneity as the source of labour–labour bargaining problems. If all unions were identical, determining the wage profile in centralized bargaining would seem easy. The central leadership would simply choose the wage rate that would maximize the objective function of all unions. This statement presupposes, implausibly, that the central union has dictatorial powers to prevent free riding. There is, however, an alternative way of looking at the process. We might view the unions as fully independent actors who are able to cooperate on wage moderation because they perceive themselves as being engaged in an iterated noncooperative game of yearly wage bargaining. In that case, moderation might be sustained by the trigger strategy discussed in Chapter 1: make moderate demands if and only if all other unions made moderate demands in the previous bargaining round. It can be shown that 'the wage level which maximizes the payoff to the cooperating unions may not be sustainable as a non-cooperative equilibrium' but that 'a less moderate agreement (with a higher wage level) may nevertheless be sustainable'.[73]

---

[72] Hersoug (1984).   [73] Holden and Raaum (1988).

Truly centralized bargaining with dictatorial leaders acting on behalf of the unions will lead to lower wages and higher welfare than the implicit mode of centralization that requires moderation to be sustainable as a trigger strategy in iterated bargaining. Implicit centralization will, in turn, induce lower wages and higher welfare than fully decentralized bargaining.

I do not know whether similar results could be proved for the more realistic case in which unions are heterogeneous and moved by norms of fair distribution in addition to pure self-interest. Yet the general point is well taken. If we look at the actual process of centralized bargaining, it is obvious that LO leaders have far from dictatorial powers. When bargaining with the employers, they have to consult with their member unions up to the last minute, since without their consent coordination may break down and decentralized bargaining take its place. The cement of centralization may well include, as one ingredient, long-term reasoning based on the self-interest of individual unions.

Up to this point I have referred to capital and labour as the only agents in the bargaining process. The government may also, however, be an explicit or implicit player in the game. As an explicit participant, government can play the benign role of offering tax rebates that substitute for wage increases without undermining employment and price stability. It has been argued that interventions by the government as an implicit player in collective bargaining have more harmful consequences.[74] If unions anticipate that the government will act as a 'current-problem solver' rather than as a 'standing-rule maker', they will take less account of the unemployment problems created by high wage claims. The government, after all, is there to clean up the mess, by creating new employment in the public sector or by subsidizing firms that cannot afford to pay the high wages. The long-term outcome may, however, be that there are more messes to clean up, that is, higher levels of unemployment than there would have been had the government adopted a nonaccommodating policy. 'The reason such policies are suboptimal is not due to myopia. The effect of this decision upon the entire future is taken into consideration. Rather, the suboptimality arises because there is no mechanism to induce *future* policymakers to take into consideration the effect of their policy, via the expectation mechanism, upon *current* decisions of agents'.[75]

---

[74] The following draws on Calmfors (1982, 1985) and Calmfors and Horn (1985, 1986).
[75] Kydland and Prescott (1977), p. 627. See also Calmfors and Horn (1985), pp. 243–4 and Schwerin (1982), pp. 471–2.

By contrast, a quasi-constitutional clause to contain the expansion of the public sector and subsidies to ailing firms would yield an intertemporally optimal outcome. The snag is that 'to achieve credibility for a non-accommodation policy, it may . . . be necessary to accept a transitory period of high unemployment in order to show the labor market organizations that the government is determined to stick to its declared intentions. Such a policy could be regarded as an investment in reputation in order to affect the future behavior of trade unions'.[76] In a complex democratic society, this kind of toughness is neither likely nor desirable. It is unlikely because governments care about reelection, not only about stabilization; indeed, they have to be reelected in order to carry out long-term stabilization. But they may not be reelected if they impose severe hardships on the citizens. In any case, standing tough would not be a good policy even if it could be credibly imposed, because of its highly uncertain efficacy. Macroeconomic theory is too undeveloped to justify large-scale, long-term experiments with reputation building that, in the end, might prove totally pointless or worse.[77]

[76] Calmfors (1985), p. 339.
[77] Elster (1989a), ch. 4, develops this point at greater length.

5. Collective action and social norms

Introduction

Writers on collective action take stands that vary from the paradoxical or heroic to the trivial. The paradoxical line is illustrated by the bootstrapping argument of Offe and Wiesenthal, discussed in the preceding chapter. The heroic line is taken by those who stipulate that no explanation of successful collective action should ever appeal to more than rational prudence, with the summit of heroism being reached by those who argue that cooperation can be selfishly rational even in a one-shot Prisoner's Dilemma. Although these writers may not really believe that all successful collective action can be thus explained, they fear that a broader concept of motivation would rob the theory of any explanatory power. This fear is amply justified by the arguments that explain collective action by assuming that the participants must be moved by a norm of cooperation or by a propensity to behave irrationally. This line of reasoning, reminiscent of the dormitive virtue of opium, is indeed utterly trivial, unless the specific norm of cooperation or the specific type of irrationality is defined in a way that is independently meaningful. This is the task of the present chapter.

I shall not assume that there is *a* norm of cooperation, whose presence and operation can be ascertained by the fact that cooperation takes place. Rather I believe that there exist several distinct norms that may, but need not, induce people to cooperate. These include moral norms, derived from utilitarianism, and the social norms of fairness and everyday Kantianism. Similarly, we can identify a specific type of irrationality – I shall refer to it as magical thinking – that plays an important role in many decisions to cooperate. I do not believe many cases of successful collective action can be explained by stipulating selfish rationality alone, be it outcome-oriented or process-oriented. But I would not argue that selfish motivations play no role in overcoming the free-rider problem. When one is confronted with successful collective action, the task is to identify the precise *mix of motivations* – selfish *and* normative, rational *and* irrational – that produced it. Motivations that taken separately would not get collective action off the ground may interact, snowball and build upon each other so that the whole exceeds the sum of its parts.

Norms of cooperation

In Chapter 1, I discussed outcome-oriented norms of cooperation, of the utilitarian or altruist kind. Here I discuss the nonconsequentialist norms of fairness and everyday Kantianism, in that order. The latter norm is considered together with its psychological foundations in what I call magical thinking. I will not inquire into the psychological foundations of the norm of fairness, a task that must be postponed until the analysis of equality and envy in the next two chapters.

The norm of fairness tells an individual to cooperate if and only everybody else, or at least a substantial number of others, cooperate. Although all members of a group may share this norm, they may have different thresholds of cooperation. For some people, the norm takes effect with a relatively small number of other cooperators. Others may require nearly universal cooperation before they join. Among the other cooperators whose presence triggers the norm of fairness for a given person, some may themselves be motivated by the same norm, with, however, a smaller number of other cooperators required. Among the latter, some may also be motivated by the norm of fairness, but as we descend the chain we shall eventually meet some people who cooperate for other reasons.[1] Cooperation could never arise in a population in which everybody was motivated by the norm of fairness.

Although the norm of fairness is not in itself consequentialist, it can coexist with consequential considerations. People motivated by fairness may be sensitive to the costs of cooperation even if they do not consider the benefits. The individual is the meeting point of several opposing forces. His own conscience and social pressure tell him to cooperate when most other people do. The costs of cooperation work in the opposite direction. If the costs are a steeply increasing function of the number of cooperators, he might actually be less likely to cooperate when a greater number of

---

[1] Note that this concept of 'unmoved movers' differs from that discussed in Chapter 3.

others do so. I assume, however, that this is not the case. In much of this chapter I use a stylized, simplified formulation that, by disregarding the costs of cooperation, exaggerates the mechanical, mindless adherence to the norm of fairness.

The principle of conditional cooperation expressed in this norm can also be generated in other ways. Utilitarian or altruist motivations can, for certain technologies of collective action, yield the same prescription. As we saw in Chapter 1, selective incentives or altruism can transform the Prisoner's Dilemma into an Assurance Game. In the latter game, defection is not a dominant strategy. Nor is cooperation dominant, as it is for the everyday Kantian. There is no dominant strategy, but cooperation is the solution that will be realized if the parties have full information about each other. In iterated games, conditional cooperation – Tit for Tat – can also be generated by purely selfish motivations, as we saw in Chapter 1. (Note, however, that Tit-for-Tat is not fully conditional since in addition to the conditional injunction to cooperate if others cooperated previously, it also includes the unconditional instruction to cooperate in the first round.) Here I am concerned with conditional cooperation generated by conformism rather than by altruism or rational prudence.

The norm of fairness makes cooperation conditional upon the actual cooperative behaviour of others, not on their anticipated cooperation. In this respect it differs crucially from conditional cooperation in the Assurance Game or in iterated games. In these, all group members can be conditional cooperators who converge on cooperation because everybody expects everybody to do so. To see why the norm of fairness does not work in the same way, consider families in a peasant community who are led, by individual rationality, to have more children than is collectively rational. If there were a social norm against large families, all would benefit from it. Could such a norm – that is, a behavioural package that involved having smaller families, punishing defectors, punishing nonpunishers and so on – be represented as the solution to an Assurance Game? I think not. Social norms cannot be sustained by instrumental reasoning of this kind. To be effective, they must be internalized, so that violating them in the presence of others is felt to be shameful and wrong, not simply a mistake or a lapse from rationality. The emotion of shame is not within the scope of rational willing.

The norm of fairness enjoins us to follow the majority, whatever it is doing. If others are not cooperating, we need not do so either. To the Kantian question 'What if everyone did that?' Yossarian in *Catch 22* an-

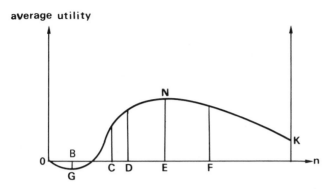

Fig. 5.1

swers, 'Then I'd be a fool to do otherwise, wouldn't I?' If others are cooperating, we are, however, under an obligation to do so too. There are innumerable instances of this reasoning in social life. Corrupt practices, for instance, are often defended by the claim that 'everybody does it' (see the concluding chapter). Conversely, the perceived obligation to do military service stems from a feeling that 'I ought to do my share'.

The obligation created by the norm of fairness does not derive from outcomes. The norm tells us to defect when there are few cooperators, even if we are on an increasing stretch of the average-benefit curve. Assume that the threshold for the norm of fairness is at D in Fig. 5.1. Although cooperation between B and D yields positive net benefits, a person motivated by the norm of fairness would not feel an obligation to cooperate. In fact, there might even be a social norm against cooperating in such cases. The general norm against sticking one's neck out could easily lead to sanctions against unilateral cooperators. *Do-gooders often make others feel bad.*

Conversely, the norm of fairness tells us to cooperate when many others do so, even when one is on a decreasing stretch of the curve. In Fig. 5.1 the outcome K under universal cooperation is substantially worse than the optimal outcome N, although still better than the noncooperative outcome 0. Even when the sum total of the benefits created by the last cooperators is well below the costs (to them)[2] of contributing, the norm of fairness might still prevent them from taking a free ride.

This problem is not, perhaps, very serious. True, there is too much

[2] If there are increasing costs of cooperation, one must also count the additional costs they impose on the inframarginal cooperators.

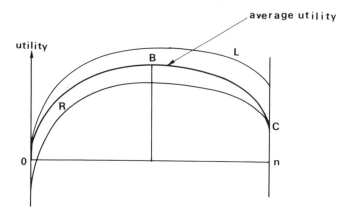

Fig. 5.2

cooperation, but not because the excessive cooperators actually harm anyone. Their contribution simply is not worth the effort. More serious problems arise when the last act of cooperation harms everybody, contributors
and noncontributors. This possibility is illustrated in Fig. 5.2. Note that
the situation remains an *n*-person Prisoner's Dilemma, although now the *L*
and *R* curves are not, as they were in Chapter 1, constrained to be monotonically increasing.

Here are some examples. A group of friends who are cleaning up after
a party might actually finish the job faster if some of them relax instead
with a drink, but the norm against free riding might overwhelm considerations of efficiency. Joining the army in wartime is a more substantial example. Those who stay home to work in vital industries may feel that they
are violating the norm of fairness. If all who want to join were allowed to
do so, the war effort as a whole might suffer. Or consider the Leninist
theory of party organization. If organizational efficacy is an increasing
function of numbers and discipline, and discipline[3] is a decreasing function
of numbers, it could happen that the optimal number of party members
falls well short of universal membership.[4] Even if there is normative pressure on workers to join the party and nonjoiners are frowned upon, not all

---

[3] Or rather the maximal level of discipline that can be achieved.
[4] This can never occur in the theories of revolution and rebellion proposed by Roemer
(1985a) and deNardo (1985), in which only numbers matter. While surely appropriate in
some cases, these theories fail to confront the problem of organizing large numbers.

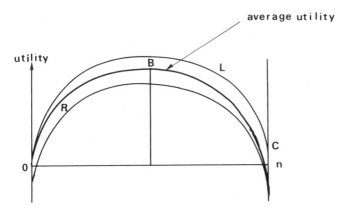

Fig. 5.3

can be allowed to join.[5] In the last two examples, universal cooperation will not occur, because there is a centralized authority that can resist the pressure to join. In situations that lack a coercive institution, the norm of fairness could drive cooperation beyond the optimal point.

It might even happen that universal cooperation is inferior to universal noncooperation, a possibility depicted in Fig. 5.3. This is not a Prisoner's Dilemma, although it is still a collective action problem in the sense that it is better for all if some cooperate than if none do.

To illustrate this case, consider the problem of cleaning up the lawn after a fête. If everybody joins in, the lawn will be trampled to destruction. It is better for all to have a lawn that is green but littered than to have it destroyed as a result of misguided solidarity. Or consider again the problem of organizing war. Suppose that the country in question initiated the war, so that universal noncooperation meant peace rather than defeat. It could then be worse for all if all joined the war effort than if nobody did, assuming that universal cooperation is so inefficient as to bring about defeat.

Collective action is defined by the feature that contributions have diffuse benefits and precise costs. In the standard theory, this provides individuals with a reason to abstain from cooperating. My idea here has been to turn this argument on its head. It is precisely because contributions are easily

[5] This suggestion is valid at most for the Leninist party at its inception, when it had to operate as a fighting unit confronting a hostile environment. Today, party membership is still restricted, but for a very different reason. As explained in Walder (1986), the main role of the Chinese Communist party, for instance, is to divide and rule the workers, by creating a deep split between activists and nonactivists within the enterprise.

identifiable that they can become the object of a social norm to cooperate. The fact that an additional contribution may actually bring about a slight decrease in the benefits from collective action has little motivating power. If I contemplate the spectacle of your getting a free ride, the thought that 'You get off more lightly than I do' may swamp the thought that 'your free riding yields an imperceptibly small increase in my utility'. I return to this perspective in the next two chapters.

I now turn to the norm of everyday Kantianism, which says that one should cooperate if and only if universal cooperation is better for everybody than universal defection. There are at least two reasons the principle should be called 'everyday' Kantianism rather than simply Kantianism. First, Kant's own formulation of the principle does not refer to what would *happen* if everyone acted in a certain way. Rather it asks whether one 'can will' that everyone will act in that way. One reason one cannot will that all will act in a certain way might appear to be that it would be worse for all if all did so. This is not Kant's view, however. Rather he argued that one cannot will X if the notion of all doing X harbours a logical or pragmatical contradiction. If breaking promises, for instance, were to be made into a universal principle, the concept of promising would lose its meaning.[6] Second, the arguments made below presuppose a naive form of Kantianism which excludes the use of mixed strategies. Some of the paradoxes of everyday Kantianism would disappear if the agents were allowed to randomize between cooperating and not cooperating. Other, more important paradoxes would, however, remain.

There are two further distinctions between everyday Kantians and true Kantians. As defined above, the everyday Kantian (like the true one) does not consider the costs to himself of cooperating. In practice, this is implausible. Like people motivated by fairness, everyday Kantians are usually outcome-insensitive with respect to benefits but not with respect to costs. Roughly speaking, they proceed in two steps. First, they use something like the categorical imperative to decide where their duty lies. Then, before acting, they consider whether the costs are prohibitive, which, on a given occasion, they may well be. The trade-off will differ across people. Some Kantians pay virtually no attention to costs, while in others the voice of duty is reduced to a whisper that is easily offset by considerations of cost. For that reason, even everyday Kantians might be sensitive to the number

---

[6] A clear and useful presentation of Kant's Kantianism is presented by Korsgaard (1985). See also Elster (1978), pp. 97–103.

of other cooperators, namely if these increased the costs of cooperation to the point where they offset the call of duty. In cases of low-cost or constant-cost cooperation (like voting), this complicating factor can largely be ignored, but in other cases it could be important.

Furthermore, in practice the everyday Kantian is somewhat sensitive to benefits. True, he does not consider the likely impact of *his* cooperation. By asking, 'What if everyone did that?' he does, however, consider the impact of universal cooperation. It seems plausible that the strength of his feeling of duty depends on the difference between universal cooperation and universal noncooperation. The smaller the difference, the lower the voice of conscience and the more likely it is to be offset by considerations of cost. Once again, this dependence will vary across people.

A case of pure and strong Kantianism during the Second World War was provided by a Protestant pastor, André Trocmé, and the other inhabitants of Le Chambon, a small village in southern France.[7] Between 1940 and 1944 these villagers provided asylum for a large number of German Jews, at great risk to themselves and under the constant surveillance of the Vichy government and later the German occupational forces. They explicitly refused to consider the consequences, to themselves *or others,* of their action. Instead, they relied on a simple principle: 'Never turn away anyone who needs help'. As early as 1934 Trocmé had written an essay on 'the opposite evil', in which

> he expressed his belief that in times of crisis, theories and predictions are a refugee for cowards. In that essay he wrote of the dangers involved in trying to predict the effects of your actions on your own life, your family's lives, the lives in your parish, and the lives of your countrymen. During the war years he did not spend precious time and energy investigating the effects of his actions on any political theory he might hold. He chose to do without intellectual systems and without fear-filled predictions. He decided simply to 'help the unjustly persecuted innocents around me'. He decided to obey God's imperious commandments

[7] The following relies on Hallie (1979). I am grateful to Michael McIntyre for drawing my attention to this case and its implications for collective action theory. Oliner and Oliner (1988) offer a large-scale study of the motivation of rescuers of Jews in Nazi Germany, with emphasis on the capacity for caring rather than on the ability to follow abstract principles. Their understanding of moral theory, however, is severely limited, as shown when they argue that the Kantian tradition in moral philosophy emphasizes fair exchange and reciprocity, while 'care endorses willingness to give more than is received' (p. 172).

against killing and betraying. With his sophisticated mind he put his sophisticated mind aside.[8]

The nonconsequentialist core of everyday Kantianism is that it does not allow consideration of the external circumstances, such as the expected number of other cooperators, that determine whether an individual act will in fact have good or bad consequences. Because it neglects these circumstances, everyday Kantianism can lead to bad outcomes in two kinds of situations. First, consider a collective action problem in which the optimal number of cooperators falls short of universal cooperation, such as in diagrams B, D and E of Fig. 1.6 or in Figs. 5.1 and 5.2. In a population of everyday Kantians there would be universal and hence more than optimal cooperation. (Sophisticated Kantians would use a mixed strategy to achieve the optimal number.) By contrast, everyday Kantians would not cooperate in situations like that depicted in Fig. 5.3, even if they represented only a small subset of the population. Even when a little cooperation would be a good thing, and they would be the only ones who could be counted on to cooperate, they would not do so, out of fear of what would happen if everyone did.

There is no reason to spell out why the problems just considered are not urgent ones, to say the least. The danger of everyday Kantianism lies elsewhere. Consider a situation, depicted in Fig. 5.4, in which unilateral cooperation is harmful to other people. Everyday Kantianism prescribes the cooperative strategy in such cases, regardless of the disastrous consequences that might ensue if few others follow suit. Unilateral disarmament could, under certain circumstances, increase the risk of war. Unilateral acts of heroism or sacrifice can give authorities or employers an excuse to crack down on nonparticipants as well as participants.[9] Unlike the disarmament example, this is more than a hypothetical case. In German-occupied countries during the Second World War, for instance, there was often considerable scepticism towards individual acts of resistance that might provoke the Germans into massive retaliation.[10] Such phenomena provide an alter-

---

[8] Hallie (1979), p. 285.

[9] In such cases, the L and R curves do not rise monotonically. Their intersections with the vertical axes still occur in the order that defines the n-person Prisoner's Dilemma.

[10] When Trocmé's wife first proposed to take in a refugee, the mayor asked her, 'Do you dare to endanger this whole village for the sake of one foreigner? Will you save one woman and destroy us all?' (Hallie 1979, p. 121). In this case, the refugee operation was successful. The Trocmés had 'moral luck' (Williams 1981, ch. 2). If, however, the Germans had retaliated ruthlessly, posterity's judgement would have differed.

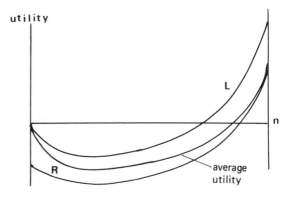

Fig. 5.4

native explanation of the negative attitude towards do-gooders. Instead of irrationally disliking do-gooders because they make us feel bad, we might dislike them on the rational ground that they actually harm us. More generally, we might dislike them on the grounds that they do not stoop to consider whether they might harm us. For someone wedded to a *Verant-wortungsethik,* their *Gesinnungsethik* is a form of moral egoism, in which all that counts is doing one's duty and damn the consequences. Needless to say, it would be ridiculous to direct this criticism at someone like Trocmé. And sometimes this instrumental criticism of do-gooders might simply be envy in disguise. But I think there are cases in which the lack of regard for consequences is indeed blamable.

The appeal of everyday Kantianism is somewhat insinuating. Two questions that embody this principle and that have strong emotional appeal are: 'If not me, who?' and 'But what if everyone did that?' Both questions suggest that there are only two possible states of the world, one in which everyone cooperates and one in which no one does so. It hints, moreover, that it is up to me which of these states will come about. If I am in a sufficiently confused state of mind, I may indeed be persuaded to believe, or to act as if I believed, that everything turns upon my behaviour. Psychologically, if not logically, there is a short step from the thought 'If *I* don't do it, why should anyone?' to the thought 'If I don't do it, nobody will'. Let me elaborate on this point, which is, I believe, of fundamental importance.

Everyday Kantianism rests on a form of magical thinking that we may call *everyday Calvinism*.[11] This is the confusion of causal and diagnostic efficacy, or the belief that by acting on the symptoms one can also change the cause. If a predeterminist doctrine like Calvinism led to entrepreneurship, it could have done so only via the magical idea that manipulation of the signs of salvation could strengthen the belief that one was among the elect. An explicit example is cited by E. P. Thompson, in his discussion of the tension among eighteenth-century British Baptists between their desire to attract new recruits and their belief in predetermination:

> It was not until 1770 that the Particular Baptists began to break out of the trap of their own dogma, issuing a circular letter (from Northhamptonshire) which offered a formula by which evangelism and the notion of election might be reconciled: 'Every soul that comes to Christ to be saved . . . is to be encouraged. . . . The coming soul need not fear that he is not elected, for none but such would be willing to come'.[12]

The example can be used to illustrate Newcomb's problem[13] (see Fig. 5.5). In this game, God moves first, deciding whether to choose me to be among the elect.[14] When it is my turn, I do not know which move God has made. I do not know, that is, whether I am facing the choice on the left or the choice on the right. It does not really matter, however, since in either case the option of staying home is preferable to that of going to church. To go involves a small cost and no possible benefit: since God has already moved there is nothing I can do to influence him. I know, however, that God in his omniscience has anticipated what I will do, and it is quite likely that he has made sure not to elect those who do not go.[15] In that case, what should I do? On the one hand, since God has already made his choice, I have nothing to lose from staying home. On the other hand, if God really makes his decision as a function of what he expects (in fact knows) that I will do, how could I stay at home?

It is not my task here to resolve this conundrum.[16] Rather I want to illustrate how people often make the equivalent decision of going to church

[11] The phrase was used in the title of an early version of Quattrone and Tversky (1986).

[12] Thompson (1969), p. 38.

[13] For extensive discussions, see the articles collected in Campbell and Sowden, eds. (1985).

[14] For other uses of game theory to illustrate theological problems, see Brams (1982).

[15] Note the deviation from the circular letter, in which going to church is cited as a sufficient but not necessary condition for being among the elect.

[16] For a possible resolution (in favour of staying home), see the brief remarks in Elster (1978), pp. 85–6.

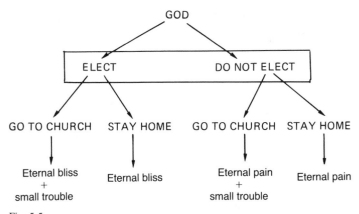

Fig. 5.5

in cases where it is uncontroversially irrational to do so. In an experiment by George Quattrone and Amos Tversky two groups of subjects were told that people with a certain kind of heart have a longer life expectancy and greater (lower) tolerance to cold water after exercise than people with a different type of heart. When later asked to keep their arm in cold water after an exercise task, they endured it for a longer (shorter) time than they had done before they were exposed to the information. The subjects, in other words, acted as if by modifying the symptoms they could, magically, alter the cause. I believe most readers, on reflection, would be able to think of occasions on which they engaged in similar practices.

There is a close connection between Newcomb's Problem and the Prisoner's Dilemma.[17] Consider two persons in a Prisoner's Dilemma who have to make their decisions independently of each other. If they are sufficiently alike, each of them may reason in the following manner. 'If I cooperate, there is a good chance that the other will cooperate too. Being like me, he will act like me. Let me, therefore, cooperate to bring it about that he does too.' Once again, the behaviour that is diagnostic of the other's cooperation is chosen as if it could have causal efficacy.

Quattrone and Tversky conducted an experiment that confirmed the hypothesis that people in fact think – or act as if they think – in this manner.[18] Subjects in each of two conditions were told that in an upcoming

[17] See the articles by Lewis, Davis and Sobel reprinted in Campbell and Sowden, eds. (1985).
[18] Quattrone and Tversky (1986), pp. 48–54.

election the electorate would consist of 4 million supporters of Party A, 4 million supporters of Party B and 4 million nonaligned. They were told, moreover, that the victorious party would win by 200 000 to 400 000 votes. Finally, all subjects were told that they were supporters of Party A. In one condition, subjects were told that party supporters would vote in approximately equal numbers, so that the nonaligned vote would be decisive. In the other condition, voters were told that the nonaligned voters would split their vote equally between the two parties, so that the turnout of the committed voters would decide the election. The second condition would seem more conducive to magical thinking, since here a supporter of Party A could deceive himself into thinking that by voting he could induce other, like-minded people to vote. This hypothesis was confirmed in the experiment, which showed, among other things, that more people in the second condition expressed an intention to vote.

Further support for the view that collective action can involve magical thinking comes from an experiment by Robyn Dawes and co-workers. Let me quote from their summary:

> The most important finding of this experiment was that having to make the cooperative or defective choice apparently did affect the estimates of what other people would do, as well as vice versa. Thus, one's choices in such a dilemma situation not only reflect beliefs about others, but also affect these beliefs. There are a number of possible explanations.
>
> First, the effect may be pure rationalization. Having decided to cooperate or defect, the group member may attempt to justify the choice by his or her estimate of what others will do. Clearly, a cooperative choice is not very wise if any other people are going to defect, while a defecting choice may be considered downright immoral if most other people cooperate . . .
>
> Second, there may be two closely related cognitive reasons for the behavior to affect the belief. Individuals may decide to use their own behavior as information about what other people would do; after all, if people from similar cultures tend to behave in similar ways in similar situations, and if I do this, it follows that my peers may do so to. In addition, there is the possibility that as I make up my mind to defect or cooperate, the reasons leading to the choice I finally make become more salient, while those leading to the other choice become less so. Then, when attempting to evaluate what other people will do, I see compelling

reasons for doing what I do and less compelling reasons for doing the opposite.[19]

The first subvariety of the second explanation corresponds to what I have called magical thinking, *except that Dawes and his co-workers explicitly characterize it as rational:* 'Given the belief that people tend to behave similarly in the same situation, a subject who decides to cooperate or defect may have a rational basis for believing others will do likewise'.[20] Hence the experimenters themselves behave as the subjects in the Quattrone–Tversky experiment, confirming how easy it is to slip into the confusion between diagnostic and causal thinking.

In the Introduction I mentioned the crash in the stock market on 19 October 1987 as a paradigm case of break-down of social order. Clearly, there is need both for coordination and for cooperation to ensure that it does not happen again. Perhaps a dose of everyday Kantianism could help? The following extract from a comment on 'the economic scene' by Leonard Silk *(New York Times,* 13 January 1988) is so wonderfully confused – and hilariously illustrative of my point – that it is worth reproducing at some length:

As the Greek philosopher Heraclitus put it about 500 B.C., you never swim in the same river twice – and it is a different market now from what it was before Oct. 19.

Indeed, an American economist, M. Louise Curley, a consultant to Scudder, Stevens & Clark, investment advisers, turns to a different philosopher to explain why the markets have not repeated the Oct. 19 crash. She finds a hint in the German philosopher Immanuel Kant (1724–1804), specifically in his Categorical Imperative. . . . This may be translated as: Never adopt a principle of action that you would not be prepared to see everyone else adopt.

The Presidential commission that investigated the Black Monday market collapse . . . has stressed the role that program trading played in causing the market to plunge by a record amount. But institutions have now presumably learned that, acting in their individual self-interest, they can be severely damaged when other institutions act as they did.

Rational self-interest dictates that they stop behaving in such a short-

---

[19] Dawes, McTavish and Shaklee (1977), pp. 10–11.   [20] Ibid., p. 8.

sighted way – that is, in the mistaken belief that they can operate in isolation from other institutional investors with similar programmed strategies for buying futures and selling stocks at their current prices.

The Categorical Imperative implies that different rules of behavior must be found in their own and the general interest. . . . Kant sought to show that the 'essential requirements of morality are really built into the concept of rationality itself'. Any rational being, Kant declared, has to recognize those requirements as binding.

But is the stock market rational? It may take further punishment before the market players recognize that their self-interest is bound up in the common interest. The sharp fall in the Dow Jones industrial average in New York on Friday, without a sign of outside cause, may imply that the Kantian lesson has not yet been learned. . . .

John von Neumann and Oskar Morgenstern, in their seminal book 'The Theory of Games and Economic Behavior', have given Kant's lesson modern form. They demonstrated that the individual economic actor must recognize that he is involved in a multi-layer or multi-firm game, in which the actions of others can make his own play self-destructive if he does not anticipate what others will do. The individual player, they counsel, needs to find a strategy that maximizes his gains, while minimizing his risks. The learning process required to master 'Minimax' is painfully proceeding in London, New York and other financial capitals.

The intellectual disarray of the last few sentences shows that even economic commentators in the world's leading newspaper might benefit from Economics 101. More interesting, symptomatic and representative is the claim that the categorical imperative coincides with rational self-interest and, more eccentrically, that von Neumann and Morgenstern give us an up-to-date version of Kant. The confusion manifest in Leonard Silk's column also underlies the spontaneous reaction of most people, myself included, when people turn up at our door Sunday evening to ask for a contribution to a television-sponsored charity drive. 'If I don't give, who will?' Being under the spell of this question, we end up contributing, at least part of the time.

Everyday Kantianism is closely related to what I described in Chapter 3 as private norms, rigid unbending rules that allow us to resist temptation. Here the operative question is: If not now, when? I might, to be sure, postpone going on the wagon or start jogging until tomorrow. The damage to my body from one day's additional indulgence is surely infinitesimal, and I can always quit (or begin) tomorrow. The snag is, of course, that since tomorrow is going to be essentially like today, the best predictor of what I will do tomorrow is what I do today. In interpersonal collective action, magical thinking amounts to believing, or acting as if I believed, that my cooperation can cause others to cooperate. In intrapersonal collective action, it amounts to believing, or acting as if I believed, that by acting prudently today I can cause myself to act prudently in the future.

One might question whether this reasoning *is* magical and irrational in the intrapersonal case.[21] Note first that in both the interpersonal and intrapersonal cases, I have tacitly assumed that there are no direct causal effects. If I can anticipate that I will cause my neighbour to change his mind when he sees me leaving for the voting booth, it is quite rational to incorporate that effect in my decision whether to vote. But I have assumed that there is no such effect to be anticipated. Similarly, if I can anticipate that the next drink will strengthen my desire for more drinks, it is quite rational to take account of that effect in my current decision whether to have a drink. Once again, however, I have assumed that there are no such effects. Although the assumption may not always be justified in the case of drinking, it is approximately correct in many cases of weakness of will. There is one effect, however, that will always be present in the intrapersonal case. The choice tomorrow will differ from today's choice in that tomorrow I shall have *more information* about earlier choices than I have today. Specifically, I will known then what I will have chosen today. Because of the asymmetry of time and the indivisibility of persons, there is in this respect a basic difference between the interpersonal and the intrapersonal cases.

The added information is relevant in that it constrains my *self-image* in a way that may ease or obstruct my ability to make the prudent choice. It has been said, correctly, that 'choices depend on tastes and tastes on past choices'.[22] Similarly, choices depend on self-image and self-image on past choices.[23] If one can *plausibly* say to oneself, 'I am not the kind of person who yields to temptation', it becomes easier to resist.[24] Conversely, yield-

[21] The following draws on Elster (1985b), p. 258.   [22] Gorman (1967).

[23] Føllesdal (1981).

[24] 'The consideration . . . that if I eat Welsh rabbit this evening, I shall much regret it tomorrow, may not suffice to deter me from the eating – if I like Welsh rabbit. But the addition of the consideration that those who obtain trivial present pleasure at the cost of future pain are gluttonous fools, or weak-minded, may suffice to turn the scale in favor of abstinence' (Lovejoy 1968, pp. 80–1). Essentially the same argument is found in C. Taylor (1976), p. 295, but in terms of cream cake rather than of Welsh rabbit.

ing often induces a kind of vertiginous feeling: 'Having yielded in the past I know that I am just a heel anyway, so why not give in again?' But why should I be constrained by my self-image? Since I am assuming that no dispositional change – mental[25] or physical – has taken place, how could the mere fact of information about the past make a rational difference for choices in the present? The answer would be that thinking about oneself as having an enduring self, over and above habits and inclinations, is part and parcel of what it is to be a person. Neo-Buddhist theories of the self[26] would argue that the belief is irrational, but even they grant that it is largely an unavoidable one. Even if persons are not constituted by an enduring self, they may be constituted by the belief that they have one. Information about past actions will then rationally constrain what *kind* of self they can believe themselves to have.

Mixed motives

All societies and groups face collective action problems. In all, at least some of the dilemmas are overcome and cooperation is achieved, frequently by coercion. Here I have considered noncoercive, voluntary cooperation. I believe that in any given case we will observe that the individuals who make a voluntary contribution have different motives. A successful campaign, strike, lobbying effort or election cannot be traced to a single, homogeneous motive that animates all the contributors. Different motivations, building upon one another, can add up to a high rate of participation. The following story can be envisaged in terms of building a social movement in which members join at successive times. For vividness, the reader may think of the movement against the Vietnam War. Later I shall discuss two cases in which decisions are made more or less simultaneously and independently of each other.

Consider once again Fig. 5.1. In this typical collective action problem, the underlying technology has constant costs of cooperation, whereas the benefits first increase slowly, then more rapidly and then more slowly again.

---

[25] One might argue, as an alternative to the present account, that choices in the present set up a mental habit or disposition that shapes future choices and that present choices could take account of that effect. I believe there is room and need for a notion of mental habit that differs both from the purely physiological facts of habituation or addiction and from the concept of self-image. I am focusing here, however, on cases in which the desire to act imprudently remains strong, so that it cannot simply be eliminated by force of habit.

[26] Kolm (1982); Parfit (1984).

I shall suppose that the population contains five main motivational types.[27] Of these, two have a dominant strategy:

1. Selfish, outcome-oriented rational individuals care exclusively about the output of collective action. Noncooperation is their dominant strategy, and hence they play no further role in the argument.

2. Everyday Kantians cooperate under all circumstances. Strictly speaking, as we have seen, this need not be true. If the costs of cooperation depend on the number of cooperators, even Kantians may make their cooperation conditional on that of others. In the story I am about to tell, however, I assume that the Kantians are insensitive to the costs of cooperation and hence, for them, cooperation is a dominant strategy.

The remaining types cooperate conditionally, depending on the number of other cooperators. There are two ways in which the number of other cooperators can influence one's propensity to cooperate. The propensity can be a direct function of the number of other cooperators, or it can be a function of the expected benefit of cooperation – a benefit which in turn depends on the number of other cooperators. Hence we may distinguish between the following:

3. Utilitarians cooperate if and only if they believe themselves to be on an increasing stretch of the average-net-benefit curve, with the number of other cooperators being between B and E in Fig. 5.1. In other words, they will not cooperate at very low and very high levels of cooperation.

4. People who derive benefits from the process of participating usually require the presence of some other cooperators, although the number can be variable. *Elite participationists* prefer that few others cooperate. Their desire is to be present at the creation, and they become bored when the movement spreads and gains strength. *Mass participationists* enjoy themselves more the larger the movement, but

---

[27] Actually, I do not believe that individuals have one and only one motivation. It is a central tenet of the present book that different motivations and norms coexist within each individual. Yet one can take only one step at a time. The admission of heterogeneous groups represents a first move towards realism. The incorporation of heterogeneous individuals will have to come later. For two attempts in this direction see Kondo (1988) and Petersen (forthcoming).

require some (variable) minimum of already-established cooperation before they join.[28]

5. People motivated by the norm of fairness will join the movement when the number of other cooperators exceeds their threshold for conditional obligation. Since people can have different thresholds, they may not all join at the same time, but come on board in successive waves.

In general, it is not possible to say anything about the dynamics of collective action with mixed motivations of this kind. The following scenario represents one possibility, chosen mainly to illustrate the possibilities and complexities. At the beginning, there are everyday Kantians, who are soon joined by elite participationists. If these two groups are between them numerous enough to get participation up to B in Fig. 5.1, the utilitarians come on board. If they are sufficiently numerous, the elite participationists begin to drop out and the mass participationists begin to join in successive waves. Assume, for specificity, that mass participationists begin to join at C. If utilitarians and mass participationists are between them numerous enough to offset the loss of the elitists, the threshold may be attained at which successive waves of people motivated by the norm of fairness also come on board. If these groups are between them sufficiently numerous to bring participation up to E, the utilitarians begin to drop out. What then happens depends on the precise mix of motivations. It could be that the loss of the utilitarians will leave the people motivated by fairness unaffected, since they can sustain each other once they have been brought out. The utilitarians will, so to speak, be the ladder which they can kick away behind themselves. It could also happen, however, that without the ladder they will fall down. When the utilitarians withdraw, the number of cooperators will become too small to sustain the norm of fairness, and the whole movement will collapse.

This scenario has been constructed on the assumption that people treat each other parametrically, as part of the given circumstances that shape the decision to cooperate. But there could also be effects of strategic anticipation. Utilitarians might not withdraw if they anticipate that their withdrawal will trigger that of others. They might enter prematurely (to the left of B in Fig. 5.1), in the hope of causing others to join. Or they might

---

[28] The elitist participationists may well be more numerous than the mass participationists. See the comments on tourism in Chapter 3.

decide not to join in the first place, if they are afraid of triggering a movement that will eventually generate so much cooperation that all will be worse off, as in Fig. 5.3. I do not think these forms of strategic reasoning occur frequently, but they are not totally implausible either.

An implication of this approach which some may find depressing is that we will never have a general theory of collective action. The variety of interacting motivations is simply too large for any equilibrium theorems to be provable. Although simulations may yield results in special cases,[29] they are not fully satisfactory explanatory devices since the results are often difficult to interpret. Historians and social scientists might, however, use the kind of framework developed here to improve their understanding of specific social movements. That, in fact, is probably as much as one can ever hope for in the social sciences. If social scientists forgot their obsession with grand theory, and looked instead for small and medium-sized mechanisms that apply across a wide spectrum of social situations, some mathematical economists and Parsonian sociologists (to name but a few) might go out of business, but the world would be a better-understood place.[30]

Two partial (other-things-being-equal) generalizations may nevertheless be suggested. There are probably not many everyday Kantians, but their presence may be an indispensable *catalyst* for cooperation. Although there are probably many people who are motivated by the norm of fairness, they cannot by themselves get cooperation off the ground. They do, however, act as a *multiplier* on the cooperation of other people.[31] The first generalization, therefore, is this: *everyday Kantianism and the norm of fairness interact to produce much more cooperation than either could do by itself.*[32]

The literature on non-selfish motivations is split on the question of the relation between individual cooperation and the general level of coopera-

---

[29] The best example known to me is Nelson and Winter (1982).

[30] Elster (1989b) makes an extended plea for a shift from theories to mechanisms in the social sciences. See also Veyne (1971).

[31] A very different multiplier effect is at work in everyday Kantianism. Magical thinking leads the individual to believe that his cooperation will effectively act as a multiplier, by causing other people to cooperate.

[32] I am grateful to Tetsuo Kondo for suggesting the characterization of Kantianism and fairness as catalyst and multiplier, respectively. In unpublished work (Kondo 1988), he has shown that the present analysis carries over to an iterated two-person Prisoner's Dilemma, when he assumes mixed motives to exist within and not across individuals. He assumes, i.e., that on any given occasion each individual follows each of the various motivations with a given probability.

tion. In Howard Margolis's model of altruistic behaviour it follows that as other people give more to good causes, I should give less.[33] The same result holds for utilitarian motivations. In Robert Sugden's model of reciprocity it follows that as other people give more, I should also give more.[34] The underlying difference is that Margolis assumes people to be outcome-oriented, whereas Sugden does not. Both may be right, but with respect to different individuals. Low levels of cooperation attract utilitarians but deter people motivated by fairness. At high levels, the opposite effects are observed. The second generalization, therefore, is this: *the strength of utilitarianism and that of fairness vary inversely with each other*,[35] because they are related in opposite ways to the number of cooperators.

In the remaining part of the chapter I look more closely at two cases of collective action – voting and tax evasion – from the mixed-motive perspective. In these cases, process benefits play little or no role, at least if we restrict ourselves, as I do, to large-scale anonymous voting. Hence we can focus on the interplay between selfishness, fairness, everyday Kantianism and utilitarianism. Of these, the last is here defined by a simple decision rule that does not presuppose high levels of moral awareness or cognitive sophistication. As just explained, the rule is, roughly speaking, the inverse of the norm of fairness: cooperate if and only if few others do. Although somewhat similar to elite participationism, the underlying motivation is different. It is derived from considerations of outcomes in situations like that depicted in Fig. 5.1. When many others cooperate, the utilitarian obligation to cooperate falls. If the level of cooperation decreases, the obligation becomes stronger.[36] Like the norm of fairness, the utilitarian decision rule must specify the exact level of cooperation (which might differ across individuals) needed to trigger cooperation or defection.

Although for convenience I shall use the language of a dichotomous independent variable, the remarks made on that point in Chapter 1 should be kept in mind. When I say, for instance, that more (or fewer) people vote when the number of voters declines, there are really two things going on. First, different persons have different thresholds. Second, for each person the 'threshold' is really a probability: it is the likelihood of his voting that is affected by the number of other voters. The costs of voting

[33] Margolis (1982).   [34] Sugden (1984).
[35] Except at very low levels of cooperation, where both motivations have an inhibiting effect.
[36] Except, once again, at very low levels of cooperation.

are essentially a random variable, depending on accidents of personal circumstance. A person might have the same pro-voting motivation in two elections, and nevertheless vote in one and abstain in the other because on the second occasion it rains too hard or he is in bed with flu. But for a given probability distribution of such events, the probability of voting depends on the strength of the motivation, which may in turn depend on the number of other voters.

Consider now the decision to vote in a large, anonymous election. Under any reasonable assumptions, selfish rationality dictates abstention, at least in the absence of selective incentives.[37] I do not think anyone ever is driven to vote by asking himself, 'My God, what if I didn't vote and my preferred candidate lost by one vote? I'd feel like killing myself'.[38] Other attempts to demonstrate equilibria with high turn-outs of selfish (or more generally outcome-oriented) voters have invariably failed.[39] Hence most writers invoke the notion of civic duty to explain patterns of voting.[40] Or, in what is essentially an equivalent explanation, they appeal to the 'expressive benefits' of voting.[41] These concepts, however, are rarely given specific content. Instead, these writers turn rapidly to a discussion of the determinants of civic duty or, more generally, of the propensity to vote. At the individual level, they explain turn-out by individual properties of voters: age, sex, marital status, income, occupation, education and so on. In addition, they explain turn-out by three external variables: direct costs and opportunity costs of voting (and of registering for voting), expected closeness of the election and perceived differences among the major alternatives. The

[37] Voting is compulsory in several countries, with small fines imposed on nonvoters.

[38] Ferejohn and Fiorina (1974), p. 535. This phrase summarizes their argument that voting is rational if voters use the principle of minimax regret in a situation of decision making under uncertainty. That principle, while not uniquely dictated by the axioms of decision making under uncertainty, is at least consistent with them (Luce and Raiffa 1957, ch. 13). The argument for seeing voting as decision making under uncertainty is that 'if a citizen calculates according to the conventional analysis, he will decide to abstain. But all citizens will arrive at the same decision; therefore, a smart citizen could vote and singlehandedly decide the decision. And yet, other citizens would also follow this strategy, so maybe he should abstain after all. But if other citizens reason similarly, maybe . . . and so forth' (ibid., p. 527). But if the selfish voter knows (as of course he does) that some people will vote regardless of the expected number of other voters, the argument collapses. For selfish voting to be rational, everyone has to be selfish. There are other flaws in the argument, but this is perhaps the simplest way of refuting it.

[39] For a survey, see Palfrey and Rosenthal (1985).

[40] Barry (1979), pp. 17–18; Wolfinger and Rosenstone (1980), p. 8 and passim; Palfrey and Rosenthal (1985).

[41] Riker and Ordeshook (1968).

importance of the latter variables shows that civic duty does not exclude some sensitivity to outcomes.

The first step towards a better understanding of turn-out rates must be to refine the notion of civic duty. In the present framework, the notion can be understood in three ways, corresponding to utilitarianism, Kantian duty and fairness. Of these, utilitarianism is essentially outcome-oriented, taking account of the benefits as well as the costs of voting. The motivations of duty and fairness are not outcome-oriented as far as the benefits of voting are concerned, although they can be sensitive to costs. The fact that the costs of voting are a major part of the explanation of low turn-outs is consistent with an interpretation of civic duty in terms of fairness or everyday Kantianism. The influence of the other external variables is consistent with everyday Kantianism but not with the norm of fairness. Because of its roots in magical thinking, everyday Kantianism becomes stronger the smaller the reference group to which it is applied. The more other people are like oneself, the more plausibly (in a psychological rather than logical sense) one can infer that they will behave like oneself. Therefore, if the election is expected to be close, the more plausible is the notion that my voting will be pivotal. Also, the smaller the perceived difference between the outcomes, the weaker is the voice of conscience. There are no similar reasons that the norm of fairness should be sensitive to the expected closeness or to the perceived difference.

The next step would be to ascertain which proportions of the electorate were motivated by which varieties of civic duty. One could ask people whether an expected increase or decrease in the turn-out would affect their own propensity to vote. As far as I know, no such studies have been carried out. Panel data for voting and abstention suggest that there are some hard-core voters, that is, everyday Kantians, but do not enable us to distinguish among the subvarieties of occasional voters.[42] Studies of bandwagon and underdog effects concern the choice of one alternative rather than the other, not to the choice of voting versus abstaining. A study of the impact on voting of broadcasting returns before the polls are closed contained an analysis of the effect on turn-out in late-closing polls in the western states.[43] The independent variable was not, however, turn-out, but election results in the eastern states. A direct impact of turn-out on turn-out in the same

---

[42]   Sigelman et al. (1985), p. 751, state in their sample 'only one Kentuckian in eight voted in as many as seven elections' out of eight.
[43]   Lang and Lang (1968), ch. 4.

election seems in any case quite unlikely. It is more plausible to think that there could be an impact of turn-out in one election on turn-out in the following election. If there is a widely perceived downward trend in turn-out, utilitarian voters should feel a strong obligation to vote, whereas those motivated by the norm of fairness have a good excuse for staying home. The net effect might be to reverse the trend or to reinforce it, depending on the precise numerical importance of the two groups.

In most countries, there are trends and cycles in turn-out. Part of the explanation probably lies in changes in individual attributes.[44] Demographic trends increase the number of young unmarried voters who are relatively unlikely to vote. Part of the explanation may lie in changes in the external variables. The effort and efficacy of the major parties in mobilizing their supporters obviously also matter. Alienation from the political system may be a factor of some importance. The question is whether, in addition to these exogenous explanations, there could be a purely endogenous component. One might construct, along the lines suggested earlier, a scenario in which utilitarianism and fairness interact to create cyclical turn-out patterns, somewhat analogous to the cobweb cycle. In the simplest model (without lags), each voter assumes that turn-out in the current election will be like turn-out in the previous one. When all act on that assumption, the outcome will in general differ from what they expected, except in the unlikely event that the effects of utilitarianism and fairness exactly offset each other. If, however, voters act on the basis of predicted turn-outs, there will usually exist a self-fulfilling turn-out prediction which leads to fairness effects and utilitarian effects that exactly offset each other.[45]

Instead of cycles, interacting motivations could also generate upward or downward trends. It is often argued that the steady decrease in American voter turn-out is due to increasing alienation from the political system. This may well be true, but the notion of alienation must be disambiguated. It could mean that people are less likely to vote because they feel less committed to a political system that fails to remove poverty and racial conflict. But political alienation could also be understood as a self-reinforcing erosion of civic duty, quite independent of substantive issues and failures.

[44] Teixeira (1987).

[45] The argument is obviously modelled on Simon (1954), who showed how it is possible to make self-fulfilling predictions of *the winner* so that bandwagon effects and underdog effects exactly offset each other. The bandwagon effect is somewhat similar to the norm of fairness. The underdog effect, however, is quite unrelated to the utilitarian motive. It is, if anything, closer to what I called elitist participationism.

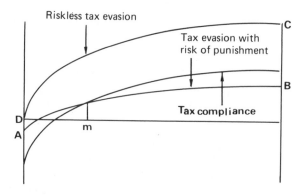

Fig. 5.6

Conversely, it might be worth while to study upward trends in this perspective. Support of the political system, as expressed in increasing turnout rates, might be due to substantive support of the decisions being made or simply to a virtuous spiral of conditional cooperation. The study of turnouts in new democracies might provide useful data for analyses of this kind.

Tax evasion as a collective action problem differs from the voting problem in a number of respects. First, the presence of negative selective incentives – penalties for detected tax evasion – alters the incentives for the taxpayer. In Fig. 5.6, we assume that the taxpayers' money is used to provide public goods and that the marginal utility from consumption of these goods is decreasing. The cost of compliance with the tax laws, that is, the earnings forgone by declaring one's income and deductions honestly, are assumed to be independent of the number of compliers. The impact of tax laws depends on the risk of detection and the severity of the fine, which in turn depend on the number of tax evaders. When there are few evaders, the risk of detection is higher and the penalty more severe. In Fig. 5.6, expected penalty for evasion in a society of compliers is BC, whereas it falls to DA when everybody engages in the practice. As a result, there are two stable equilibria – universal compliance and universal evasion – and one unstable equilibrium in which exactly m people comply with the tax laws.

The preceding analysis may be controversial. For one thing, why should the risk of being detected be higher when there are few evaders? If there is a tax inspection force of a given size, the conclusion follows, but is it not reasonable to assume that the force will expand pari passu with the number of evaders? Against this, however, there is the argument – widely made in the literature on tax evasion – that 'increasing the authoritative zeal of tax authorities may be counterproductive'.[46] Below I discuss a mechanism that could support this hypothesis.

For another thing, why should the severity of punishment decrease with the number of evaders? In one, obvious sense it does not: keeping tax laws constant, the legal penalty for detected tax evasion does not depend on the number of actual or detected evaders. This is not true, however, of the informal penalties – social stigma – associated with detection. The fewer tax evaders there are, the larger is the social stigma. (This is discussed further later.) But the objection might also take a different form, paralleling the argument about expanding the inspection force. Why should tax laws not change pari passu with the number of evaders, increasing the legal penalty so as to offset the decrease in informal sanctions? The counterargument is also parallel: increased severity might be self-defeating.

A major finding in the literature on tax evasion is that people are more likely to evade taxes if they believe many others do so. 'Well, everyone else does it, so why shouldn't I?'[47] For obvious reasons, however, it is much more difficult for an individual to estimate the proportion of tax evaders than to estimate the proportion of voters. One major source of information lies in the prevalence of tax evasion among one's personal acquaintances. The propensity to evade taxes increases with the number of evaders personally known to one.[48] Government behaviour provides another source. People are likely to reason as follows. 'Since the government is taking stronger measures against tax evasion, it must be so widespread that there is no reason to feel ashamed of doing it. Being rational, I shall certainly take account of these measures, but the strength of the measures also tells me that I don't need to take account of anything else'. In addition, we can adduce an argument from 'the psychology of tyranny';[49] if the government takes very harsh measures against tax evaders, the ensuing loss of legitimacy may partially offset the deterrence effect.

It is sometimes suggested that appeals to conscience are more effective than threats of punishment in preventing tax evasion.[50] It is certainly true

[46] Lewis (1982), p. 180.   [47] Ibid., p. 175; see also Laurin (1986), p. 190.
[48] Grasmick and Scott (1982), p. 223; Laurin (1986), p. 191.   [49] Roemer (1985).
[50] Lewis (1982), pp. 281–7. Schwartz and Orleans (1967) confirm this idea, but only with respect to low-income groups.

that the argument from the psychology of tyranny does not apply to appeals
to conscience. The information argument does, however, apply with equal
force:

> In one of the more intriguing studies in the deterrence literature, Tittle
> and Rowe injected a 'moral appeal' onto a college classroom situation
> in which cheating on exams was widespread. The researchers expected
> that a public appeal to the students' obligation to be honest would instill
> a threat of guilt feelings among students and, thus, reduce the prevalence
> of cheating. To the contrary, the moral appeal, rather than inhibiting
> those students who had been cheating, seemed to inspire the formerly
> honest students to cheat. The authors speculated that the moral appeal
> suggested to the honest students that cheating had become so customary
> that it was out of control and that the norm against it had lost its moral
> force. Consequently, after the moral appeal, the formerly honest stu-
> dents joined their classmates and began to cheat. We would not be sur-
> prised if a moral appeal to tax payers, stressing their duty to be honest,
> would have the same effect as the moral appeal in the classroom.[51]

So far I have considered two motives for tax compliance: self-interested
fear of punishment and the norm of fairness.[52] In addition, there might
conceivably be a utilitarian mechanism: 'Knowledge of widespread tax
evasion and the perception of a significant problem may motivate one not
to add to the problem'.[53] With one possible exception, I have not found
any support for this hypothesis in the literature. Even if there is an effect
of this kind, it might be swamped by the oppositely directed fairness effect.
This points to a general problem in explaining compliance and cooperation. Economists 'tend to aggregate data even though they have been gathered from heterogeneous groups. The homogeneity assumptions are mis-
placed, [George Katona] argues. Individual differences do not cancel each
other out; consistent, independent psychological variables are important
aspects of improving predictions'.[54] Hence an econometric study might

---

[51] Grasmick and Scott (1982), p. 228, citing Tittle and Row (1973).

[52] This refers to the norm of fairness in the technical sense defined earlier in this chapter.
Other conceptions of fairness are also relevant to the study of tax evasion (Keenan and Dean
1980, pp. 212–13; Dean, Keenan and Kenney 1980, p. 30).

[53] Kaplan and Reckers (1985), p. 97. They go on to say that 'on the other hand, it may
suggest that since so many others are evading she/he should also engage in the behavior'.

[54] Lewis (1982), p. 32.

find a mild fairness effect when the underlying reality is that some people are strongly motivated by fairness while others are strongly motivated by utilitarian reasoning.

The exception just referred to comes from a study[55] that used two measures of the dependent variable, that is, attitude towards tax evasion, and two measures of the independent variable, that is, extent of tax evasion. Subjects were asked whether they would evade taxes under certain circumstances. They were also asked about the appropriate penalty for tax evasion under the same circumstances. The dependent variable was manipulated by stipulating that prevalence of tax evasion was 'low' in one condition and 'great and becoming still greater' in another. In addition, subjects were asked to estimate the precise numerical percentage of others engaging in evasion. The finding was that high estimates of evasion were associated with less severe penalties and (in one of two studies) with higher intentions to evade. Nevertheless, high prevalence was associated with severe penalties for evasion: 'Suggesting that tax evasion is a widespread problem that is getting worse may also suggest that something must be done about it'.[56] With increasing evasion the citizen would like penalties to be harsher, but he would be more likely to evade at any given level of penalty. A utilitarian effect of a sort would be implied if increasing evasion caused the citizen to desire penalties that were severe enough to make him less likely to evade than under the penalties appropriate for lower levels of evasion.[57]

Everyday Kantianism – plain moral outrage at tax evasion, regardless of its prevalence – is an important if somewhat elusive phenomenon. Urban Laurin's study of attitudes towards tax evasion in Sweden reveals an interesting connection between morality and beliefs about others. A strong moral attitude may be caused by the belief that few others are cheating, although the attitude itself is not formulated in conditional terms.[58] In practice, this will seem very much like the norm of fairness: the citizen complies if and only if he believes that most others comply. But the underlying psychology differs: the citizen adopts an attitude of unconditional compliance if and only if he believes that most others comply. The behaviour of others is the

[55] Kaplan and Reckers (1985).   [56] Ibid., p. 99.

[57] I say utilitarianism 'of a sort', since it is not the same utilitarian effect as described earlier in the chapter. That effect would require the citizen to be less likely to evade taxes when the number of evaders increased, independently of any effects mediated by changes in legal sanctions.

[58] Laurin (1986), p. 384.

cause of his moral stance, not an element of it. To the extent that this is the case, everyday Kantians are not bedrocks of morality.

The problem of causal direction is central in studying attitudes towards tax evasion. First, people who are strongly opposed to tax evasion may be 'rationalizers' who simply have no opportunities to cheat.[59] Second, the belief that many others are evading may be the effect of one's own evasion rather than its cause.[60] The underlying mechanism – cognitive dissonance reduction – bears a perverse resemblance to the magical thinking in everyday Kantianism. 'By doing it I can cause others to do it too, thus justifying my doing it'. Third, a lax moral attitude towards tax evasion may also be an effect rather than the cause of evading behaviour.[61] All three arguments suggest that norms are mere rationalizations with no independent motivating power. I argued in Chapter 3 that the view, if carried to extremes, is self-defeating. There seems to be evidence that people often comply even when they have an opportunity to evade at low or little risk. Unfortunately, the nature of the case makes robust evidence hard to come by. Explaining tax behaviour is much more difficult than explaining voting. Yet I hope that the concepts developed in this chapter can suggest some new ways of framing hypotheses and questions in future studies of tax evasion.

[59] Hochstein (1985).   [60] Laurin (1986), p. 181.   [61] Ibid., p. 359.

6. Bargaining and social norms

Introduction

Norms of equality, equity and fair division shape the outcome of bargaining generally and of collective wage bargaining in particular. Sometimes appeal to a norm of distribution facilitates agreement, both in labour–capital bargaining and in labour–labour bargaining. Norms of fairness can force agreement on the division of earnings between shareholders and workers. The task of coordinating separate labour–capital negotiations is itself a bargaining problem which can sometimes be resolved by appeal to a norm of equity or equality. But norms can also be an obstacle to agreement. In the presence of competing norms that favour different groups, the self-righteousness conferred by belief in a norm can lead to a bargaining impasse.

The role of norms in bargaining, therefore, is twofold. On the one hand, norms can help us overcome the problem created by a *plurality of cooperative arrangements*. On the other hand, the *plurality of norms* may in turn create new problems. In some cases, therefore, *norm-free bargaining* – negotiating from credible threats – is more likely to force agreement. All parties might then benefit from a tacit agreement to abstain from appealing to norms. If one believes, as I do, that such cases are becoming increasingly frequent, one might even wish for a social norm against the appeal to norms of distribution.

I shall consider norms regulating labour–labour relations as well as those governing labour–capital relations. Among the former, two norms stand out. On the one hand, there is the norm of *equality* – equal pay for everyone, regardless of type of work. In practice, implementing this norm means to move towards equality, not all the way to that end. On the other hand, there are norms of *equity* – ranging from norms of proportionality of the form 'to each according to his *X*' to the norm of 'equal pay for equal work'.

Among the norms regulating capital–labour relations, two also stand out. *Reference-level* norms give a privileged position to the status quo. Norms of *fair division* are rules for sharing the surplus between workers and the firm.

In what follows, I use 'bargaining strength' to denote the determinants of the outcome of norm-free bargaining. As explained in Chapter 2, these determinants include the risk aversion and time preferences of the parties, the earning power of the firm, the inside options of labour and management, their outside options (insofar as they constrain the outcome) and the temporal organization of the bargaining process. One might want to say that norms can also enhance one's bargaining strength, but I have chosen not to do so. This is a purely terminological decision, with no substantive implications, since I certainly do believe that norms affect outcomes. I distinguish, in other words, between norm-free and normative determinants of outcomes and refer to the former as bargaining strength.

I shall use collective bargaining to illustrate the basic proposition of this chapter: *norms interact with self-interest and with other norms.* I do not offer a general theory of these ambiguous and elusive interactions, but limit myself mainly to typology and illustration. I doubt that a general theory will ever be forthcoming, not because I hold the obscurantist view that one cannot have a precise theory of ambiguity,[1] but because there are so many variables involved that it is hardly feasible to go beyond ceteris paribus propositions. Laboratory experiments have the great value of isolating and controlling factors so that we can see the mechanisms in their pure form, but they are of limited help in explaining the tug of war between mechanisms that is the rule in social life.

In this chapter I focus mainly on wage bargaining, neglecting other aspects of collective bargaining. The typology of wage goals shown in Fig. 6.1 may serve as a point of departure.

Standard bargaining theory – cooperative or noncooperative – is concerned only with absolute wage levels. Relative levels – be they wage differences across firms or wage increases within firms – are deduced from independently determined absolute levels. Each negotiation starts from a clean slate, independently of the past and of what happens in other nego-

---

[1] See Elster (1978), pp. 68 and 91 n.10, for arguments against the similarly obscurantist view that a theory of psychological or social contradictions must be self-contradictory. The cliché that 'art in a splintered world must itself be splintered' reflects, I think, the same confusion.

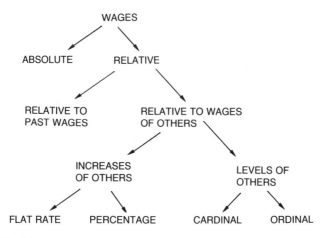

Fig. 6.1

tiations. Nobody who has looked at actual wage bargaining believes in this view. It is obvious to the most casual observer that relativities matter.

Wage relativities can be illuminated by two bodies of literature. Work on 'reference points' in cognitive psychology shows that people assess options in terms of changes from a reference point rather than in terms of the end state.[2] The status quo tends to harden into a normative principle, almost like a property right. For instance, 'as western US cities develop, successive rings of new developments generate successively increasing water costs. Residents and businesses often feel it is only fair that they should continue to pay the rates that prevailed before more recent development on the grounds that the new developments caused the higher water costs'.[3]

Experimental studies suggest that similar principles obtain in labour markets.[4] The status quo determines a reference level of profit and a reference level of wages. Here the basic principle of perceived fairness is that it is unfair for the firm to reduce wages below the reference level unless it has to do so to preserve the reference level of profits. One implication is that the firm can legitimately cut wages when it would otherwise see a loss in profits, but that it cannot fairly use local unemployment as an excuse for cutting wages. Another is that although the firm can legitimately pass on losses to the workers, it is not obliged to let them share in the gains. These are answers to questions phrased in terms of individual worker–employer

---

[2] See notably Tversky and Kahneman (1981).   [3] Zajac (1985), p. 140.

[4] The following draws on Kahneman, Knetsch and Thaler (1986a).

relations. As we shall see, the same results do not obtain in collective wage bargaining. Yet the notion of a status quo and the idea of a right to one's wage are as powerful in the collective as in the individual case. In particular, 'nominal-wage cuts rate newspaper headlines'.[5]

Reference points are important mainly for understanding the labour–capital relationship. For labour–labour relations, we can turn to the theory of reference groups.[6] Often, what matters to a union is to preserve and if possible to improve wage differentials, or to achieve parity with another group. These goals can be achieved by improving one's own position, *but also by preventing others from getting ahead*. In Sweden, LO has often tried to reduce the compensation of other groups for wage drift. Here it may be difficult to distinguish fear of inflation from relative wage goals. But when in 1983 LO economists proposed that reductions in progressive taxation for high-income groups be given up to forestall compensation demands from low-income groups, desire to preserve relativities must be the explanation. In such cases, *envy* seems to be the appropriate characterization of union behaviour.

In many cases wage–wage linkages can be explained without invoking envy, namely if the types of labour in question are substitutes for each other.[7] As mentioned in Chapter 4, higher wages for A labour will increase demand and thus wages for the substitute B labour. Also, the linkages might simply be due to competitive pressures. The presence of highly productive firms can force other firms to follow suit and pay high wages, if the workers in the latter can make a credible threat to take up a job in the former. In the limit, a single vacant job in a single high-wage firm is sufficient to force high wages for all workers in all other firms. This explanation, while plausible in many cases, cannot explain the full force of relativities. 'The keen attention that the steel industry gives to wages paid by the automotive industry is out of proportion when compared with the competitive attraction of jobs in auto firms for steel workers. . . . Apparently workers and firms need a standard to guide their judgments of *fairness* more than they need a precise indicator of market pressures'.[8]

---

[5] Mitchell (1986), p. 47. The money illusion is also observed in Kahneman, Knetsch and Thaler (1986a), pp. 731–2. An alternative explanation of the money illusion is that workers are concerned about relative wages. 'It might be suggested, for example, that workers' morale depends on relative wage-standing, and that with asynchronous wage-setting nominal wage-cuts are inherently relative wage cuts. . . . Each individual employer would be reluctant to cut wages despite falling demand because of the adverse productivity effects' (Mitchell 1986, p. 63; see also Keynes 1936, p. 26).

[6] Merton (1957); Runciman (1966).   [7] Oswald (1979).   [8] Okun (1981), p. 94.

The force of relativities is enhanced when a group finds itself lagging behind with respect to several reference groups. In Sweden, the LKAB miners' strike in 1969 was triggered by the fact that miners compared themselves unfavorably both with functionaries in mining and with other blue-collar workers. Miners, who traditionally had been among the highest paid blue-collar workers, had suffered from the solidaristic wage policy. By contrast, functionaries in mining had benefited from the fact that white-collar pay raises 'tended to follow aggregate blue-collar increases, not simply those received by high-pay wage earners like miners'.[9] In addition to being doubly badly off in terms of relative wage *increases,* the miners could also represent their claims as a demand for parity of *level.* They could argue (and Prime Minister Palme argued on their behalf after the final concessions) that the high wages of miners were offset by their harsh working conditions so that, all in all, they were lagging behind other groups. The combination was unbeatable.

Relativities may themselves be measured in absolute or relative terms – as flat differences or as per cent differences. Similarly, preservation of wage differentials can be stated in terms of a constant absolute difference or a constant per cent difference. When wages are increasing, keeping the flat difference constant is a way of compressing the relative differential – simultaneously, as it were, maintaining differences and reducing them. It is not surprising that this has been a frequent compromise formula between the equality demands of low-income groups and the equity demands of high-income groups. Another frequently used compromise is a 'kinked-line formula' that combines elements of flat-rate increases and per cent increases. Thus in 1952 LO negotiated across-the-board wage increases of 8 per cent, constrained by a minimum increase of 10 öre if present wages could not be brought up with at least that amount by the per cent increase.

So far I have taken it for granted that wage comparisons concern cardinal differences. Workers are interested in *how much* more they earn than others. Robert Frank has argued, however, that ordinal difference or *status* is also highly valued, so much, in fact, that people are willing to trade it off against absolute income. As evidence, he adduces the fact that an academic may remain in a medium-rank university even when he has a higher offer from a top-ranked university.[10] The satisfaction of being a big fish in a small pond offsets the loss in income. This observation rings true: being

---

[9] Swenson (1989), p. 87.   [10] Frank (1985), pp. 75–82.

the best-paid member of a department has an importance that is relatively independent of the size of the gap to the next-best-paid member, just as being the winner of the 100-yard sprint matters vastly more than the distance to the runner-up.[11] Frank also cites the striking fact that the earning profile of car salesmen is much flatter than their marginal productivity profile, so that the most efficient salesmen seem to be paying for their place at the top.[12]

Concentrating on cardinal wage differences might also be misleading for another reason. Consider the question whether wage comparisons focus on before-tax or after-tax income. The use of tax reforms as an instrument in combined wage settlements suggests that after-tax income is often crucial. Against this, however, we may note 'the envy sometimes observable in the lesser man of someone who stands so high in the esteem of his employers that they will pay him a seemingly exorbitant sum, though with prevailing income tax rates he may end up having hardly more in his pocket than the man who envies him'.[13] In less contentious language, before-tax income is a measure of *prestige*. After-tax income has material value, but before-tax income can have an important symbolic value. In some contexts, this may well compete for attention with real-wage comparisons.[14] (In addition, of course, union leaders can choose the representation most likely to appeal to their members.)

Before-tax comparisons need not be a bad thing. Joseph Carens has argued that a system in which people maximize prestige, as measured by before-tax income, could combine the virtues of equality (achieved by redistributive taxation) and efficiency.[15] While other utopian proposals are vulnerable to the objection that people would work too little, this one is open to the charge that it could make them work too hard.[16] Any system in which people are motivated by relativities tends to be inefficient, with people running as fast as they can to remain in the same place. Everybody could be better off if everybody reduced their efforts.[17] The problem, of

[11] In fact, a close victory may be more satisfactory than a crushing one.

[12] Frank (1985), pp. 68–71, 84–6.   [13] Schoeck (1987), p. 367.

[14] On the symbolic value of pay see Hyman and Brough (1975), p. 55.

[15] Carens (1981).

[16] Carens (1981) assumes that before-tax income would be an absolute rather than relative goal. But the emphasis he places on social approval as a motive suggests that in practice the members of his utopia would maximize relative before-tax income.

[17] Haavelmo (1970). In the concluding chapter I suggest that this proposition may not be universally true, however.

course, is one of allocating these reductions among people with different skills and preferences. Once again, the bargaining problem is a more serious obstacle to Pareto improvement than is the free-rider problem.

Norms in capital–labour bargaining

The main norms of distribution invoked in bargaining between capital and (organized or unorganized labour) appear to be the following:

1. The norm of maintaining the reference wage
2. The norm of maintaining the reference wage, except when cuts are needed to maintain reference profits
3. The norm that both labour and capital should benefit from any gains in the firm's earnings
4. The norm that gains from luck (e.g., improved market conditions) should be shared between capital and labour
5. The norm that gains due to increased skills should accrue mainly to the skill holder, be it labour or management
6. The Kalai–Smorodinsky norm that gains should be divided proportionally to the maximal feasible gains of the parties.

A first question concerns the choice of reference wage. If the firm pays its workers a fixed wage and a bonus, there are two possible reference wages, with or without the bonus.[18] The workers' choice between these levels might depend on their offensive or defensive posture. The higher reference wage will be selected to justify a claim, the lower to rationalize a defeat or an imposed wage cut. This distinction applies quite generally. Choice of norm or of reference group may be dictated by strategic ambition or by resignation.

Next, the second reference wage norm embodies an asymmetry between capital and labour. Capital is allowed to pass on losses to workers, but it is not required to pass on gains. While appropriate for individual bargaining, this norm is not a good description of collective bargaining. Here the question is rather one of *which* gains and losses to share with the workers. Management will certainly resist appropriation of gains due to entrepreneurial skill, relying either on arguments from desert[19] or on the argument that such practices, by destroying the incentive to innovate, have socially

---

[18] Kahneman, Knetsch and Thaler (1986a).   [19] Sher (1987).

detrimental effects.[20] Workers can use symmetrical arguments with respect to the gains due to increased worker effect. With respect to gains due to sheer luck, neither party can claim any merit or invoke incentive effects in its favour. Sometimes the parties have distinguished between 'good' and 'bad' wage drift – due, respectively, to productivity increase and market conditions – and agreed to keep the latter to a minimum and to subtract it from next year's increases.[21]

Although unions usually demand a share in gains created by entrepreneurial skill, they are not willing to share the losses caused by managerial ineptitude. Indeed, by refusing to do so they may force the firm to mend its ways. If the firm says that there is no room for a wage raise, the union can reply with Marx: 'Impossible! Ne me dites jamais ce bête de mot'.[22] In a 1958 document, the American Federation of Labor expressed what is probably a prevalent opinion.

> There is of course a question of principle, of whether it is a responsibility of workers to subsidize a company by accepting wages which lag far behind those paid elsewhere. . . . The financial difficulties of some companies are due to reasons which cannot begin to be met by restricting wages. . . . Unions are aware that, if an employer knows they will relax efforts to raise wages, he will be more inclined to let his business slide along as in the past, hoping that some broad economic changes will come along to better his position. But if the union keeps pushing firmly for wage advances, the employer is forced to find better ways to run his business to offset the costs of higher wages.[23]

To some extent, of course, this requires the workers to gamble with their own future. The firm might, after all, not be able to mend its ways, and the workers might lose their jobs. In Sweden, this problem has been solved by what amounts to an insurance scheme. In the 1950s, LO embraced the policy 'equal pay for equal work', with the explicit intention of weeding the least efficient firms out of business. The policy was supported by government labour market programs subsidizing training and labour mobility,

---

[20] Slichter (1947), p. 26. Observe that this argument differs from the proposition, discussed in Chapter 4, that confiscatory wage claims, by reducing profits, reduce both the incentive and the opportunity to invest.

[21] Elvander (1988), p. 225.

[22] Marx (1867), p. 477, citing Mirabeau. He is discussing demands on the firm by the state, not by the workers.

[23] Cited after Foley and Maunders (1977), pp. 123–4.

thus reducing the risk for workers who lost their jobs when their employer was forced into bankruptcy.

In sum, there seems to be a consensus that workers have a right to share the gains created by an increase in their effort. There is an approximate consensus that either both parties share both windfall gains and losses or both fall upon the firm. There is little consensus as to how to share the gains and losses caused by managerial skill or ineptitude. In Sweden, unions have successfully imposed an asymmetrical norm: to get a share of the gains, but not partake of the losses.

I should add that the earnings of the firm are not merely a target for norm-guided claims. They are also a source of bargaining power. Here, as elsewhere, high earnings are a mixed blessing.[24] On the one hand, they enhance the *ability* to innovate, to participate in collective action or – as here – to weather a strike. On the other hand, high earnings reduce the *motivation* for these actions. Note, however, that ability is linked to past earnings and motivation to expected profits in the future. We might expect, therefore, firms to be maximally resistant to wage claims at the peak of the business cycle, when past earnings enhance the ability to weather a strike and the prospect of lower profits in the future promotes the motivation to do so. Unions, by contrast, will tend to base their claims on past earnings, which are more easily verified and not as subject to misrepresentation by the management.[25]

The Kalai–Smorodinsky norm differs from the other norms regulating capital–labour relations, being directed towards wage *levels* rather than *increases*. In practice this norm often amounts to a requirement that each party to bargaining make some concessions, that is, that neither can expect to get his most preferred outcome. This norm can easily have perverse effects. A union might insist on an outcome ranked third in its own preferences and second in management's preferences, rejecting an outcome ranked second by itself and top-ranked by management. This is a bit like envy, cutting off one's nose to spite one's face, yet not quite the same phenomenon. Rather it is part of a *bargaining culture,* in which conces-

---

[24] Elster (1985d), pp. 352–3.

[25] Mitchell (1986), p. 61, reaches the same conclusion from different premises when he writes, 'A union might seek to establish a position that it wanted to achieve a given nominal-wage increase at least partially protected from inflation by an escalator clause. Management might seek to establish a role for prospective profitability as a guide for wage adjustments. These positions would systematically clash at the peak of the business cycle when inflation might be high but the future downturn was beginning to loom'.

sions in face-to-face confrontation are inherently valuable. For Swedish workers, for instance, wage increases obtained in industry-level bargaining count for more than gains obtained in central bargaining;[26] direct wage increases more than increases which follow from automatic index clauses;[27] and wage increases in any form more than tax reductions.[28]

Norms in labour–labour bargaining

Often, unions or bargaining cartels engage in protracted internal bargaining before they agree on a wage profile to be presented to the employers as their common demand. In these internal negotiations, sheer bargaining power appears to count for less than various norms of fair wages. These include, notably, the following:

1. The norm of equal wage regardless of type of work
2. Norms of strong equity: to each proportionately to his X, where X could include effort, hardship, skill, education, seniority or contribution to output
3. The norm of weak equity, or equal wage for equal work
4. The norm of differential equity, or maintenance of wage differences in percentage terms
5. The norm of maintenance of wage differences in absolute terms
6. The norm of payment according to need, as measured, say, by the number of family dependents or the local cost of living

Of these, the most important are the norm of equality and the norms of equity. The norm of equality has many applications to labour markets. In periods of unemployment, for instance, work sharing to provide equal but smaller amounts of work for all is regularly proposed as an alternative to layoffs.[29] Random layoffs would also be a form of work sharing, with probabilistic rather than physical equality as the norm.[30] In practice, layoffs are governed by a rule of equity: first in, last out. The main application of the equality norm, however, is to wage setting. In this context, the norm of equality dictates equal wages per hour, regardless of the nature of the work and the characteristics of the worker.[31] The norm of equality does

[26] de Geer (1986), p. 167.   [27] Ibid., p. 114.   [28] Elvander (1988), pp. 290, 300.
[29] Hoel (1986); Drèze (1987); Calmfors (1987b).
[30] See Elster (1989a), ch. 2, for a discussion of this principle in various contexts.
[31] This norm was advocated, e.g., by the Ricardian socialists (Pagano 1985, pp. 27–36).

not require equal wages regardless of the number of hours worked, as in the parable of the labourers in the vineyard. The reward system in that parable, although based on a form of equality, was felt to be inequitable. Among the many equity norms, the least controversial says that each should be rewarded proportionally to the number of hours worked. The norm of equal hourly wages is consistent at least with that norm of equity.

The norm of equality can be defined at many levels, to dictate equality within groups, equality among groups and overall equality among all members of all groups. In Sweden, targets for equalization have included (a) low-wage groups within a given industry, (b) low-wage firms within a given industry, (c) low-wage industries and (d) low-income workers regardless of industry.[32] Not surprisingly, it may not be possible to achieve all of these goals simultaneously. Trade-offs and choices have to be made.

Sometimes one can achieve both inter- and intragroup equality in one fell stroke. In the 1930s, the Swedish metal workers demanded and obtained parity with building workers as a condition for levelling within their own group.[33] More frequently, the goals cannot be achieved or approximated simultaneously. In Sweden today, private functionaries have a policy of equality with industrial workers as well as a policy of compression of the wage differential within the group.[34] The former amounts to an equalization of averages, the latter to a reduction of spread. It is usually not possible to achieve both goals simultaneously. Equalization within one group of workers often occurs at the expense of a lower average growth for the group as a whole, because employers require concessions on the average wage to offset the frustration of their desire for differentials (as discussed later).

When employers trade off average against spread, the impact of intragroup equalization on overall wage equality may also be negative. Thus in 1981 the Metal Workers' Union declared that 'the wage differences within the LO-collective have become so small that further evening-out will no longer lead to decreased income disparity in the whole of society. The equalization policy should continue, but it has to embrace all wage-earner groups'.[35] For a numerical illustration, suppose that there are two groups of equal size, each of them divided into three subgroups of equal size. Initially, the within-group distributions are $X = [(4, 6, 8), (6, 8, 10)]$. After

[32] De Geer (1986), pp. 340–1, asserts that in addition to the traditional support for (a), the concern for (b), (c) and (d) was added in, respectively, 1963–4, 1965–6 and 1968–9.
[33] Swenson (1989), p. 46.   [34] Elvander (1988), p. 40.
[35] Cited after Lash (1985), p. 222.

a round of collective bargaining, the new distributions emerge as $Y = [(6, 7, 8), (9, 11, 14)]$. If the first union had not insisted on a solidaristic settlement, the outcome would have been $Z = [(6, 8, 10), (9, 11, 14)]$. On any reasonable measure of equality, the overall inequality of Y is greater than that of either X or Z.

Conversely, an increase in intergroup equality can occur at the expense of a decrease both in overall equality and in intragroup equality. Assume that one group of workers accept a settlement with higher average and larger spread, so as to achieve the same average wage as some reference group. Specifically, assume that the initial distributions were $U = [(5, 6, 7), (6, 8, 10)]$. After negotiations in which the first union abandons the solidaristic policy, the distributions are $V = [(5, 8, 11), (7, 9, 11)]$. If it had kept the solidaristic policy, the outcome would have been $W = [(6, 7, 8), (7, 9, 11)]$. Although the union averages are closer to each other in V than in U or W, both overall inequality and inequality within the first union are greater in V.[36]

The implications of the norm of equality depend on the context. In constant-sum situations, it simply says that the given total is to be divided equally among the members. In variable-sum situations, we can distinguish among three norms of equality. *Nonenvious egalitarianism* tells us to divide equally up to the point where further equalization would make some worse off without making anyone better off. *Weakly envious egalitarianism* tells us to divide equally up to the point where further equalization would make everybody worse off. This norm is consistent with changes that make some worse off without making anyone better off ('If I can't have it, nobody will'). *Strongly envious egalitarianism* insists on absolute equality even if it makes everyone worse off ('cutting off one's nose to spite one's face'). Numerical illustrations are provided in the following paragraphs.

Collective wage bargaining is sometimes portrayed as variable-sum bargaining between capital and labour followed by constant-sum bargaining among the workers to divide up the wage kitty. Often, however, the two processes are related, since the employer is frequently willing to accept a higher average in return for larger wage differentials which are deemed

---

[36] This paradox can also arise in attempts to equalize average income of men and women or the average incomes of different countries. If one believes (as I do) in a principle of ethical individualism, attempts to create equality among groups are basically misguided if they cause greater inequality among individuals.

necessary to attract or retain certain categories of workers. Labour–labour bargaining then also becomes variable-sum. Suppose there are three equal-size groups of workers and that the union must formulate a preference over the following wage profiles: $A = (5, 6, 7)$, $B = (5, 6, 8)$ and $C = (4, 7, 8)$. In the absence of envy, the union will prefer B over A. An envious union would have the opposite preference. (A strongly envious union would even prefer $D = (4, 4, 4)$ over any other profile. In the following I assume the absence of strong envy.) Any egalitarian union will rank C at the bottom. The employers, let us assume, prefer C over B and A. Their top-ranked alternative is the egalitarian union's least preferred option. We can safely predict that it will not be chosen.

Assume first that employers prefer A over B because A is cheaper overall and B is not sufficiently differentiated. If the union has nonenvious egalitarian preferences, the outcome is likely to be A. Whenever a conflict of interest includes an alternative that is both parties' second choice, that option is likely to be the outcome.[37] If the union has weakly envious preferences, A might appear to be even more likely to be chosen, being the first choice of the union and the second choice of the employers. Assume next that employers prefer B over A and that the union has nonenvious egalitarian preferences. In that case, B is likely to be chosen, being the union's top-ranked option and the second-ranked option of the employers. If the union is weakly envious, B is still likely to be chosen, as each party's second-best alternative.

In this analysis I made the seemingly innocent assumption that if one alternative is chosen when it is the second choice of both parties, its likelihood of being chosen cannot decrease when it becomes the first option of one party. *The intuition behind the Kalai–Smorodinsky analysis of bargaining is that this assumption may be false.* The bargaining culture makes it easier to reach agreement when the conflict of interest is so strong that neither party can gets its first choice than when their interests converge to the point where one party's first choice is the other's second choice.

Consider now norms of equity. A norm of equity singles out some feature of the worker or his work by virtue of which he is entitled to a certain level of wages. If the feature is measurable on a ratio scale, the norm might take the form 'To each proportionately to his X', referred to earlier as norms of strong equity. In practice, such norms are often impracticable or

---

[37] This is why, for instance, two royal pretenders to a throne may be able to agree on a president as a compromise (Marx 1852, p. 166).

irrelevant. Many relevant criteria, such as effort or hardship, cannot be measured on a ratio scale. When a relevant criterion can be thus measured, the norm of proportionality may not be plausible. Length of education or duration of employment, for instance, is frequently used to set wages, but never by proportionality.[38] In such cases, the norm of strong equity takes the form 'To each proportionately to $f(X)$', where f is a monotonically increasing function.

In addition, three other norms of equity, which are implied by strong equity without implying it, are important in bargaining. First, the norm might say, 'Higher wages for higher X', without requiring proportionality. Call this *ordinal equity*. This norm requires that X be measurable on an ordinal scale. It explains, for instance, why highly skilled engineers are usually not allowed to earn more than the managers from whom they take orders.[39] Second, there is the important norm of 'Equal wages for equal X', referred to above as the norm of *weak equity*. This norm does not require any ability to measure X on a scale, but simply the ability to identify a given job as member of an equivalence class. Third, there is a norm of *differential equity:* the maintenance of constant (per cent) wage differences between given X categories. It is often complained that the maintenance of wage differentials has become a goal in itself that prevents the establishment of an equitable system. In practice, however, the focal-point quality of the status quo ensures that differential equity has a strong grip on the mind. One can subvert it to some extent by choosing absolute differences rather than per cent differences as the focus of comparison.

The substance of an equity norm is given by the choice of X. (a) Marx argued that in the lower stage of socialism one should follow the norm of strong equity, with X defined as contribution.[40] (b) Equity theorists in social psychology have also equated X with contribution, usually operationalized as time, effort or achievement.[41] (c) The neoclassical theory of income distribution says that under perfect competition each factor of production will be rewarded according to its contribution, defined as mar-

[38] An exception occurs when X is the number of hours worked. As mentioned earlier, this equity norm is so weak that it is usually consistent with the norm of equality. A conflict might arise, however, if the determinant of the number of hours worked is ability rather than motivation (Dworkin 1981).

[39] Or perhaps we should put it the other way around: it explains why managers have to earn more than the highly skilled engineers to whom they give orders.

[40] See Elster (1985d), sec. 4.3, for a discussion of these principles.

[41] Messick and Cook, eds. (1983); see also Deutsch (1985).

ginal product.[42] Since perfect competition is a desirable state, because of its efficiency properties, distribution according to marginal productivity also has normative force. (d) The functionalist theory of social inequality predicts and recommends that people be rewarded according to the social value of their skills.[43] (e) In Sweden, LO has for many years advocated a 'difficulty-grading' of work that would allow an equality wage system. The grading would take account of skills, education, risks and hardships, seasonal unemployment and other factors. No consensus on details has been reached, and it is safe to bet that none will ever be.[44] (f) Ideological correctness (*biaoxian*) has been and remains a major factor in reward allocation in China.[45] (g) Reward according to seniority is a major principle in many industrial systems. (h) Reward according to age also has a role to play, as when older workers are allowed to take longer holidays. But age is rarely a factor in wage determination. (i) Finally, reward according to one's place in the hierarchy is an important norm of equity.

Arguments to use a given X as the basis for an equity norm are of three kinds. First, there are the *pure backward-looking systems:* reward according to entitlement, desert or moral worth.[46] Rewarding according to age is a pure example. Reward according to ideological merit also fits this category. Sometimes reward according to seniority is also justified on these grounds. Second, there are the *pure forward-looking systems* that allocate wages where they will produce the most good. A differentiated wage system enables the firm to allocate higher wages to attract or retain the most scarce – but not necessarily the most skilled – types of labour power. Third, there are a number of *mixed backward-forward-looking systems.* Schematically speaking, these operate as follows. At time t_1 it becomes known that at time t_3 rewards will be allocated according to effort, skill or contribution at time t_2. The creation of a backward-looking system is justified by a forward-looking argument from incentives: if people know they

---

[42] Bronfenbrenner (1971).   [43] Davis and Moore (1945).

[44] Elvander (1988), ch. 5, has a full account of these chimerical attempts.

[45] Walder (1986), ch. 4 and passim. Allocation according to *biaoxian* coexists with and is tempered by the principle of *guanxi* explained in Chapter 3. In Walder's phrase, *biaoxian* is a form of *principled particularism,* while guanxi represents the more familiar unprincipled particularism.

[46] A good example is the demobilization system used in the U.S. Army at the end of the Second World War (Stouffer et al. 1949, vol. 2, ch. 11). Here soldiers were graded on a point system that took account of length and danger of service, soldiers with higher scores being demobilized before others.

will be rewarded according to past effort, they have a reason to work hard. If they know they will be rewarded by seniority, they have an incentive to stay in the firm. Pure backward-looking systems tend to become mixed. Religious doctrines that promise salvation in return for good works usually add that the reward will not be forthcoming if the works are undertaken for the sake of salvation.[47] In practice, the warning is rarely heeded.[48] Conversely, some mixed systems over time can also be perceived as pure backward-looking ones. Reward by seniority and the finders-keepers rule are examples of principles that have been justified both on mixed (or rule-utilitarian) grounds and on backward-looking, rights-based grounds.

Like the norm of equality, norms of equity can be sustained by envy. When A is paid more than B for work requiring the same qualifications, B may feel indignant even if the excess does not occur at his expense. It is quite possible that public functionaries ultimately benefit from the higher wages of their private counterparts. Public functionaries are largely paid out of taxes levied on workers and firms in private industries. Some wage differentiation in the latter is probably good for productivity, since solidaristic wage policies tend to increase youth unemployment with long-term adverse effects.[49] If public functionaries use a backward-looking criterion of equity, like education or effort, they might still believe that private functionaries are rewarded in excess of what they deserve. For the envious, there is no such thing as what Leibniz called 'the right to innocent utility' – the right to benefits that do not occur at anyone else's expense.[50] I have more to say about envy in the final chapter.

Norms of equality and equity are substantive norms that prescribe specific outcomes. Procedural norms of equal treatment are also important in the labour market. To illustrate the operation of procedural norms, one may cite the massive legitimacy of devaluations and wage and price freezes as tools of economic policy. Following the large devaluation of the Swedish currency in 1982, the unions agreed to abstain from demanding compensation for the increase in the cost of living. Similarly, wage and price freezes are rarely contested on grounds of distributive unfairness. Although these measures have definite winners and losers, their blind, mechanical

---

[47] Salvation, in other words, is essentially a by-product (Elster 1983a, p. 74).

[48] A similar degeneration of reward according to ideological merit is described by Walder (1986).

[49] Flanagan (1987), p. 150.

[50] For an account of Leibniz's view, see Elster (1975), pp. 135–8.

and impersonal character make it clear that they are not motivated by these gains and losses.

By contrast, selective measures of economic policy are always vulnerable to suspicion. It may or may not be true that lower taxes for high-income groups will eventually benefit everybody, but it is certain that their immediate effect is to benefit the rich. Efficiency may require selectivity, but perceived fairness demands blind universality. It is not quite true that tightening is acceptable only if the burdens are equitably shared ex post.[51] What matters is rather the absence of any intentional selectivity ex ante. Unequal outcomes that would be intolerable if they were thought to be deliberately engineered are calmly accepted if perceived as a matter of chance and luck. Devaluations and freezes are tools that must be used sparsely, since otherwise their effects will be undone by anticipation, but they can be quite effective.

Norms versus self-interest in bargaining

The purpose of the preceding sections was mainly descriptive. I have been concerned to bring out the variety of norms that are invoked in collective bargaining. In this section I discuss some analytical issues related to the explanation of norms and their impact on the outcome of bargaining. In particular, I consider four views of the relation between norms and self-interest. (a) Norms operate within a range of indeterminacy left by market interaction based on self-interest. (b) Norms are not taken seriously by anyone, but are deliberately invoked to promote and rationalize self-interest. (c) Norms are taken seriously, but self-interest provides the (unconscious) mechanism that explains why any particular norm is (sincerely) invoked in a given situation. (d) Norms that work against one's self-interest can have motivating power. Assuming that norms are not all-powerful, the problem then becomes one of understanding how norms and self-interest interact to produce the final outcome.

A widespread view, especially among British writers on collective bargaining, is that norms and custom operate in the labour market to fill the 'indeterminacy left by market forces'.[52] On this view, social norms have no power that could oppose market forces and cause the outcome to differ

---

[51] As argued in Schwerin (1980), p. 80, and Schwerin (1982), p. 469.
[52] Brown and Simon (1975), p. 24; Willman (1982), p. 10; Marsden (1986), pp. 112, 137.

from what it would be if the market reigned supreme. Rather they take up the slack left by strictly economic forces. The nature and cause of this indeterminacy are, however, never made quite clear. Perhaps what these writers have in mind is the alleged indeterminacy of bargaining or, if you prefer, the indeterminacy of the 'thin' markets created by collective bargaining as distinct from perfect markets with individual wage bargaining. Competition forces determinacy, whereas a small number of sellers and buyers makes for indeterminacy. From the discussion in Chapter 2, it is clear enough that bargaining often involves considerable uncertainty that cannot be resolved by rational, norm-free negotiations. Norms of equality and equity, or the norm of maintaining established reference levels, can then indeed fill the gap.

The role of social norms is more important, however, than this account would suggest. Norms can replace rationality, not just supplement it. In Chapter 2 I argued that the monotonicity axiom and the Kalai–Smorodinsky solution concept cannot be defended on grounds of individual rationality. Rather they are rooted in perceptions of fairness. 'It is not *fair* that you should get nearly the best outcome you could hope for while I fall far short of my maximum. Fairness requires proportionality to maximal achievement'. The importance of reference points in bargaining is also inconsistent with self-interested rationality. Rationality would dictate that bygones be bygones. Each new round of bargaining should start from a clean slate, so that wage differences across firms and wage increases within firms would be explained in the same manner. The downward stickiness of wages is extremely hard to square with this view.[53] The willingness of strong unions to accept wage increases that are smaller in relative *and* absolute terms than those granted to other unions would also be a mystery for theories in which outcomes are dictated exclusively by bargaining strength.

Other writers grant the widespread appeal to norms but deny that norms ever make a difference to the outcome.[54] The plethora of norms that are

[53] Many explanations of the stickiness of wages have been proposed, not all of them involving normative considerations. For surveys, see Stiglitz (1986) and the essays in Beckerman, ed. (1986). Some of the non-normative explanations seem implausible and contrived compared with the much simpler explanation that the resistance to lose what one has is much stronger than the resistance to accept less in the first place. Other non-normative explanations, such as the theory of efficiency wages, are more plausible. (For a survey of these theories, see Akerlof and Yellen, eds. 1986.) As noted earlier, however, some efficiency-wage theories incorporate fairness motives.

[54] See, e.g., Lockwood (1955) and Wootton (1962). Other representatives of this view are cited in Hyman and Brough (1975), p. 79.

relevant to the labour market is such, they argue, that virtually any claim can be backed up by a suitable norm. Labour and management consciously pick the norms that favour their interest. Although I shall end up denying both this view and the closely related view that self-interest provides the unconscious mechanism that explains why certain norms are more salient than others, both ideas contain an important element of truth.

To see the strength of the reductionist views, recall that we have defined six norms regulating capital–labour relations and an equal number of norms regulating labour–labour relations. Most of these norms can be presented in several versions and refined in various ways. (a) The wage may be defined in real or nominal terms. (b) It may be defined in terms of the contract wage or in terms that also include normal income from overtime. (c) The wage may be defined in before-tax or after-tax terms. (d) The reference group for wage comparisons can be other workers in the firm, other workers in the industry, other workers with similar education, other workers in the local wage area or still other groups. (e) Norms of equity can invoke a large number of substantive criteria (effort, skill, seniority, etc.).

Moreover, for each norm there arise questions of interpretation and implementation, which are themselves a matter of normative considerations.[55] Any 'standard of comparison' must be supplemented by a 'standard of distribution'.[56] For instance, the norm of reward according to need may be defined by number of dependents,[57] but it can also be understood by personal characteristics such as health or by local costs of living. The norm of reward according to contribution is relatively unambiguous if the different kinds of labour interact additively. If, however, they interact multiplicatively (as in standard production functions), the identification of individual contributions is much more controversial.[58] Even the apparently simple rule of seniority turns out to harbour a morass of complexities.[59]

Taking account of all possible permutations, the number of plausible-sounding norms is certainly well into three figures. It would be a particularly unfortunate or inept group that did not find some norm with which to justify *its* claim to a larger share. There is no lack of opportunity to engage

[55] Zajac (1985), p. 130.   [56] Selten (1978a, 1987).

[57] As suggested by Marx in the *Critique of the Gotha Program*.

[58] Camerer and MacCrimmon (1983).

[59] For an overview of the 'circumstances under which seniority may be acquired, transferred, modified, lost and, if such be permitted, regained', see U.S. Department of Labor (1972). The concept of seniority used in competitive allocations (promotions and layoffs) is not the same as the concept used in noncompetitive situations (vacations and pensions).

in conscious manipulation of norms. And there is no doubt that workers and managers often do invoke or exploit norms in a purely opportunistic fashion. In addition to the labour market norms enumerated earlier, they can exploit general social norms such as the norm of reciprocity. Howard Raiffa observes that if you want to sell your house and go out to dinner with a prospective buyer, you should always insist on paying for yourself.[60] Otherwise, the norm of reciprocity might cause you to accept $10 000 less for your house in return for the $10 dinner. LO took a risk when, after some hesitation, it accepted the principle that bargaining should take place in localities provided by the employers' association.

Against this we can set the argument made in Chapter 3, that the cynical view of norms, if taken to extremes, is self-defeating. The point is often made in the industrial relations literature. 'If appeals to fairness were not at times made sincerely, their insincere use would have no point'.[61] 'It is difficult to explain the continued use of moral arguments if it is assumed that they are merely a façade. Presumably, continued cynical use of such arguments in an unjustifiable fashion would so devalue the "moral currency" of industrial relations that sympathy and support would cease to be encouraged by their use'.[62]

I believe these arguments are essentially right. A counterexample might be the 'culture of hypocrisy', which, or so I argued in Chapter 3, predominates in the Soviet Union and in China. Even when it is common knowledge that nobody believes in the norms, they may still be useful tools for manipulation and self-promotion.[63] The system might crumble overnight if a person of high authority said that the emperor had no clothes on, but as long as this does not happen everyone goes along. I do not fully understand the psychological processes that sustain this feat of collective self-deception, but in any case they do not seem to operate in the labour market. Most workers (and managers) sincerely believe in *all* the norms enumerated earlier, in the sense that there are frames of mind in which their violation by oneself or others induces guilt, shame or anger. The righteous indignation that leads workers to strike has no resemblance to the make-believe enthusiasm of workers in socialist countries.

---

[60] Raiffa (1982), p. 36.   [61] Hyman and Brough (1975), p. 80.
[62] Willman (1982), p. 1.
[63] Walder (1986) and Sabel and Stark (1982) argue that managers in Communist countries are victims of the official egalitarian ideology, which provides workers with strong leverage in informal shop-floor bargaining.

There is, nevertheless, the possibility that people unconsciously choose the distributive norm that favours them. In support of this hypothesis, let me first cite two allocative problems from outside the labour market. When asked their opinion about the fairness of different criteria of admission to medical school, students with a bad scholarly record ranked an even-chance lottery over a lottery weighted by grades, and the latter over a pure merit-based system, whereas those with a better record ranked the pure lottery at the bottom.[64] When asked their opinion about the fairness of different criteria for demobilization from the army at the end of World War II, the principle that married men with children should be let out first was most popular among married men with children, less popular among married men without children and least popular among single men.[65]

Blue-collar and white-collar workers tend to invoke different norms of equity, the former arguing that work should be rewarded according to the burdens imposed on the workers and the latter that wages should reflect skills and benefit to society.[66] Although norm-free bargaining will also reflect these aspects of work, they may gain extra force if embodied in explicit norms. The following experimental finding may be understood in light of this difference. 'Subjects who worked for ten hours when another person worked seven, judged that the mean fair pay for themselves was $35.24 when the other person had been paid $25. However, when they themselves had worked seven hours and had been paid $25, subjects judged the fair pay to others to be $30.29'.[67] In the first condition, subjects might naturally focus on the increasing disutility of work, with a corresponding norm of reward according to toil. In the latter condition, the decreasing productivity of effort might be more salient, with a norm of reward according to output. The diverging perceptions of the striking LKAB miners – were they underdogs or part of the aristocracy of labour? – can perhaps be understood in this perspective.

Probably the most widely cited example from the labour market is the adherence of low-wage groups to the norm of equality and of high-wage groups to norms of equity. On the one hand, women argue for higher wages for the low-income occupations in which they are disproportionately represented. On the other hand, higher functionaries argue that wages must reflect education. Both groups explicitly refer to norms of fairness, albeit

[64] Hofstee (1983).   [65] Stouffer et al. (1949), vol. 2, ch. 11.
[66] Hyman and Brough (1975), p. 49.   [67] Messick and Sentis (1983), p. 70.

to different norms – namely the norms that happen to coincide with their self-interest. Here, too, experiments yield similar results. There is a clear tendency for low-efficiency subjects to prefer the norm of equality over the norm of equity, while high-efficiency subjects have the opposite preference.[68]

It is hardly surprising that the appeal to norms has a self-serving aspect. It is more interesting to note that many individuals espouse norms that go against their material interests. Some experimental studies[69] find evidence of a 'norm of modesty' that leads low achievers to prefer equity and high achievers to prefer equality. Among the students with good scholastic records, a majority preferred the weighted lottery and a non-negligible chance of rejection over merit selection and certain acceptance. Among married men with children, only 60 per cent thought married men with children should be demobilized first, whereas 27 per cent of single men held this preference. There is a correlation between self-interest and conceptions of fairness, but it is far from perfect.

This conclusion also appears to be borne out in the labour market. In the 1960s and 1970s, the norm of equality had a strong hold in the LO unions whose members were being asked to moderate their claims in favour of low-income groups.[70] On purely self-interested grounds, the adherence of high-wage unions to solidaristic wage policies might seem inexplicable. What is in it for them, except the satisfaction of seeing justice done? As we saw in Chapter 4, they do have an interest in cooperative policies, which reduce inflation and unemployment and create more investment and public goods. The terms of trade, however, remain to be decided: will the wage profile be more or less egalitarian than it would have been under decentralized labour–capital bargaining?

There are three possibilities. (a) If the labour–labour bargaining on this issue were purely a matter of bargaining power, the profile would be *less egalitarian* than a decentralized profile. Highly paid workers can credibly claim to survive even in the jungle of decentralized bargaining, following the general 'Matthew effect' in bargaining. Hence they can credibly demand the lion's share of the benefits from collective restraint. (b) The norm of equity would suggest *the same profile* of relative wages as that which would obtain under decentralized conditions, assuming that decentralized

---

[68] Messick and Sentis (1983) is the most complete statement and defence of this view.
[69] See references in note 95 to Chapter 3.   [70] Elvander (1988), p. 265.

bargaining would reward workers more strictly according to contribution. Here the determinant of the profile is the bargaining power of unions vis-à-vis employers, not vis-à-vis each other. (c) Nevertheless, high-income workers often end up embracing solidaristic policies, which impose a *more egalitarian* wage profile. A plausible explanation (but not the only one, as we shall see) is that they actually share the norm of equality. At any rate, it is clear that something is preventing them from exploiting their bargaining power to the hilt.

The problem is that what seems like non-self-interested subscription to a norm that favours another group may turn out to be self-interest in disguise. Consider the striking stability of flat-rate income differentials in many industries. H. A. Turner notes that in Britain 'the average differential between the various engineering district rates for labourers and fitters, for instance, was constant from 1926 to 1948 at 16/- per week, although rates nearly doubled in this period'.[71] Among the considerations he adduces to explain this striking constancy, one relies squarely on the norm of equality: 'Among craftsmen (and particularly in the building trades where skilled men and labourers work in close co-operation) one meets the argument that the labourer needs as much to live as any other'. Another consideration, however, is couched in terms of self-interest and refers to 'the craftsman's fear of undercutting by the unskilled worker'.[72] Better-paid workers have an interest in increasing the income of the lower-paid groups to reduce employers' incentive to substitute.[73] An agent who exercises his monopoly powers stands the risk of losing it,[74] and one may pull one's punch out of self-interest as well as of solidarity.

In a loosely analogous manner, it may be in the self-interest of high-wage workers in Sweden to embrace solidaristic wage policies. Assume, namely, that the norm of equality is so strong among low-wage workers that they would rather not have any central agreement at all than one that did not have a low-wage profile. In that case, high-income workers have to accommodate themselves to the strongly held norms of low-income groups, whether or not they believe in the norm for themselves. We saw in Chapter 3 that if belief in a norm enables the weak to say, credibly, that they will cut off their nose to spite their face, the strong will have to yield, at least if they are rational. True, the strong may also be moved by a norm. Per-

---

[71] Turner (1952), pp. 241–2.   [72] Ibid., p. 248.   [73] Swenson (1989), p. 27.
[74] This lies behind the 'imperialism of free trade' (Kindleberger 1975).

haps high-income groups genuinely believe in a norm of reward according to contribution. Yet if, as is probable, that norm's grip on their mind is too weak to sustain similar sacrifices, they will end up yielding to the norm of equality.[75]

I do not really believe in the argument just sketched. I am confident, that is, that high-income workers, too, feel the pull of the norm of equality, because of its central place in the working-class movement. The purpose of the argument was simply to show that even if they do not, they may have to act as if they did. A similar and more plausible analysis can be made with respect to the 'efficiency-wage' argument that it is in the employer's interest to raise wages so as to motivate the workers. Usually, the argument relies on deterrence effects. By raising wages, employers ensure that workers have more to lose if they are caught shirking and are fired.[76] The argument can also, however, invoke 'morale' effects. Workers whose wages drop below their reference point[77] or who earn less than other members of their reference group[78] might be demoralized to the point where productivity is adversely affected. In that case, it may be in the firm's interest to raise their wages, thus acting 'as if' it shared the norms of the workers. 'If workers exhibit such irrationalities, it pays for firms to reflect those irrationalities in their wage-setting policies'.[79]

I have argued that in labour–labour bargaining or in capital–labour bargaining, a norm-guided agent often does better than a purely rational interlocutor because of his willingness to suffer irrational sacrifices. Robert Frank uses a similar observation to argue that norms of fairness are self-interest in disguise.[80] Suppose that A and B are bargaining over $1000, and that A is somehow able to precommit himself to an insistent offer of $900. Under those circumstances, it is clearly in B's interest to accept the $100, although the distribution is very unfair to himself. Yet if he feels sufficiently strongly about the unfairness of the distribution, he may refuse the deal altogether, forgoing the $100 rather than accept the unfair distri-

[75] There is, however, a difference between this case and that discussed by Turner. In his analysis, the pulled-punch argument did not rely on anyone believing in any norms. In the conjectural analysis of the Swedish case, the apparent espousal by high-wage groups of the norm of equality relies on the low-wage groups sincerely espousing it.

[76] Shapiro and Stiglitz (1984).   [77] Stiglitz (1986), p. 192.

[78] Oswald (1981), p. 271. This article considers the interaction of the 'morale' effect and the 'implicit threat' effect discussed in Chapter 4.

[79] Stiglitz (1986), p. 192.   [80] Frank (1985), p. 21; see also Frank (1988), ch. 9.

bution. There is evidence that people behave like this in experimental situations,[81] and it is easy to think of real-life analogues. The knowledge that B might react in this way provides A with a reason for not precommitting himself. Hence B ends up better off as a result of his desire for fair distribution. So far, so good. Frank goes too far, however, when he suggests that norms of fairness can be *explained* by these benefits. In the first place, he would have to show that the overall effect of believing in fairness is beneficial, rather than citing one example in which it is useful to do so. When people have incompatible notions of what is fair, they may not be able to reach any agreement at all. Rigid adherence to a norm can be disastrous in the face of rigid adherence to another norm. In the second place, even had he demonstrated a positive net effect, it would still not follow that it explains the behaviour that causes it.

Hence we see that the relation between norms and self-interest is twofold. On the one hand, because and to the extent that people adhere to norms, they are willing to act against their self-interest. On the other hand, norm-induced willingness to break off negotiations rather than accept an unfair outcome may compensate for lack of bargaining power. Hence adherence to norms can also serve one's self-interest. One should not infer, however, that it is rational to believe in norms, any more than one should infer that it is rational to be a homicidal maniac. Although the maniac often gets his way, his fate is, in general, not an enviable one.[82]

An additional argument for the reality of norms relies on the need for consistency in appealing to them. As I remarked in Chapter 3, it is difficult to invoke a norm in one situation where it serves my interest and then refuse its relevance in another, similar situation where it works against me. My self-image as a person constrained by social norms will not allow me to act in this way:

The representative [bargaining on behalf of union members] may be able to pick and choose between comparisons in the interest of a seductive negotiating case, but a workforce, although it may shift the emphasis of its attention between more than one salient reference group, cannot flit around a range of them or adopt fresh ones with any nimbleness. . . .

[81] Kahneman, Knetsch and Thaler (1986b).
[82] See also Elster (1985c) for the general issue of the rationality of the emotions.

few employees take aggressive action against their employers without a sense of legitimate grievance.[83]

Equally importantly, others will not allow me to get away with ad hoc invocation of norms. There is a clear social norm to the effect that if one party opens up a certain line of argument or invokes a certain social norm, it stays on the table forever. Legal rules for cross-examination of witnesses reflect this norm: a line of inquiry may be closed to the prosecution unless the defence brings it up.

This principle – one may think of it as the 'Pandora's box' principle – has several applications to wage bargaining. Consider first the obligation to disclose information. Under U.S. labour law, 'attempts by management to show "inability to pay" may create a potential entitlement, on the part of the unions, to a wide range of organizational information'.[84] More generally, 'employees will eventually become suspicious of management which sees fit to "open the books" only when the firm is in trouble'.[85] A firm may end up in better shape if, as a matter of principle, it never opens its book than if it lets itself be tempted to open them on one occasion in which it is in its interest to do so.

The ability-to-pay criterion itself is a two-edged sword, in the hands of either party. From the union's point of view, 'although ability to pay may appear merely to have a "ratchet" influence in that it appears to be used in wage demand rationalizations only when it is favourable to the union case, in fact "inability to pay" may also depress the union's expectations'.[86] As another writer says, 'Labor cannot expect to have its cake and eat it too. If wages are to be pushed up when and as each employer has or appears likely to have especially high profits, then it would seem only logical that wages paid by any employer should go down when his profits decline'.[87]

From the employers' point of view, the appeal to the ability-to-pay criterion during the Great Depression may, in the long run, have set a dangerous precedent. 'Once it became clear that the post-war period would not feature a return to the Great Depression, the business community lost its interest in ability to pay as a criterion for wage setting'.[88] Yet bygones

---

[83] Brown and Simon (1975), p. 32.
[84] Foley and Maunders (1977), p. 149.   [85] Ibid., p. 39.   [86] Ibid., p. 124.
[87] Fairchild (1946), p. 40.   [88] Mitchell (1986), p. 69.

are not always bygones; the past cannot be undone; and what has been will be. 'If the Great Depression had never occurred, if certain government policies had not been adopted, notions of fairness might be different'.[89] Departures from equilibrium may bring into existence new social norms that persist when equilibrium is restored.[90]

The Great Depression had a similar effect on norms of collective bargaining in Sweden. In the 1930s, wages of metal workers lagged behind those of construction workers. The strong dissatisfaction of the metal workers with the existing wage differentials was a major cause of the move towards centralized bargaining.[91] Later, when the metal workers became the high-wage outliers, they were bound by their past appeals to solidarity. As early as 'the beginning of the war, there were already some who thought that Metall had blundered by becoming the standard bearer for the idea of solidaristic wage policy in 1936. Certainly, it had been the underdog then, but now that they were better off, it gave them the moral obligation to show solidarity even when it was to their disadvantage'.[92]

The final view to be discussed is that norms of fair distribution and self-interest jointly determine the outcome of bargaining. This view seems to me obviously correct, but it does not pack much punch until we have specified the precise mechanism of interaction. One general observation is that normative considerations seem to be more important at the central level, whereas plant-level negotiations are more exclusively determined by bargaining strength. In particular, relative-wage considerations seem to matter less in local bargaining.[93] Centrally determined solidaristic wage policies are to a considerable extent offset by local wage drift. There is little doubt, however, that sometimes normative and norm-free elements interact at the same level of bargaining. How do they interact?

The task is to measure normative appeal x and bargaining strength y, and to determine the outcome of bargaining as a function $f(x, y)$ of these arguments. Looking back to the discussion of Chapter 2, there are several ways in which normative considerations might be captured. 'Irrelevant al-

---

[89] Ibid., p. 72.

[90] A similar, better-known proposition applies to social institutions. The redistributive institutions of contemporary societies also owe much to the temporary disequilibrium in the 1930s.

[91] Swenson (1989), pp. 43–53.   [92] Gösta Rehn, cited after Swenson (1989), p. 60.

[93] Calmfors (1986). Nilsson (1987) cites, however, several instances in which wage drift is influenced by wage relativities.

ternatives', that is, the outside options of the parties, can have a normative effect if the workers are motivated by the desire to preserve income differentials. The best feasible outcomes of the parties could also affect normative strength, as in the Kalai–Smorodinsky solution. In addition, reference earnings could be used as an indicator of x. Bargaining strength could be captured by the inside options of the parties or by cruder indicators such as the size of the strike funds. What could the function f look like? The following passage amounts to saying that in capital–labour bargaining, $f(x, y) = g(\min[x, y])$, where g is an increasing function of its argument:

> If material and ideological factors are both of importance in influencing the process of pay determination, however, it would appear that they interact in a manner singularly unfavourable to the interests of trade unionists. . . . employee groups without adequate collective strength are unlikely to benefit significantly from moral righteousness; yet the limited availability of normative rationale for pay demands of stronger groups is likely to inhibit the effective exercise of their power.[94]

In other words, normative power constrains the strong but does not help the weak. The argument is made for British collective bargaining, about which I know little.[95] It does not sound plausible, however; and it certainly does not apply to collective bargaining in the Scandinavian countries. Here it would be more tempting to say that $f(x, y) = g(\max[x, y])$. Strong groups play on their bargaining strength and weak groups on the normative appeal of equality. But this does not seem quite right, either. The strong are to some extent constrained by normative considerations, as I have argued. It is plausible to assume, therefore, that f is sensitive to changes in both arguments. One could write, for instance, $f(x, y) = ax + by$. An additive-interaction assumption of this kind is made by Max Bazerman in his attempt to determine the weights of various factors that arbitrators take into account when making their decision.[96] More plausibly, perhaps, we may assume that the impact of norms depends on the level of bargaining strength, so that there is an element of multiplicative interaction. A Cobb–Douglas

---

[94] Hyman and Brough (1975), pp. 82–3.

[95] A similar argument (also about Britain) is made by Brown and Simon (1975), p. 29: 'When a workforce has sufficient bargaining strength to influence the level of its wage, its efforts are likely to be influenced most by what it sees to be "fair" '

[96] Bazerman (1985).

Nature of the constraints

		Economic possibility	Social norms
Impact of the con-straints	Only when binding	Nash	Case I
	Also when not binding	Kalai-Smorodinsky	Case II

Fig. 6.2

function $f(x, y) = x^r y^{1-r}$ is implausible since it assigns no weight to pure bargaining strength. A better suggestion might be $f(x, y) = ax + by + cxy$.

These are, however, very mechanical proposals. A more intuitively meaningful approach to the question can be derived from Fig. 6.2.[97] Action takes place under constraints. Hard constraints are those given by the laws of physics, biology, or economics: we cannot walk on water or spend more than we earn. As mentioned in Chapter 3, social norms may to some extent be perceived as soft constraints on action. To this distinction between different types of constraints we may add a distinction between different modes of operation of the constraints. The standard view is that constraints do not affect outcomes unless they are binding. Thus, changes in 'irrelevant alternatives', that is, alternatives that would not be realized under any circumstances, cannot affect the outcome. Against this, we may set the view that constraints can 'act at a distance', so that changes in irrelevant alternatives can affect the outcome. In Chapter 3, this distinction was used to contrast the Nash and Kalai–Smorodinsky solution concepts. In that discussion, however, it was taken for granted that the constraints in question were hard, economic ones. Now we may admit the possibility of soft or social constraints, and make a similar distinction between two ways in which they can affect action. In Case I, norms affect outcomes only when they are binding. Let us assume that the managers have a reference level of profits and the workers a reference level of wages. If the outcome of norm-free bargaining respects both reference levels, the norms have no

---

[97] The following is inspired largely by Barth and Iversen (1988).

role. In Case II, by contrast, norms can affect the outcome even when they are not binding. The workers might say to themselves, 'It's not fair that we should just get our reference level of wages whereas the firm gets a large increase in profits compared with the reference level'. In that case, norms enter doubly into the explanation of the outcome: both as constraints and as part of the mode of operation of the constraints. In Case I and in the Kalai–Smorodinsky solution, they enter only once, albeit differently in the two cases.

Norm conflicts in bargaining

We may distinguish among the following cases of two-party bargaining. (a) The bargaining is merely a matter of bargaining strength, with no place for norms. (b) One party believes so strongly in a norm of fair distribution that the other party is constrained by its self-interest to accept the outcome dictated by that norm. (c) Both parties believe in a norm that favours one of them. (d) The two parties believe in different norms. The most frequent case arises if each party subscribes to a norm that favours its interest, but other cases may also occur.

The first case, norm-free bargaining, can easily lead to an impasse, because the parties are uncertain about each other's preferences or have pre-committed themselves to incompatible positions. The parties may eventually reach agreement, but only after considerable losses have been incurred. Cases (b) and (c) are more likely to yield a negotiated solution. Case (b) may for practical purposes be represented as a precommitment by one party that preempts similar tactics by the other. Case (c) does not require further comment. The last case, norm conflict, is less likely to yield negotiated solutions. In norm-free bargaining, the only thing at stake is self-interest, a mild if mean-spirited passion. In norm conflict, the parties argue in terms of their honour, a notoriously strong passion capable of inspiring self-destructive and self-sacrificial behavior.[98] Belief in incompatible norms is a bit like precommitment to incompatible positions, although less irrevocable as an obstacle to agreement. It *is* possible to back down from a norm-motivated claim, whereas the very point of a precommitment is to make it impossible to back down.[99] The norm of never retreating is less binding

---

[98] Hirschman (1977) is the *locus classicus* for this distinction.

[99] But see Crawford (1982) for a notion of precommitment that allows for backing down, at some cost.

than the action of actually burning one's bridges. Compromises are possible between opposing norms, if one or both parties pour some water in their wine and let self-interest override honour.

I shall use the norm of equality and the various equity norms to illustrate norm conflict. The relation between equality and ordinal equity is indeterminate and not very interesting. Since this concept of equity is purely ordinal, it is consistent with nearly equal remuneration for all jobs as well as with highly differentiated wage systems. The relations between equality, on the one hand, and strong equity, weak equity and differential equity, on the other, are more important. I shall discuss them in this order, with a view to the possibility and modalities of reconciliation and compromise.

Consider first the conflict between equality and proportionality. This conflict appears clearly in the allocation of ministries to the members of a coalition government, where equality dictates that each party get the same number of ministries whereas equity demands that ministries be allocated proportionately to seats in parliament or to the percentage of the vote. *A priori,* we might expect a compromise to be reached: the smaller members of the coalition get a more than proportional number of ministries, yet fewer than the larger parties.[100] I believe that the internal power structure of central labour unions also reflects this principle: the smaller unions carry more weight than size alone would suggest, yet less weight than the larger ones. As a consequence, centrally negotiated wage agreements tend to be somewhere in-between equality and strong equity.[101] A different type of compromise is reached in the U.S. Congress, where the norm of equality is embodied in the Senate and the norm of proportionality in the House of Representatives.

Consider next the conflict between equality and the weak norm of equity. Sometimes, these two goals can be reconciled. In Sweden, as in many other countries, there is a 'double imbalance' between private and public functionaries. Higher functionaries in private industries earn more and lower functionaries earn less than their public counterparts. To restore equity, one could either compress the differentials in the private sector or increase them in the public sector. The former course would also be a move towards equality, whereas the latter would create equity at the expense of greater inequality.

---

[100] Support for this view is adduced in Komorita and Chertkoff (1973). It is difficult to test the hypothesis directly, since not all ministries are equally valuable.

[101] For a similar experimental finding see Mikula and Uray (1973).

Consider finally the relation between equality and differential equity. These goals can also be reconciled, albeit mainly in a cosmetic way. Equal flat-rate wage increases can be presented as equalizing, insofar as they reduce per cent differentials, and as equitable insofar as they preserve absolute differentials. In Sweden, the 1984 bargaining round was constrained (very loosely, as it turned out) by a 5 per cent ceiling on wage increases. This constraint could be presented as a differential-preserving measure. Since the per cent increase was calculated on the average wage, so that it gave higher per cent increases for low-income groups, it could also be made to appear as a step towards equality.

Usually, however, equality and ultraweak or differential equity cannot be reconciled. One might expect, therefore, some kind of compromise. What we observe instead are oscillations. In Sweden, there has been a clear cyclical movement over the past four or five decades. Before 1950, the norm of equality was very strong within the labour movement. At the LO congress in 1951 the principle of equal pay for equal work became the dominant principle. In the 1960s, there was a return to solidaristic wage policies. In the 1980s, the weak equity norm seems to be coming back. The cycle may well correspond to underlying changes in public opinion, but I do not believe this is the whole explanation. In addition, there is the lesson from advertising: *never split the message*. At any given time, the labour movement needs a single unifying principle, not an uneasy compromise between two norms.

In Western societies the appeal to norms of fair distribution is widespread. Increasingly, wage negotiations take place in a public arena that makes it difficult to appeal to naked self-interest. Here arguments must be backed by principles rather than sheer bargaining strength.[102] I have been arguing that this shift from norm-free to normative bargaining can make it more difficult to reach agreement. In other decision-making contexts, public discussion can facilitate agreement. A properly structured political process may enable the parties to reach or approach consensus.[103] Bargaining is not, however, a deliberative process. Here norms are branded as weapons, not advanced as arguments. Once put on the table, their effect is to make it more difficult to back down rather than easier to reach agreement.

[102] Elster (1983a), sec. 1.5.   [103] Ibid.

Another effect of the shift to normative bargaining tends, however, to attenuate this problem. The plethora of norms in the labour market encourages some scepticism and cynicism as to how strongly and deeply the parties believe in the principles they advocate, and probably undermines the depth and strength of feeling in the parties themselves.[104] As normative wage bargaining becomes less similar to an irresistible force meeting an immovable object, the risk that appeal to incompatible norms may produce a bargaining impasse is reduced. Other things being equal, the proliferation of norms makes it more difficult to reach agreement. By weakening the belief in norms, that proliferation itself ensures that other things will not be equal, thus facilitating agreement. The net effect is anybody's guess.

[104] Recall the distinction made in Chapter 3 between strength and depth of feeling.

Conclusion: the cement of society

Introduction

There are no societies, only individuals who interact with each other. Yet the structure of interaction allows us to identify clusters of individuals who interact more strongly with each other than with people in other clusters.[1] These clusters are hierarchically arranged. Imagine a series of concentric circles or, more generally, of nested closed curves, covering a given territory. For the area enclosed by any given curve, we can calculate – at least in principle – a *coefficient of cohesion,* defined as the number of transactions between individuals in the area divided by the total number of transactions in which these individuals are involved. As we move up in the hierarchy, from smaller to larger areas, the coefficient will increase, decrease, increase again and so on. In the Roman Empire, the coefficient decreases as we move from the city to the province, increases as we move from the province to the empire and decreases again as we move outside the empire to include the barbarian environment.[2] In the following, the term 'society' refers to any area which has a local maximum of cohesiveness, so that any slightly smaller or slightly larger area has a lower coefficient. There is no presumption that a society in this sense is well ordered. The interaction that defines a society can be destructive – the war of all against all – as well as cooperative.[3]

Superimposed upon these hierarchical clusters of interaction are cultural fields. The vehicles of culture are tradition and social norms. As a paradigm of culture we may take language. I use the term 'field' to suggest a continuous gradient of change and variation, dialect shading into dialect in an imperceptible manner. Imagine that the United Nations successfully

[1] Elster (1978), p. 109; Faia (1986), p. 31; citing Sztompa (1974), p. 60. David Laitin has pointed out to me the relevance to this issue of the work of Karl Deutsch, usefully summarized in Foltz (1981).
[2] Veyne (1976), pp. 103–10.   [3] Faia (1986), p. 31.

imposed Esperanto as the common language throughout the world, inculcated by a pill that also obliterated from memory the formerly spoken languages. It would not take long before local dialects emerged. Neutral *drift* due to imperfect imitation would break down the initial uniformity, and after a few centuries we would be back to Babel. Culture in this sense also includes belief systems and religion. It would be misleading to say that people throughout the Roman Empire believed in the 'same' gods, while perhaps worshipping them in different ways, as people who live in different parts of a country see the 'same' mountain from different perspectives.[4] Rather there was a continuously variable field of practices, each of them overlapping strongly with those of neighbours and parents while coinciding fully with neither. Practices at opposite ends of the empire might have little but the names of the gods in common.

Cultures do not form clusters to the same extent as do societies. Culture is a product of local imitations, whereas a society is defined by a larger set of interactions. Consider a social border, defined as a curve enclosing a society. People living near the border interact to a greater extent with people on the other side of the border than with people living at the other geographical extreme of their own society. Obviously, the clusters of interaction shape cultures to some extent, so that the slope of the gradient is steeper at some points than at others. It is nonetheless impossible to define a cultural notion of border analogous to the idea of a social border.

Superimposed upon societies and cultures are states and, more generally, administrative units. Unlike societies and cultures, they have strict boundaries. To a large extent, they shape societies and cultures, by regulating interaction and imposing uniformity. Tariff barriers and immigration laws make social borders more impenetrable. Laws imposing state religions or forbidding the teaching of minority languages in public schools make cultural gradients steep to the point of discontinuity.

In trying to identify the 'cement of society' I am inquiring into the sources of social order, as defined in the Introduction. How are expectations coordinated? How is cooperation for mutual advantage achieved? Often, the state is responsible for social order. The French idea of *indicative planning,* for example, highlighted the role of the state in coordinating expectations rather than in forcing or inducing specific forms of behaviour.[5] More obviously, the state induces cooperation within its boundaries through

---

[4] Taylor (1971) is an exponent of the view I am arguing against here.
[5] See Meade (1970) for a survey and discussion of these two alternatives.

selective incentives, by taxing and punishing undesirable activities and occasionally (though with less effect) encouraging desirable ones. I am mainly concerned, however, with decentralized, spontaneous mechanisms for coordination and cooperation. In any attempt to understand these mechanisms, both society and culture are important. Roughly speaking, society provides the larger reference groups and culture the local reference groups with respect to which norms, altruism, envy and other social motivations operate. Culture is local and allows for strong bonds to a small number of persons. Society is global and allows for weaker ties to a larger number of persons.[6]

The investigation of this problem – *How is spontaneous order possible?* – is sometimes referred to as the 'Hayek programme'.[7] The present analysis differs in two ways from most other attempts to implement the programme.[8] First, I have distinguished between two problems of social order, whereas most other writers have concentrated on the problem of achieving cooperation. Second, I have invoked a larger variety of individual motivations. Most writers try to make do with rational self-interest as a sole motivational assumption, while I have invoked a broader range of motives. Though I share their preference for a parsimonious explanation and their hesitation to get into a morass of ad hoc assumptions, I have concluded, with some reluctance, that there is no way in which the programme can be brought forward on this narrow basis. Ultimately, parsimony must take second place to realism. In physics, truth may be simple. In chemistry, it is likely to be messy. Social science, to repeat what I said in the Introduction, is closer to chemistry than to physics.

In this book I have sketched a relatively fine grained typology of human motivations.[9] In Chapter 6, for instance, I said that the number of potentially relevant norms in collective bargaining is well into three figures. In this conclusion I want to step back from this bewildering variety. Using a more robust classification, I shall distinguish among three varieties of human motivation: (a) envy, (b) opportunism, or self-interest with guile, and

---

[6] For different views about the impact of weak and strong ties on cooperative behaviour see Granovetter (1973) and Marwell, Oliver and Prahl (1988).

[7] See notably Hayek (1978), vols. 1–3. For comments, see Gray (1986) and Vanberg (1986).

[8] Attempts to implement the Hayek programme include those of Nozick (1974), Ullman-Margalit (1977), Schotter (1981), Hardin (1982), Axelrod (1984), Sugden (1986) and M. Taylor (1987).

[9] This is not to say that it could not be refined and extended in many directions, as in Holmes (forthcoming).

(c) codes of honour, or the ability to make credible threats and promises. Each of these has been taken to provide the 'cement of society', without which chaos and anarchy would prevail.[10]

The defence of envy and opportunistic self-interest is a variation on Mandeville's theme, 'private vices, public benefits'. Nobody has ever argued that envy, sorcery, witchcraft, cheating, stealing, bribery and corruption are virtues or virtuous actions. Envy is often said to be the *rust* of the soul. 'As oxide eats up iron, so is the envious devoured by this passion', wrote Antisthenes, founder of the Cynics.[11] 'Envy is a beast that will gnaw its own leg if it can't get anything else', says a German proverb. An envious person will cut off his nose to spite his face. He 'prefers the equality of hell to the hierarchies of heaven'.[12] Similarly, corruption 'is linked with actions which erode the mind of the individual'.[13] The first victim of corruption is the corruptor.

The social consequences of these traits and actions are more controversial. Some modern Mandevillians argue that envy is the 'glue' that keeps society together.[14] Similarly, it has been argued that corruption can 'serve as a cement – "a *hyphen* which joins, a *buckle* which fastens" the otherwise separate and conflicting elements of a society into a body politic'.[15] The 'common interests in spoils may provide cement for effective political unity'.[16] An analogy belonging to a different realm is that corruption acts as 'oil', 'grease' or 'lubricant', which by loosening the clogged points in the system ensures free play for the gears of society.[17] Against this is the view that corruption is a form of 'cancer'[18] and that selfishness is 'the rust of societies'.[19] Other metaphors could be used to describe the social effects of envy: it is a dead hand, a drag on the foot, a straightjacket that hinders movement.[20] These, perhaps, are consistent with the glue metaphor: a so-

---

[10] Actually, in what follows three sorts of analogies are cited, referring to the coherence of matter (cement, glue, dissolvent), the smooth functioning of a machine (oil, lubricant, rust) and the normal functioning of an organism (cancer), respectively. Some of these are metaphors for predictability, others for cooperation.

[11] Mora (1987), p. 6. The same phrase was used by Basil of Caesarea (ibid., p. 23).

[12] Mme de Staël, quoted in Mora (1987), p. 48. [13] Katsenelinboigen (1983), p. 222.

[14] Mora (1987), p. 84, characterizing the views of Schoeck (1987).

[15] Leys (1965), p. 54. [16] Bayley (1966), p. 948; see also J. C. Scott (1969), p. 276.

[17] Some of these metaphors are taken from Becquart-Leclerc (1984), pp. 191–2. (She ends up, however, arguing against this benign view of corruption.) See also Huntington (1968), p. 386.

[18] Wertheim (1963), p. 207. [19] Tocqueville (1969), p. 274.

[20] These ideas, if not the expressions, run through the expositions of envy in Mora (1987) and Schoeck (1987). Both writers are right-wing, illiterate in political philosophy, well read in the history of thought and endowed with considerable psychological acumen (Mora) and sociological knowledge (Schoeck).

ciety may be so well cemented by envy that no internal movement or outward expansion is possible. In that case, the corrosive force of corruption may be welcome.

The notion of credibility is closely related to that of *trust,* which is frequently characterized as a social 'lubricant',[21] without which the wheels of society would soon come to a standstill. Unlike envy and opportunism, trust is unambiguously welcome at the individual as well as the social level. Credibility, I shall argue, is more complex. Almost by definition, it enhances predictability. In its effects on cooperation, however, it cuts both ways. By allowing people to believe in each other's promises, it promotes cooperation. By lending credibility to threats, it undermines cooperation and promotes violence.

Envy

The phenomenology of envy and its converse, spite, malice or *Schadenfreude,* is complex. The basic source of envy is that when we attempt to take stock of ourselves, the first impulse is to look at others.[22] The serenity of mind that allows us to determine whether we are happy without comparing ourselves with others is rare. If the comparison is unfavourable, we feel a pang of envy, a fleeting rage, soon suppressed because of the recognition that the feeling is ignoble. Here is Ovid on envy:

> The residence of Envy, spattered with black pus, is at the end of a pit, empty of sun, whereas the air does not reach, sad, flooded by an inert cold, lacking fire and covered with fog. The heroic Minerva, who seeds fear on battle, as soon as she reached there stopped at the door, for she was forbidden to enter; she tapped it with the tip of her spear and it opened. She saw Envy inside devouring the flesh of vipers, the food of her vices, and she cast her eyes aside. Envy rose slowly from the ground as she left the half eaten bodies of the snakes fall off her, and moved forward with dying steps. As soon as she saw the goddess Minerva, dressed with her weapons and so beautiful, she cried with mourning gestures. Her face was pale, her whole body appeared emaciated, her gaze was always to the side, the teeth of pale oxide; her breasts flowered bile, her tongue was dripping poison, and smiled only at the sight of

---

[21] Dasgupta (1988), pp. 49, 64; Lorenz (1988), p. 198. The relation between credibility and trust is further discussed later.
[22] Festinger (1954).

pain. She never slept, she always lay awake with multiple cares, and she suffered deeply at the successes of men. She devoured and devoured herself. . . . She took a staff all covered with thorns, she covered herself with a black cloud, and wherever she crossed she smashed the flowering fields, burned the grass and lowered the high peaks. Her breath contaminated nations, cities and homes.[23]

The first urge of envy is not 'I want what he has', but 'I want him not to have what he has, because it makes me feel that I am less'. As explained in the preceding chapter, a weakly envious person does not want anyone to have what he cannot have.[24] A strongly envious person is even willing to give up a part of what he has if that is a condition for bringing others down to his level.[25] In both cases, the concern with self-respect is primary, and redistributive concerns are secondary. This distinction is blurred in John Rawls, for whom self-respect *is* a good – indeed, the most important of all goods – and as such is subject to redistribution. Let us assume, for simplicity, that there are two primary goods, wealth and self-respect, and that the self-respect of an individual is a function of the difference between the wealth of others and his own. Two profiles of distribution of these goods between two individuals might be $A = [(6, 4), (3, 2)]$ and $B = [2, 3), (2, 3)]$, with self-respect as the second good. From the premises that self-respect is the most important primary good[26] and that one ought to prefer the distribution which is most favourable to the worst off,[27] one must infer that B is to be preferred over A.

Rawls is unique among moral philosophers in finding excuses for envy. 'When envy is a reaction to the loss of self-respect in circumstances where it would be unreasonable to expect someone to feel differently, I shall say that it is excusable'.[28] He then argues that a well-ordered society is unlikely to give rise to feelings of envy, both because material inequalities are likely to be relatively small[29] and because the worst off are more likely to accept them since they know they work to their advantage and, indeed, are allowed to exist only because they work to their advantage.[30] The second argument, however, is implausible. Compare the following distributions of a bundle of primary goods (which may or may not include self-

---

[23] Cited after Mora (1987), pp. 15–16.
[24] This is the definition of envy proposed by Nozick (1974), p. 239.
[25] This is the definition of envy proposed by Rawls (1971), p. 532.   [26] Ibid., p. 440.
[27] Ibid., pp. 75–80.   [28] Ibid., p. 534.   [29] Ibid., pp. 536–7.
[30] Ibid., pp. 177–9, 496–9.

respect) among three groups: $A = (12, 8, 3)$, $B = (8, 7, 5)$ and $C = (9, 4, 6)$. Rawls's difference principle tells us to choose B, which makes the worst off better off than the worst off in any other state. The argument just stated fails, however, because the worst off in B, that is, the third group, would be better off in C. This could be a breeding ground for envy.

Envy of other people's excellence can also be excused on other grounds. In itself, the fact that another is richer or more gifted than myself cannot harm me. I might fear, however, that he might put his wealth and talents to dangerous use. The debate over the Greek practice of ostracism illustrates the point. Svend Ranulf argues that the basic root of ostracism was envy, conceived of as a general propensity of the lower middle class: 'There will, in a class of petty bourgeois, who (though they may vehemently maintain the contrary) feel their conditions of life to be burdensome and humiliating, arise a disinterested tendency to inflict punishment rooted in jealousy'.[31] Against this, others have explained ostracism by supposing that the Greeks had a justified fear of demagoguery, oligarchy and tyranny.[32] Most likely there is an element of truth in both views. The inadmissible feeling of envy needs more acceptable arguments to latch onto.

While envy begins as an emotion, it has consequences for belief formation as well as for action. Consider first the implications for belief formation. When the contemplation of the success of others brings my own failure home to me with inescapable vividness, I cannot help enquiring into the causes of my failure. Who or what caused my failure? Is there anyone I can blame? The main possibilities seem to be the following: (a) I can, truthfully, blame myself. This option is open mainly to those who otherwise enjoy enough success to ensure the self-esteem needed to admit mistakes and responsibility. (b) I can, irrationally, blame myself. 'I should have figured out that the stock market was about to crash. Certainly, all my smart friends did'. (c) I can, with justification, blame others, whether or not they also are the individuals whose superiority made me aware of my failure in the first place. Because of the mechanisms of envy-enjoyment and envy-provocation (as discussed later) this belief will sometimes be true. (d) I can, without justification, blame others. Usually the targets of comparison turn into causes of my inferiority: 'Our factual inability to

---

[31] Ranulf (1934), p. 282. The view that envy is particularly characteristic of the lower middle class is explored by Ranulf (1938).

[32] For references to writers who have held this view, see Ranulf (1933), pp. 136–7.

acquire a good is wrongly interpreted as a positive action against our desire'.[33] The plausibility of this belief is greater if one believes in magic than if one believes only in mechanical, billiard-ball-like causality. (e) I may believe, correctly, that I have simply had bad luck. 'You win some, you lose some'. (f) I may believe, wrongly, that I have simply had bad luck. Unforeseen circumstances might well have been anticipated if I had exercised normal caution. (g) I may blame the gods. For Christians, who believe God to be good and just, this is tantamount to blaming oneself. The Greeks had a more complex attitude towards misfortune sent by the gods. It might be punishment for guilt, but the gods could also cause misfortune for no particular reason or out of envy for the happy man.[34] (h) I may blame the stars. In several respects, this is a most satisfactory solution:

> No doubt it was more comforting to learn that one had been crossed at birth than to be told that one had no one to blame for one's misfortunes but oneself. . . . Astrology could thus appeal as a means of evading responsibility, removing guilt from both sufferer and society at large. Like religion, it also combated the notion that misfortune was purely random in its incidence. . . . Those who rejected [astrology] were left with a choice between two equally unattractive doctrines, the rule of blind chance or the sovereignty of a capricious deity.[35]

I may also entertain similar beliefs about the causes of the success of others. These beliefs will influence the nature and strength of my envy, as well as my willingness and my belief in my ability to seek redress. If I believe that others have caused my misfortune by magic, I may try to turn the tables on them by countermagic. A belief that others have achieved success at my expense will enhance my motivation to seek redress or, failing that, to destroy their good fortune. By contrast, the belief that others have succeeded by good luck, hard work or favours from the gods does not suggest that countermeasures are appropriate.

Consider next the relation between feelings of envy and acts of envy. According to Thomas Aquinas, the tendency to feel envy is universal,

---

[33] Scheler (1972), p. 52. I argue in Elster (1983a), p. 70, that the substance of the argument in Bourdieu (1979) is a theoretical analogue of the operation described by Scheler. Like the books by Schoeck and Mora, Scheler's work must be read with a strong dose of scepticism. For some well-taken objections, see Ranulf (1938), pp. 199–204.

[34] Ranulf (1933), p. 91.   [35] Thomas (1973), pp. 390–1.

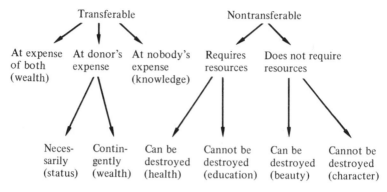

Fig. 1

spontaneous and ethically neutral.[36] It becomes noxious only when it leads to action. Kant distinguishes between one who finds pleasure in another's misfortune and one who actively promotes it.[37] The distinction is morally important: one is responsible for one's actions, but not (or to a lesser extent) for one's emotions.[38] Many who find a titillating pleasure in a friend's misfortune would be horrified at the thought of going out of their way to provoke it. Doing so by omission or abstention might be easier. It is very hard to admit to oneself that one is envious: it does not take a moralist to recognize that it is an ignoble feeling. Acting on envy would leave one with a bad taste in the mouth. Not acting to prevent misfortune, however, could be justified to oneself and others by more acceptable motives, such as 'sturdy self-reliance' – 'I don't ask for help nor do I give any'.

The target of envy is another person's fortune – his intelligence, health, good looks, sunny disposition, knowledge, wealth, spouse, title, job, status or luck. One might even envy another for his utility function – his ability to derive pleasure from consumption goods.[39] Targets of envy can be classified according to the scheme presented in Fig. 1.

---

[36] Mora (1987), pp. 29–30.   [37] Schoeck (1987), p. 201.

[38] This is controversial. Sabini and Silver (1987) argue that we do find other people responsible for their emotions and judge them accordingly, but that the judgement is aesthetic rather than moral. Aristotle argued that I am responsible for involuntary emotions, because at some earlier time I could have decided to become the kind of person that is not subject to these feelings. See also Elster (1985c).

[39] As explained in Roemer (1985b), this is one of several reasons the theory of 'envy-freeness' (see Foley 1967; Varian 1975) is not an attractive notion of distributive justice. I might not envy your consumption of meat if I am allergic to it, but I might envy you the absence of the allergy.

There are two main categories: transferable and nontransferable goods. Some goods can be transferred and shared without any loss of value. Knowledge is the classic example. Suppose I am about to go out, not knowing that rain has been forecast. A friend who knows nevertheless does not tell me, relishing the idea that I will get wet. Most transfers of goods make one or both parties worse off, however. The case in which both are made worse off arises when distribution has a negative impact on production. Redistribution by progressive taxation, when carried to extremes, might have this effect. This case is the converse of the previous one. Abstention from giving when nobody would lose shows a mean, spiteful attitude. Similarly, the demand for a gift when both would lose from the transfer can be explained only by strong envy, 'cutting off one's nose to spite one's face'.

In less extreme cases, transfers of goods benefit the recipient at the expense of the donor. This is, however, a contingent conflict of interest. It would not arise if the recipient, by receiving the good, were made so much more productive that both donor and recipient ended up gaining. A necessary conflict of interest arises if the good is a positional one, like status. These cases are not central for the present purposes. The desire to benefit at another's expense may be greedy and selfish, but it is neither envious nor spiteful. True, the desire to acquire more in absolute terms often goes together with, and may be hard to distinguish from, the desire to acquire more in relative terms. Emulation, as distinct from envy, is a blend of both.

A pervasive theme in the literature on envy is that people are envied both for what they *are* and for what they *have*. The fact that health, beauty, education and character cannot be transferred does not prevent them from being targets of envy. Sometimes the development of personal properties in one person requires resources that might have been spent on developing similar properties in another. I might have had your glowing health or your cultural skills if my parents had been as wealthy or educated as yours. In such cases, a weakly envious person might welcome the destruction of the qualities he envies. A levelling transfer being impossible, he would welcome a levelling destruction. The belief that an injustice has been done could lend some legitimacy to the claim that 'if I can't have it, nobody shall'.[40] Other qualities – beauty or personal integrity – are inborn or ac-

---

[40] It should be mentioned, however, that the all-or-none principle can also be defended on higher grounds. In Jewish ethics, for instance, the principle that scarce life-saving resources should not be given to anyone if they cannot be given to everyone is defended on the grounds

quired in a way that carries no opportunity costs for others. Yet the sight of them might so inflame an envious person that he would welcome their destruction. Here the innocent pedigree of the properties makes it difficult for envy to come into the open.

A distinction at right angles to the one just made is that between the nontransferable properties which can be destroyed and those which are indestructible. These correspond, roughly speaking, to bodily and mental properties, respectively. Health and beauty are destroyed with time which can be some consolation for the envious, who are naturally inclined to think these properties so important that it must be even worse to lose them than to lack them. They might think with Donne, 'Less grief to be foul than to have been fair'. If natural decay is too slow, the envious might decide to lend nature a hand, although such tactics as disfiguring a rival's face is more common in jealousy than in envy.[41] The thrower of acid will say, 'If I can't get him, you shall not either', not 'If I can't be beautiful, you shan't either'. An educated mind and integrity of character, by contrast, are not subject to decay or to destruction, except perhaps by corruption. If an envious person can find a wedge or a crack in the character of the envied, he can use promises of wealth, fame or power as a lever to open it further. Complete integrity can be destroyed only through destruction of the body. 'Therefore when they were gathered together, Pilate said unto them, Whom will ye that I release unto you? Barabbas, or Jesus which is called Christ? For he knew that for envy they had delivered him' (Matt. 27:17–18).

Innocent, indestructible goodness attracts envy, although it harms nobody, occurs at nobody's expense and cannot be destroyed short of destroying the body. Nietzsche observed that what especially galls the envious is that the envied does not himself envy anyone.[42] Many writers have

---

of sanctity of human life (Cahn 1955, pp. 61–71; Jakobovits 1959, p. 98; Rosner 1986). The related principle that it is better that all Jews be killed by the tyrant than for them to hand over any one among themselves to be killed (Daube 1965, 1987, pp. 75–114) is justified on different grounds. By agreeing to select the individual who is to be killed, they would collaborate with the oppressor as they would not, for instance, if he asked them to hand over a named person.

[41] The distinction between the two-party relation of envy and the three-party relation of jealousy is hard to draw in some cases. A might be jealous of the fact that C envies B. Why doesn't C envy *him*? C's envy, like C's love, may be a feeling directed to only one target at a time. If A enjoys being envied, he might be jealous of B. But A might also be envious of the fact that B attracts universal envy. In such cases A is really envious of B's success, and there is no element of jealousy.

[42] Mora (1987), p. 53.

observed that attempts by the nonenvious envied to restore equality by sharing some of their goods with the envious stimulates envy rather than assuages it.[43] If we follow Kant in thinking that ingratitude can stimulate giving, because the benefactor 'may well be convinced that the very disdain of any such reward as gratitude only adds to the moral worth of his benefaction',[44] a vicious–virtuous spiral is set up. The more you give, the greater my resentment at the superior character manifested in your giving, and the more, therefore, you give.

This mechanism should be distinguished from two others to which it bears a partial resemblance. First, I may give to assuage the feeling of guilt that your envy causes me to have. I might even abstain from becoming superior in the first place, to prevent any envy from arising. This is the mechanism of *envy-avoidance,* which has a prominent place in many writings on the topic.[45] Second, I may give to enjoy your humiliation, knowing and intending your envy to become stronger rather than weaker as a result. A different but related line of thought is the following. While I do indeed enjoy your envy at the sight of my success, your envy is not really worth having if you are too great a failure.[46] Hence it is in my interest to keep you from slipping down to the level at which your envy would be merely pathetic and no longer give me the thrill of superiority.[47] These arguments rely on the mechanisms of *envy-provocation* and *envy-enjoyment,* which have a central role in writings on conspicuous consumption.[48]

The social consequences of the private vice of envy depend on the reactions of the envied or potentially envied to the fact of envy. Envy-avoidance is closely related to witchcraft and, especially, to accusations of witchcraft. In many societies, successful people have been branded as witches. This is a central theme in Clyde Kluckhohn's work on the Navaho. As an extended quotation from his work will show, he believed envy to be adaptive as well as maladaptive:

> Witchcraft, however, not only provides 'scapegoats' against whom hostile impulses may be displaced. Under some circumstances, witchcraft provides a means for attack upon the actual targets of my hostile feel-

[43] Mora (1987) and Schoeck (1987) have numerous references.
[44] Schoeck (1987), p. 204.   [45] See notably Kluckhohn (1944) and Schoeck (1987).
[46] This is related to Hegel's master–slave paradox, as discussed, e.g., in Elster (1978), ch. 4.
[47] As Stephen Holmes has pointed out to me, this was the attitude of the Athenians to their vassal states.
[48] Veblen (1970); Bourdieu (1979).

ings. If I am a singer and smarting under professional jealousy of another singer I can whisper accusations of witchcraft against my rival. . . . Or I can mitigate the burning of my envy of a rich neighbor by suggesting that perhaps the way his riches were obtained would not bear too careful scrutiny. If my wife runs off with another man, I can often say to my relatives, 'Oh, he got her by Frenzy Witchcraft'. This both permits intensified and socially justified indignation on my part and also reduces my shame: it is not that the seducer is a better man than I – *he* used magical powers. . . .

[C]redence in witchcraft likewise has many specific 'latent' functions which make for preservation of the group's and the society's equilibrium. It tends, along with other social mechanisms, to prevent undue accumulation of wealth and tempers too ready a rise in social mobility. A rich man knows that if he is stingy with his relatives or fails to dispense generous hospitality to all and sundry he is likely to be spoken of as a witch. Individuals know also that if they accumulate wealth too rapidly the whisper will arise that they got their start by robbing the dead of their jewelry. In a society like the Navaho which is competitive and capitalistic, on the one hand, and still familistic on the other hand, any ideology which has the effect of slowing down economic mobility is decidedly adaptive. . . .

At the same time, witchcraft has its *costs* for the individual and for the group. Given the conditions of Navaho life and the Navaho socialization process, given the conditions in the background that the Indian Service will prevent wholesale slaughter of 'witches', Navaho witchcraft does constitute an adjustive and adaptive structure. Its *cost* is projected aggression and some social disruption. Probably, as a natural consequence of the insistence that witchcraft *does* have important adaptive and adjustive effects, the *cost* has been too little stressed. In many cases, witchcraft does more to promote fear and timidity than to relieve aggressive tendencies. The fears consequent upon witchcraft tend to restrict life activities of some persons, to curtail their social participation.[49]

Using more trenchant language, Keith Thomas suggests a similar analysis:

---

[49] Kluckhohn (1944), pp. 56, 63, 68.

In a primitive society, witch-beliefs of this kind can act as a severe check to technical progress by discouraging efficiency and innovation. A man who gets ahead in a tribal society is likely to awaken the suspicion of his neighbours. Among the Bemba of Northern Rhodesia, for example, it is said that to find a beehive with honey in the woods is good luck; to find two beehives is very good luck; to find three is witchcraft. In such an environment, witch-beliefs help to sustain a rough egalitarianism. They are a conservative force, acting as a check on undue individual effort. Similarly, in twelfth-century England the chronicler William Malmesbury could complain that the common people disparaged excellence in any sphere by attributing it to demonic aid.[50]

The relation between success and witchcraft is more complex, however, than what these passages suggest. Success can attract witches: 'If you have become unusually prosperous, the witches will probably be attacking you, because they always go for people whose good fortune they envy'.[51] Related to this fact is a social norm that the poor must be treated kindly lest they turn into witches.[52] Finally, witchcraft is invoked to explain failure as well as success. 'We think them bewitched that wax suddenly poor, not them that grow hastily rich', wrote Reginald Scot.[53] In other words, both rich and poor can be sources as well as victims of witchcraft. All four mechanisms conspire to bring about egalitarianism. The rich are deterred from getting too rich by the fear that they will be accused of witchcraft or become the targets of witchcraft. The poor are prevented from getting too poor by the fear that they may be provoked into witchcraft. The idea that the poor are victims of witchcraft can sustain a more favourable attitude towards them than would otherwise obtain.[54] In these societies, therefore, egalitarianism results from a combination of envy and altruism, with the latter in turn being largely the effect of envy-avoidance.[55]

Shorn of its functionalist overtones, there is certainly something to this picture. It suggests a sense in which envy does indeed serve as the glue and cement of society, by relentlessly repressing deviants and, more fundamentally, the desire to deviate in the first place. The evil eye of envy is

---

[50] Thomas (1973), pp. 643–4.   [51] Mayer (1954), p. 65.
[52] Kluckhohn (1944), p. 67.   [53] Thomas (1973), p. 644.
[54] This argument is more speculative than the first three.
[55] A formal model of utility functions incorporating altruism towards the poor and envy towards the rich is presented by R. H. Scott (1972). He does not, however, suggest that the altruism might be caused by fear of envy.

not limited to preindustrial societies and does not need witchcraft to make itself felt. Inhabitants of small towns everywhere will recognize the 'law of Jante', written down (in 1933) by one who got away:

1. Thou shalt not believe thou *art* something.
2. Thou shalt not believe thou art as good as *we*.
3. Thou shalt not believe thou art more wise than *we*.
4. Thou shalt not fancy thyself better than *we*.
5. Thou shalt not believe thou knowest more than *we*.
6. Thou shalt not believe thou art greater than *we*.
7. Thou shalt not believe *thou* amountest to anything.
8. Thou shalt not laugh at *us*.
9. Thou shalt not believe that anyone is concerned with *thee*.
10. Thou shalt not believe thou canst teach *us* anything.[56]

Envy-avoidance provides a solution to the first problem of social order. By enforcing rigid uniformity and punishing the most harmless deviations, it ensures that behaviour will be predictable. Yet it does little to solve the second problem and to ensure cooperation. Deviations that might eventually benefit everybody are ruthlessly punished, because the would-be innovator is afraid that success will cause envy and that failure will expose him to spite.[57] The overarching norm, *don't stick your neck out*, acts as a deterrent to socially useful risk taking and to hard work.

Envy-avoidance is only part of the story. Envy-enjoyment is the other part. Francisco de Quevodo said that 'whoever does not want to be envied, he does not want to be a man'.[58] Many people are simultaneously motivated by the desire to stand out *and* by the norm against sticking one's neck out. In the closed atmosphere of a small town or a small group, the two desires are reconciled by *virtuoso conformism*. The one-upmanship of the holier than thou is illustrated in Stendhal's description of the theological seminary in Besançon. Initially, Julien Sorel sought to distinguish himself from his fellows by his scholastic abilities, until he understood that 'être le premier dans les différents cours de dogme, d'histoire ecclésiastique, etc., etc., que l'on suit au séminaire, n'était à leurs yeux qu'un péché *splendide*'.[59] He came to see that the path of distinction was elsewhere. 'Au séminaire, il est une façon de manger un oeuf à la coque qui

[56] Sandemose (1936), pp. 77–8.   [57] Schoeck (1987), pp. 75, 101.
[58] Mora (1987), p. 37.   [59] Stendal (1952), p. 384.

annonce les progrès faits dans la vie dévote'.[60] The virtuoso distinguishes himself by *setting* the norm to which he conforms.

With social mobility and economic progress come more flamboyant forms of envy-enjoyment. These, in turn, create incentives to work hard. Keeping up with the Joneses is important when you know that Jones and his wife are basking in your inferiority and enjoying your envy. Via this mechanism, envy may cause people to work too much rather than too little. As I mentioned in Chapter 6, nobody gets ahead when everybody tries to get ahead. Excessive investment in education is often cited as an example.[61] This case also suggests, however, that the ultimate effect of envy-enjoyment could be beneficial. When all take one more year of education, nobody gets ahead in the rat race, but they contribute to a more skilled work force and a more productive and efficient economy.[62] When all are motivated by relative levels of welfare, they end up being better off, not because they make an extra effort but because they benefit from the extra effort of others. The erroneous belief that education will make one better off than others induces, if universally shared, behaviour that makes all better off than they would otherwise have been.[63] By this mechanism envy could induce cooperative behavior.

Opportunism

Many people would assent to the proposition that self-interest is the cement of society, until they reflect more closely on the implications. Acting according to self-interest means never telling the truth or keeping one's promise unless it pays to do so; stealing and cheating if one can get away with it or, more generally, if the expected value of doing so is larger than the expected value of the alternative; treating punishment merely as the price of crime, and other people merely as means to one's own satisfaction. We

---

[60] Ibid., p. 388.   [61] Boudon (1973).

[62] I am assuming that education acts not merely as a screening device, but actually improves performance.

[63] This statement does not turn upon an ambiguity in what counts as 'better off'. People have an interest in both relative and absolute levels of welfare. Each person acts on the assumption that the sum of the absolute and relative benefits conferred by an extra year of education exceeds the costs of education. When all act in this way, two things happen. First, nobody gets the relative benefits. Second, everybody gets absolute benefits in excess of what they expected, because they benefit from the investment of others. I am claiming that the net effect of these unintended consequences, as evaluated by people who are concerned with both relative and absolute levels, could be positive.

may use the term *opportunism* for this relentless pursuit of self-interest and distinguish it from honest self-interest, which is constrained by the law and by norms of honesty and truthfulness.[64] When people refer to the wonderful effects of self-interest, what they usually have in mind is the latter. On the one hand, they can point to the superior efficiency of self-interest as compared with altruism and cite Adam Smith, who had 'never known much good done by those who affected to trade for the public good'. On the other hand, they can cite the liberating effects of self-interest as compared with the claustrophobic world of envy and revenge. From the present perspective, however, the view that honest self-interest is the cement of society already concedes too much. Why be honest, unless it is out of respect for a moral or social norm? I shall explore, therefore, the more radical view that opportunism glues people together, using corruption and bribery as the vehicle of the argument.[65]

Social scientists like paradoxes. From Mandeville onwards, they have been attracted to the ideas that less is more, weakness is strength, vice is virtue, helping is cruel, error is useful, irrationality is rational and the like. Often, these turn out to be second-best propositions. If I act irrationally in one respect, I might be better off if I deviate from rationality in other respects too. In a world in which some agents deviate from the socially desirable behaviour, the socially best outcome may be produced if other people deviate too.[66] The 'approximation assumption',[67] that one can approach the good society by acting as if it were already a fact, is not justified. Evil must be fought with evil, and one ill driven out by another. Perhaps the world would be a perfect place if everyone were motivated by honest if naked self-interest. Human nature being what it is, however, we can be sure that deviations from honest self-interest will occur. Religious fanaticism and ethnic prejudice lead to savage, mutually destructive warfare. The dead hand of tradition and envy keeps entrepreneurs in chains even when all might have benefited from their activities. Under these circumstances, corruption can be a useful countervailing power. To oppose it is to confuse the conditions of first-best morality with the realities of a second-best world.

---

[64] On this contrast, see also Williamson (1985), pp. 64–7.

[65] Most of the defences of corruption discussed here were written in the 1960s. Today, the realist line in political science seems to be not that opportunism is good but that it is inevitable.

[66] Lipsey and Lancaster (1956–7), p. 12.   [67] Margalit (1983).

This argument is frequently made with respect to developing countries. 'For two hundred and fifty years before 1688, Englishmen had been killing each other to obtain power. . . . The settlements of 1660 and 1688 inaugurated the Age of Reason, and substituted a system of patronage, bribery, and corruption for the previous method of bloodletting'.[68] As Albert Hirschman has argued, the substitution of 'le doux commerce' for the harsher passions provided a 'political argument for capitalism before its triumph'.[69] Although it appears that Hirschman mainly has in mind honest self-interest (he does not mention corruption), the argument could easily be extended to opportunistic behaviour. The opportunist, too, might use violence, but only when it pays to do so, never out of a pointless desire to get even. Significantly, there was less corruption under Stalin's terror regime than under subsequent leadership.[70] Nevertheless, corruption is rarely fully free of violence. Against witnesses and judges who cannot be bought, there is no alternative to violence or threats of violence.[71] (And if everyone can be bought, it is not quite clear what one is buying. I return to this point.)

Sometimes corruption can undo damage caused by envy. It 'may provide the means of overcoming discrimination against members of a minority group, and allow an entrepreneur to gain access to the political decisions necessary for him to provide the skills. In East Africa, for instance, corruption may be prolonging the effective life on an important economic asset – the Asian minority entrepreneur – beyond what political conditions would otherwise allow'.[72] Along similar lines, it is argued that 'if cynicism acts as a solvent on traditional inhibitions, and increased self-seeking leads to new ambitions, economic development may be furthered'.[73] Also, corruption may be a good thing in the face of administrative rigidity. 'In terms of economic growth, the only thing worse than a society with a rigid, overcentralized, dishonest bureaucracy is one with a rigid, overcentralized, honest bureaucracy'.[74] In a society where favouritism is rampant, efficiency is promoted by corruption. There is no presumption that relatives and friends of the bureaucrats will be good entrepreneurs, but there *are*

---

[68] Wraith and Simpkins (1963), p. 60.   [69] Hirschman (1977).

[70] Katsenelinboigen (1983), p. 234.

[71] Gambetta (1988a) cites this as one of four reasons for the rational use of violence by the Sicilian mafiosi. The most important, in his opinion, derives from the fact that the main task of the mafiosi is to 'sell trust' to people who deal in illegal commodities. To do so, they must be stronger than their protégés, who, because they deal outside the law, are already likely to be violent.

[72] Nye (1967), p. 968.   [73] Leff (1964), p. 400.   [74] Huntington (1968), p. 386.

reasons to think that the highest bidders for a public contract will also be the most efficient firms.[75]

Corruption can also enhance the moral cohesion and strength of society. Several writers have argued that 'the scandals associated with corruption can sometimes have the effect of strengthening a value system as a whole'.[76] In societies with strong ethnic or religious divisions, the cash nexus may provide the missing link: 'Nepotism and spoils enhance political development. . . . Involvement sparks a sense of belonging, offers the first step toward commitment. The bureaucracy becomes an important ladder for social mobility and therefore also a unifying and stabilizing force'.[77] By reducing unemployment, nepotism defuses social unrest and the risk of rebellion.[78] Finally, by reducing uncertainty, corruption alleviates what I have called the first problem of social order. In early capitalism, 'production for the market, fraught with uncertainty and subject to extortion, was often politically less attractive than the guaranteed returns offered by a system of politically oriented capitalism'.[79] With respect to today's developing countries, the argument that corruption reduces uncertainty takes a different form:

> The possible dangers arising from the government's extensive role in the economy are increased because of the failure of representative government to put an effective check on arbitrary action. The personalist and irrational style of decision-making, and the frequent changes in government personnel and policies add to the risks. Consequently, if entrepreneurs are to make investments, they must have some assurance that the future will not bring harmful intervention in their affairs. We can see an illustration of these difficulties in the fact that in periods of political uncertainty and crisis, investment shrinks, and economic stagnation occurs. By enabling entrepreneurs to control and render predictable this important influence on their environment, corruption can increase the rate of investment.[80]

Before evaluating the argument in this Panglossian medley, I shall consider the list of defences of bribery discussed (and refuted) by John Noonan in his massive study of the subject.[81] These include both attempts to justify

---

[75] Bayley (1966), p. 945.
[76] Nye (1967), p. 964, drawing on Gluckman (1955), p. 135.
[77] Abueva (1966), p. 537.   [78] Bayley (1967), p. 947.   [79] J. C. Scott (1972), p. 51.
[80] Leff (1964), p. 396.   [81] Noonan (1984), pp. 685–702.

bribery as consistent with subjective morality and arguments that the effects of bribery are socially desirable.

First, 'everybody does it'. From the subjective point of view, this may indeed appear to justify corrupt practices. As we shall see, however, the social benefits (if any) of corruption tend to disappear when everybody engages in the practice.

Second, it is sometimes necessary to do it. Was it wrong to bribe Nazi officials to get Jews out of the country? Was Lincoln wrong to use presidential patronage to get the necessary Democratic votes or abstentions for the Thirteenth Amendment? How can American firms survive abroad unless they accept the local mores and offer bribes? Is bribery not a functional necessity in new nations today?

Third, bribes cannot be distinguished from gifts, tips, access payments and campaign contributions. 'The Greeks did not have a word for bribes because all gifts are bribes. All gifts are given by way of reciprocation for favors past or to come'.[82] Whoever wants to condemn one of these practices has to condemn them all. And who would want to do that?

Fourth, and following closely on the preceding point, accusations of bribery and corruption usually stem from motives at least as murky as the practices they denounce. 'When certain exchanges are categorized as bribes, enforcement of their condemnation is inconsistent; intemperate; hypocritical; an expression of envy'.[83] Accusations of bribery resemble accusations of witchcraft, with respect both to their causes and to their consequences. Both can stem from envy. 'Just as accusations of witchcraft sometimes worked to clarify and strengthen the social structure, so have accusations of bribery. . . . Just as accusations of witchcraft sometimes confused and weakened the structure, so have accusations of bribery'.[84] The two types of accusations differ in one respect, however. For accusations of bribery to be both credible and damaging, the practice must be neither too rare (otherwise it will not be credible) nor too frequent (otherwise it will do no damage).[85] No similar statement is true of accusations of witchcraft.

Finally, corruption is insignificant and the amount involved is trivial. *'Lex non curat de minimis.* ''The law pays no attention to trifles'', runs the old adage. What is true of law is *a fortiori* true of morality. Morals are concerned with what aids or impedes the fulfillment of basic human needs.

---

[82] Ibid., p. 687.   [83] Ibid., p. 690.   [84] Ibid., p. xviii.

[85] Counterexamples of the last claim are provided by the 'cultures of hypocrisy' discussed in earlier chapters. Even when everybody knows that everybody is corrupt, a credible accusation might still be damaging.

A small increase in the cost of government, an increase probably less than what is due to sheer waste and inefficiency, is not the sort of thing with which morality concerns itself'.[86]

I refer the reader to Noonan's work for a detailed discussion of these arguments. Their self-serving nature is fairly obvious. Many of them have in common a feature that also characterized some of the earlier arguments. They defend corruption, bribery and opportunism by the good effects they *can* have, in special cases or under special assumptions. Needless to say, this falls vastly short of a demonstration that these practices tend systematically to have good net effects.[87] Similarly, to denounce critics of corruption by referring to the bad motives they *may* have is to show neither that these motives are universally present nor that the critics are wrong.

The main objection to the argument that corruption is socially useful can be derived from two premises. First, corruption is useful only when there is not too much of it. 'A developed traditional society may be improved – or at least modernized – by a little corruption; a society in which corruption is already pervasive, however, is unlikely to be improved by more corruption'. Another advocate of corruption recognizes that 'for the benefits of corruption to outweigh the costs depends on its being limited in various ways' and goes on to cite Mandeville to the effect that 'Vice is beneficial found when it's by Justice lopt and bound'.[88] For one thing, corruption requires a minimum of honesty in the corruptee. It has been said that an honest politician is a politician who stays bought. General Vernon Walters remarked of former President Noriega of Panama that 'he cannot be bought, only rented'. In highly developed systems of corruption, the honesty of the corruptee is enforced by specialized go-betweens, like the Sicilian mafiosi.[89] For another, corruption often requires a minimum of honesty among third parties. When corruption is 'top-heavy',[90] A corrupts B so that B will use his authority to make C act for A's benefit. Unless C accepts B's authority as legitimate, B's promise to A is not credible. If B has to bribe or threaten C to get him to execute a legitimate command, the system has broken down beyond repair.

The second premise is that corruption feeds on itself. The critical attitude towards the noncorrupt in a corrupt society is a main mechanism behind this snowball effect. Sometimes 'a top politician who is not known

---

[86] Noonan (1984), p. 692.
[87] Nye (1967) is a rare attempt to move from possibilities to probabilities.
[88] The first observation is Huntington's (1968), p. 499; the second is Nye's (1967), p. 574.
[89] Gambetta (1988).   [90] Huntington (1968), pp. 497–8.

to have acquired a vast fortune is singled out for praise as some kind of ascetic',[91] but this is probably an exception. The same author observes that although honesty may be appreciated by the public, it is less favourably looked upon by colleagues: 'A person whose probity and sense of duty show his colleagues in a bad light will be slandered and pushed out'.[92] Although opportunism can sometimes undo the damage caused by envy, envy can also act as a multiplier on opportunism. The latter effect seems, in fact, much more plausible.

Edward Banfield argued that 'in a society of amoral familists, the claim of any person or institution to be inspired by zeal for public rather than private advantage will be regarded as fraud'.[93] A recent study of corruption in Sicily suggests a more complicated picture.[94] It argues that society is not uniformly amoral, but divided into *furbi* and *fessi*, or, in American parlance, wiseguys and mugs.[95] For the *furbi*, 'an act of disinterested altruism is either eccentric *fesseria*, or a more sophisticated form of *furberia*'. Brooklyn wiseguys have a similar attitude towards ordinary citizens: 'They were the timid, law-abiding, pension-plan creatures neutered by compliance and awaiting their turn to die. To wiseguys, "working guys" were already dead'.[96] In the United States, wiseguys are a small subset of the population, and hence a large proportion of their transactions can be undertaken with mugs they can exploit. In Sicily, the *furbi* presumably form a larger proportion of the population, and hence more of their encounters take place among themselves.[97]

---

[91] Andreski (1968), p. 347. He probably intended to refer to those 'known not to have acquired vast fortunes', since if nothing is known people will assume the worst (Banfield 1958, p. 99).

[92] Andreski (1968), p. 349.   [93] Banfield (1958), p. 95.   [94] Smart (1983), pp. 130–1.

[95] Although Smart (1983) does not spell it out fully, it would appear that the *fessi* believe that the world is made up of *fessi*, while the *furbi* know that it is made up of both *fessi* and *furbi*. This provides an interesting contrast to the hypothesis that there are two sorts of people, competitors and noncompetitors, and that 'competitors would tend to believe that other people are also and uniformly competitive, whereas cooperators would believe other people are heterogeneous in this respect, some being cooperative and some competitive' (Kelley and Stahelski 1970, p. 69).

[96] Pileggi (1986), p. 36.

[97] As mentioned in Chapter 3, such cases look like a frequency-dependent polymorphism similar to those discussed by evolutionary biologists. In equilibrium, *furbi* and *fessi* would do equally well, the gains of the *furbi* in their encounters with the *fessi* being offset by their losses in encounters with other *furbi*. Parental transmission of values together with differential survival could produce a mechanism whereby the equilibrium would be reached or approximated. The reason for the smaller proportion of *furbi* in the United States than in Sicily might be that equilibrium has not yet been reached in the former country or that other features of the two countries make for a different equilibrium. Needless to say, however, this is little more than a 'just-so story'.

Even in the absence of ostracism of the honest, corruption feeds upon itself. The norm of fairness suggests that it is perfectly all right to engage in corrupt practices when others do so. Members of the 'plundering generation' in American politics could argue that 'importing illegal voters was legitimate if the other side started it'.[98] As in the closely related case of tax evasion (Chapter 5), attempts to fight corruption may unintentionally promote it:

> It is certain that fear of bolstering [the impression of the prevalence of corruption] influenced Nehru consistently to resist demands for bolder and more systematic efforts to cleanse his government and administration of corruption. 'Merely shouting from the house-tops that everybody is corrupt creates an atmosphere of corruption', he said. 'People feel they live in a climate of corruption and they get corrupted themselves. The man in the street says to himself: *"well, if everybody seems corrupt, why shouldn't I be corrupt?"* That is the climate sought to be created which must be discouraged'.[99]

Also, the more corruption there is, the more officials will go out of their way to solicit bribes and to make difficulties for those unwilling to pay them. What may have started as payment of 'speed-up' money to get to the head of the queue – a practice arguably justified on efficiency grounds – invites deliberate procrastination and delay for the purpose of increasing the size and number of bribes. In addition, the practice of corruption may undermine predictability to an extent that can be overcome only by more corruption. It is often argued, for instance, that central planning in Soviet-type economies requires corruption to deal with the bottlenecks that arise in production.[100] Against this one might want to consider the possibility that without corruption there would be fewer bottlenecks.[101]

The conclusion we derive from these two premises is that the optimal[102] intermediate solution (moderate corruption) may be unfeasible. In practice, we are constrained to choose between the corner solutions: little corruption or heavy corruption. 'If truth, honesty and altruism are valuable traits in some areas of social life, they may be impossible to preserve if dishonesty is openly tolerated elsewhere'.[103] Beyond a certain threshold, the whole

---

[98] Summers (1987), p. 13.   [99] Myrdal (1968), pp. 408–9.
[100] Johnston (1986), p. 995.
[101] See the similar arguments in Chapter 3 with respect to the alleged benefits of revenge.
[102] At least I assume it is optimal, for the sake of argument.
[103] Rose-Ackerman (1978), p. 8.

fabric of society may unravel. In Chapter 5 I argued that the likelihood of unravelling depends on the technology of collective action and on the particular motivational mix in the population. In any given case, it may be difficult to predict what will happen if some corruption is tolerated. Some regimes – Thailand is sometimes cited as an example – seem to tolerate stable levels of moderate corruption.[104] The United States also seems to have a moderate and fairly constant level of corruption. As a policy prescription, however, experimenting with corruption would be disastrous. When broken bones set, they become stronger than before, but no responsible doctor would prescribe a fracture for people who depend on their strength. There are simply too many things that could go wrong.

In a recent study of corruption and the decline of Rome, Ramsay MacMullen found the privatization of public offices to have been a major element in the regime's decay. A central mechanism was that whereby illicit exactions of money from the citizens became part of acceptable custom (*consuetudo*). Commenting on two texts from the fourth century, MacMullen writes that they 'not only make plain how completely the ethics of taking pervaded the judicial system, but how irresistibly; first, it eluded control; then, when confronted, it asserted its right to exist against the conventional ethics'.[105] Corruption can be kept in check as long as it pays homage to the virtue of hiding itself. Even when everybody knows that corrupt practices exist, the need to keep them secret imposes a limit on their extent. As observed in Chapter 3, social norms often have this effect. When office-holders openly claim rights to the spoils, so that offices are used as collateral for loans,[106] it is a sign that the norm has lost its grip.

Further on, MacMullen summarizes the transition in a comment on a late-fourth-century text that is worth citing at some length:

Contemporaries speak tolerantly, or at least make little or no complaint, about the exaction of small sums by small bureaucrats in the later empire. That wasn't the problem. Libanius puts his finger on something more serious when he declares his acceptance of a certain degree of extortion, in the triangle that joins himself, his peasants, and the local military commander. It is all right, he says, 'for the masters to offer something to the powerful, on behalf of the laborers, rather than the laborers as a check on the masters. The one gives solidity to the owners'

---

[104] J. C. Scott (1972), pp. 79–84.　　[105] MacMullen (1988), p. 157.　　[106] Ibid., p. 169.

world, while the other, leaving no place for trust [in the master], under-mines its very foundations'. And he goes on to speak of the need to preserve due order and rank. He is ready to meet the demands of the local commandant – to pay 'protection'. What he finds intolerable is the destruction of the patron-dependent relationship that had for so long maintained a village under his control.

The owners' world is the old world. . . . You knew where and who you were and where you would be tomorrow – which is really what Libanius is getting at when he speaks of *taxis*, 'assigned position and proper order'. A world in which, by contrast, assistance from the pow-erful is given for money establishes no structure at all. Rather, it dis-solves all ties: no sense of obligation or honor, 'no *fides* can remain, where all that people are considering is the size of their profits'. . . . Each purchase is a thing in itself. Before and after, no one owes anybody anything. Therefore it is not suited to long-term or complicated neces-sities; and relationships involving anything other than the wish for ma-terial possessions have no chance to develop. In both the new and the old world there was ample room for greed and self-interest; but only in the old (many characteristics of which survived into the later empire, of course) was there also room for the Roman species of honor.[107]

This is an argument that norms are needed to solve both problems of social order. When profit replaces honour and power is for sale, transac-tions become less predictable and less cooperative. Could not, however, long-term self-interest substitute for social norms? Clearly, in the Roman world it did not. Let us look more closely at this proposal.

Credibility

An important condition for predictable behaviour is the ability to make credible communications about what one will do under future circum-stances. Societies in which such statements of intention are ipso facto cred-ible enjoy more stability than do those in which credibility depends on

---

[107] Ibid. Libanius' Oration 47 is cited again in the powerful conclusion to the book (pp. 196–7). I lift a very similar passage on the breakdown on machine politics in Chicago from a recent mystery novel: 'The old patronage Machine is dead. The line of continuity has been broken. . . . There's no standing debts in the Party anymore. *Every deal you cut is a fresh deal*' (Campbell 1988, p. 153, italics added).

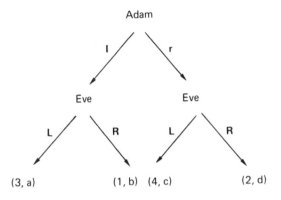

Fig. 2

whether it will be in the speaker's future self-interest to do what he has announced that he will do. The ability to make credible communications also affects the second problem of social order, that of cooperative behaviour, although the net impact is ambiguous. The ability to make credible promises enables people to cooperate more than they would otherwise have done. The ability to make credible threats reduces the level of cooperation from what it would otherwise have been.

There are, I believe, five ways in which a threat or promise to act against one's immediate self-interest can be made credible: investment in bargaining power, precommitment, long-term self-interest, social norms and investment in reputation. Of these mechanisms, the first three are variations on the theme of rational self-interest. The fourth, or so I have argued, differs radically from instrumental rationality. The last mechanism trades on people's uncertainty about each other's rationality. In a society in which it is known that some people are moved by rationality and others by social norms, but there is some uncertainty as to which people belong to which category, it may be rational to invest in a reputation for being irrational.

The rest of this chapter tries to substantiate these assertions. I proceed in three steps. First, I discuss the concept of credibility and its relation to the concepts of trust and trustworthiness. Second, I survey the sources or causes of credibility. Finally, I consider the effects of credibility on the transacting parties and, more generally, on the problem of social order.

To illustrate the problem of credibility, let us assume that we are dealing with a one-shot game between two rational players, Eve and Adam (Fig. 2).

The payoffs to Eve are assumed to be constrained by $a > c$ and $a > d$. She has an incentive, therefore, to induce Adam to move left, using a threat, a promise or a combination. Assume first that $a > b > c > d$. Then Eve can threaten to move right if Adam moves right. But this threat is not credible. He knows that she will not cut off her nose to spite her face by moving right; hence he moves right, knowing that she will move left. The outcome will be worse for Eve and better for Adam than it would have been had the threat been credible. Assume next that $b > a > d > c$. Then Eve can promise to move left if Adam moves left. Once again, however, this promise is not credible. Adam knows that once he has moved left it will be in Eve's self-interest to move right. As a result he will move right and Eve will move right, leaving them both worse off than they would have been had her promise been credible. Assume finally that $b > a > c > d$. Here Eve can brandish both the carrot and the stick, promising to move left if he moves left and threatening to move right if he moves right. Neither communication is credible; Adam moves right, Eve moves left; he is better off and she is worse off than they would have been had the promise/threat been credible. Note that the lack of credibility can affect efficiency as well as distribution. In this case noncredible threats affect distribution only, whereas noncredible promises also affect efficiency.[108]

Figure 3 presents a more complicated example. In the natural order of things, player I would move right and then II would end the game by behaving similarly. However, II might try to force the outcome (3, 6) by threatening to move left. Anticipating that move, I might then threaten to move right if II moves left. If both are rational, neither threat is credible. If, however, both threats are (somehow) made and carried out, the outcome (1, 1) is worse for both than it would have been had no threats been made. Hence the credibility of bilateral threats affects efficiency and not just distribution.

We may compare the concept of credibility with that of *trust*, which has recently been discussed at great and interesting length in a volume of essays edited by Diego Gambetta.[109] On one conception, trust and trustwor-

---

[108] Another difference is that a threat is efficacious only if there is no need to carry it out, whereas a promise has an effect only if actually kept. A noncredible threat would be dismissed by the argument 'You wouldn't do it', whereas a noncredible promise would be met by the argument 'You won't do it'.

[109] Gambetta, ed. (1988).

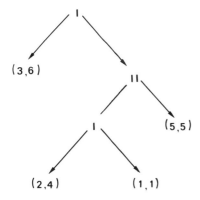

Fig. 3

thiness amount to the ability to make credible promises.[110] We might then want to ask, as I do later, about the other side of the coin. Trust might be part of a code of honour (Chapter 3) which also includes the desire not to be taken advantage of, the desire for preeminence and the like.[111] Although trust in itself is desirable, the package as a whole might not be. On another conception, however, trust goes beyond mere credibility, to include a belief that the other party will act honourably even under unforeseen circumstances not covered by contract or promises.[112] People may feel bound, that is, by the agreements they would have reached had the unanticipated development been foreseen. It has been argued that trust in this sense requires something like friendship, whereas credibility can obtain in relations between pure strangers.[113] Yet trust in this wider sense could also be sustained by arguments from long-term self-interest similar to those developed later. Social norms against taking advantage of the bad luck of others might bring about the same outcome. All in all, therefore, I believe that most arguments about the causes and consequences of trust are also captured by my discussion of credibility.

Drawing on earlier chapters, the further analysis of credibility will use examples from capital–labour relations. Consider first wage bargaining. Let us assume that the firm announces its intention to stand firm and to meet demands for higher wages with a lock-out. If the firm has high fixed

[110] This seems, for instance, to be the central idea in Dasgupta (1988).
[111] Hawthorn (1988), p. 114.   [112] Lorenz (1988), p. 201.
[113] Lorenz (1988) argues (p. 208) that the relation between managers in the contracting and subcontracting firms he studied are 'at an intermediate level between friends and strangers'.

payments because it has invested heavily in expensive capital equipment, this threat lacks credibility, since the union will know that the firm cannot afford a protracted work stoppage. Similarly, if the firm's inventories are low, the union will know that the firm cannot risk losing its customers. The case is, of course, more complex than that illustrated in Fig. 2, since the union, too, would suffer from a lock-out. The outcome depends, as explained in Chapter 2, on who will suffer most from a work stoppage. The general point, however, stands: a threat of lock-out is not credible if the union knows that it would not be in the firm's interest to carry it out.

Suppose now that the union and the firm reach an agreement. In the Rubinstein bargaining model, the agreement is simply assumed to be binding. In this sense the bargaining game is actually cooperative rather than noncooperative.[114] In the context of labour–management bargaining in the real world, this is a reasonable assumption to make. Agreements are binding because enforceable by the courts. In a more general discussion, the assumption is inappropriate, since the establishment of courts and enforcing agencies is itself a problem that falls within its scope. The fundamental problem of social order – why we are not in the state of nature – cannot be solved by reference to the existence of highly evolved juridical institutions. The question, therefore, is whether the wage agreed upon by Rubinstein-type bargaining can be sustained without third-party enforcement. The following discussion suggests a negative answer.

If wages are paid at the end of the production period, the following game arises. At the beginning of the period, workers have the choice between working and not working. If they decide to work, the firm has the choice, at the end of the period, between paying them the agreed-upon wage and not paying them. If this was all there was to the story, it would be clear that a rational firm would decide not to pay them and that rational workers, anticipating nonpayment, would decide not to work. Any promise of payment that the firm might make would lack credibility. As a consequence, both the firm and the workers would end up worse off than they would have had the promise of payment been credible.

Let us now go back to the bargaining problem and ask what the firm might do to make its threat more credible. For one thing, it might forgo capital-intensive techniques and work instead with inferior, labour-intensive methods. True, in doing so it would cause the total volume of produc-

---

[114] Friedman (1986), p. 171. I am indebted to Adam Przeworski for making me see the implications of this fact.

tion to fall, but it would still be rational if the loss were offset by the higher share accruing to the firm due to its greater bargaining power. For another, it might decide to build up larger stocks. Once again, the costs involved in building larger warehouses and the like might be offset by the gains from larger bargaining power. Although investments in bargaining power are socially wasteful, they may well be individually rational.

The workers would be doubly hurt by such tactics. There would be less to share, and their relative share would be smaller. To prevent this loss, they might promise not to use any bargaining leverage that would be created by capital-intensive techniques or low inventories. Specifically, they might promise to let the firm keep at least the level of profits it would make with inferior techniques or higher inventories. But this promise would not be credible. The firm would know that once it had invested in capital-intensive techniques, it would be in the workers' interest to use their bargaining power to depress profits below the promised level. The workers' promise to abstain from making credible threats would not be credible.[115]

Hence we see that even unilateral threats can affect efficiency, not only distribution. An actual threat affects distribution only, but the anticipation of a threat may induce behaviour, designed to reduce the credibility of the threat, that reduces the total to be distributed. The anticipation of this behaviour may, in turn, induce a promise not to carry out the threat. But this promise will not be credible. More generally, there are many promises – not only those designed to reduce wasteful strategic adaptation – that, if respected, would benefit both parties but are not made or, if made, are not believed.

Layoff policies present a similar problem. It might seem to be unambiguously in the interest of firms to be able to lay off workers whenever business conditions are bad and, moreover, to be able to choose which workers to lay off. Workers, however, have a clear interest in job security. Moreover, to the extent that layoffs sometimes have to be made, a majority of the workers would want them to be governed by seniority. On reflection,

---

[115] We may note at this point that credible threats differ from credible *warnings*. The 'morale' effect discussed in Chapter 6 could never be parleyed into a bargaining chip, since the workers cannot threaten to become demoralized if their wages fall below the reference level or fall behind the wages of some reference group. For one thing, the 'decision to be demoralized' is paradoxical and probably nonfeasible, like a decision to believe or a decision to forget (Elster 1983a, ch. 2). For another, even if the workers could make themselves demoralized, it would not be in their interest to do so. But the workers or their leaders could credibly issue a warning that lower wages would lead to a fall in morale, work effort and productivity.

however, the firm also has an interest in job security and layoffs by seniority, since these practices reduce turn-over and thereby increase productivity and (other things being equal) profit.[116] Nonunionized firms may not,
however, be able to make credible promises that layoffs will be made by
seniority. If the firm gets into trouble, it will usually want to lay off the
least productive workers or, more generally, use the layoff policy that
maximizes its chances of surviving. Knowing this, workers will not believe in promises that layoffs will be made by seniority. Acting on that
knowledge, they will tend to quit more frequently, thereby reducing productivity and making it more likely that the firm will in fact get into trouble. In unionized firms, by contrast, the union can act as an enforcer of the
promise and thereby make it less likely that the occasion to keep it will
ever arise. Unionization is to some extent in the firm's interest since it
needs the union in order to make credible promises that layoffs will be
made by seniority. However, since unions also seek to raise the wages of
their members, the firm may decide that on the whole it is better off without them.[117]

As this example suggests, *precommitment* is a generic technique for
lending credibility to threats and promises.[118] If Eve can enlist the assistance of the snake and write an enforceable contract that the snake will
punish her if she fails to carry out her threat or promise, Adam will know
that she has an interest in sticking to her announced intention. One reason
workers expect to be paid by the firm at the end of the production period
is that the wage contract will be enforced by the courts if the firm fails to
respect it. The firm might even volunteer to post a bond in order to per-
suade the workers that the managers will not simply abscond from the
premises. Similarly, a threat to strike can be made more credible if the
union takes steps to incur extra costs if it fails to do so. Union leaders
might, for instance, assert publicly that they will strike unless their demands are met, to ensure that by not striking they will suffer a loss of
prestige that will offset the costs of striking and hence add credibility to
their threat.

Let me turn to the impact of social norms on credibility. I shall refer to
Figs. 3.2 (p. 124) and 3.3 (p. 135), together with some of the earlier
observations prompted by those games.

---

[116] Freeman and Medoff (1984), ch. 11.   [117] Ibid., ch. 12.
[118] Schelling (1963) remains an invaluable and inexhaustible source of insights on this
topic.

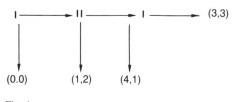

Fig. 4

With rational players the outcome of the game in Fig. 3.3 will be (2, 2). Player I will move right, anticipating that II will then move left. Although II might threaten to move right if I moves right, the threat is not credible. Assume now that II is a 'person of honour', known for never making an empty threat or breaking a promise. In that case, the threat to move right if I moves right *is* credible, and I will move left if he is rational. If I, too, is moved by a code of honour that tells him never to be taken advantage of, he will move right and take a loss rather than yield to the threat. As a result, both are worse off than if I had been rational.

Similar effects may be produced by norms of distribution. Consider Fig. 3.2. Rational players will converge on (3, 1). Any threat by II to go right will not be credible. Assume, however, that II is moved by an egalitarian norm. In that case, he might be willing to cut off his nose to spite his face: he would rather take nothing than accept the inegalitarian distribution. Knowing this, I will move left, if he is rational. Once again, however, I might also be moved by normative considerations. He might, for instance, believe in a norm of equity that justifies unequal reward by unequal contributions. If I believes himself to have made a greater contribution to the dividendum than II, he, too, might take nothing rather than accept the egalitarian distribution.

Similarly, promises that would otherwise not be credible may become so if backed by norms of honesty. In the game depicted in Fig. 4, rational players will end up at (1, 2). Player II will anticipate that if she moves across so that I is able to make his second move, I will move down and leave II with 1, which is less than what II will get if she moves down. If, however, I is known to be utterly honest, he can make a credible promise to move across on the last move, thus ensuring (3, 3). Here unilateral honesty ensures gains for both parties. The example of wage payment il-lustrates this case. If the firm is known to be honest, it is in the self-interest of the workers to come to work.

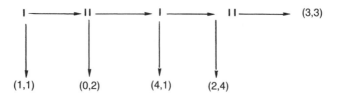

Fig. 5

In other cases, both parties have to be honest. In Fig. 5, both parties must believe each other to be honest for an outcome Pareto-superior to (1, 1) to be realized. (At least, I shall tell a story in which this is a plausible conclusion.) Assume first that I is honest but believes II to be rational rather than a person of honour. In that case I could move across at the first node and promise to move across at the third node, knowing that II will then move down at the last node. But if I is a person of honour, he will not accept the unequal outcome (2, 4), but rather move down at the first node to ensure an outcome in which he is not taken advantage of. Assume next that II is honest but believes I to be rational. Then II will anticipate that at the penultimate node I will play down rather than across, even if II has made a credible promise to play across at the last node. Knowing this, II will play down at the second node. Knowing this, I will play down at the first node.

Note that honesty is not the same as altruism. In the game of Fig. 5, assume that I is an altruist in the sense of always maximizing the sum of the two rewards but that II is purely selfish. Neither is honest, that is, neither can be counted on to keep a promise unless it is in his (altruistic or selfish) interest to do so. This will ensure the outcome (2, 4). Player II will know that at the penultimate mode, I will play across to ensure a joint gain of 6 rather than 5. Knowing this, II will play across at the second node. Knowing this, I will play across at the first node. Altruism may yield socially desirable outcomes even in the absence of honesty.

Conversely, cutthroat competitiveness in the market may coexist with stable norms of honesty, if the agents are motivated by self-interest without guile. Indeed, this has always been considered to be the ideal form of capitalism.[119] Cutthroat competitiveness without honesty, that is, self-interest with guile or opportunism, is a much uglier creature. Superficially, most

---

[119] Examples of this attitude are cited in Coleman (1982).

advanced industrial societies would seem to exhibit more honest behaviour than what the opportunism model would predict. Yet we must be wary of inferring from the fact that observed behaviour is consistent with norms of honesty that it is actually *sustained* by these norms. It could also be sustained by a motivation neglected up to this point in the argument, namely long-term self-interest.

Consider again the wage payment problem. If there is a single period of production and wages are paid at the end of that period, the promise to pay will not be credible. If, however, there are many periods and wages are paid at the end of each of them, the promise can be sustained even if managers are known not to be honest. They will know, namely, that if they do not pay the workers, the latter will not come to work in the next week. More precisely, workers can follow the rule 'Always work in the first week. In later weeks, work if and only if wages were paid at the end of the preceding week'. Against this 'Tit-for-Tat' strategy (a variant of that discussed in Chapter 1) the rational response of management usually is to pay wages. Long-term self-interest can mimic the norm of honesty. It can also mimic codes of honour. A threat that would not be credible in a one-shot game may become so if the threatener follows the strategy of executing it if and only if the other party failed to be deterred by it in the previous game.

Let us, however, consider this problem more carefully. For long-term self-interest to induce the firm to pay wages, it must not be too myopic. In fact, a myopic firm will be doubly tempted to defect. In the first place, we saw in Chapter 2 that a myopic bargainer is at a disadvantage. By his impatience he will be forced to concede more than he would otherwise have done. If the union is less impatient, it may claim and get high wages. The combination of high wages and myopia may then, in the second place, induce the firm to defect at the end of the first period. I asserted in Chapter 1 that cooperation in an iterated Prisoner's Dilemma is rational only if the parties do not discount the future too heavily, and a similar consideration obviously carries over to the present case. In general, cooperation in iterated games depends both on the reward parameters and on the rate of time discounting. In this special case, the reward parameters themselves are influenced by time discounting, which has a crucial role in determining the outcome of bargaining.

Assume, then, that both the firm and the union know that the firm is so myopic that it will not keep its promise of paying wages at the end of the period. No agreement will be struck, to the detriment of both parties. But there is an alternative: an agreement to pay wages at the beginning of each period. The firm can use the strategy of paying wages in the first week and then, in later weeks, to pay if and only if the workers actually performed in the previous week. If the workers' rate of time discounting is suitably low, their best reply is to come to work each Monday. It may be easier for the parties to reach agreement if they can bargain over the institutional set-up of wage payment, as well as over the actual amount of wages.

It could well happen, of course, that neither institutional arrangement will induce cooperation. Both parties might be too myopic to be trusted. But what if both are sufficiently patient to be trusted? What will determine whether workers will be paid at the beginning or at the end of the period? More generally, which self-enforcing agreement will be realized when there are several such arrangements none of which dominates the others? We seem to be thrown back into a bargaining problem, but at a deeper level at which there are not, to my knowledge, any appropriate theoretical tools available.

The central idea in the preceding argument was that rationality may have different implications in one-shot games and in iterated games. In addition, iterated games can be exploited to create doubts about one's rationality. In a one-shot game, it can never (by definition) be rational to carry out a threat if doing so is contrary to one's interest. In iterated games, it may be rational to act contrary to one's interest, in order to build up a reputation for toughness that will pay off in later games.[120] Often, it will not be clear whether a person is, in fact, moved by a code of honour that will not allow him to back down. Not everybody wears his norms on his face, as mafiosi are supposed to do. If, for instance, I have to make strong demands on behalf of my union, I cannot simply assert that I am a man of honour. To impose myself, I may have to act in irrational ways, effectively cutting off my nose to spite my face. My bargaining opponent will then have to think twice before insulting me by refusing to give in to my demands. All that is required is an initial belief that there is some chance (it may be quite small) that I am, in fact, irrational. By acting irrationally, I then force him to upgrade the probability that I am, in fact, irrational. But if he *knows* me

---

[120] Kreps and Wilson (1982). As briefly mentioned in Chapter 3, the assumptions behind their argument are somewhat artificial.

to be rational, he will conclude that my apparently irrational behaviour is just faking, and my investment will have been wasted. A similar argument applies to investment in a reputation for being cooperative.[121]

I now turn to the consequences of these credibility-enhancing procedures. On the one hand, we have to enquire into the costs and risks of achieving credibility. On the other hand, we must ascertain the costs and benefits of credibility once achieved by whatever means. Individually rational procedures for achieving credibility may not be socially desirable.

As emphasized in Chapter 2, *investment in bargaining power* is never socially desirable. *Precommitment to promises* is always socially desirable, unless the costs of precommitment exceed the joint gains from credibility. It does not follow, however, that it will always be undertaken when the costs are smaller than the joint gains, only if the gains to the promiser exceed the costs. There might, for this reason, be underinvestment in credibility.[122] From the social point of view, *precommitment to threats* is usually bad or disastrous. Since the costs of precommitment have to be deducted from the total to be shared, precommitment to threats affects efficiency as well as distribution. More seriously, if both parties precommit themselves, the threats may actually have to be carried out, perhaps at great cost to both and to third parties. I can think of only one case in which precommitment to a threat is desirable, namely if the certainty that the threat will be carried out deters the other party from wasteful investments in bargaining power that it might otherwise have made. *Investment in reputation* can also be costly. Nuclear deterrence, for instance, is more credible if the other side can be led to believe that one's own side is led by a madman who would rather blow up the whole world than give in to an attack. To cultivate a credible image of madness, national leaders might have to impose severe costs on their nations.

When more threats and promises are credible, two things follow. First, people will do more harm to each other.[123] This conclusion requires a

---

[121] Kreps et al. (1982). For a summary of the extensive literature on reputation effects see Wilson (1985).

[122] Dasgupta (1988), p. 64, makes essentially the same point.

[123] For the impact of threats on the level of cooperation, see Deutsch and Krauss (1960), who find that there is less cooperation when both parties have threat technologies available to them than when only one party has this option, and less cooperation in the latter case than when neither party has it. Since the feasibility of threats is a necessary condition for their credibility, enhancing the former ought, other things being equal, also to enhance the latter.

couple of intermediate steps: when threats are more credible, more threats will be made; and when more threats are made, more threats will actually be carried out. The last premise is plausible in light of the fact that the social norms that make threats credible may also lead their targets to ignore them, as was observed earlier. Societies with strong norms of vengeance have more death from violence than others.[124] Second, people will help one another to a larger extent when it is to their mutual advantage to do so. Free riding on the efforts of others will be deterred both by credible promises to reciprocate and by credible threats to punish lack of reciprocation. Needless to say, these large claims are highly speculative. Although I believe they are roughly plausible, they do not allow of anything like empirical or deductive demonstration.

Let me conclude with another speculative argument, to the effect that scientific, technical, economic and social development tends to erode the ability to make credible threats and promises, by undermining social norms and reducing the scope for long-term self-interest. This historical argument, taken together with the theoretical argument sketched in the preceding paragraph, suggests that modern societies are safer and bleaker than their traditional counterparts. They are safer because fewer threats are made and carried out, and bleaker because fewer promises are made and kept. People are less violent, but also less helpful and cooperative. In addition, bonds of altruism and solidarity may also be weaker. It will be clear from the next few paragraphs that the historical part of this argument is not only speculative but open to numerous counterexamples. I am not claiming that the trend is unambiguously towards a society in which credible threats and promises can no longer be made, only that the net effect of several opposing tendencies may well be in that direction.

In traditional, prescientific societies, people are more likely to be swayed by social norms than by means–ends considerations, simply because less is known about ends–means relations. People need guidance for their actions. When lack of understanding of natural or social causality makes it hard to predict the outcome of action, rationality may not provide much help. Social norms, by focusing directly on action rather than on its consequences, are more useful. They can tell people what to do when they are

---

[124] In Chapter 3 I reported the estimate in Chagnon (1988) that 30% of deaths among adult males among the Yanomamö Indians were due to violence. Boehm (1984), p. 177, reports that between 1901 and 1905 the percentage of deaths from violent causes in northern Albania averaged around 25% and adds that most were probably due to feuding rather than warfare.

ignorant of, and therefore unable to compare, the outcomes of the courses of action that confront them.[125] Now, this argument is suspiciously functionalist. It seems to say that social norms can be explained by their ability to guide action, but it does not provide a mechanism by which that consequence of norms helps to bring them into being or to maintain them. Because I have no idea what the mechanism would be like, the argument is conjectural and does not bear much weight.

A second reason that social norms may lose their grip on the mind in the modern world derives from the social and geographical mobility that is part and parcel of industrial societies. Mobility tends to weaken social norms.[126] When people spend more of their time with strangers, the external sanctions that are so important for sustaining norms lose their force. Why should I mind being ostracized by someone whom in any case I am unlikely to meet again? However, new norms emerge to regulate relations among strangers. Queuing, for instance – Sartre's paradigmatic example of 'serial existence' – is guided by a number of complex norms.[127]

Increased social mobility has two additional effects. First, it tends to undermine bonds of altruism and solidarity, simply because people are not around each other long enough for these to develop. Second, social mobility reduces the scope of arguments from long-term self-interest. It is generally recognized that Tit-for-Tat arguments work best in small and stable societies, in which there is a high probability that the same people will interact over and over again.[128] Conversely, in modern societies interaction is often too ephemeral for implicit promises and threats to ensure cooperation. Altogether, therefore, the low turn-over rates in traditional communities enforce cooperation in three distinct ways: by promoting stronger emotional bonds among the members, by providing more effective sanctions for promise breaking and by increasing the scope for long-term self-

---

[125] Commenting on the 1938 Munich agreement with Hitler, William Pfaff speculates about what might have happened if Czechoslovakia had fought, and then goes on to write: 'Speculation aside, there is a policy counsel in this: When you cannot know how something will come out, principle is the safest guide. It is better to do what is honorable. If in 1938 everyone had done what was honorable, *however blindly* they acted, it could have spared us a world war' (*International Herald Tribune,* 24 September 1988; my italics). Whether or not it makes sense as policy advice (see Elster 1989a, sec. 4.4), the observation may have some explanatory power: when people do not know how something will come out, they turn instead to 'blind' nonconsequentialist principles.

[126] Tocqueville (1969), p. 308; Tumin (1957).

[127] See e.g., Czwartosz (1988), as well as the discussion in Chapter 3 of the norm against buying into a queue.

[128] M. Taylor (1987), p. 105; Axelrod (1984), p. 174.

interest. In many actual cases, all three mechanisms are inextricably inter-twined, but they can and do also occur separately. Remember, however, the other side of this coin. Hate as well as love is more likely to emerge in small, tightly knit communities. Threats as well as promises are more cred-ible when people play iterated games with one another. Social norms add credibility to threats as well as to promises.

How does the decline of the Roman Empire, as explained by Mac-Mullen, fit in with this argument? A central part of the process was the decline of patron–client relations and their replacement by a more merce-nary relationship between soldiers and peasants. The former amounted to an implicit long-term contract, in which protection against uncertainty was exchanged against tribute, not unlike American machine politics. Here, long-term self-interest could reinforce and act in concert with notions of honour and loyalty. The question is whether the time horizon of the Roman army commanders was long enough to allow for an implicit contract with the peasantry to emerge. What was their life expectancy? How long was their time of office? Were they frequently rotated? How frequently did the army itself move around? The evidence for the later part of the empire is scanty,[129] but perhaps we can infer, from the fact of the observed decline, that the peasant–army relationship was too unstable for long-term relations to emerge.

A third reason for believing in the weakening of social norms also has to do with the incessant change in the modern world. Norms that tell peo-ple what to do have no force when the prescribed or proscribed action ceases to be feasible, as may well happen in a state of flux. The norm against rate busting disappears when individual piece work is replaced by team work. The norm against nobles marrying commoners disappears when there are no more nobles. The norm of helping neighbours with the harvest disappears if market changes force the community to shift to animal hus-bandry. In a constantly changing society the new practices will themselves disappear after a while, before any new social norms have had the time to emerge and regulate them. When change is the rule, however, norms emerge that regulate people's attitudes towards change. We have seen, for in-stance, that wage setting is guided by the norm that employers can reduce wages when profits are threatened because of declining demand, but not when the worker's bargaining power is reduced by unemployment.

---

[129] Ramsay MacMullen, personal communication.

The title of this book embodies a large problem, which I have split up into two slightly smaller but still enormously large questions. What is it that enables people to predict each other's behaviour? What is it that enables them to cooperate with one another? The partial answers I have provided are several sizes smaller than the questions. Altruism, envy, social norms and self-interest all contribute, in complex, interacting ways to order, stability and cooperation. Some mechanisms that promote stability also work against cooperation. Some mechanisms that facilitate cooperation also increase the level of violence. Each society and each community will be glued together, for better and for worse, by a particular, idiosyncratic mix of these motivations. But the basic ingredients that go into the cement seem to be more or less the same in all societies, even if they can be combined in innumerable ways.

References

Abbott, A. (1983). Professional ethics. *American Journal of Sociology* 88: 855–85.

Abueva, J. V. (1966). The contribution of nepotism, spoils, and graft to political development. *East–West Center Review* 3: 45–54. Cited after the reprint in A. Heidenheimer, ed. (1970), *Political corruption: Readings in comparative analysis*, pp. 534–9. New York: Holt, Rinehart & Winston.

Ainslie, G. (1975). Specious reward. *Psychological Bulletin* 82: 463–96.

(1982). A behavioral economic approach to the defense mechanisms: Freud's energy theory revisited. *Social Science Information* 21: 735–79.

(1984). Behavioral economics. II: Motivated involuntary behavior. *Social Science Information* 23: 247–74.

(1986). Beyond microeconomics. In J. Elster, ed., *The multiple self*, pp. 133–76. Cambridge University Press.

Akerlof, G. (1976). The economics of caste and of the rat race and other woeful tales. *Quarterly Journal of Economics* 90: 599–617.

(1980). A theory of social custom, of which unemployment may be one consequence. *Quarterly Journal of Economics* 94: 749–75.

Akerlof, G. and Yellen, J., eds. (1986). *Efficiency wage models of the labor market*. Cambridge University Press.

Andreski, S. (1968). Kleptocracy as a system of government in Africa. In *The African predicament*, pp. 201–9. New York: Atherton. Cited after the reprint in A. Heidenheimer, ed. (1970), *Political corruption: Readings in comparative analysis*, pp. 346–57. New York: Holt, Rinehart & Winston.

Andvig, J. and Moene, K. O. (1988). How corruption corrupts (unpublished manuscript).

Aoki, M. (1984). *The co-operative game theory of the firm*. New York: Oxford University Press.

Arbetsmarknadsdepartementet (1988). *Fach och samhälle*. Stockholm: Allmänna Förlaget.

Aronson, E. (1984). *The social animal*, 4th ed. New York: Freeman.

Arrow, K. (1971). Political and economic evaluation of social effects and externalities. In M. Intriligator, ed., *Frontiers of quantitative economics*, pp. 3–25. Amsterdam: North-Holland.

(1982). Risk perception in psychology and economics. *Economic Inquiry* 20: 1–9.

Axelrod, R. (1984). *The evolution of cooperation.* New York: Basic Books.

(1986). An evolutionary approach to norms. *American Political Science Review* 80: 1095–1111.

Baldwin, C. Y. (1983). Productivity and labor unions. *Journal of Business* 56: 155–85.

Banfield, E. G. (1958). *The moral basis of a backward society.* New York: Free Press.

Barry, B. (1979). *Sociologists, economists and democracy,* 2d ed. University of Chicago Press.

(1985). Comment on Elster. *Ethics* 96: 156–8.

Barth, E. (1988). The sequence of moves in wage bargaining. Working paper, Institute for Social Research, Oslo.

Barth, E. and Iversen, T. (1988). Rasjonalitet og sosiale normer. Qualifying paper, University of Oslo, Department of Economics.

Baumol, W. J. and Quandt, R. E. (1985). Chaos models and their implications for forecasting. *Eastern Journal of Economics* 11: 3–15.

Bayley, D. H. (1966). The effects of corruption on developing nations. *Western Political Quarterly* 19: 719–32. Cited after the reprint in A. Heidenheimer, M. Johnston and V. T. LeVine, eds. (1989), *Political corruption: A handbook,* pp. 935–52. New Brunswick, N.J.: Transaction Books.

Bazerman, M. (1985). Norms of distributive justice in interest arbitration. *Industrial and Labor Relations Review* 38: 558–70.

Bazerman, M. and Carroll, J. S. (1987). Negotiator cognition. In L. L. Cummings and B. M. Staw, eds., *Research in Organizational Behavior* 9: 247–88. Greenwich, Conn.: JAI Press.

Becker, G. (1976). *The economic approach to human behavior.* University of Chicago Press.

Beckerman, W., ed. (1986). *Wage rigidity and unemployment.* London: Duckworth.

Becquart-Leclerc, J. (1984). Paradoxes de la corruption politique. Cited after the translation in A. Heidenheimer, M. Johnston and V. T. LeVine, eds. (1989), *Political corruption: A handbook,* pp. 191–210.

Begg, D. K. H. (1982). *The rational expectations revolution in macroeconomics.* Oxford: Allan.

Besnard, P. (1987). *L'anomie,* Paris: Presses Universitaires de France.

Bhaduri, A. and Harris, D. J. (1987). The complex dynamics of the simple Ricardian system. *Quarterly Journal of Economics* 102: 893–902.

Bicchieri, C. (1987). Self-refuting theories of strategic interaction: A paradox of common knowledge. Working Paper, University of Chicago, Center for Ethics, Rationality and Society.

Binmore, K. (1987a). Modeling rational players. *Economics and Philosophy* 3: 179–214.

(1987b). Nash bargaining theory I. In K. Binmore and P. Dasgupta, eds., *The economics of bargaining,* pp. 27–46. Oxford: Blackwell Publisher.

Binmore, K. and Dasgupta, P., eds. (1987). *The economics of bargaining*. Oxford: Blackwell Publisher.

Binmore, K., Rubinstein, A. and Wolinsky, A. (1986). The Nash bargaining solution in economic modelling. *Rand Journal of Economics* 17: 176–88.

Black-Michaud, J. (1975). *Cohesive force: Feud in the Mediterranean and the Middle East*. New York: St. Martin's Press.

Boehm, C. (1984). *Blood revenge: The anthropology of feuding in Montenegro and other tribal societies*. Lawrence: University of Kansas Press.

Boudon, R. (1973). *Education, opportunity, and social inequality*. New York: Wiley.

Bourdieu, P. (1966). The sentiment of honour in Kabyle society. In J. G. Peristiany, ed., *Honour and shame: The values of Mediterranean society*, pp. 191–241. University of Chicago Press.

(1979). *La distinction*, Paris: Presses Universitaires de France.

Bowles, S. (1986). The production process in a competitive economy: Walrasian, Neo-Hobbesian, and Marxian models. *American Economic Review* 75: 16–36.

Bowman, J. (1989). *Capitalist collective action*. Cambridge University Press.

Brams, S. (1982). *Biblical games*. Cambridge, Mass.: MIT Press.

Bronfenbrenner, M. (1971). *Income distribution theory*. London: Macmillan Press.

Brown, W. and Simon, K. (1975). The use of comparison in workplace wage determination. *British Journal of Industrial Relations* 13: 23–53.

Burawoy, M. (1979). *Manufacturing consent*. University of Chicago Press.

Busquet, J. (1920). *Le droit de la vendetta et les paci corses*. Paris: Pedone.

Cahn, E. (1955). *The moral decision*. Bloomington: Indiana University Press.

Calmfors, L. (1982). Employment policies, wage formation and trade union behavior in a small open economy. *Scandinavian Journal of Economics* 84: 345–73.

(1985). The role of stabilization policy and wage setting for macroeconomic stability: The experience of economies with centralized bargaining. *Kyklos* 38: 329–47.

(1986). Arbetsmarknadsorganisationerna och lönerna. *Ekonomisk Debatt* 14: 51–8.

(1987a). Comments [on Flanagan (1987)]. In B. P. Bosworth and A. Rivlin, eds., *The Swedish economy*, pp. 174–80. Washington, D.C.: Brookings Institution.

(1987b). Comments [on Drèze (1987)]. In R. Layard and L. Calmfors, eds., *The fight against unemployment*, pp. 198–204. Cambridge, Mass.: MIT Press.

Calmfors, L. and Forslund, A. (1988). Wage setting in Sweden. Prepared for the conference Nordic Wage Formation in Stockholm, 11–13 April 1988.

Calmfors, L. and Horn, H. (1985). Classical unemployment, accommodation policies and the adjustment of real wages. *Scandinavian Journal of Economics* 87: 234–61.

(1986). Employment policies and centralized wage-setting. *Economica* 53: 281–302.

Camerer, C. F. and MacCrimmon, K. R. (1983). Underground and overpaid: Equity theory in practice. In D. M. Messick and K. Cook, eds., *Equity Theory*, pp. 295–326. New York: Praeger.

Camic, C. (1986). The matter of habit. *American Journal of Sociology* 91: 1039–87.

Campbell, R. (1988). *Hip deep in alligators*. New York: New American Library.

Campbell, R. and Sowden, L., eds. (1985). *Paradoxes of rationality and cooperation*. Vancouver: University of British Columbia Press.

Cancian, F. (1975). *What are norms?* Cambridge University Press.

Caplow, T. (1984). Rule enforcement without visible means: Christmas giving in Middletown. *American Journal of Sociology* 89: 1306–23.

Carens, J. (1981). *Equality, moral incentives, and the market*. University of Chicago Press.

Chagnon, N. (1988). Life histories, blood revenge, and warfare in a tribal population. *Science* 239: 985–92.

Chandler, A. (1977). *The visible hand*. Cambridge, Mass.: Harvard University Press.

Chen, Y. (1986). *Making revolution: The Communist movement in Eastern and Central China, 1937–1945*. Berkeley and Los Angeles: University of California Press.

Coddington, A. (1968). *Theories of the bargaining process*. London: Allen & Unwin.

Cohen, G. A. (1978). *Karl Marx's theory of history: A defence*. Oxford: Oxford University Press.

Cohen, M. D. and Axelrod, R. (1984). Coping with complexity: The adaptive value of changing utility. *American Economic Review* 74: 30–42.

Coleman, J. S. (1982). Systems of trust. *Angewandte Sozialforschung* 10: 277–300.

(forthcoming). *Foundations of social theory*. Cambridge, Mass.: Harvard University Press.

Coleman, J. and Silver, C. (1986). Justice in settlements. *Social Philosophy and Policy* 4: 102–44.

Coser, L. (1986). *The functions of social conflict*. New York: Free Press.

Crawford, V. (1982). A theory of disagreement in bargaining. *Econometrica* 50: 607–38.

(1985). The role of arbitration and the theory of incentives. In A. Roth, ed., *Game-theoretic models of bargaining*, pp. 363–90. Cambridge University Press.

Crawford, V. and Varian, H. (1979). Distortion of preferences and the Nash theory of bargaining. *Economic Letters* 3: 203–6.

Cross, J. (1965). A theory of the bargaining process. *American Economic Review* 60: 67–94. Cited after the reprint in O. Young, ed. (1975), *Bargaining*, pp. 191–218. Urbana: University of Illinois Press.

Crott, H. W. (1971). Experimentelle Untersuchungen zum Verhandlungsverhalten in kooperativen Spielen. *Zeitschrift für Sozialpsychologie* 2: 61–74.

Cwartosz, Z. (1988). On queuing. *Archives Européennes de Sociologie* 29: 3–11.

Dalton, M. (1948). The industrial 'rate-buster': A characterization. *Applied Anthropology* (Winter): 5–18. Cited after the reprint in T. Lupton, ed., *Payment Systems*, pp. 64–91. Harmondsworth: Penguin.

Dasgupta, P. (1988). Trust as a commodity. In D. Gambetta, ed. (1988), *Trust: Making and Breaking of Cooperative Relationships*, pp. 49–72. Oxford: Blackwell Publisher.

Dasgupta, P. and Ray, D. (1986). Inequality as a determinant of malnutrition and unemployment: Theory. *Economic Journal* 96: 1011–34.

(1987). Inequality as a determinant of malnutrition and unemployment: Policy. *Economic Journal* 97: 177–88.

Dasgupta, P. and Stiglitz, J. (1980). Uncertainty, industrial structure, and the speed of R & D. *Bell Journal of Economics* 11: 1–28.

Daube, D. (1965). *Collaboration with tyranny*. New York: Oxford University Press.

(1987). *Appeasement or resistance*. Berkeley and Los Angeles: University of California Press.

Davidson, D. (1980). *Essays on actions and events*. New York: Oxford University Press.

(1986). Judging interpersonal interests. In J. Elster and A. Hylland, eds., *Foundations of social choice theory*, pp. 195–212. Cambridge University Press.

Davis, K. and Moore, W. (1945). Some principles of stratification. *American Sociological Review* 10: 242–9.

Dawes, R., McTavish, J. and Shaklee, H. (1977). Behavior, communication, and assumptions about other people's behavior in a common dilemma situation. *Journal of Personality and Social Psychology* 35: 1–11.

Dawes, R., Orbell, J., Simmons, J. T. and van de Kragt, A. J. C. (1986). Organizing groups for collective action. *American Political Science Review* 80: 1171–85.

Day, R. (1983). The emergence of chaos from classical economic growth. *Quarterly Journal of Economics* 98: 201–13.

Dean, P., Keenan, T. and Kenney, F. (1980). Taxpayers' attitudes to income tax evasion. *British Tax Review* 1: 28–44.

de Nardo, J. (1985). *Power in numbers*. Princeton, N.J.: Princeton University Press.

Deutsch, M. (1985). *Distributive justice*. New Haven, Conn.: Yale University Press.

Deutsch, M. and Krauss, R. M. (1960). The effect of threat upon interpersonal bargaining. *Journal of Abnormal and Social Psychology* 61: 181–9.

Drèze, J. (1987). Work-sharing. In R. Layard and L. Calmfors, eds., *The fight against unemployment*, pp. 139–92. Cambridge, Mass.: MIT Press.

Dworkin, R. (1981). What is equality? Part 2: Equality of resources. *Philosophy and Public Affairs* 10: 283–345.

Edelman, R. J. (1987). *The psychology of embarrassment*. New York: Wiley.

Edgerton, R. (1985). *Rules, exceptions and the social order.* Berkeley and Los Angeles: University of California Press.

Eissinger, J. R. (1975). The right-to-work imbroglio. *North Dakota Law Review* 51: 71–96.

Elster, J. (1975). *Leibniz et la formation de l'esprit capitaliste.* Paris: Aubier-Montaigne.

(1978). *Logic and society.* New York: Wiley.

(1980). [Review of Cohen (1978).] *Political Studies* 28: 121–8.

(1981). Snobs [review of Bourdieu (1979)] *London Review of Books* 3(20): 10–12.

(1982). Marxism, functionalism and game theory. *Theory and Society* 11: 453–82.

(1983a). *Sour grapes.* Cambridge University Press.

(1983b). *Explaining technical change.* Cambridge University Press.

(1983c). The crisis in economic theory [review of Nelson and Winter (1982) and Roemer (1982)]. *London Review of Books* 20 October–2 November.

(1984). *Ulysses and the sirens*, rev. ed. Cambridge University Press.

(1985a). Rationality, morality and collective action. *Ethics* 96: 136–55.

(1985b). Weakness of will and the free-rider problem. *Economics and Philosophy* 1: 231–65.

(1985c). Sadder but wiser? Rationality and the emotions. *Social Science Information* 24: 375–406.

(1985d). *Making sense of Marx.* Cambridge University Press.

(1986). Introduction to J. Elster, ed., *Rational choice*, pp. 1–33. Oxford: Blackwell Publisher.

(1988). Is there (or should there be) a right to work? In A. Guttman, ed., *Democracy and the welfare state*, pp. 53–78. Princeton, N.J.: Princeton University Press.

(1989a). *Solomonic judgements.* Cambridge University Press.

(1989b). *Nuts and bolts for the social sciences.* Cambridge University Press.

Elvander, N. (1988). *Den svänska modellen.* Stockholm: Almánna Fórlaget.

Engel, H. (1986). *A city called July.* New York: Penguin Books.

Evans-Pritchard, E. (1940). *The Nuer.* New York: Oxford University Press.

Faia, M. A. (1986). *Dynamic functionalism: Strategy and tactics.* Cambridge University Press.

Fairchild, F. R. (1946). *Profit and the ability to pay wages.* Irvington-on-Hudson, N.Y.: Foundation for Economic Education.

Feinberg, J. (1984). *Harm to others.* New York: Oxford University Press.

Fenichel, O. (1945). *The psychoanalytic theory of neurosis.* New York: Norton.

Ferejohn, J. and Fiorina, M. (1974). The paradox of not voting. *American Political Science Review* 68: 525–36.

Festinger, L. (1954). A theory of social comparison processes. *Human Relations* 7: 117–40.

Finley, M. I. (1981). *Economy and society in ancient Greece.* London: Chatto & Windus.

Fischhoff, B. (1982). For those condemned to study the past: Heuristics and biases in hindsight. In D. Kahneman, P. Slovic and A. Tversky, eds. (1982), *Judgment under Uncertainty: Heuristics and biases*, pp. 335–51. Cambridge University Press.

(1983). Predicting frames. *Journal of Experimental Psychology: Learning, Memory and Cognition* 9: 103–16.

Flanagan, R. J. (1987). Efficiency and equality in Swedish labor markets. In B. P. Bosworth and A. Rivlin, eds., *The Swedish economy*, pp. 125–73. Washington, D.C.: Brookings Institution.

Foley, B. and Maunders, K. (1977). *Accounting information disclosure and collective bargaining*. London: Macmillan Press.

Foley, D. (1967). Resource allocation in the public sector. *Yale Economic Essays* 7: 73–6.

Føllesdal, D. (1981). Sartre on freedom. In P. A. Schilpp, ed., *The philosophy of Jean-Paul Sartre*, pp. 392–407. La Salle, Ill.: Open Court.

Foltz, W. J. (1981). Modernization and nation building. In R. L. Merritt and B. M. Russett, eds., *From national development to global community*, pp. 25–45. London: Allen & Unwin.

Frank, R. (1985). *Choosing the right pond*. New York: Oxford University Press.

(1987). If *homo economicus* could choose his own utility function, would he want one with a conscience? *American Economic Review* 77: 593–604.

(1988). *Passions within reason*. New York: Norton.

Freeman, R. and Medoff, J. (1984). *What do unions do?* New York: Basic Books.

Fried, C. (1984). Individual and collective rights in work relations. *University of Chicago Law Review* 51: 1012–40.

Friedman, J. (1986). *Game theory with applications to economics*. New York: Oxford University Press.

Frohlich, N. and Openheimer, J. (1970). I get by with a little help from my friends. *World Politics* 23: 104–20.

Galasi, P. and Kertesi, G. (1987). The spread of bribery in a Soviet-type economy. Unpublished manuscript.

Gambetta, D. (1987). *Did they jump or were they pushed?* Cambridge University Press.

(1988a). Fragments of an economic theory of the mafia. *Archives Européennes de Sociologie* 28: 127–45.

(1988b). Mafia: The price of distrust. In D. Gambetta, ed., *Trust: Making and breaking of cooperative relationships*, pp. 158–75. Oxford: Blackwell Publisher.

Gambetta, D., ed. (1988). *Trust: Making and breaking of cooperative relationships*. Oxford: Blackwell Publishers.

Gauthier, D. (1986). *Morals by agreement*. New York: Oxford Press.

Gazzaniga, M. S. (1988). *Mind matters*. Boston: Houghton Mifflin.

Geer, H. de (1986). *SAF i förhandlingar*. Stockholm: SAFs Förlag.

Gleick, J. (1987). When chaos rules the market. *New York Times*, 22 November.

Gluckman, M. (1955). *Custom and conflict in Africa*. New York: Oxford University Press.

Golden, M. (1988). Heroic defeats (unpublished manuscript).

Gorman, W. M. (1967). Tastes, habits and choices. *International Economic Review* 8: 218–22.

Gouldner, A. (1960). The norm of reciprocity. *American Sociological Review* 25: 161–78.

Granovetter, M. (1973). The strength of weak ties. *American Journal of Sociology* 78: 1360–80.

Grasmick, H. G. and Scott, W. P. (1982). Tax evasion and mechanisms of social control. *Journal of Economic Psychology* 2: 213–30.

Gray, J. (1986). *Hayek on liberty*, 2d ed. Oxford: Blackwell Publisher.

Griffin, J. (1985). Some problems of fairness. *Ethics* 96: 100–19.

Grout, P. A. (1984). Investment and wages in the absence of binding contracts: A Nash bargaining approach. *Econometrica* 52: 449–60.

Güth, W., Schmittberger, R. and Schwarze B. (1982). An experimental analysis of ultimatum bargaining. *Journal of Economic Behavior and Organization* 3: 367–88.

Haavelmo, T. (1970). Some observations on welfare and economic growth. In W. A. Eltis, M. Scott and N. Wolfe, eds., *Induction, growth and trade: Essays in honour of Sir Roy Harrod*, pp. 65–75. New York: Oxford University Press.

Habermas, J. (1982). *Zur Theorie des kommunikativen Handelns*. Frankfurt a.M.: Suhrkamp.

Haggard, T. R. (1980). Right-to-work laws in the Southern States. *North Carolina Law Review* 59: 29–69.

Hallie, P. (1979). *Lest innocent blood be shed*. New York: Harper & Row.

Hampton, J. (1987). Free-rider problems in the production of collective goods. *Economics and Philosophy* 3: 245–74.

Hardin, R. (1982). *Collective action*. Baltimore: Johns Hopkins University Press.

(1988). *Morality within the limits of reason*. University of Chicago Press.

Harris, R. J. and Joyce, M. A. (1980). What's fair? It depends on how you phrase the question. *Journal of Personality and Social Psychology* 38: 165–79.

Harsanyi, J. (1956). Approaches to the bargaining problem before and after the theory of games. *Econometrica* 24: 144–57.

(1977a). *Rational behavior and bargaining equilibrium in games and social situations*. Cambridge University Press.

(1977b). Advances in understanding rational behavior. In R. E. Butts and J. Hintikka, eds., *Foundational problems in the special sciences*, pp. 315–43. Dordrecht: Reidel.

Harsanyi, J. and Selten, R. (1988). *A general theory of equilibrium selection in games*. Cambridge, Mass.: MIT Press.

Hasluck, M. (1954). *The unwritten law in Albania*. Cambridge University Press.

Hawthorn, G. (1988). Three ironies in trust. In D. Gambetta, ed., *Trust: Making and breaking of cooperative relationships*, pp. 111–26. Oxford: Blackwell Publisher.

Hayek, F. (1978). *Law, legislation and liberty*, vols. 1–3. University of Chicago Press.

Heidenheimer, A., Johnston, M. and LeVine, V. T., eds. (1989). *Political corruption: A handbook*. New Brunswick, N.J.: Transaction Books.

Heiner, R. (1983). The origin of predictable behavior. *American Economic Review* 83: 560–95.

(1988). The origin of predictable dynamic behavior. *Journal of Economic Behavior and Organization* 10: 29–55.

Hersoug, T. (1984). Forbundsvise versus samordnede oppgjør: Hvem har fordelen? *Sosialøkonomen* no. 9: 25–8.

Hey, J. D. (1981). Are optimal search rules reasonable? *Journal of Economic Behavior and Organization* 2: 47–70.

Hirschleifer, J. (1987). On the emotions as guarantors of threats and promises. In J. Dupré, ed., *The latest on the best*, pp. 307–26. Cambridge, Mass.: MIT Press.

Hirschman, A. (1977). *The passions and the interests*. Princeton, N.J.: Princeton University Press.

(1982). *Shifting involvements*. Princeton, N.J.: Princeton University Press.

Hochstein, M. (1985). Tax ethics: Social values and noncompliance. *Public Opinion* (February–March): 11–14.

Hoel, M. (1986). Employment and allocation effects of reducing the length of the working day. *Economica* 53: 75–85.

Hofstee, W. K. B. (1983). The case for compromise in educational selection and grading. In S. B. Anderson and J. S. Helmick, eds., *On educational testing*, pp. 109–27. San Francisco: Jossey-Bass.

Höglund, B. (1987). Om blandekonomins beslutsmekanismer. Paper presented at the Arne Ryde Symposium on Political Economy, Marienlyst, 11–12 June.

Holden, S. (1987a). Wage drift in Norway: A bargaining approach. Memorandum from the University of Oslo, Department of Economics, no. 20, 4 November.

(1987b). Local and central wage bargaining. *Scandinavian Journal of Economics* 90: 93–99.

Holden, S. and Raaum, O. (1988). Does union moderation make sense? (unpublished manuscript).

Hollis, M. and Lukes, S., eds. (1982). *Rationality and relativism*. Oxford: Blackwell Publisher.

Holmes, S. (forthcoming). The secret history of self-interest. In J. Mansbridge, ed., *Against self-interest*. University of Chicago Press.

Horn, H. and Wolinsky, A. (1988). Worker substitutability and patterns of unionisation. *Economic Journal* 98: 484–97.

Howard, N. (1971). *Paradoxes of rationality*. Cambridge, Mass.: MIT Press.

Hume, D. (1751). *An enquiry concerning the principles of morals*.

Huntington, S. (1968). Modernization and corruption. In *Political order in changing societies*, pp. 59–71. New Haven, Conn.: Yale University Press. Cited after the reprint in A. Heidenheimer, M. Johnston and V. T. LeVine, eds.,

Political Corruption: A Handbook, pp. 377–88. New Brunswick, N.J.: Transaction Books.

Hwang, K.-K. (1987). Face and favor. *American Journal of Sociology* 92: 944–74.

Hyman, R. and Brough, I. (1975). *Social values and industrial relations.* Oxford: Blackwell Publisher.

Jakobovits, I. (1975). *Jewish medical ethics.* New York: Bloch.

Johansen, L. (1979). The bargaining society and the inefficiency of bargaining. *Kyklos* 32: 497–522.

Johnston, P. (1986). The political consequences of corruption. *Comparative Politics* 18: 459–77. Cited after the reprint in A. Heidenheimer, M. Johnston and V. T. LeVine, eds., *Political corruption,* pp. 985–1006.

Jones, S. F. (1984). *The economics of conformism.* Oxford: Blackwell Publisher.

Kahn, A., Lamm, H. and Nelson, R. (1977). Preferences for an equal or equitable allocator. *Journal of Personality and Social Psychology* 35: 837–44.

Kahneman, D., Knetsch, J. and Thaler, R. (1986a). Fairness as a constraint on profit-seeking. *American Economic Review* 76: 728–41.

  (1986b). Fairness and the assumptions of economics. *Journal of Business* 59: S285–S300.

Kalai, E. (1985). Solutions to the bargaining problem. In L. Hurwicz, D. Schmeidler and H. Sonnenscheein, eds., *Social goals and social organization,* pp. 77–106. Cambridge University Press.

Kalai, E. and Smorodinsky, M. (1975). Other solutions to Nash's bargaining problems. *Econometrica* 43: 513–18.

Kaplan, S. E. and Reckers, P. M. J. (1985). A study of tax evasion judgments. *National Tax Journal* 38: 97–102.

Katselinboigen, A. (1983). Corruption in the USSR: Some methodological issues. In M. Clarke, ed., *Corruption: Causes, consequences and control,* pp. 220–38. London: Pinter.

Keenan, A. and Dean, P. N. (1980). Moral evaluations of tax evasion. Social Policy Administration 14: 209–20.

Keillor, G. (1986). *Lake Wobegon days.* New York: Penguin Books.

Kelley, H. H. and Stahelski, A. J. (1970). Social interaction basis of cooperators' and competitors' beliefs about others. *Journal of Personality and Social Psychology* 16: 66–91.

Keynes, J. M. (1936). *The general theory of interest, employment and money.* London: Macmillan Press.

Kindleberger, C. (1975). The rise of free trade in Western Europe 1820–75. *Journal of Economic History* 35: 20–55.

Kitcher, P. (1985). *Vaulting ambition.* Cambridge, Mass.: MIT Press.

Kluckhohn, C. (1944). *Navaho witchcraft.* Papers of the Peabody Museum, Harvard University.

Knesper, D. J., Pagnucco, D. J. and Wheller, J. R. C. (1985). Similarities and differences across mental health service providers and practice settings in the United States. *American Psychologist* 40: 1352–69.

Koch, K.-F. (1974). *War and peace in Jalémo: The management of conflict in Highland New Guinea.* Cambridge, Mass.: Harvard University Press.

Kolakowski, L. (1978). *Main currents of Marxism.* New York: Oxford University Press.

Kolm, S.-C. (1982). *Le bonheur-liberté.* Paris: Presses Universitaires de France.

Komorita, S. S. and Chertkoff, J. M. (1973). A bargaining theory of coalition formation. *Psychological Review* 80: 149–62.

Kondo, T. (1988). Is normative behavior needed to maintain social order? Qualifying paper, University of Chicago, Department of Political Science.

Korsgaard, C. (1985). Kant's formula of universal law. *Pacific Philosophical Quarterly* 66: 24–47.

Kragt, A. J. C. van de, Orbell, J. M. and Dawes, R. M. (1983). The minimal contribution set as a solution to the public goods problem. *American Political Science Review* 77: 112–22.

Kreps, D. M. and Wilson, R. (1982). Reputation and imperfect information. *Journal of Economic Theory* 27: 253–79.

Kreps, D. M., Milgrom, P., Roberts, J. and Wilson, R. (1982). Rational cooperation in the finitely repeated Prisoners' Dilemma. *Journal of Economic Theory* 27: 245–52.

Kuran, T. (1983). Behavioral norms in Islam. *Journal of Economic Behavior and Organization* 4: 353–79.

Kurtz, E. (1979). *Not-God: A history of Alcoholics Anonymous.* Center City, Minn.: Hazelden Educational Services.

Kydland, F. and Prescott, E. (1977). Rules rather than discretion: The inconsistency of optimal plans. *Journal of Political Economy* 85: 473–921.

Lancaster, K. (1873). The dynamic inefficiency of capitalism. *Journal of Political Economy* 81: 1092–1109.

Lang, K. and Lang, G. E. (1968). *Voting and nonvoting.* Waltham, Mass.: Blaisdell.

Lash, S. (1985). The end of neo-corporatism? The breakdown of centralised bargaining in Sweden. *British Journal of Industrial Relations* 23: 215–39.

Laurin, U. (1986). *På heder och samvete.* Stockholm: Norstedts.

Leff, N. H. (1964). Economic development through bureaucratic corruption. *American Behavioral Scientist* 8: 8–14. Cited after the reprint in A. Heidenheimer, M. Johnston and V. T. LeVine, eds., *Political corruption: A handbook,* pp. 389–403. New Brunswick, N.J.: Transaction Books.

Leontief, W. (1946). The pure theory of the guaranteed annual wage contract. *Journal of Political Economy* 54: 76–9.

Levenson, J. (1968). *Confucian China and its modern fate.* Berkeley and Los Angeles: University of California Press.

Levi, I. (1986). *Hard choices.* Cambridge University Press.

Levy, R. (1973). *The Tahitians.* University of Chicago Press.

Lewis, A. (1982). *The psychology of taxation.* New York: St. Martin's Press.

Lewis, D. (1969). *Convention.* Cambridge, Mass.: Harvard University Press.

Leys, C. (1965). What is the problem about corruption? *Journal of Modern African*

Studies 3: 215–24. Cited after the reprint in A. Heidenheimer, M. Johnston and V. T. LeVine, eds., *Political corruption: A handbook,* pp. 51–66. New Brunswick, N.J.: Transaction Books.

Lincoln-Keiser, R. (1986). Death enmity in Thull. *American Ethnologist* 13: 489–505.

Lindbeck, A. and Snower, D. J. (1986). Wage rigidity, union activity and unemployment. In W. Beckerman, ed., *Wage rigidity and unemployment,* pp. 97–126. London: Duckworth.

(1988). Cooperation, harassment and involuntary unemployment. *American Economic Review* 78: 167–88.

Lindgren, A. (1985). *Brothers Lionheart.* New York: Penguin Books.

Lipsey, R. G. and Lancaster, K. (1956–7). The general theory of the second-best. *Review of Economic Studies* 24: 11–32.

Lipson, C. (1986). Bankers' dilemmas: Private cooperation in rescheduling sovereign debts. In K. A. Oye, ed., *Cooperation under anarchy,* pp. 200–25. Princeton, N.J.: Princeton University Press.

Lockwood, D. (1955). Arbitration and industrial conflict. *British Journal of Sociology* 6: 335–47.

Lorenz, E. H. (1988). Neither friends nor strangers: Informal networks of subcontracting in French industry. In D. Gambetta, ed., *Trust: Making and breaking of cooperative relationships,* pp. 194–210. Oxford: Blackwell Publisher.

Lovejoy, A. O. (1968). *Reflections on human nature.* Baltimore, Md.: Johns Hopkins University Press.

Luce, R. D. and Raiffa, H. (1957). *Games and decisions.* New York: Wiley.

Lupton, T., ed. (1972). *Payment systems.* Harmondsworth: Penguin.

MacIntyre, A. (1988). *Whose justice? Which rationality?* Notre Dame, Ind.: University of Notre Dame Press.

MacMullen, R. (1988). *Corruption and the decline of Rome.* New Haven, Conn.: Yale University Press.

Malouf, M. and Roth, A. (1981). Disagreement in bargaining: An experimental study. *Journal of Conflict Resolution* 25: 329–48.

Margalit, A. (1983). Ideals and second-best. In S. Fox, ed., *Philosophy for education,* pp. 77–90. Jerusalem: Van Leer Foundation.

Margolis, H. (1982). *Selfishness, altruism and rationality.* Cambridge University Press.

Marsden, D. (1986). *The end of economic man? Custom and competition in labour markets.* Brighton: Wheatsheaf Books.

Marwell, G. (1982). Altruism and the problem of collective action. In V. J. Derlega and J. Grzelak, eds., *Cooperation and helping behavior,* pp. 207–26. New York: Academic Press.

Marwell, G., Oliver, P. and Prahl, R. (1988). Social networks and collective action: A theory of the critical mass III. *American Journal of Sociology* 94: 502–34.

Marx, K. (1852). *The eighteenth Brumaire of Louis Bonaparte.* In *Marx and Engels: Collected works,* vol. 11. London: Lawrence & Wishart.

(1865). *Results of the immediate process of production.* Cited after the English translation in the Appendix to Karl Marx, *Capital: Volume One,* translated by Ben Fowkes. New York: Vintage Books (1977).

(1867). *Capital I.* New York: International Publishers.

Mayer, P. (1954). Witches. Cited after the reprint in M. Marwick, ed., *Witchcraft and sorcery,* pp. 54–70. Harmondsworth: Penguin.

Maynard-Smith, J. (1982). *Evolution and the theory of games.* Cambridge University Press.

McDonald, I. M. and Solow, R. (1981). Wage bargaining and employment. *American Economic Review* 71: 896–908.

Meade, J. (1970). The theory of indicative planning. In *The collected papers of James Meade,* vol. 2, pp. 109–57. London: Unwin Hyman; reprinted 1988.

Meisner, M. (1967). *Li Ta-ch'ao and the origins of Chinese communism.* Cambridge, Mass.: Harvard University Press.

Merton, R. (1957). *Social theory and social structure.* New York: Free Press.

Messick, D. M. and Cook, K., eds. (1983). *Equity theory.* New York: Praeger.

Messick, D. M. and Sentis, K. (1983). Fairness, preference, and fairness biases. In D. M. Messick and K. Cook. eds., *Equity theory,* pp. 61–94. New York: Praeger.

Midgaard, K. (1980). On the significance of language and a richer concept of rationality. In L. Lewin and E. Vedung, eds., *Politics as rational action,* pp. 83–97. Dordrecht: Reidel.

Mikula, G. (1972). Gewinnaufteilung in Dyaden bei variiertem Leistungsverhältnis. *Zeitschrift für Sozialpsychologie* 3: 126–33.

Mikula, G. and Uray, H. (1973). Die Vernachlässigung individueller Leistungen bei der Lohnaufteilung in Sozialsituationen. *Zeitschrift für Sozialpsychologie* 4: 136–44.

Mills, J. (1946). *The engineer in society.* New York: Nostrand.

Mill, J. S. (1976). *Principles of political economy.* Fairfield: Kelley.

Mitchell, D. J. (1986). Explanations of wage inflexibility. In W. Beckerman, ed., *Wage rigidity and unemployment,* pp. 43–76. London: Duckworth.

Moene, K. O. (1988a). Union militancy and plant design (unpublished manuscript).

(1988b). Employment incentives and income generation of different wage bargaining environments. *Economic Journal* 98: 471–83.

Moene, K. O. and Ognedal, T. (1987). Utbyttedeling og medarbeidereie (unpublished manuscript).

Mora, G. F., de la (1987). *Egalitarian envy.* New York: Paragon.

Moran, T. H. (1987). Managing an oligopoly of would-be sovereigns. *International Organization* 41: 575–607.

Müllensiefen, H. (1963). Kartelle als Produktionsförderer. In L. Kastl (ed.), *Kartelle in der Wirklichkeit,* pp. 71–88. Cologne: Carl Heymanns.

Myerson, R. (1984). Two-person bargaining problems with incomplete information. *Econometrica.* 52: 461–87.

(1985). Analysis of two bargaining problems with incomplete information. In A. Roth, ed., *Game-theoretic models of bargaining*, pp. 115–47. Cambridge University Press.

Myrdal, G. (1968). *Asian drama*. Harmondsworth: Penguin. Cited after the reprint in A. Heidenheimer, M. Johnston and V. T. LeVine, eds., *Political corruption: A handbook*, pp. 405–21. New Brunwsick, N.J.: Transaction Books.

Najemy, J. (1982). *Corporatism and consensus in Florentine electoral politics, 1280–1400*. Chapel Hill: University of North Carolina Press.

Nash, J. (1950). The bargaining problem. *Econometrica* 18: 155–62.

(1951). Non-cooperative games. *Annals of Mathematics* 64: 286–95.

(1953). Two-person cooperative games. *Econometrica* 21: 128–40.

Nelson, R. and Winter, S. (1982). *An evolutionary theory of economic change*. Cambridge, Mass.: Harvard University Press.

Neurath, O. (1913). Die verrirten des Cartesius und das Auxiliarmotiv: Zur Psychologie des Entschlusses. Cited after the translation in O. Neurath (1983), *Philosophical Papers, 1913–1946*, pp. 1–12. Dordrecht: Reidel.

Nilsson, C. (1987). *Lokal lönebildning och inflation*. Stockholm: Trade Union Institute for Economic Research.

Nisbett, L., Borgida, E., Crandell, R. and Reed, H. (1982). Popular induction: Information is not necessarily informative. In D. Kahneman, P. Slovic and A. Tversky, eds., *Judgment under uncertainty: Heuristics and biases*, pp. 101–16. Cambridge University Press.

Noonan, J. T. (1984). *Bribes*. Berkeley and Los Angeles: University of California Press.

Norges Offentlige Utredninger (1988). *Inntektsdannelsen i Norge*. Oslo: Statens Trykningskontor.

North, D. (1981). Structure and change in economic history. New York: Norton.

Nozick, R. (1974). *Anarchy, state and utopia*. New York: Basic Books.

Nydegger, R. V. and Owen, F. (1975). Two-person bargaining: An experimental test of the Nash axioms. *International Journal of Game Theory* 4: 239–49.

Nye, J. (1967). Corruption and political development: A cost–benefit analysis. *American Political Science Review* 61: 417–27. Cited after the reprint in A. Heidenheimer, M. Johnston and V. T. LeVine, eds., *Political corruption: A handbook*, pp. 963–83. New Brunswick, N.J.: Transaction Books.

Offe, C. and Wiesenthal, H. (1980). Two logics of collective action. *Political Power and Social Theory* 1: 67–115.

Okun, A. (1981). *Prices and quantities*. Washington, D.C.: Brookings Institution.

Oliner, S. B. and Oliner, P. (1988). *The altruistic personality*. New York: Free Press.

Oliver, P. (1980). Rewards and punishments as selective incentives for collective action. *American Journal of Sociology* 85: 1356–75.

Oliver, P., Marwell, G. and Teixeira, R. (1985). A theory of the critical mass. I: Interdependence, group heterogeneity, and the production of collective action. *American Journal of Sociology* 91: 522–56.

Olson, M. (1965). *The logic of collective action*. Cambridge, Mass.: Harvard University Press.

(1982). *The rise and decline of nations.* New Haven, Conn.: Yale University Press.

Ortuño-Ortin, I. and Roemer, J. (1987). Deducing interpersonal comparability from local expertise. Working paper, University of California, Davis, Department of Economics.

Oswald, A. J. (1979). Wage determinations in an economy with many trade unions. *Oxford Economic Papers* 31: 369–85.

(1981). Threat and morale effects in the theory of wages. *European Economic Review* 16: 269–83.

(1985). The economic theory of trade unions: An introductory survey. *Scandinavian Journal of Economics* 87: 160–93.

(1986). Is wage rigidity caused by 'lay-offs by seniority'? In W. Beckerman, ed., *Wage rigidity and unemployment,* pp. 77–96. London: Duckworth.

Pagano, U. (1985). *Work and welfare in economic theory.* Oxford: Blackwell Publisher.

Palfrey, T. and Rosenthal, H. (1985). Voter participation and strategic uncertainty. *American Political Science Review* 79: 62–78.

Parfit, D. (1984). *Reasons and persons.* New York: Oxford University Press.

Pears, D. (1984). *Motivated irrationality.* New York: Oxford University Press.

Pemberton, J. (1988). A 'managerial' model of the trade union. *Economic Journal* 98: 755–71.

Pen, J. (1959). *The wage rate under collective bargaining.* Cambridge, Mass.: Harvard University Press.

Petersen, R. (forthcoming). Rationality, ethnicity, and military enlistment. *Social Science Information.*

Peyre, H. (1967). *The failures of criticism.* Ithaca, N.Y.: Cornell University Press.

Piddocke, S. (1965). The Potlatch system of the southern Kwakiutl. *Southwestern Journal of Anthropology* 21: 244–64.

Pileggi, N. (1987). *Wiseguy.* New York: Pocket Books.

Ploeg, F. van der (1987). Trade unions, investment, and employment. *European Economic Review* 31: 1465–92.

Pollak, R. (1976). Interdependent preferences. *American Economic Review* 66: 309–20.

Popkin, S. (1979). *The rational peasant.* Berkeley and Los Angeles: University of California Press.

Przeworski, A. and Wallerstein, M. (1987). Corporatism, pluralism and market competition (unpublished manuscript).

Putterman, L. (1986). On some recent explanations of why capital hires labor. In L. Putterman, ed., *The economic nature of the firm,* pp. 312–28. Cambridge University Press.

Quattrone, G. and Tversky, A. (1986). Self-deception and the voter's illusion. In J. Elster, ed., *The multiple self,* pp. 35–58. Cambridge University Press.

Raiffa, H. (1982). *The art and science of negotiation.* Cambridge, Mass.: Harvard University Press.

Ranulf, S. (1933). *The jealousy of the gods and criminal law at Athens*, vol. 1. London: Williams & Norgate.

(1934). *The jealousy of the gods and criminal law at Athens*, vol. 2. London: Williams & Norgate.

(1938). *Moral indignation and middle class psychology*. Copenhagen: Munksgaard.

Rawls, J. (1971). *A theory of justice*. Cambridge, Mass.: Harvard University Press.

Rice, O. (1982). *The Hatfields and the McCoys*. Lexington: University Press of Kentucky.

Rigden, J. S. (1987). *Rabi: Scientist and citizen*. New York: Basic Books.

Riker, W. and Ordeshook, P. (1968). A theory of the calculus of voting. *American Political Science Review* 62: 25–42.

Roemer, J. (1982). *A general theory of exploitation and class*. Cambridge, Mass.: Harvard University Press.

(1985a). Rationalizing revolutionary ideology. *Econometrica* 53: 85–108.

(1985b). A note on interpersonal comparability and the theory of fairness. Working paper no. 261, University of California, Davis, Department of Economics.

Roethlisberger, F. J. and Dickson, W. J. (1939). *Management and the worker*. Cambridge, Mass.: Harvard University Press.

Rose-Ackerman, S. (1978). *Corruption: A study in political economy*. New York: Academic Press.

Rosner, F. (1986). *Modern medicine and Jewish ethics*. New York: Yeshiva University Press.

Roth, A. (1987). Bargaining phenomena and bargaining theory. In A. Roth, ed., *Laboratory experimentation in economics*, pp. 14–41. Cambridge University Press.

Roth, A. and Malouf, M. (1979). Game-theoretic models and the role of information in bargaining. *Psychological Review* 86: 574–94.

Roth, A. and Rothblum, U. (1982). Risk aversion and Nash's solution for bargaining games with risky outcomes. *Econometrica* 50: 639–47.

Roy, D. (1952). Quota restriction and goldbricking in a machine shop. *American Journal of Sociology* 67: 427–42. Cited after the reprint in T. Lupton, ed., *Payment systems*, pp. 35–63. Harmondsworth: Penguin.

Royce, J. E. (1981). *Alcohol problems and alcoholism*. New York: Free Press.

Rubinstein, A. (1982). Perfect equilibrium in a bargaining model. *Econometrica* 50: 97–109.

(1985a). The choice of conjectures in a bargaining game with incomplete information. In A. Roth, ed., *Game-theoretic models of bargaining*, pp. 99–114. Cambridge University Press.

(1985b). A bargaining model with incomplete information about time preferences. *Econometrica* 53: 1151–72.

(1988a). Comments on the interpretation of game theory. Discussion paper, London School of Economics and Political Science, Suntory Toyota International Centre for Economics and Related Disciplines.

(1988b). The electronic mail game: Strategic behavior under 'almost common knowledge' (unpublished manuscript).

Runciman, W. G. (1966). *Relative deprivation and social justice.* London: Routledge & Kegan Paul.

Sabel, C. F. and Stark, D. (1982). Planning, politics and shop-floor power: Hidden forms of bargaining in Soviet-imposed state socialist societies. *Politics and Society* 11: 439–75.

Sabini, J. and Silver, M. (1987). Emotions, responsibility and character. In F. Schoeman, ed., *Responsibility, character and the emotions,* pp. 165–75. Cambridge University Press.

Samuelson, W. (1985). A comment on the Coase theorem. In A. Roth, ed., *Game-theoretic models of bargaining,* pp. 321–39. Cambridge University Press.

Samuelson, W. and Bazerman, M. (1985). The winner's curse in bilateral negotiations. *Research in Experimental Economics* 3: 105–37.

Sandemose, A. (1936). *A fugitive crosses his track.* New York: Knopf.

Sapsford, D. (1982). The theory of bargaining and strike activity. *International Journal of Social Economics* 9: 3–31.

Scheffler, S. (1982). *The rejection of consequentialism.* New York: Oxford University Press.

Scheler, M. (1972). *Ressentiment.* New York: Schocken Books.

Schelling, T. C. (1963). *The strategy of conflict.* Cambridge, Mass.: Harvard University Press.

(1978). *Micromotives and macrobehavior.* New York: Norton.

Scheppele, K. (1988). *Legal secrets.* University of Chicago Press.

Schoeck, H. (1987). *Envy.* Indianapolis, Ind.: Liberty Press.

Schotter, A. (1981). *The economic theory of social institutions.* Cambridge University Press.

Schwartz, R. D. and Orleans, S. (1967). On legal sanctions. *University of Chicago Law Review* 34: 274–300.

Schwerin, D. (1980). The limits of organization as a response to wage–price problems. In R. Rose, ed., *Challenge to governance,* pp. 73–104. Beverly Hills, Calif.: Sage.

(1982). Incomes policy in Norway: Second-best corporate institutions. *Polity* 14: 464–80.

Scott, J. C. (1969). Corruption, machine politics and political change. *American Political Science Review* 63: 1142–49. Cited after the reprint in A. Heidenheimer, M. Johnston and V. T. LeVine, eds., *Political corruption: A handbook,* pp. 275–86. New Brunswick, N.J.: Transaction Books.

(1972). *Comparative political corruption.* Englewood Cliffs, N.J.: Prentice-Hall.

Scott, R. H. (1972). Avarice, altruism and second party preferences. *Quarterly Journal of Economics* 86: 1–18.

Selten, R. (1975). Re-examination of the perfectness concept for equilibrium points in extensive games. *International Journal of Game Theory* 4: 25–55.

(1978a). The equity principle in economic behavior. In H. Gottinger and W.

Leinfellner, eds., *Decision theory and social ethics*, pp. 289–301. Dordrecht: Reidel.

(1978b). The chain store paradox. *Theory and Decision* 9: 127–59.

(1987). Equity and coalition bargaining in experimental three-person games. In A. Roth, ed., *Laboratory experimentation in economics*, pp. 42–98. Cambridge University Press.

Sen, A. (1967). Isolation, assurance and the social rate of discount. *Quarterly Journal of Economics* 80: 112–24.

(1977). Rational fools. *Philosophy and Public Affairs* 6: 317–44.

(1980–1). Plural utility. *Proceedings of the Aristotelian Society* n.s. 81: 193–215.

(1986). Prediction and economic theory. *Proceedings of the Royal Society* 407: 3–213.

(1987). *On ethics and economics*. Oxford: Blackwell Publisher.

Shapiro, C. and Stiglitz, J. (1984). Equilibrium unemployment as a worker discipline device. *American Economic Review* 74: 433–44.

Shapley, L. and Shubik, M. (1967). Ownership and the production function. *Quarterly Journal of Economics* 80: 88–111.

Sher, G. (1987). *Desert*. Princeton, N.J.: Princeton University Press.

Shubik, M. (1982). *Game theory in the social sciences*. Cambridge, Mass.: MIT Press.

Sigelman, L., Roeber, P. W., Jewell, M. E. and Baer, M. A. (1985). Voting and nonvoting: A multi-election perspective. *American Journal of Political Science* 29: 747–65.

Simmel, G. (1978). *The philosophy of money*. London: Routledge & Kegan Paul.

Simon, H. (1954). Bandwagon and underdog effects in election predictions. *Public Opinion Quarterly* 69: 99–118.

Simpson, A. K. (1984). *Cannibalism and the common law*. University of Chicago Press.

Singer, G., Carr, P. L., Mulley, A. G. and Thibault, G. E. (1983). Rationing intensive care: Physician response to a resource shortage. *New England Journal of Medicine* 19: 1155–60.

Sjölund, M. (1987). *Statens kaka*. Stockholm: Allmänna Förlaget.

Slichter, S. H. (1947). *Basic criteria used in wage negotiations*. Chicago Association of Commerce and Industry.

Smart, N. (1983). Classes, clients and corruption in Sicily. In M. Clarke, ed., *Corruption: Causes, consequences and control*. London: Pinter.

Sobel, J. (1981). Distortion of utilities and the bargaining problem. *Econometrica* 49: 597–617.

Solomon, R. and Corbit, J. (1974). An opponent-process theory of motivation. *Psychological Review* 81: 119–45.

Sperber, D. (1984). Anthropology and psychology: Towards an epidemiology of representations. *Man* n.s. 20: 73–89.

Ståhl, I. (1972). *Bargaining theory*. Stockholm School of Economics.

Ståhl, I. (1988). A comparison between the Rubinstein and Ståhl bargaining models. Paper presented at the University of Oslo, 11 May.

Steedman, I. and Krause, U. (1986). Goethe's *Faust*, Arrow's possibility theorem and the individual decision-taker. In J. Elster, ed., *The multiple self*, pp. 197–233. Cambridge University Press.

Stendhal (1952). *Le rouge et le noir*. In *Romans et nouvelles*, vol. 1, ed. Pléiade. Paris: Gallimard.

Stiglitz, J. (1986). Theories of wage rigidity. In J. L. Butkiewitz, K. J. Koford and J. B. Miller, eds., *Keynes' economic legacy: Contemporary economic theories*, pp. 153–206. New York: Praeger.

Stone, L. (1972). *The causes of the English revolution*. New York: Harper & Row.

Stouffer, S. et al. (1949). *The American soldier*. Princeton, N.J.: Princeton University Press.

Stroll, A. (1987). Norms. *Dialectica* 41: 7–22.

Sugden, R. (1984). Reciprocity: The supply of public goods through voluntary contributions. *Economic Journal* 94: 772–87.

(1986). *The economics of rights, co-operation and welfare*. Oxford: Blackwell Publisher.

Summers, M. W. (1987). *The plundering generation*. New York: Oxford University Press.

Sundt, E. (1974–8). *Verker i Utvalg*. Oslo: Gyldendal.

Sutton, J. (1986). Non-cooperative bargaining theory: An introduction. *Review of Economic Studies* 53: 709–24.

Sutton, J., Shaked, A. and Binmore, K. (1986). An outside option experiment. Working paper, London School of Economics.

Svejnar, J. (1986). Bargaining power, fear of disagreement, and wage settlements. *Econometrica* 54: 1055–78.

Swenson, P. (1987). Employer power and the shape of the unions in Sweden. Paper prepared for the Conference on Union Policy, Labor Militancy and Capital Accumulation, Cornell University, 2–5 April.

(1989). *Fair shares*. Ithaca, N.Y.: Cornell University Press.

Sziráczki, G. (1989). Internal subcontracting in Hungarian enterprises. In J. Elster and K. O. Moene, eds., *Alternatives to capitalism*, pp. 39–60. Cambridge University Press.

Sztompa, P. (1974). *System and function*. New York: Academic Press.

Taylor, C. (1971). Interpretation and the sciences of man. *Review of Metaphysics* 25: 3–51.

(1976). Responsibility for self. In A. Rorty, ed., *The identities of persons*, pp. 281–300. Berkeley and Los Angeles: University of California Press.

Taylor, M. (1987). *The possibility of cooperation*. Cambridge University Press.

Taylor, M., ed. (1988). *Rationality and revolution*. Cambridge University Press.

Taylor, M. and Ward, H. (1982). Chickens, whales and lumpy goods: Alternative models of public goods provision. *Political Studies* 3: 350–70.

Teixeira, R. (1987). *Why Americans don't vote*. New York: Greenwood Press.

Thaler, R. (1980). Towards a positive theory of consumer behavior. *Journal of Economic Behavior and Organization* 1: 39–60.

(1988). The winner's curse. *Journal of Economic Perspectives* 2: 191–202.

Thomas, K. (1973). *Religion and the decline of magic*. Harmondsworth: Penguin.

Thompson, E. P. (1969). *The making of the English working class*. Harmondsworth: Penguin.

Tittle, C. R. and Rowe, A. R. (1973). Moral appeal, sanction threats, and deviance: An experimental test. *Social Problems* 20: 488–98.

Tocqueville, A. de (1969). *Democracy in America*. New York: Anchor Books.

Trivers, R. E. (1971). The evolution of reciprocal altruism. *Quarterly Review of Biology* 46: 35–57.

Tumin, M. (1957). Some unapplauded consequences of social mobility in a mass society. *Social Forces* 15: 32–7.

Turnbull, C. (1961). *The forest people*. New York: Simon & Schuster.

(1972). *The mountain people*. New York: Simon & Schuster.

Turner, H. A. (1952). Trade unions, differentials and the levelling of wages. *Manchester School of Economic and Social Studies* 20: 227–82.

Tversky, A. and Kahneman, D. (1981). The psychology of choice and the framing of preferences. *Science* 211: 4353–8.

Ullmann-Margalit, E. (1977). *The emergence of norms*. New York: Oxford University Press.

U.S. Department of Labor (1972). Administration of Seniority. Bulletin 1425-14. Washington, D.C.

Vanberg, V. (1986). Spontaneous market order and social rules: A critical examination of F. A. Hayek's theory of cultural evolution. *Economics and Philosophy* 2: 75–100.

Varian, H. (1975). Distributive justice, welfare economics, and the theory of fairness. *Philosophy and Public Affairs* 4: 223–47.

Veblen, T. (1970). *The theory of the leisure class*. London: Allen & Unwin.

Veyne, P. (1971). *Comment on écrit l'histoire*. Paris: Editions du Seuil.

(1976). *Le pain et le cirque*. Paris: Editions du Seuil.

(1979). L'Hellénisation de Rome et la problématique des acculturations. *Diogène* no. 106, 3–29.

Walder, A. G. (1986). *Communist neo-traditionalism*. Berkeley and Los Angeles: University of California Press.

Waller, W. (1937). The rating and dating complex. *American Sociological Review* 2: 727–34.

Wallerstein, M. (1985). Working class solidarity and rational behavior. Ph.D. dissertation, University of Chicago, Department of Political Science.

(1987). Unemployment, collective bargaining, and the demand for protection. *American Journal of Political Science* 31: 729–52.

Walzer, M. (1983). *Spheres of justice*. New York: Basic Books.

Weitzman, L. (1985). *The divorce revolution*. New York: Free Press.

Wertheim, W. F. (1963). Sociological aspects of corruption in Southeast Asia. *Sociologica Neerlandica* 1: 129–52. Cited after the reprint in A. Heidenheimer, ed., *Political corruption: Readings in comparative analysis.* New York: Holt, Rinehart & Winston.

Williams, B. (1973). A critique of utilitarianism. In J. J. C. Smart and B. Williams, *Utilitarianism: For and against.* Cambridge University Press.

(1981). *Moral luck.* Cambridge University Press.

Williamson, O. (1975). *Markets and hierarchies.* New York: Free Press.

(1985). *The economic institutions of capitalism.* New York: Free Press.

Willman, P. (1982). *Fairness, collective bargaining and incomes policy.* New York: Oxford University Press.

Wilson, R. (1985). Reputations in games and markets. In A. Roth, ed., *Game-theoretic models of bargaining,* pp. 27–62. Cambridge University Press.

Winslow, G. (1982). *Justice by triage.* Berkeley and Los Angeles: University of California Press.

Wolf, E. (1966). Kinship, friendship and patron–client relations in complex societies. In M. P. Banton, ed., *The social anthropology of complex societies,* pp. 1–22. London: Tavistock.

Wolfinger, R. and Rosenstone, S. (1980). *Who votes?* New Haven, Conn.: Yale University Press.

Wootton, B. (1962). *The social foundations of wage policy.* London: Allen & Unwin.

Wraith, R. and Simpkins, E. (1963). *Corruption in developing countries.* London: Allen & Unwin.

Yaari, M. and Bar-Hillel, M. (1984). On dividing justly. *Social Choice and Welfare* 1: 1–14.

(1987). Judgments of justice (unpublished manuscript).

Zajac, E. P. (1985). Perceived economic justice: The example of public utility regulation. In H. P. Young, ed., *Cost Allocation,* pp. 119–53. Amsterdam: North-Holland.

Zermelo, E. (1912). Ueber eine anwendung der Mengenlehre auf die Theorie des Schachspiels. *Proceedings of the Fifth International Congress of Mathematics,* Cambridge.

Index

nceton to pick up a car—Bill Woodward, one of
 students there, lent me his station wagon. I fixed
 tle ambulance, with a mattress and sheets in the
 ne could lie down in case she got tired. Although
 of the periods when the disease was apparently
 d she was at home, Arlene had been in the county
 , and she was a little weak.

 to Cedarhurst and picked up my bride. Arlene's
 d goodbye, and off we went. We crossed Queens
 , then went to Staten Island on the ferry—that
 ntic boat ride—and drove to the city hall for the
 ichmond to get married.

 p the stairs, slowly, into the office. The guy there
 e. He did everything right away. He said, "You
 y witnesses," so he called the bookkeeper and an
 rom another room, and we were married accord-
 ws of the State of New York. Then we were very
 e smiled at each other, holding hands.

 eeper says to me, "You're married now. You should
 !"

 shful character kissed his bride lightly on the

 ne a tip and we thanked them very much. We got
 ar, and drove to Deborah Hospital.

 end I'd go down from Princeton to visit Arlene.
 bus was late, and I couldn't get into the hospital.
 t any hotels nearby, but I had my old sheepskin
 was warm enough), and I looked for an empty lot
 was a little worried what it might look like in the

pital or Bell Labs. We could get married in a few months, in New York. We worked everything out that afternoon.

For some months now Arlene's doctors had wanted to take a biopsy of the swelling on her neck, but her parents didn't want it done—they didn't want to "bother the poor sick girl." But with new resolve, I kept working on them, explaining that it's important to get as much information as possible. With Arlene's help, I finally convinced her parents.

A few days later, Arlene telephones me and says, "They got a report from the biopsy."

"Yeah? Is it good or bad?"

"I don't know. Come over and let's talk about it."

When I got to her house, she showed me the report. It said, "Biopsy shows tuberculosis of the lymphatic gland."

That really got me. I mean, that was the first goddamn thing on the list! I passed it by, because the book said it was easy to diagnose, and because the doctors were having so much trouble trying to figure out what it was. I assumed they had checked the obvious case. And it *was* the obvious case: the man who had come running out of the meeting room asking "Do you spit up blood?" had the right idea. He knew what it probably was!

I felt like a jerk, because I had passed over the obvious possibility by using circumstantial evidence—which isn't any good—and by assuming the doctors were more intelligent than they were. Otherwise, I would have suggested it right off, and perhaps the doctor would have diagnosed Arlene's disease way back then as "tuberculosis of the lymphatic gland—?" I was a dope. I've learned, since then.

Anyway, Arlene says, "So I might live as long as seven years. I may even get better."

"So what do you mean, you don't know if it's good or bad?"

"Well, now we won't be able to get married until later."

Knowing that she only had two more years to live, we had solved things so perfectly, from her point of view, that she was disturbed to discover she'd live longer! But it didn't take me long to convince her it was a better circumstance.

So we knew we could face things together, from then on. After going through that, we had no difficulty facing any other problem.

When the war came, I was recruited to work on the Manhattan Project at Princeton, where I was finishing up my degree. A few months later, as soon as I got my degree, I announced to my family that I wanted to get married.

My father was horrified, because from the earliest times, as he saw me develop, he thought I would be happy as a scientist. He thought it was still too early to marry—it would interfere with my career. He also had this crazy idea: if a guy was in some difficulty, he used to always say, "Cherchez la femme"—look for the woman behind it. He felt that women were the great danger to a man, that a man always has to watch out and be tough about women. And when he sees me marrying a girl with tuberculosis, he thinks of the possibility that I'm going to get sick, too.

My whole family was worried about that—aunts, uncles, everyone. They brought the family doctor over to our house. He tried to explain to me that tuberculosis is a dangerous disease, and that I'm bound to get it.

I said, "Just tell me how it's transmitted, and we'll figure it out." We were already very, very careful: we knew we must not kiss, because there's a lot of bacteria in the mouth.

Then they very carefully e promised to marry Arlene, I d body would understand that I and that it didn't represent a

I never had that feeling, tha I was getting married because *thought* of that. It wasn't a que thing; we had stalled around, not being formally married, b already married, emotionally.

I said, "Would it be sensible his wife has tuberculosis to lea

Only my aunt who ran the be all right for us to get mar against it. But this time, since kind of advice before and it ha much stronger position. It was proceed. So there was no probl similar circumstance, they wer anything any more. Arlene and we were doing.

Arlene and I worked everythin New Jersey just south of Fort Di I was at Princeton. It was a cha the name of it—supported by the Union of New York. Arlene was didn't make any difference. And I ing on this project for the govern low. But this way I could take care

We decided to get married on th

I went to the gradua it up like a back, so A this was o not so bad hospital a I drove family wa and Brook was our r Borough

We we was very don't hav accounta ing to th happy, a

The b kiss the

So th cheek.

I gave e back in

Ever One tir There coat or to slee

morning when people looked out of their windows, so I found a place that was far enough away from houses.

The next morning I woke up and discovered I'd been sleeping in a garbage dump—a landfill! I felt foolish, and laughed.

Arlene's doctor was very nice, but he would get upset when I brought in a war bond for $18 every month. He could see we didn't have much money, and kept insisting we shouldn't contribute to the hospital, but I did it anyway.

One time, at Princeton, I received a box of pencils in the mail. They were dark green, and in gold letters were the words "RICHARD DARLING, I LOVE YOU! PUTSY." It was Arlene (I called her Putsy).

Well, that was nice, and I love her, too, but—you know how you absentmindedly drop pencils around: you're showing Professor Wigner a formula, or something, and leave the pencil on his desk.

In those days we didn't have extra stuff, so I didn't want to waste the pencils. I got a razor blade from the bathroom and cut off the writing on one of them to see if I could use them.

The next morning, I get a letter in the mail. It starts out, "WHAT'S THE IDEA OF TRYING TO CUT THE NAME OFF THE PENCILS?"

It continues: "Aren't you proud of the fact that I love you?" Then: "WHAT DO YOU CARE WHAT OTHER PEOPLE THINK?"

Then came poetry: "If you're ashamed of me, dah dah, then Pecans to you! Pecans to you!" The next verse was the same kind of stuff, with the last line, "Almonds to you! Almonds to you!" Each one was "Nuts to you!" in a different form.

So I had to use the pencils with the names on them. What else could I do?

It wasn't long before I had to go to Los Alamos. Robert Oppenheimer, who was in charge of the project, arranged for Arlene to stay in the nearest hospital, in Albuquerque, about a hundred miles away. I had time off every weekend to see her, so I would hitchhike down on a Saturday, see Arlene in the afternoon, and stay overnight in a hotel there in Albuquerque. Then on Sunday morning I would see Arlene again, and hitchhike back to Los Alamos in the afternoon.

During the week I would often get letters from her. Some of them, like the one written on a jigsaw-puzzle blank and then taken apart and sent in a sack, resulted in little notes from the army censor, such as "Please tell your wife we don't have time to play games around here." I didn't tell her anything. I *liked* her to play games—even though she often put me in various uncomfortable but amusing conditions from which I could not escape.

One time, near the beginning of May, newspapers mysteriously appeared in almost everybody's mailbox at Los Alamos. The whole damn place was full of them—hundreds of newspapers. You know the kind—you open it up and there's this headline screaming in thick letters across the front page: ENTIRE NATION CELEBRATES BIRTHDAY OF R.P. FEYNMAN!

Arlene was playing her game with the world. She had a lot of time to think. She would read magazines, and send away for this and that. She was always cooking up something. (She must have got help with the names from Nick Metropolis or one of the other guys at Los Alamos who would often visit her.) Arlene was in her room, but she was in the world, writing me crazy letters and sending away for all kinds of stuff.

One time she sent me a big catalog of kitchen equipment—the kind you need for enormous institutions like prisons, which have a lot of people in them. It showed everything from blowers and hoods for stoves to huge pots and pans. So I'm thinking, "What the hell is this?"

It reminded me of the time I was up at MIT and Arlene sent me a catalog describing huge boats, from warships to ocean liners—great big boats. I wrote to her: "What's the idea?"

She writes back: "I just thought that maybe, when we get married, we could buy a boat."

I write, "Are you crazy? It's all out of proportion!"

Then another catalog comes: it's for big yachts—forty-foot schooners and stuff like that—for very rich people. She writes, "Since you said no to the other boats, maybe we could get one of these."

I write, "Look: you're way out of scale!"

Soon another catalog comes: it's for various kinds of motor boats—Chriscraft this and that.

I write, "Too expensive!"

Finally, I get a note: "This is your last chance, Richard. You're always saying no." It turns out a friend of hers has a rowboat she wants to sell for $15—a used rowboat—and maybe we could buy it so we could row around in the water next summer.

So, yes. I mean, how can you say no after all that?

Well, I'm still trying to figure out what this big catalog for institutional kitchen equipment is leading to, when another catalog comes: it's for hotels and restaurants—supplies for small and medium-sized hotels and restaurants. Then a few days later, a catalog for the kitchen in your new home comes.

When I go down to Albuquerque the next Saturday, I find

out what it's all about. There's a little charcoal broiler in her room—she's bought it through the mail from Sears. It's about eighteen inches across, with little legs.

"I thought we could have steaks," Arlene says.

"How the hell can we use it in the room, here, with all the smoke and everything?"

"Oh, no," she says. "All you have to do is take it out on the lawn. Then you can cook us steaks every Sunday."

The hospital was right on Route 66, the main road across the United States! "I can't do that," I said. "I mean, with all the cars and trucks going by, all the people on the sidewalk walking back and forth, I can't just go out there and start cookin' steaks on the lawn!"

"What do *you* care what other people think?" (Arlene *tortured* me with that!) "Okay," she says, opening a drawer, "we'll compromise: you don't have to wear the chef's hat and the gloves."

She holds up a hat—it's a real chef's hat—and gloves. Then she says, "Try on the apron," as she unfolds it. It has something silly written across it, like "BAR-B-Q KING," or something.

"Okay, okay!" I say, horrified. "I'll cook the steaks on the lawn!" So every Saturday or Sunday, I'd go out there on Route 66 and cook steaks.

Then there were the Christmas cards. One day, only a few weeks after I had arrived at Los Alamos, Arlene says, "I thought it would be nice to send Christmas cards to everybody. Would you like to see the ones I picked out?"

They were nice cards, all right, but inside they said Merry

Christmas, from Rich & Putsy. "I can't send these to Fermi and Bethe," I protested. "I hardly even know them!"

"What do *you* care what other people think?"—naturally. So we sent them.

Next year comes around, and by this time I know Fermi. I know Bethe. I've been over at their houses. I've taken care of their kids. We're all very friendly.

Somewhere along the line, Arlene says to me, in a very formal tone, "You haven't asked me about our Christmas cards this year, Richard . . ."

FEAR goes through me. "Uh, well, let's see the cards."

The cards say Merry Christmas and a Happy New Year, from Richard and Arlene Feynman. "Well, that's fine," I say. "They're very nice. They'll go fine for everybody."

"Oh, no," she says. "They won't do for Fermi and Bethe and all those other famous people." Sure enough, she's got another box of cards.

She pulls one out. It says the usual stuff, and then: From Dr. & Mrs. R. P. Feynman.

So I had to send them those.

"What's this formal stuff, Dick?" they laughed. They were happy that she was having such a good time out of it, and that I had no control over it.

Arlene didn't spend all of her time inventing games. She had sent away for a book called *Sound and Symbol in Chinese*. It was a lovely book—I still have it—with about fifty symbols done in beautiful calligraphy, with explanations like "Trouble: three women in a house." She had the right paper, brushes, and ink, and was practicing calligraphy. She had also bought a Chinese dictionary, to get a lot of other symbols.

One time when I came to visit her, Arlene was practicing these things. She says to herself, "No. That one's wrong."

So I, the "great scientist," say, "What do you mean, 'wrong'? It's only a human convention. There's no law of nature which says how they're supposed to look; you can draw them any way you want."

"I mean, artistically it's wrong. It's a question of balance, of how it feels."

"But one way is just as good as another," I protest.

"Here," she says, and she hands me the brush. "Make one yourself."

So I made one, and I said, "Wait a minute. Let me make another one—it's too blobby." (I couldn't say it was wrong, after all.)

"How do you know how blobby it's supposed to be?" she says.

I learned what she meant. There's a particular way you have to make the stroke for it to look good. An aesthetic thing has a certain set, a certain character, which I can't define. Because it couldn't be defined made me think there was nothing to it. But I learned from that experience that there *is* something to it—and it's a fascination I've had for art ever since.

Just at this moment, my sister sends me a postcard from Oberlin, where she's going to college. It's written in pencil, with small symbols—it's in Chinese.

Joan is nine years younger than I am, and studied physics, too. Having me as her older brother was tough on her. She was always looking for something I couldn't do, and was secretly taking Chinese.

Well, I didn't know any Chinese, but one thing I'm good

at is spending an infinite amount of time solving a puzzle. The next weekend I took the card with me to Albuquerque. Arlene showed me how to look up the symbols. You have to start in the back of the dictionary with the right category and count the number of strokes. Then you go into the main part of the dictionary. It turns out each symbol has several possible meanings, and you have to put several symbols together before you can understand it.

With great patience I worked everything out. Joan was saying things like, "I had a good time today." There was only one sentence I couldn't figure out. It said, "Yesterday we celebrated mountain-forming day"—obviously an error. (It turned out they did have some crazy thing called "Mountain-forming Day" at Oberlin, and I had translated it right!)

So it was trivial things like you'd expect to have on a postcard, but I knew from the situation that Joan was trying to floor me by sending me Chinese.

I looked back and forth through the art book and picked out four symbols which would go well together. Then I practiced each one, over and over. I had a big pad of paper, and I would make fifty of each one, until I got it just right.

When I had accidentally made one good example of each symbol, I saved them. Arlene approved, and we glued the four of them end to end, one on top of the other. Then we put a little piece of wood on each end, so you could hang it up on the wall. I took a picture of my masterpiece with Nick Metropolis's camera, rolled up the scroll, put it in a tube, and sent it to Joan.

So she gets it. She unrolls it, and she can't read it. It looks to her as if I simply made four characters, one right after the other, on the scroll. She takes it to her teacher.

The first thing he says is, "This is written rather well! Did you do this?"

"Uh, no. What does it say?"

"Elder brother also speaks."

I'm a real bastard—I would never let my little sister score one on me.

When Arlene's condition became much weaker, her father came out from New York to visit her. It was difficult and expensive to travel that far during the war, but he knew the end was near. One day he telephoned me at Los Alamos. "You'd better come down here right away," he said.

I had arranged ahead of time with a friend of mine at Los Alamos, Klaus Fuchs, to borrow his car in case of an emergency, so I could get to Albuquerque quickly. I picked up a couple of hitchhikers to help me in case something happened on the way.

Sure enough, as we were driving into Santa Fe, we got a flat tire. The hitchhikers helped me change the tire. Then on the other side of Santa Fe, the spare tire went flat, but there was a gas station nearby. I remember waiting patiently for the gas station man to take care of some other car, when the two hitchhikers, knowing the situation, went over and explained to the man what it was. He fixed the flat right away. We decided not to get the spare tire fixed, because repairing it would have taken even more time.

We started out again towards Albuquerque, and I felt foolish that I hadn't thought to say anything to the gas station man when time was so precious. About thirty miles from Albuquerque, we got another flat! We had to abandon the car, and we hitchhiked the rest of the way. I called up a towing company and told them the situation.

I met Arlene's father at the hospital. He had been there for a few days. "I can't take it any more," he said. "I have to go home." He was so unhappy, he just left.

When I finally saw Arlene, she was very weak, and a bit fogged out. She didn't seem to know what was happening. She stared straight ahead most of the time, looking around a little bit from time to time, and was trying to breathe. Every once in a while her breathing would stop—and she would sort of swallow—and then it would start again. It kept going like this for a few hours.

I took a little walk outside for a while. I was surprised that I wasn't feeling what I thought people were supposed to feel under the circumstances. Maybe I was fooling myself. I wasn't delighted, but I didn't feel terribly upset, perhaps because we had known for a long time that it was going to happen.

It's hard to explain. If a Martian (who, we'll imagine, never dies except by accident) came to Earth and saw this peculiar race of creatures—these humans who live about seventy or eighty years, knowing that death is going to come—it would look to him like a terrible problem of psychology to live under those circumstances, knowing that life is only temporary. Well, we humans somehow figure out how to live despite this problem: we laugh, we joke, we live.

The only difference for me and Arlene was; instead of fifty years, it was five years. It was only a quantitative difference— the psychological problem was just the same. The only way it would have become any different is if we had said to ourselves, "But those other people have it better, because they might live fifty years." But that's crazy. Why make yourself miserable saying things like, "Why do we have such bad luck? What has God done to us? What have we done to deserve this?"—all of which, if you understand reality and take it completely into your heart, are irrelevant and unsolvable. They are just things that nobody can know. Your situation is just an accident of life.

We had a hell of a good time together.

I came back into her room. I kept imagining all the things that were going on physiologically: the lungs aren't getting enough air into the blood, which makes the brain fogged out and the heart weaker, which makes the breathing even more difficult. I kept expecting some sort of avalanching effect, with everything caving in together in a dramatic collapse. But it didn't appear that way at all: she just slowly got more foggy, and her breathing gradually became less and less, until there was no more breath—but just before that, there was a very small one.

The nurse on her rounds came in and confirmed that Arlene was dead, and went out—I wanted to be alone for a moment. I sat there for a while, and then went over to kiss her one last time.

I was very surprised to discover that her hair smelled exactly the same. Of course, after I stopped and thought about it, there was no reason why hair should smell different in such a short time. But to me it was a kind of a shock, because in my mind, something enormous had just happened—and yet nothing had happened.

The next day, I went to the mortuary. The guy hands me some rings he's taken from her body. "Would you like to see your wife one last time?" he asks.

"What kind of a—no, I don't want to see her, no!" I said. "I just saw her!"

"Yes, but she's been all fixed up," he says.

This mortuary stuff was completely foreign to me. Fixing up a body when there's nothing there? I didn't want to look at Arlene again; that would have made me more upset.

I called the towing company and got the car, and packed Arlene's stuff in the back. I picked up a hitchhiker, and started out of Albuquerque.

It wasn't more than five miles before . . . BANG! Another flat tire. I started to curse.

The hitchhiker looked at me like I was mentally unbalanced. "It's just a tire, isn't it?" he says.

"Yeah, it's just a tire—and another tire, and again another tire, and another tire!"

We put the spare tire on, and went very slowly, all the way back to Los Alamos, without getting the other tire repaired.

I didn't know how I was going to face all my friends at Los Alamos. I didn't want people with long faces talking to me about the death of Arlene. Somebody asked me what happened.

"She's dead. And how's the program going?" I said.

They caught on right away that I didn't want to moon over it. Only one guy expressed his sympathy, and it turned out he had been out of town when I came back to Los Alamos.

One night I had a dream, and Arlene came into it. Right away, I said to her, "No, no, you can't be in this dream. You're not alive!"

Then later, I had another dream with Arlene in it. I started in again, saying, "You can't be in this dream!"

"No, no," she says. "I fooled you. I was tired of you, so I cooked up this ruse so I could go my own way. But now I like you again, so I've come back." My mind was really working against itself. It had to be explained, even in a goddamn *dream*, why it was possible that she was still there!

I must have done something to myself, psychologically. I didn't cry until about a month later, when I was walking past a department store in Oak Ridge and noticed a pretty dress in the window. I thought, "Arlene would like that," and then it hit me.

IT'S AS SIMPLE AS
ONE, TWO, THREE . . .

When I was a kid growing up in Far Rockaway, I had a friend named Bernie Walker. We both had "labs" at home, and we would do various "experiments." One time, we were discussing something—we must have been eleven or twelve at the time—and I said, "But thinking is nothing but talking to yourself inside."

"Oh yeah?" Bernie said. "Do you know the crazy shape of the crankshaft in a car?"

"Yeah, what of it?"

"Good. Now, tell me: how did you describe it when you were talking to yourself?"

So I learned from Bernie that thoughts can be visual as well as verbal.

Later on, in college, I became interested in dreams. I wondered how things could look so real, just as if light were hitting the retina of the eye, while the eyes are closed: are the nerve cells on the retina actually being stimulated in some other way—by the brain itself, perhaps—or does the brain have a "judgment department" that gets slopped up during dreaming? I never got satisfactory answers to such questions from psychology, even though I became very interested in how the brain works. Instead, there was all this business about interpreting dreams, and so on.

When I was in graduate school at Princeton a kind of dumb psychology paper came out that stirred up a lot of discussion. The author had decided that the thing controlling the "time sense" in the brain is a chemical reaction involving iron. I thought to myself, "Now, how the hell could he figure that?"

Well, the way he did it was, his wife had a chronic fever which went up and down a lot. Somehow he got the idea to test her sense of time. He had her count seconds to herself (without looking at a clock), and checked how long it took her to count up to 60. He had her counting—the poor woman—all during the day: when her fever went up, he found she counted quicker; when her fever went down, she counted slower. Therefore, he thought, the thing that governed the "time sense" in the brain must be running faster when she's got fever than when she hasn't got fever.

Being a very "scientific" guy, the psychologist knew that the rate of a chemical reaction varies with the surrounding temperature by a certain formula that depends on the energy of the reaction. He measured the differences in speed of his wife's counting, and determined how much the temperature changed the speed. Then he tried to find a chemical reaction whose rates varied with temperature in the same amounts as his wife's counting did. He found that iron reactions fit the pattern best. So he deduced that his wife's sense of time was governed by a chemical reaction in her body involving iron.

Well, it all seemed like a lot of baloney to me—there were so many things that could go wrong in his long chain of reasoning. But it *was* an interesting question: what *does* determine the "time sense"? When you're trying to count at an even rate, what does that rate depend on? And what could you do to yourself to change it?

I decided to investigate. I started by counting seconds—without looking at a clock, of course—up to 60 in a slow, steady rhythm: 1, 2, 3, 4, 5 . . . . When I got to 60, only 48 seconds had gone by, but that didn't bother me: the problem was not to count for exactly one minute, but to count at a standard rate. The next time I counted to 60, 49 seconds had passed. The next time, 48. Then 47, 48, 49, 48, 48 . . . . So I found I could count at a pretty standard rate.

Now, if I just sat there, without counting, and waited until I thought a minute had gone by, it was very irregular—complete variations. So I found it's very poor to estimate a minute by sheer guessing. But by counting, I could get very accurate.

Now that I knew I could count at a standard rate, the next question was—what affects the rate?

Maybe it has something to do with the heart rate. So I began to run up and down the stairs, up and down, to get my heart beating fast. Then I'd run into my room, throw myself down on the bed, and count up to 60.

I also tried running up and down the stairs and counting to myself *while* I was running up and down.

The other guys saw me running up and down the stairs, and laughed. "What are you doing?"

I couldn't answer them—which made me realize I couldn't talk while I was counting to myself—and kept right on running up and down the stairs, looking like an idiot.

(The guys at the graduate college were used to me looking

like an idiot. On another occasion, for example, a guy came into my room—I had forgotten to lock the door during the "experiment"—and found me in a chair wearing my heavy sheepskin coat, leaning out of the wide-open window in the dead of winter, holding a pot in one hand and stirring with the other. "Don't bother me! Don't bother me!" I said. I was stirring Jell-O and watching it closely: I had gotten curious as to whether Jell-O would coagulate in the cold if you kept it moving all the time.)

Anyway, after trying every combination of running up and down the stairs and lying on the bed, surprise! The heart rate had no effect. And since I got very hot running up and down the stairs, I figured temperature had nothing to do with it either (although I must have known that your temperature doesn't really go up when you exercise). In fact, I couldn't find anything that affected my rate of counting.

Running up and down stairs got pretty boring, so I started counting while I did things I had to do anyway. For instance, when I put out the laundry, I had to fill out a form saying how many shirts I had, how many pants, and so on. I found I could write down "3" in front of "pants" or "4" in front of "shirts," but I couldn't count my socks. There were too many of them: I'm already using my "counting machine"—36, 37, 38—and here are all these socks in front of me—39, 40, 41 . . . . How do I count the socks?

I found I could arrange them in geometrical patterns—like a square, for example: a pair of socks in this corner, a pair in that one; a pair over here, and a pair over there—eight socks.

I continued this game of counting by patterns, and found I could count the lines in a newspaper article by grouping the lines into patterns of 3, 3, 3, and 1 to get 10; then 3 of those patterns, 3 of those patterns, 3 of those patterns, and 1 of those patterns made 100. I went right down the newspaper like that. After I had finished counting up to 60, I knew where I was in the patterns and could say, "I'm up to 60, and there are 113 lines." I found that I could even *read* the articles while I counted to 60, and it didn't affect the rate! In fact, I could do anything while counting to myself—except talk out loud, of course.

What about typing—copying words out of a book? I found that I could do that, too, but here my time was affected. I was excited: finally, I've found something that appears to affect my counting rate! I investigated it more.

I would go along, typing the simple words rather fast, counting to myself 19, 20, 21, typing along, counting 27, 28, 29, typing along, until—What the hell is that word?—Oh, yeah— and then continue counting 30, 31, 32, and so on. When I'd get to 60, I'd be late.

After some introspection and further observation, I realized what must have happened: I would interrupt my counting when I got to a difficult word that "needed more brains," so to speak. My counting rate wasn't slowing down; rather, the counting itself was being held up temporarily from time to time. Counting to 60 had become so automatic that I didn't even notice the interruptions at first.

The next morning, over breakfast, I reported the results of all these experiments to the other guys at the table. I told them all the things I could do while counting to myself, and said the only thing I absolutely could not do while counting to myself was talk.

One of the guys, a fella named John Tukey, said, "I don't believe you can read, and I don't see why you can't talk. I'll bet you I can talk while counting to myself, and I'll bet you you can't read."

So I gave a demonstration: they gave me a book and I read it for a while, counting to myself. When I reached 60 I said, "Now!"—48 seconds, my regular time. Then I told them what I had read.

Tukey was amazed. After we checked him a few times to see what his regular time was, he started talking: "Mary had a little lamb; I can say anything I want to, it doesn't make any difference; I don't know what's bothering you"—blah, blah, blah, and finally, "Okay!" He hit his time right on the nose. I couldn't believe it!

We talked about it a while, and we discovered something. It turned out that Tukey was counting in a different way: he was visualizing a tape with numbers on it going by. He would say, "Mary had a little lamb," and he would *watch* it! Well, now it was clear: he's "looking" at his tape going by, so he can't read, and I'm "talking" to myself when I'm counting, so I can't speak!

After that discovery, I tried to figure out a way of reading out loud while counting—something neither of us could do. I figured I'd have to use a part of my brain that wouldn't interfere with the seeing or speaking departments, so I decided to use my fingers, since that involved the sense of touch.

I soon succeeded in counting with my fingers and reading out loud. But I wanted the whole process to be mental, and not rely on any physical activity. So I tried to imagine the feeling of my fingers moving while I was reading out loud.

I never succeeded. I figured that was because I hadn't practiced enough, but it might be impossible: I've never met anybody who can do it.

By that experience Tukey and I discovered that what goes

on in different people's heads when they *think* they're doing the same thing—something as simple as *counting*—is different for different people. And we discovered that you can externally and objectively test how the brain works: you don't have to ask a person how he counts and rely on his own observations of himself; instead, you observe what he can and can't do while he counts. The test is absolute. There's no way to beat it; no way to fake it.

It's natural to explain an idea in terms of what you already have in your head. Concepts are piled on top of each other: this idea is taught in terms of that idea, and that idea is taught in terms of another idea, which comes from counting, which can be so different for different people!

I often think about that, especially when I'm teaching some esoteric technique such as integrating Bessel functions. When I see equations, I see the letters in colors—I don't know why. As I'm talking, I see vague pictures of Bessel functions from Jahnke and Emde's book, with light-tan *j*'s, slightly violet-bluish *n*'s, and dark brown *x*'s flying around. And I wonder what the hell it must look like to the students.

GETTING AHEAD

One time, back in the fifties, when I was returning from Brazil by boat, we stopped off in Trinidad for a day, so I decided to see the main city, Port of Spain. In those days, when I visited a city I was most interested in seeing the poorest sections—to see how life works at the bottom end.

I spent some time off in the hills, in the Negro section of town, wandering around on foot. On the way back a taxi stopped and the driver said, "Hey, mon! You want to see the city? It only cost five biwi."

I said, "Okay," and got in the taxi.

The driver started right off to go up and see some palace, saying, "I'll show you all the fancy places."

I said, "No, thank you; that's similar in every city. I want to see the bottom part of the city, where the poor people live. I've already seen the hills up there."

"Oh!" he said, impressed. "I'll be glad to show you around. And I have a question for you when we're through, so I want you to look at everything carefully."

So he took me to an East Indian neighborhood—it must

have been some housing project—and he stopped in front of a house made of concrete blocks. There was practically nothing inside. A man was sitting on the front steps. "You see that man?" he said. "He has a son studyin' medicine in Maryland."

Then he picked up someone from the neighborhood so I could better see what they were like. It was a woman whose teeth had a lot of decay.

Further along we stopped and he introduced me to two women he admired. "They got enough money together to buy a sewing machine, and now they do sewing and tailoring work for people in the neighborhood," he said, proudly. When he introduced me to them, he said, "This man is a professor, and what's interesting is, he wants to see our neighborhoods."

We saw many things, and finally the taxi driver said to me, "Now, Professor, here is my question: you see the Indian people are just as poor, and sometimes even poorer than the Negro people, but they're getting somewhere, somehow—this man has sent his son to college; those women are building up a sewing business. But my people aren't getting anywhere. Why is that?"

I told him, of course, that I didn't know—which is my answer to almost every question—but he wouldn't accept that, coming from a professor. I tried to guess at something which I thought was possible. I said, "There's a long tradition behind life in India that comes from a religion and philosophy that is thousands of years old. And although these people are not in India, they still pass on those traditions about what's important in life—trying to build for the future and supporting their children in the effort—which have come down to them for centuries."

I continued, "I think that your people have unfortunately

not had a chance to develop such a long tradition, or if they did, they lost it through conquest and slavery." I don't know if it's true, but it was my best guess.

The taxi driver felt that it was a good observation, and said he was planning to build for the future, too: he had some money on the horses, and if he won, he would buy his own taxicab, and *really* do well.

I felt very sorry. I told him that betting on the horses was a bad idea, but he insisted it was the only way he could do it. He had such good intentions, but his method was going to be luck.

I wasn't going to go on philosophizing, so he took me to a place where there was a steel band playing some great calypso music, and I had an enjoyable afternoon.

HOTEL CITY

One time, when I was in Geneva, Switzerland, for a Physical Society meeting, I was walking around and happened to go past the United Nations buildings. I thought to myself, "Gee! I think I'll go in and look around." I wasn't particularly dressed for it—I was wearing dirty pants and an old coat—but it turned out there were tours you could go on where some guy would show you around.

The tour was quite interesting, but the most striking part was the great big auditorium. You know how everything is overdone for these big international characters, so what would ordinarily be a stage or a dais was in several layers: you have to climb up whole sequences of steps to this great, big, monstrous wooden thing that you stand behind, with a big screen in back of you. In front of you are the seats. The carpets are elegant, and the big doors with brass handles at the back are beautiful. On each side of the great auditorium, up above, are windowed booths for the translators of different languages to work in. It's a fantastic place, and I kept thinking to myself, "Gee! How it must be to give a talk in a place like this!"

Right after that, we were walking along the corridor just outside the auditorium when the guide pointed through the window and said, "You see those buildings over there that are under construction? They'll be used for the first time at the Atoms for Peace Conference, in about six weeks."

I suddenly remembered that Murray Gell-Mann and I were supposed to give talks at that conference on the present situation of high-energy physics. My talk was set for the plenary session, so I asked the guide, "Sir, where would the talks for the *plenary* session of that conference be?"

"Back in that room that we just came through."

"Oh!" I said in delight. "Then I'm gonna give a speech in that room!"

The guide looked down at my dirty pants and my sloppy shirt. I realized how dumb that remark must have sounded to him, but it was genuine surprise and delight on my part.

We went along a little bit farther, and the guide said, "This is a lounge for the various delegates, where they often hold informal discussions." There were some small, square windows in the doors to the lounge that you could look through, so people looked in. There were a few men sitting there talking.

I looked through the windows and saw Igor Tamm, a physicist from Russia that I know. "Oh!" I said. "I know that guy!" and I started through the door.

The guide screamed, "No, no! Don't go in there!" By this time he was *sure* he had a maniac on his hands, but he couldn't chase me because he wasn't allowed to go through the door himself!

Tamm's face lit up when he recognized me, and we talked a little bit. The guide was relieved and continued the tour without me, and I had to run to catch up.

At the Physical Society meeting my good friend Bob Bacher said to me, "Listen: it's going to be hard to get a room when that Atoms for Peace Conference is going on. Why don't you have the State Department arrange a room for you, if you haven't already made a reservation?"

"Naw!" I said. "I'm not gonna have the State Department do a damn thing for me! I'll do it myself."

When I returned to my hotel I told them that I would be leaving in a week, but I'd be coming back at the end of summer: "Could I make a reservation now for that time?"

"Certainly! When will you be returning?"

"The second week in September . . ."

"Oh, we're terribly sorry, Professor Feynman; we are already completely booked for that time."

So I wandered off, from one hotel to another, and found they were all booked solid, six weeks ahead of time!

Then I remembered a trick I used once when I was with a physicist friend of mine, a quiet and dignified English fellow.

We were going across the United States by car, and when we got just beyond Tulsa, Oklahoma, there were supposed to be big floods up ahead. We came into this little town and we saw cars parked everywhere, with people and families in them, trying to sleep. He says, "We had better stop here. It's clear we can go no further."

"Aw, come on!" I say. "How do you know? Let's see if we can *do* it: maybe by the time we get there, the water will be down."

"We shouldn't waste time," he replies. "Perhaps we can find a room in a hotel if we look for it now."

"Aw, don't worry about it!" I say. "Let's go!"

We drive out of town about ten or twelve miles and come to

an arroyo. Yes, even for me, there's too much water. There's no question: we aren't going to try to get through *that*.

We turn around: my friend's muttering about how we'll have no chance of finding a room in a hotel now, and I tell him not to worry.

Back in town, it's absolutely *blocked* with people sleeping in their cars, obviously because there are no more rooms. All the hotels must be packed. I see a small sign over a door: it says "HOTEL." It was the kind of hotel I was familiar with in Albuquerque, when I would wander around town looking at things, waiting to see my wife at the hospital: you have to go up a flight of stairs and the office is on the first landing.

We go up the stairs to the office and I say to the manager, "We'd like a room."

"Certainly, sir. We have one with two beds on the third floor."

My friend is amazed: The town is packed with people sleeping in cars, and here's a hotel that has room!

We go up to our room, and gradually it becomes clear to him: there's no door on the room, only a hanging cloth in the doorway. The room was fairly clean, it had a sink; it wasn't so bad. We get ready for bed.

He says, "I've got to pee."

"The bathroom is down the hall."

We hear girls giggling and walking back and forth in the hall outside, and he's nervous. He doesn't want to go out there.

"That's all right; just pee in the sink," I say.

"But that's unsanitary."

"Naw, it's okay; you just turn the water on."

"I can't pee in the sink," he says.

We're both tired, so we lie down. It's so hot that we don't

use any covers, and my friend can't get to sleep because of the noises in the place. I kind of fall asleep a little bit.

A little later I hear a creaking of the floor nearby, and I open one eye slightly. There he is, in the dark, quietly stepping over to the sink.

Anyway, I knew a little hotel in Geneva called the Hotel City, which was one of those places with just a doorway on the street and a flight of stairs leading up to the office. There were usually some rooms available, and nobody made reservations.

I went up the stairs to the office and told the desk clerk that I'd be back in Geneva in six weeks, and I'd like to stay in their hotel: "Could I make a reservation?"

"Certainly, sir. Of course!"

The clerk wrote my name on a piece of paper—they hadn't any book to write reservations in—and I remember the clerk trying to find a hook to put the paper on, to remember. So I had my "reservation," and everything was fine.

I came back to Geneva six weeks later, went to the Hotel City, and they *did* have the room ready for me; it was on the top floor. Although the place was cheap, it was clean. (It's Switzerland; it was *clean!*) There were a few holes in the bedspread, but it was a clean bedspread. In the morning they served a European breakfast in my room; they were rather delighted to have this guest who had made a reservation six weeks in advance.

Then I went over to the U.N. for the first day of the Atoms for Peace Conference. There was quite a line at the reception desk, where everyone was checking in: a woman was taking down everybody's address and phone number so they could be reached in case there were any messages.

"Where are you staying, Professor Feynman?" she asks.

"At the Hotel City."

"Oh, you must mean the Hotel Cité."

"No, it's called 'City': C-I-T-Y." (Why not? We would call it "Cité" here in America, so they called it "City" in Geneva, because it sounded foreign.)

"But it isn't on our list of hotels. Are you *sure* it's 'City'?"

"Look in the telephone book for the number. You'll find it."

"Oh!" she said, after checking the phone book. "My list is incomplete! Some people are still looking for a room, so perhaps I can recommend the Hotel City to them."

She must have got the word about the Hotel City from someone, because nobody else from the conference ended up staying there. Once in a while the people at the Hotel City would receive telephone calls for me from the U.N., and would *run up* the two flights of stairs from the office to tell me, with some awe and excitement, to come down and answer the phone.

There's an amusing scene I remember from the Hotel City. One night I was looking through my window out into the courtyard. Something, in a building across the courtyard, caught the corner of my eye: it looked like an upside-down bowl on the windowsill. I thought it had moved, so I watched it for a while, but it didn't move any. Then, after a bit, it moved a little to one side. I couldn't figure out what this thing was.

After a while I figured it out: it was a man with a pair of binoculars that he had against the windowsill for support, looking across the courtyard to the floor below me!

There's another scene at the Hotel City which I'll always remember, that I'd love to be able to paint: I was returning one night from the conference and opened the door at the bottom of the stairway. There was the proprietor, standing there, trying to look nonchalant with a cigar in one hand while he pushed something up the stairs with the other. Farther up, the woman who brought me breakfast was pulling on this same heavy object with both hands. And at the top of the stairs, at the landing, there *she* was, with her fake furs on, bust sticking out, hand on her hip, *imperiously waiting*. Her customer was a bit drunk, and was not very capable of walking up the steps. I don't know whether the proprietor knew that *I* knew what this was all about; I just walked past everything. He was ashamed of his hotel, but, of course, to me, it was delightful.

WHO THE HELL IS HERMAN?

One day I got a long-distance telephone call from an old friend in Los Alamos. She says in a very serious voice, "Richard, I have some sad news for you. Herman died."

I'm always feeling uncomfortable that I don't remember names, and then I feel bad that I don't pay enough attention to people. So I said, "Oh?"—trying to be quiet and serious so I could get more information, but thinking to myself, "Who the hell is Herman?"

She says, "Herman and his mother were both killed in an automobile accident near Los Angeles. Since that is where his mother is from, the funeral will be held in Los Angeles at the Rose Hills Mortuary on May 3rd at three o'clock." Then she says, "Herman would have liked it very, very much to know that you would be one of his pallbearers."

I still can't remember him. I say, "Of course I'd be happy to do that." (At least this way I'll find out who Herman is.)

Then I get an idea: I call up the mortuary. "You're having a funeral on May 3rd at three o'clock . . ."

"Which funeral do you mean: the Goldschmidt funeral, or the Parnell funeral?"

"Well, uh, I don't know." It still doesn't click for me; I don't think it's either one of them. Finally, I say, "It might be a double funeral. His mother also died."

"Oh, yes. Then it's the Goldschmidt funeral."

"Herman Goldschmidt?"

"That's right; Herman Goldschmidt and Mrs. Goldschmidt."

Okay. It's Herman Goldschmidt. But I still can't remember a Herman Goldschmidt. I haven't any idea what it is I've forgotten; from the way she talked, my friend was sure that Herman and I knew each other well.

The last chance I have is to go to the funeral and look into the casket.

I go to the funeral, and the woman who had arranged everything comes over, dressed in black, and says in a sorrowful voice, "I'm *so* glad you're here. Herman would be so happy if he knew"—all this serious stuff. Everybody's got long faces about Herman, but I still don't know who Herman is—though I'm sure that if I knew, I'd feel very sorry that he was dead!

The funeral proceeded, and when it came time for everybody to file past the caskets, I went up. I looked into the first casket, and there was Herman's mother. I looked into the second casket, and there was Herman—and I swear to you, I'd never seen him before in my life!

It came time to carry the casket out, and I took my place among the pallbearers. I very carefully laid Herman to rest in his grave, because I knew he would have appreciated it. But I haven't any idea, to this day, who Herman was.

Many years later I finally got up enough courage to bring it up to my friend. "You know that funeral I went to, about ten years ago, for Howard . . ."

"You mean Herman."

"Oh yeah—Herman. You know, I didn't know who Herman was. I didn't even recognize him in the casket."

"But Richard, you knew each other in Los Alamos just after the war. You were both good friends of mine, and we had many conversations together."

"I still can't remember him."

A few days later she called and told me what might have happened: maybe she had met Herman just after I had left Los Alamos—and therefore got the timing mixed up somehow—but because she was such good friends with each of us, she thought we must have known each other. So she was the one who had made the mistake, not me (which is usually the case). Or was she just being polite?

FEYNMAN SEXIST PIG!

A few years after I gave some lectures for the freshmen at Caltech (which were published as the *Feynman Lectures on Physics*), I received a long letter from a feminist group. I was accused of being anti-woman because of two stories: the first was a discussion of the subtleties of velocity, and involved a woman driver being stopped by a cop. There's a discussion about how fast she was going, and I had her raise valid objections to the cop's definitions of velocity. The letter said I was making the woman look stupid.

The other story they objected to was told by the great astronomer Arthur Eddington, who had just figured out that the stars get their power from burning hydrogen in a nuclear reaction producing helium. He recounted how, on the night after his discovery, he was sitting on a bench with his girlfriend. She said, "Look how pretty the stars shine!" To which he replied, "Yes, and right now, I'm the only man in the world who knows *how* they shine." He was describing a kind of wonderful loneliness you have when you make a discovery.

The letter claimed that I was saying a woman is incapable of understanding nuclear reactions.

I figured there was no point in trying to answer their accusations in detail, so I wrote a short letter back to them: "Don't bug me, man!"

Needless to say, that didn't work too well. Another letter came: "Your response to our letter of September 29th is unsatisfactory . . ."—blah, blah, blah. This letter warned that if I didn't get the publisher to revise the things they objected to, there would be trouble.

I ignored the letter and forgot about it.

A year or so later, the American Association of Physics Teachers awarded me a prize for writing those books, and asked me to speak at their meeting in San Francisco. My sister, Joan, lived in Palo Alto—an hour's drive away—so I stayed with her the night before and we went to the meeting together.

As we approached the lecture hall, we found people standing there giving out handbills to everybody going in. We each took one, and glanced at it. At the top it said, "A PROTEST." Then it showed excerpts from the letters they sent me, and my response (in full). It concluded in large letters: "FEYNMAN SEXIST PIG!"

Joan stopped suddenly and rushed back: "These are interesting," she said to the protester. "I'd like some more of them!"

When she caught up with me, she said, "Gee whiz, Richard; what did you do?"

I told her what had happened as we walked into the hall.

At the front of the hall, near the stage, were two prominent women in the American Association of Physics Teachers. One was in charge of women's affairs for the organization, and the other was Fay Ajzenberg, a professor of physics I knew, from Pennsylvania. They saw me coming down towards the stage accompanied by this woman with a fistful of handbills, talking to me. Fay walked up to her and said, "Do you realize that Professor Feynman has a *sister* that he encouraged to go into physics, and that *she* has a Ph.D. in physics?"

"Of course I do," said Joan. "I'm that sister!"

Fay and her associate explained to me that the protesters were a group—led by a man, ironically—who were always disrupting meetings in Berkeley. "We'll sit on either side of you to show our solidarity, and just before you speak, I'll get up and say something to quiet the protesters," Fay said.

Because there was another talk before mine, I had time to think of something to say. I thanked Fay, but declined her offer.

As soon as I got up to speak, half a dozen protesters marched down to the front of the lecture hall and paraded right below the stage, holding their picket signs high, chanting, "Feynman sexist pig! Feynman sexist pig!"

I began my talk by telling the protesters, "I'm sorry that my short answer to your letter brought you here unnecessarily. There are more serious places to direct one's attention towards improving the status of women in physics than these relatively trivial mistakes—if that's what you want to call them—in a textbook. But perhaps, after all, it's good that you came. For women do indeed suffer from prejudice and discrimination in physics, and your presence here today serves to remind us of these difficulties and the need to remedy them."

The protesters looked at one another. Their picket signs began to come slowly down, like sails in a dying wind.

I continued: "Even though the American Association of Physics Teachers has given me an award for teaching, I must confess I don't know how to teach. Therefore, I have nothing to say about teaching. Instead, I would like to talk about something that will be especially interesting to the women in the audience: I would like to talk about the structure of the proton."

The protesters put their picket signs down and walked off. My hosts told me later that the man and his group of protesters had never been defeated so easily.

(Recently I discovered a transcript of my speech, and what I said at the beginning doesn't seem anywhere near as dramatic as the way I remember it. What I remember saying is much more wonderful than what I actually said!)

After my talk, some of the protesters came up to press me about the woman-driver story. "Why did it have to be a woman driver?" they said. "You are implying that all women are bad drivers."

"But the woman makes the cop look bad," I said. "Why aren't you concerned about the cop?"

"That's what you expect from cops!" one of the protesters said. "They're all pigs!"

"But you *should* be concerned," I said. "I forgot to say in the story that the cop was a woman!"

I JUST SHOOK HIS HAND,
CAN YOU BELIEVE IT?

For some years now the Kyoto University has been inviting me to visit Japan. But every time I accepted their invitation, I would happen to get sick and not be able to go.

In the summer of 1986 there was going to be a conference in Kyoto and the university again invited me to come. Although I love Japan and wanted very much to visit, I felt uncomfortable at the invitation because I had no paper to give. The university said it would be all right for me to give a summary paper, but I said I don't like to do that. But then they said they would be honored if I would be the chairman of one session of the conference—that's all I would have to do. So I finally said okay.

I was lucky this time and didn't get sick.* So Gweneth and I went to Kyoto, and I was chairman of one session.

The chairman is supposed to make sure that the speakers

---

* Feynman was suffering from abdominal cancer. He had surgery in 1978 and 1981. After he returned from Japan, he had more surgery, in October 1986 and October 1987.

only talk for a certain length of time, in order to leave enough time for the next speaker. The chairman occupies a position of such high honor that there are two co-chairmen to assist him. My co-chairmen said they would take care of introducing the speakers, as well as telling them when it's time to stop.

Things went smoothly for most of the session until one speaker—a Japanese man—didn't stop talking when his time was up. I look at the clock and figure it's time he should stop. I look over at the co-chairmen and gesture a little bit.

They come up to me and say, "Don't do anything; we'll take care of it. He's talking about Yukawa.* It's all right."

So I was the honorary chairman of one session, and I felt I didn't even do my job right. And for that, the university paid my way to Japan, they took care of arranging my trip, and they were all very gracious.

One afternoon we were talking to the host who was arranging our trip. He shows us a railroad map, and Gweneth sees a curved line with lots of stops in the middle of the Ise Peninsula—it's not near the water; it's not near anywhere. She puts her finger on the end of the line and says, "We want to go here."

He looks at it, and says, "Oh! You want to go to ... Iseokitsu?"

She says, "Yes."

"But there's *nothing* in Iseokitsu," he says, looking at me as if my wife is crazy, and hoping I'll bring her back to her senses.

So I say, "Yes, that's right; we want to go to Iseokitsu."

Gweneth hadn't talked to me about it, but I knew what

---

* Hideki Yukawa. Eminent Japanese physicist; Nobel Prize, 1949.

she was thinking: we enjoy traveling to places in the middle of nowhere, places we've never heard of, places which have nothing.

Our host becomes a little bit upset: he's never made a hotel reservation for Iseokitsu; he doesn't even know if there's an inn there.

He gets on the telephone and calls up Iseokitsu for us. In Iseokitsu, it turns out, there are no accommodations. But there's another town—about seven kilometers beyond the end of the line—that has a Japanese-style inn.

We say, "Fine! That's just what we want—a Japanese-style inn!" They give him the number and he calls.

The man at the inn is very reluctant: "Ours is a very small inn. It's a family-run place."

"That's what they want," our host reassures him.

"Did he say yes?" I ask.

After more discussion, our host says, "He agrees."

But the next morning, our host gets a telephone call from this same inn: last night they had a family conference. They decided they can't handle the situation. They can't take care of foreigners.

I say, "What's the trouble?"

Our host telephones the inn and asks what the problem is. He turns to us and says, "It's the toilet—they don't have a Western-style toilet."

I say, "Tell them that the last time my wife and I went on a trip, we carried a small shovel and toilet paper, and dug holes for ourselves in the dirt. Ask him, 'Shall we bring our shovel?'"

Our host explains this over the telephone, and they say, "It's okay. You can come for one night. You don't need to bring your shovel."

The innkeeper picked us up at the railroad station in Iseokitsu and took us to his inn. There was a beautiful garden outside our room. We noticed a brilliant, emerald-green tree frog climbing a metal frame with horizontal bars (used for hanging out the wet clothes), and a tiny yellow snake in a shrub in front of our *engawa* (veranda). Yes, there was "nothing" in Iseokitsu—but everything was beautiful and interesting to us.

It turned out there was a shrine about a mile away—that's why this little inn was there—so we walked to it. On our way back, it began to rain. A guy passed us in his car, then turned around and came back. "Where are you going?" he asked in Japanese. "To the inn," I said. So he took us there.

When we got back to our room, we discovered that Gweneth had lost a roll of film—perhaps in the man's car. So I got the dictionary out and looked up "film" and "lost," and tried to explain it to the innkeeper. I don't know how he did it, but he found the man who had given us the ride, and in his car we found the film.

The bath was interesting; we had to go through another room to get to it. The bathtub was wooden, and around it were all kinds of little toys—little boats and so on. There was also a towel with Mickey Mouse on it.

The innkeeper and his wife had a little daughter who was two, and a small baby. They dressed their daughter in a kimono and brought her up to our room. Her mother made origami things for her; I made some drawings for her, and we played with her.

A lady across the street gave us a beautiful silk ball that she had made. Everything was friendly; everything was very good.

The next morning we were supposed to leave. We had a reservation at one of the more famous resorts, at a spa somewhere. I looked in the dictionary again; then I came down and showed the innkeeper the receipt for our reservation at the big resort hotel—it was called the Grand View, or something like that. I said, "We don't want stay big hotel tomorrow night; we want stay *here* tomorrow night. We happy here. Please you call them; change this."

He says, "Certainly! Certainly!" I could tell he was pleased by the idea that these foreigners were canceling their reservation in this big, fancy hotel in order to stay in his little inn another night.

After we returned to Tokyo, we went to the University of Kanazawa. Some professors arranged to drive us along the coast of nearby Noto Peninsula. We passed through several delightful fishing villages, and went to visit a pagoda in the middle of the countryside.

Then we visited a shrine with an enclave behind it, where one could go only by special invitation. The Shinto priest there was very gracious and invited us into his private rooms for tea, and he did some calligraphy for us.

After our hosts had taken us a little farther along the coast, they had to return to Kanazawa. Gweneth and I decided to stay in Togi for two or three days. We stayed in a Japanese-style hotel, and the lady innkeeper there was very, very nice to us. She arranged for her brother to take us by car down the coast to several villages, and then we came back by bus.

The next morning the innkeeper told us there was something important happening in town. A new shrine, replacing an old one, was being dedicated.

When we arrived at the grounds we were invited to sit on a bench, and were served tea. There were many people milling around, and eventually a procession came out from behind the shrine. We were delighted to see the leading figure was the head priest from the shrine we had visited a few days before. He was dressed in a big, ceremonial outfit, and was obviously in charge of everything.

After a little while the ceremony began. We didn't want to intrude into a religious place, so we stayed back from the shrine itself. But there were kids running up and down the steps, playing and making noise, so we figured it wasn't so formal. We came a little closer and stood on the steps so we could see inside.

The ceremony was wonderful. There was a ceremonial cup with branches and leaves on it; there was a group of girls in special uniforms; there were dancers, and so on. It was quite elaborate.

We're watching all these performances when all of a sudden we feel a tap on the shoulder. It's the head priest! He gestures to us to follow him.

We go around the shrine and enter from the side. The head priest introduces us to the mayor and other dignitaries, and invites us to sit down. A *noh* actor does a dance, and all kinds of other wonderful things go on.

Then there are speeches. First, the mayor gives a speech. Then the head priest gets up to speak. He says, "Unano, utsini kuntana kanao. Untanao uni kanao. Uniyo zoimasu doi zinti Fain-man-san-to unakano kane gozaimas . . ."—and he points to "Fain-man-san" and tells me to say something!

My Japanese is very poor, so I say something in English: "I love Japan," I say. "I am particularly impressed by your tremendous rate of technological change, while at the same time your traditions still mean so much, as you are showing with this shrine dedication." I tried to express the mixture I saw in Japan: change, but without losing respect for traditions.

The head priest says something in Japanese which I do not believe is what I said (although I couldn't really tell), because he had never understood anything I had said to him previously! But he *acted* as if he understood *exactly* what I said, and he "translated" it with complete confidence for everyone. He was much like I am, in this respect.

Anyway, the people politely listened to whatever it was that I said, and then another priest gave a speech. He was a young man, a student of the head priest, dressed in a wonderful outfit with big, wide pant legs and a big, wide hat. He looked so gorgeous, so wonderful.

Then we went to lunch with all the dignitaries, and felt very honored to be included.

After the shrine dedication ceremony was over, Gweneth and I thanked the head priest and left the dining hall to walk around the village for a while. After a bit we found some people pulling a big wagon, with a replica of the shrine in it, through the streets. They're all dressed up in outfits with symbols on the back, singing, "Eyo! Eyo!"

We follow the procession, enjoying the festivities, when a policeman with a walkie-talkie comes up to us. He takes off his white glove and puts out his hand. I shake hands with him.

As we leave the policeman and begin to follow the procession again, we hear a loud, high-pitched voice behind us, speaking very rapidly. We turn around and see the policeman clutching his walkie-talkie, speaking into it with great excitement: "O gano fana miyo ganu Fain-man-san iyo kano muri tono muroto kala . . ."—and I could just imagine him telling the person at the other end: "Do you remember that Mr. Fainman who spoke at the shrine dedication? I just shook his hand, can you believe it?"

The priest must have "translated" something very impressive!

LETTERS

October 11, 1961
Hotel Amigo, Brussels

Hello, my sweetheart,

Murray and I kept each other awake arguing until we could stand it no longer. We woke up over Greenland, which was even better than last time because we went right over part of it. In London we met other physicists and came to Brussels together. One of them was worried—in his guidebook the Hotel Amigo was not even mentioned. Another had a newer guide—five stars, and rumored to be the best hotel in Europe!

It is very nice indeed. All the furniture is dark red polished wood, in perfect condition; the bathroom is grand, etc. It is really too bad you didn't come to this conference instead of the other one.

At the meeting next day things started slowly. I was to talk in the afternoon. That is what I did, but I didn't really have enough time. We had to stop at 4 pm because of a reception scheduled for that night. I think my talk was OK though—what I left out was in the written version anyway.

So that evening we went to the palace to meet the king and queen. Taxis waited for us at the hotel—long black ones—and off we went at 5 pm, arriving through the palace gates with a guard on each side, and driving under an arch where men in red coats and white stockings with a black band and gold tassel under each knee opened the doors. More guards at the entrance, in the hallway, along the stairs, and up into a sort of ballroom. These guards, in dark grey Russian-type hats with chin straps, dark coats, white pants, and shiny black leather boots, stand very straight—each holding a sword straight up.

In the "ballroom" we had to wait perhaps 20 minutes. It has inlaid parquet floors with an L in each square (for Leopold—the present king is Baudoin, or something). The gilded walls are 18th century and on the ceiling are pictures of naked women riding chariots among the clouds. Lots of mirrors and gilded chairs with red cushions around the outside edge of the room—just like so many of those palaces we have seen, but this time it's no museum: it's alive, with everything clear and shining, and in perfect condition. Several palace officials were milling around among us. One had a list and told me where to stand but I didn't do it right and was out of place later.

The doors at the end of the hall open. Guards are there with the king and queen; we all enter slowly and are introduced one by one to the king and queen. The king has a young semi-dopey face and a strong handshake; the queen is very pretty. (I think her name is Fabriola—a Spanish countess she was.) We exit into another room on the left where there are lots of chairs arranged like in a theatre, with two in front, also facing forward, for K & Q. A table at the front with six seats is for illustrious scientists—Niels Bohr, J. Perrin (a Frenchman), J. R. Oppenheimer etc.—see drawing.

It turns out the king wants to know what we are doing, so the old boys give a set of six dull lectures—all very solemn—no jokes. I had great difficulty sitting in my seat because I had a very stiff and uncomfortable back from sleeping on the plane.

That done, the K & Q pass through the room where we met them and into a room on right (marked R). (All these rooms are very big, gilded, Victorian, fancy, etc.) In R are many kinds of uniforms: guards at door in red coats, waiters in white coats (to serve drinks and hors d'oeuvres), military khaki and medals, and black coats—undertaker's type (palace officials).

On the way out of L into R, I am last because I walk slowly from stiff back. I find myself talking to a palace official—nice man. He teaches math part time at Louvain University, but his main job is secretary to the queen. He had also tutored the K when K was young and has been in palace work 23 years. Now, at least, I have somebody to talk to.

Some others are talking to K or to Q; everybody is standing up. After a while the professor who is head of the conference (Prof. Bragg) grabs me and says K wants to talk to me. Bragg says, "K, this is Feynman." I pull boner #1 by wanting to shake hands again—apparently wrong: no hand reaches up. After an embarrassed pause K saves day by shaking my hand. K makes polite remarks on how smart we must all be and how hard it must be to think. I answer, making jokes (having been instructed to do so by Bragg, but what does he know?)—apparently error #2. Anyway, strain is relieved when Bragg brings over some other professor—Heisenberg, I think. K forgets F and F slinks off to resume conversation with sec'y of Q.

After considerable time—several orange juices and many very good hors d'oeuvres later—a military uniform with medals comes over to me and says, "Speak to the queen!" Nothing I should like to do better (pretty girl, but don't worry, she's married). F arrives at scene: Q is sitting at table surrounded by three other occupied chairs—no room for F. There are several low coughs, slight confusion, etc., and lo!—one of the chairs has been reluctantly vacated. Other two chairs contain one lady and one Priest in Full Regalia (who is also a physicist) named LeMaître.

We have quite a conversation (I listen, but hear no coughs, and am not evacuated from seat) for perhaps 15 minutes. Sample:

Q: "It must be very hard work thinking about those difficult problems . . ."

F: "No, we all do it for the fun of it."

Q: "It must be hard to learn to change all your ideas"—(a thing she got from the six lectures).

F: "No, all those guys who gave you those lectures are old

fogeys—all that change was in 1926, when I was only eight. So when I learned physics I only had to learn the new ideas. The big problem now is, do we have to change them again?"

Q: "You must feel good, working for peace like that."

F: "No, that never enters my head, whether it is for peace or otherwise. We don't know."

Q: "Things certainly change fast—many things have changed in the last hundred years."

F: "Not in this palace." (I thought it, but controlled myself.) "Yes," and then launched into lecture on what was known in 1861 and what we found out since—adding at end, laughingly, "Can't help giving a lecture, I guess—I'm a professor, you see. Ha, ha."

Q, in desperation, turns to lady on her other side and begins conversation with same.

After a few moments K comes over and whispers something to Q, who stands up—they quietly go out. F returns to sec'y of Q who personally escorts him out of palace past guards, etc.

I'm so terribly sorry you missed it. I don't know when we'll find another king for you to meet.*

I was paged in the hotel this morning just before leaving with the others. I returned to the others and announced, "Gentlemen, that call was from the queen's secretary. I must leave you now." All are awestruck, for it did not go unnoticed that F talked longer and harder to Q than seemed proper. I didn't tell them, however, that it was about a meeting we arranged—he was inviting me to his home to meet his wife and two (of four) of his daughters, and to see his house. I had invited him to

---

* Four years later Richard and Gweneth met the king of Sweden—at the Nobel Prize ceremony.

visit us in Pasadena when he came to America and this was his response.

His wife and daughters are very nice and his house is positively beautiful. You would have enjoyed that even more than visiting the palace. He planned and built his house in a Belgian style, somewhat after an old farmhouse style, but done just right. He has many old cabinets and tables inside, right beside newer stuff, very well combined. It is much easier to find antiques in Belgium than in Los Angeles as there are so many old farms, etc. The house is slightly bigger than ours and the grounds are much bigger but not yet landscaped, except for a vegetable garden. He has a bench that he made for himself in the garden, hidden under trees, to go and sit on and look at the surrounding countryside. He has a dog— from Washington—that somebody gave to the king and the K gave to him. The dog has a personality somewhat like Kiwi* because I think he is equally loved.

I told the secretary I had a queen in a little castle in Pasadena that I would like him to see, and he said he hoped he would be able to come to America and see us. He would come if the Q ever visits America again.

I am enclosing a picture of his house, and his card, so I don't lose it.

I know you must feel terrible being left out this time—but I'll make it up someday somehow. But don't forget I love you very much and am proud of my family that is and my family that is to be.† The secretary and his wife send their best wishes to you and our future.

---

* The Feynmans' dog.

† Gweneth was expecting Carl at the time.

I wish you were here, or, next best thing, that I were there. Kiss SNORK* and tell Mom all about my adventures and I will be home sooner than you think.

Your husband loves you.
Your husband.

                              Grand Hotel
                              Warsaw

Dearest Gweneth,
   To begin with, I love you.
   Also I miss you and the baby† and Kiwi, and really wish I were home.
   I am now in the restaurant of the Grand Hotel. I was warned by friends that the service is slow, so I went back for pens and paper to work on my talk for tomorrow—but what could be better than to write to my darling instead?
   What is Poland like? My strongest impression—and the one which gives me such a surprise—is that it is almost exactly as I pictured it (except for one detail)—not only in how it looks, but also in the people, how they feel, what they say and think about the government, etc. Apparently we are well informed in the US and magazines such as <u>Time</u> and <u>Atlas</u> are not so bad. The detail is that I had forgotten how completely destroyed Warsaw was during the war and therefore that, with few exceptions (which are easily identified by the bullet holes all over them), all the buildings are built since the war. In fact it

---

* Kiwi.
† Carl. This letter was written in 1963.

is a rather considerable accomplishment—there are very many new buildings: Warsaw is a big city, all rebuilt.

The genius of builders here is to be able to build old buildings. There are buildings with facings falling off (walls covered with concrete with patches of worn brick showing thru), rusted window bars with streaks of rust running down the building, etc. Further, the architecture is old—decorations sort of 1927 but heavier—nothing interesting to look at (except one building).

The hotel room is very small, with cheap furniture, a very high ceiling (15 feet), old water spots on the walls, plaster showing through where bed rubs wall, etc. It reminds me of an old "Grand Hotel" in New York—faded cotton bedspread covering bumpy bed, etc. But the bathroom fixtures (faucets etc.) are bright and shiny, which confused me: they seem relatively new in this old hotel. I finally found out: the hotel is only three years old—I had forgotten about their ability to build old things. (No attention at all yet from waiter, so I break down and ask a passing one for service. A confused look—he calls another over. Net result: I am told there is no service at my table and am asked to move to another. I make angry noises. The response: I am put at another table, given a menu, and have 15 seconds to make up my mind. I order Sznycel Po Wiedensku—Wiener Schnitzel.)

On the question of whether the room is bugged: I look for covers of old sockets (like the one in the ceiling of the shower). There are five of them, all near the ceiling—15 feet. I need a ladder and decide not to investigate them. But there is a similar large square plate in the lower corner of my room near the telephone. I pull it back a little (one screw is loose). I have rarely seen so many wires—like the back of a radio.

What is it? Who knows! I didn't see any microphones; the ends of the wires were taped, like connections or outlets no longer in use. Maybe the microphone is in the tape. Well, I haven't a screwdriver so I don't take the plate off to investigate further. In short, if my room isn't bugged they are wasting a lot of wires.

The Polish people are nice, poor, have at least medium style in (soup arrives!) clothes, etc. There are nice places to dance, with good bands, etc., etc. So Warsaw is not very heavy and dull, as one hears Moscow is. On the other hand, you meet at every turn that kind of dull stupid backwardness characteristic of government—you know, like the fact that change for $20 isn't available when you went to get your card renewed at the US Immigration Office downtown. Example: I lost my pencil, and wanted to buy a new one at the kiosk here. "A pen costs $1.10."

"No, I want a pencil—wooden, with graphite."

"No, only $1.10 pens."

"OK, how many Zlotys is that?"

"You can't buy it in Zlotys, only for $1.10." (Why? Who knows!)

I have to go upstairs for American money. I give $1.25.

Clerk at kiosk cannot give change—must go to cashier of hotel. The bill for my pen is written in quadruplicate: the clerk keeps one, the cashier one, and I get two copies. What shall I do with them? On the back it says I should keep them to avoid paying US customs duties. It is a Papermate pen made in the USA. (The soup dish is removed.)

The real question of government versus private enterprise is argued on too philosophical and abstract a basis. Theoretically, planning may be good. But nobody has ever figured out the cause of government stupidity—and until they do (and find the cure), all ideal plans will fall into quicksand.

I didn't guess right the nature of the palace in which the meetings are held. I imagined an old, forbidding, large room from 16th century or so. Again, I forgot that Poland was so thoroughly destroyed. The palace is brand new: we meet in a round room with white walls, with gilded decorations on the balcony; the ceiling is painted with a blue sky and clouds. (The main course comes. I eat it; it is very good. I order dessert: pastries with pineapple, 125 g. Incidentally, the menu is very precise: the "125 g" is the weight—125 grams. There are things like "filet of herring, 144 g," etc. I haven't seen anybody checking for cheating with a scale; I didn't check if the schnitzel was the claimed 100 grams.)

I am not getting anything out of the meeting. I am learning nothing. Because there are no experiments this field is not an active one, so few of the best men are doing work in it. The result is that there are hosts of dopes here (126) and it is not good for my blood pressure: such inane things are said and seriously discussed that I get into arguments outside the formal sessions (say, at lunch) whenever anyone asks me a question or starts to tell me about his "work." The "work" is always: (1) completely un-understandable, (2) vague and indefinite, (3) something correct that is obvious and self-evident, but worked out by a long and difficult analysis, and presented as an important discovery, or (4) a claim based on the stupidity of the author that some obvious and correct fact, accepted and checked for years, is, in fact, false (these are the worst: no argument will convince the idiot), (5) an attempt to do something probably impossible, but certainly of no utility, which, it is finally revealed at the end, fails (dessert arrives and is eaten), or (6) just plain wrong.

There is a great deal of "activity in the field" these days, but this "activity" is mainly in showing that the previous "activity" of somebody else resulted in an error or in nothing useful or in something promising. It is like a lot of worms trying to get out of a bottle by crawling all over each other. It is not that the subject is hard; it is that the good men are occupied elsewhere. Remind me not to come to any more gravity conferences!

I went one evening to the home of one of the Polish professors (young, with a young wife). People are allowed seven square yards per person in apartments, but he and his wife are lucky: they have twenty-one*—for living room, kitchen, bathroom. He was a little nervous with his guests (myself, Professor and Mrs. Wheeler, and another) and seemed apologetic that his apartment was so small. (I ask for the check. All this time the waiter has had two or three active tables, including mine.) But his wife was very relaxed and kissed her Siamese cat "Booboosh" just like you do with Kiwi. She did a wonderful job of entertaining—the table for eating had to be taken from the kitchen, a trick requiring the bathroom door to be first removed from its hinges. (There are only four active tables in the whole restaurant now, and four waiters.) Her food was very good and we all enjoyed it.

Oh, I mentioned that one building in Warsaw is interesting to look at. It is the largest building in Poland: the "Palace of Culture and Science," given as a gift by the Soviet Union. It was designed by Soviet architects. Darling, it is unbelievable! I cannot even begin to describe it. It is the craziest monstrosity on land! (The check comes—brought by a different waiter. I await the change.)

---

* About 200 square feet.

This must be the end of my letter. I hope I don't wait too long for the change. I skipped coffee because I thought it would take too long. Even so, see what a long letter I can write while eating Sunday dinner at the Grand Hotel.

I say again I love you, and wish you were here—or better I were there. Home is good.

(The change has come—it is slightly wrong (by 0.55 Zloty = 15¢) but I let it go.)

Good bye for now.
Richard.

Saturday, June 29(?) 3pm
Royal Olympic Hotel. Poolside.

Dear Gweneth, and Michelle* (and Carl?),

This is my third day in Athens.

I'm writing by the side of the hotel pool with the paper in my lap because the tables are too high and the chairs too low.

The trip was all on time but uncomfortable anyway because the plane from New York to Athens was absolutely full—every seat. I was met by Prof. Illiapoulos, a student, and his nephew, who is just Carl's age.

I was surprised to find the weather here is just like in Pasadena, but about 5 degrees cooler: the vegetation is very similar, the hills look bare and desert-like—same plants, same cactuses, same low humidity and same cool nights. But there the similarity ends. Athens is a sprawling, ugly, noisy, exhaust-

---

* Daughter Michelle was about eleven when this letter was written, in 1980 or 1981.

filled mess of streets filled with nervous traffic jumping like rabbits when the lights go green and stopping with squealing brakes when they go red—and blowing horns when they go yellow. Very similar to Mexico City, except the people don't look as poor—there are only occasional beggars in the streets. You, Gweneth, would love it because there are so many shops (all small), and Carl would love walking around in the arcades with their rabbit-warren twists and surprises, especially in the old part of town.

Yesterday morning I went to the archeological museum. Michelle would like all the great Greek statues of horses—especially one of a small boy on a large galloping horse, all in bronze, that is a sensation. I saw so much stuff my feet began to hurt. I got all mixed up—things are not labeled well. Also, it was slightly boring because we have seen so much of that stuff before. Except for one thing: among all those art objects there was one thing so entirely different and strange that it is nearly impossible. It was recovered from the sea in 1900 and is some kind of machine with gear trains, very much like the inside of a modern wind-up alarm clock. The teeth are very regular and many wheels are fitted closely together. There are graduated circles and Greek inscriptions. I wonder if it is some kind of fake. There was an article on it in the <u>Scientific American</u> in 1959.

Yesterday afternoon I went to the Acropolis, which is right in the middle of the city—a high rock plateau on which was built the Parthenon and other shrines and temples. The Parthenon looks pretty good, but the Temple at Segesta, which Gweneth and I saw in Sicily, is just as impressive because you are allowed to walk around in it—you can't go up to or walk around among the Parthenon columns. Prof. Illiapoulos' sister came with us and with a notebook she had—she is a professional archeologist—guided our tour with all kinds of details, dates, quotations from Plutarch, etc.

It appears the Greeks take their past very seriously. They study ancient Greek archeology in their elementary schools for 6 years, having to take 10 hours of that subject every week. It is a kind of ancestor worship, for they emphasize always how wonderful the ancient Greeks were—and wonderful indeed they were. When you encourage them by saying, "Yes, and look how modern man has advanced beyond the ancient Greeks"—thinking of experimental science, the development of mathematics, the art of the Renaissance, the great depth and understanding of the relative shallowness of Greek philosophy, etc., etc.—they reply, "What do you mean? What was wrong with the ancient Greeks?" They continually put their age down and the old age up, until to point out the wonders of the present seems to them to be an unjustified lack of appreciation for the past.

They were very upset when I said that the development of greatest importance to mathematics in Europe was the discovery by Tartaglia that you can solve a cubic equation: although it is of very little use in itself, the discovery must have been psychologically wonderful because it showed that a modern man could do something no ancient Greek could do. It therefore helped in the Renaissance, which was the freeing of man from the intimidation of the ancients. What the Greeks are learning in school is to be intimidated into thinking they have fallen so far below their super ancestors.

I asked the archeologist lady about the machine in the museum—whether other similar machines, or simpler machines leading up to it or down from it, were ever found—but she hadn't heard of it. So I met her and her son of Carl's age (who looks at me as if I were a heroic ancient Greek, for he is studying physics) at the museum to show it to her. She required some explanation from me why I thought such a machine was interesting and surprising because, "Didn't Eratosthenes measure the distance to the sun, and didn't that require elaborate scientific instruments?" Oh, how ignorant are classically educated people. No wonder they don't appreciate their own time. They are not of it and do not understand it. But after a bit she believed maybe it *was* striking, and she took me to the back rooms of the museum—surely there were other examples, and she would get a complete bibliography. Well, there were no other examples, and the complete bibiography was a list of three articles (including the one in the <u>Scientific American</u>)—all by one man, an <u>American</u> from Yale!

I guess the Greeks think all Americans must be dull, being only interested in machinery when there are all those beautiful statues and portrayals of lovely myths and stories of gods and goddesses to look at. (In fact, a lady from the museum staff remarked, when told that the professor from America wanted to know more about item 15087, "Of all the beautiful things in this museum, why does he pick out <u>that</u> particular item? What is so special about it?")

Everyone here complains of the heat, and concerned about whether you can stand it, when in fact it is just like Pasadena but about 5 degrees cooler on the average. So all stores and offices close from perhaps 1:30 pm to 5:30 pm ("because of the heat"). It turns out to be really a good idea (everyone takes a nap) because then they go late into the night—supper is between 9:30 and 10 pm, when it is cool. Right now, people here are seriously complaining about a new law: to save energy, all restaurants and taverns must close at 2 am. This, they say, will spoil life in Athens.

It is the witching hour between 1:30 and 5:30 pm now, and I am using it to write to you. I miss you, and I would really be happier at home. I guess I really have lost my bug for travelling. I have a day and a half yet here and they have given me all kinds of literature about a beautiful beach (of pebbles) here, of an important ancient site (although in rather complete ruins) there, etc. But I will go to none of them, for each, it turns out, is a long, two- to four-hour ride each way on a tour bus. No. I'll just stay here and prepare my talks for Crete. (They have me giving an extra three lectures to some twenty Greek university students who are all coming to Crete just to hear me. I'll do something like my New Zealand lectures,* but I haven't got any notes! I'll have to work them out again.)

I miss you all, especially when I go to bed at night—no dogs to scratch and say good night to!

Love, Richard.

P.S. IF YOU CAN'T READ THE ABOVE HANDWRITING, HAVE NO FEAR—IT IS UNIMPORTANT RAMBLINGS. I AM WELL & IN ATHENS.

---

* The "New Zealand lectures," delivered in 1979, are written up in *QED: The Strange Theory of Light and Matter* (Princeton University Press, 1985).

MacFaddin Hall
Cornell University
Ithaca, NY
November 19, 1947*

My Dear Family:

Just a brief letter before we go off to Rochester. We have every Wednesday a seminar at which somebody talks about some item of research, and from time to time this is made a joint seminar with Rochester University. To-day is the first time this term that we are going over there for it.

It is a magnificent day, and it should be a lovely trip; Rochester is northwest of here, on the shores of Lake Ontario, and we go through some wild country. I am being taken in Feynman's car, which will be great fun if we survive. Feynman is a man for whom I am developing a considerable admiration; he is the first example I have met of that rare species, the native American scientist. He has developed a private version of the quantum theory, which is generally agreed to be a good piece of work and may be more helpful than the orthodox version for some problems; in general he is always sizzling with new ideas, most of which are more spectacular than helpful, and hardly any of which get very far before some newer inspiration eclipses it. His most valuable contribution to physics is as a sustainer of morale; when he bursts into the room with his latest brain-wave and proceeds to expound on it with the most lavish sound effects and waving about of the arms, life at least is not dull.

* These letters were contributed by Freeman Dyson. They are the first and last letters he wrote that mention Richard Feynman. Other letters are referred to in Dyson's book *Disturbing the Universe*.

Weisskopf, the chief theoretician at Rochester, is also an interesting and able man, but of the normal European type; he comes from Munich, where he was a friend of Bethe from student days.

The event of the last week has been a visit from Peierls, who ... stayed two nights with the Bethes before flying home .... On Monday night the Bethes gave a party in his honor, to which most of the young theoreticians were invited. When we arrived we were introduced to Henry Bethe, who is now five years old, but he was not at all impressed. In fact, the only thing he would say was "I want Dick! You told me Dick was coming!" Finally he had to be sent off to bed, since Dick (alias Feynman) did not materialize.

About half an hour later, Feynman burst into the room, just had time to say, "So sorry I'm late—had a brilliant idea just as I was coming over," and then dashed upstairs to console Henry. Conversation then ceased while the company listened to the joyful sounds above, sometimes taking the form of a duet and sometimes of a one-man percussion band. ...

Much Love,
Freeman

Urbana, Illinois
April 9, 1981

Dear Sara,*

I just spent a marvelous three days with Dick Feynman and wished you had been there to share him with us. Sixty years

* A family friend.

and a big cancer operation have not blunted him. He is still the same Feynman that we knew in the old days at Cornell.

We were together at a small meeting of physicists organized by John Wheeler at the University of Texas. For some reason Wheeler decided to hold the meeting at a grotesque place called World of Tennis, a country club where Texas oil-millionaires go to relax. So there we were. We all grumbled at the high prices and the extravagant ugliness of our rooms. But there was nowhere else to go—or so we thought. But Dick thought otherwise: he just said, "To hell with it. I am not going to sleep in this place," picked up his suitcase, and walked off alone into the woods.

In the morning he reappeared, looking none the worse for his night under the stars. He said he did not sleep much, but it was worth it.

We had many conversations about science and history, just like in the old days. But now he had something new to talk about, his children. He said, "I always thought I would be a specially good father because I wouldn't try to push my kids into any particular direction. I wouldn't try to turn them into scientists or intellectuals if they didn't want it. I would be just as happy with them if they decided to be truck drivers or guitar players. In fact, I would even like it better if they went out in the world and did something real instead of being professors like me. But they always find a way to hit back at you. My boy Carl, for instance. There he is in his second year at MIT, and all he wants to do with his life is to become a goddamn philosopher!"*

* As it turned out, Feynman was not to be disappointed: Carl works at the Thinking Machines Company, and daughter Michelle is studying to become a commercial photographer.

As we sat in the airport waiting for our planes, Dick pulled out a pad of paper and a pencil and started to draw the faces of people sitting in the lounge. He drew them amazingly well. I said I was sorry I have no talent for drawing. He said, "I always thought I have no talent either. But you don't need any talent to do stuff like this." . . .

Yours,
Freeman

February 17, 1988
London, England*

Dear Mrs. Feynman,

We have not met, I believe, frequently enough for either of us to have taken root in the other's conscious memory. So please forgive any impertinence, but I could not let Richard's death pass unnoticed, or to take the opportunity to add my own sense of loss to yours.

Dick was the best and favorite of several "uncles" who encircled my childhood. During his time at Cornell he was a frequent and always welcome visitor at our house, one who could be counted on to take time out from conversations with my parents and other adults to lavish attention on the children. He was at once a great player of games with us and a teacher even then who opened our eyes to the world around us.

My favorite memory of all is of sitting as an eight- or nine-year-old between Dick and my mother, waiting for the distinguished naturalist Konrad Lorenz to give a lecture. I was

---

* This letter was contributed by Henry Bethe.

itchy and impatient, as all young are when asked to sit still, when Dick turned to me and said, "Did you know that there are twice as many numbers as numbers?"

"No, there are not!" I was defensive as all young of my knowledge.

"Yes there are; I'll show you. Name a number."

"One million." A big number to start.

"Two million."

"Twenty-seven."

"Fifty-four."

I named about ten more numbers and each time Dick named the number twice as big. Light dawned.

"I see; so there are three times as many numbers as numbers."

"Prove it," said Uncle Dick. He named a number. I named one three times as big. He tried another. I did it again. Again.

He named a number too complicated for me to multiply in my head. "Three times that," I said.

"So, is there a biggest number?" he asked.

"No," I replied. "Because for every number, there is one twice as big, one three times as big. There is even one a million times as big."

"Right, and that concept of increase without limit, of no biggest number, is called 'infinity'."

At that point Lorenz arrived, so we stopped to listen to him.

I did not see Dick often after he left Cornell. But he left me with bright memories, infinity, and new ways of learning about the world. I loved him dearly.

Sincerely Yours,
Henry Bethe

PHOTOS AND DRAWINGS

Richard and Arlene on the board-
walk in Atlantic City.

On their wedding day.

Arlene in the hospital.

Coffee hour at Winnett Student Center, 1964. (CALTECH)

Gesturing at a Caltech Alumni Day lecture, 1978. (CALTECH)

In the Caltech production of *Fiorello*, 1978. (CALTECH)

The chief from Bali Hai in *South Pacific*, 1982. (CALTECH)

With Michelle, 3, and Carl, 10, in Yorkshire, England. (BBC, YORKSHIRE
TELEVISION)

With son Carl on the day Richard
won the Nobel Prize, 1965.
(CALTECH)

Richard and Gweneth on their silver wedding anniversary, 1985. (PHOTO BY
YASUSHI OHNUKI)

Richard Feynman began taking art lessons at the age of 44, and continued drawing for the rest of his life. These sketches include portraits of professional models, his friend Bob Sadler, and his daughter Michelle (at the age of 14). Feynman rarely signed his artwork. When he did, he used "Ofey"—his pseudonym as an artist.

Dot Sadler

Mr. Feynman Goes to Washington: Investigating the Space Shuttle *Challenger* Disaster

PRELIMINARIES

In this story I'm going to talk a lot about NASA,* but when I say "NASA did this" and "NASA did that," I don't mean all of NASA; I just mean that part of NASA associated with the shuttle.

To remind you about the shuttle, the large central part is the tank, which holds the fuel: liquid oxygen is at the top, and liquid hydrogen is in the main part. The engines which burn that fuel are at the back end of the orbiter, which goes into space. The crew sits in the front of the orbiter; behind them is the cargo bay.

During the launch, two solid-fuel rockets boost the shuttle for a few minutes before they separate and fall back into the sea. The tank separates from the orbiter a few minutes later—much higher in the atmosphere—and breaks up as it falls back to earth.

The solid rocket boosters are made in sections. There are two types of joints to hold the sections together: the perma-

---

* The National Aeronautics and Space Administration.

nent "factory joints" are sealed at the Morton Thiokol factory in Utah; the temporary "field joints" are sealed before each flight—"in the field"—at the Kennedy Space Center in Florida.

Figure 1. The space shuttle *Challenger*. The fuel tank, flanked by two solid-fuel rocket boosters, is attached to the orbiter, whose main engines burn liquid hydrogen and liquid oxygen. (© NASA.)

Igniter Joints　　　　　Field Joints　　　　　Nozzle-to-case Joint

Figure 2. Locations and close-up views of booster-rocket field joints.

COMMITTING SUICIDE

As you probably know, the space shuttle *Challenger* had an accident on Tuesday, January 28, 1986. I saw the explosion on TV, but apart from the tragedy of losing seven people, I didn't think much about it.

In the newspaper I used to read about shuttles going up and down all the time, but it bothered me a little bit that I never saw in any scientific journal any results of anything that had ever come out of the experiments on the shuttle that were supposed to be so important. So I wasn't paying very much attention to it.

Well, a few days after the accident, I get a telephone call from the head of NASA, William Graham, asking me to be on the committee investigating what went wrong with the shuttle! Dr. Graham said he had been a student of mine at Caltech, and later had worked at the Hughes Aircraft Company, where I gave lectures every Wednesday afternoon.

I still wasn't exactly sure who he was.

When I heard the investigation would be in Washington, my immediate reaction was not to do it: I have a principle of not going anywhere near Washington or having anything to do with government, so my immediate reaction was—how am I gonna get out of this?

I called various friends like Al Hibbs and Dick Davies, but they explained to me that investigating the *Challenger* accident was very important for the nation, and that I should do it.

My last chance was to convince my wife. "Look," I said. "Anybody could do it. They can get somebody else."

"No," said Gweneth. "If you don't do it, there will be twelve people, all in a group, going around from place to place together. But if you join the commission, there will be eleven people— all in a group, going around from place to place together— while the twelfth one runs around all over the place, checking all kinds of unusual things. There probably won't be anything, but if there is, you'll find it." She said, "There isn't anyone else who can do that like you can."

Being very immodest, I believed her.

Well, it's one thing to figure out what went wrong with the shuttle. But the next thing would be to find out what was the matter with the organization of NASA. Then there are questions like, "Should we continue with the shuttle system, or is it better to use expendable rockets?" And then come even bigger questions: "Where do we go from here?" "What should be our future goals in space?" I could see that a commission which started out trying to find out what happened to the shuttle could end up as a commission trying to decide on national policy, and go on forever!

That made me quite nervous. I decided to get out at the end of six months, no matter what.

But I also resolved that while I was investigating the accident, I shouldn't do anything else. There were some physics problems I was playing with. There was a computer class at Caltech I was teaching with another professor. (He offered to take over the course.) There was the Thinking Machines Company in Boston I was going to consult for. (They said they would wait.) My physics would have to wait, too.

By this time it was Sunday. I said to Gweneth, "I'm gonna commit suicide for six months," and picked up the telephone.

THE COLD FACTS

When I called Graham and accepted, he didn't know exactly what the commission was going to do, who it was going to be under, or even if I would be accepted onto it. (There was still hope!)

But the next day, Monday, I got a telephone call at 4 P.M.: "Mr. Feynman, you have been accepted onto the commission"—which by that time was a "presidential commission" headed by William P. Rogers.

I remembered Mr. Rogers. I felt sorry for him when he was secretary of state, because it seemed to me that President Nixon was using the national security adviser (Kissinger) more and more, to the point where the secretary of state was not really functioning.

At any rate, the first meeting would be on Wednesday. I figured there's nothing to do on Tuesday—I could fly to Washington Tuesday night—so I called up Al Hibbs and asked him to get some people at JPL* who know something about the shuttle project to brief me.

On Tuesday morning I rush over to JPL, full of steam, ready to roll. Al sits me down, and different engineers come in, one after the other, and explain the various parts of the shuttle. I don't know *how* they knew, but they knew all about the shuttle. I got a very thorough, high-speed, intense briefing. The guys at JPL had the same enthusiasm that I did. It was really quite exciting.

When I look at my notes now, I see how quickly they gave me hints about where to look for the shuttle's problems. The first line of my notes says "Inhibit burning. Liner." (To inhibit propellant from burning through the metal wall of each booster rocket, there's a liner, which was not working right.) The second line of my notes says "O-rings show scorching in clevis check." It was noticed that hot gas occasionally burned past the O-rings in booster-rocket field joints.

On the same line it says "$ZnCrO_4$ makes bubbles." (The zinc chromate putty, packed as an insulator behind the O-rings, makes bubbles which can become enlarged very fast when hot gas leaks through, eroding the O-rings.)

The engineers told me how much the pressures change inside the solid rocket boosters during flight, what the propellant is made of, how the propellant is cast and then baked at different temperatures, the percentages of asbestos, polymers, and whatnot in the liner, and all kinds of other stuff. I learned about the thrusts and forces in the engines, which are the most powerful engines for their weight ever built. The engines

---

* NASA's Jet Propulsion Laboratory, located in Pasadena; it is administered by Caltech.

Figure 3. The beginning of Feynman's notes from his informal JPL briefing.

had many difficulties, especially cracked turbine blades. The engineers told me that some of the people who worked on the engines always had their fingers crossed on each flight, and the moment they saw the shuttle explode, they were sure it was the engines.

If the engineers didn't know something, they'd say something like, "Oh, Lifer knows about that; let's get *him* in." Al would call up Lifer, who would come right away. I couldn't have had a better briefing.

It's called a briefing, but it wasn't brief: it was *very* intense, very fast, and very complete. It's the only way I know to get technical information quickly: you don't just sit there while they go through what *they* think would be interesting; instead,

Figure 4. Detailed diagram of a field joint.

Figure 5. Photograph of bubbles in zinc chromate putty, which can lead to erosion of the O-rings.

you ask a lot of questions, you get quick answers, and soon you begin to understand the circumstances and learn just what to ask to get the next piece of information you need. I got one hell of a good education that day, and I sucked up the information like a sponge.

That night I took the red-eye* to Washington, and got there early Wednesday morning. (I never took the red-eye again—I learned!)

I checked into the Holiday Inn in downtown Washington, and got a cab to take me to the first meeting of the commission.

"Where to?" the driver says.

All I have is a little piece of paper. "1415 8th Street."

We start off. I'm new in Washington. The Capitol is over here, the Washington Monument is over there; everything seems very close. But the taxi goes on and on, farther and farther into worse and worse territory. Buildings get smaller, and they begin to look run down a little bit. Finally, we get onto 8th Street, and as we go along, the buildings begin to disappear altogether. Finally we find the address—by interpolation: it's an empty lot between two buildings!

By this time I realize something is completely cockeyed. I don't know what to do, because I've only got this slip of paper, and I don't know where to go.

I say to the taxi driver, "The meeting I'm going to has something to do with NASA. Can you take me to NASA?"

---

* A flight that leaves the West Coast around 11 P.M. and arrives on the East Coast around 7 A.M., five hours and three time zones later.

"Sure," he says. "You know where it is, don't you? It's right where I picked you up!"

It was true. NASA I could have walked to from the Holiday Inn: it was right across the street! I go in, past the guard at the gate, and start wandering around.

I find my way to Graham's office, and ask if there's a meeting about the shuttle.

"Yes, I know where it is," somebody says. "I'll take you down there."

They take me to a room and, sure enough, there's a big meeting going on: there are bright lights and television cameras down in front; the room is completely full, bursting with people, and all I can do is barely squash my way into the back. I'm thinking, "There's only one door to this place. How the hell am I gonna get down to the front from here?"

Then I overhear something a little bit—it's so far down there that I can't make out exactly what it is—but it's evidently a different subject!

So I go back to Graham's office and find his secretary. She calls around and finds out where the commission is meeting. "I don't know, either," she says to the person on the other end. "He simply wandered in here!"

The meeting was in Mr. Rogers' law offices, at 1415 *H* Street. My slip of paper said 1415 *8th* Street. (The address had been given over the telephone.)

I finally got to Mr. Rogers' office—I was the only one late—and Mr. Rogers introduced me to the other commissioners. The only one I had ever heard of besides Mr. Rogers was Neil Armstrong, the moon man, who was serving as vice-chairman.

(Sally Ride was on the commission, but I didn't realize who she was until later.*) There was a very handsome-looking guy in a uniform, a General Kutyna (pronounced Koo-TEE-na). He looked formidable in his outfit, while the other people had on ordinary suits.

This first meeting was really just an informal get-together. That bothered me, because I was still wound up like a spring from my JPL briefing the day before.

Mr. Rogers did announce a few things. He read from the executive order that defined our work:

The Commission shall:
1. Review the circumstances surrounding the accident and establish the probable cause or causes of the accident; and
2. Develop recommendations for corrective or other action based upon the Commission's findings and determinations.

Mr. Rogers also said we would complete our investigation within 120 days.

That was a relief: the scope of our commission would be limited to investigating the accident, and our work might be finished before I was done committing suicide!

Mr. Rogers asked each of us how much of our time we could spend on the commission. Some of the commissioners were retired, and almost everybody said they had rearranged their

---

* Sally Ride was the first American woman in space.

schedules. I said, "I'm ready to work 100 percent, starting right now!"

Mr. Rogers asked, "Who will be in charge of writing the report?"

A Mr. Hotz, who had been the editor of *Aviation Week* magazine, volunteered to do that.

Then Mr. Rogers brought up another matter. "I've been in Washington a long time," he said, "and there's one thing you all must know: no matter what we do, there will always be leaks to the press. The best we can do is just try to minimize them. The proper way to deal with leaks is to have public meetings. We will have closed meetings, of course, but if we find anything important, we will have an open meeting right away, so the public will always know what is going on."

Mr. Rogers continued, "To start things off right with the press, our first official meeting will be a public meeting. We'll meet tomorrow at 10 A.M."

As we were leaving the get-together, I heard General Kutyna say, "Where's the nearest Metro station?"

I thought, "This guy, I'm gonna get along with him fine: he's dressed so fancy, but inside, he's straight. He's not the kind of general who's looking for his driver and his special car; he goes back to the Pentagon by the Metro." Right away I liked him, and over the course of the commission I found my judgment in this case was excellent.

The next morning, a limousine called for me—someone had arranged for us to arrive at our first official meeting in limousines. I sat in the front seat, next to the driver.

On the way to the meeting, the driver says to me, "I under-stand a lot of important people are on this commission . . ."

"Yeah, I s'pose . . ."

"Well, I collect autographs," he says. "Could you do me a favor?"

"Sure," I say.

I'm reaching for my pen when he says, "When we get there, could you point out to me which one Neil Armstrong is, so I can get his autograph?"

Before the meeting started, we were sworn in. People were milling around; a secretary handed us each a badge with our picture on it so we could go anywhere in NASA. There were also some forms to sign, saying you agree to this and that so you can get your expenses paid, and so on.

After we were sworn in, I met Bill Graham. I did recognize him, and remembered him as a nice guy.

This first public meeting was going to be a general brief-ing and presentation by the big cheeses of NASA—Mr. Moore, Mr. Aldrich, Mr. Lovingood, and others. We were seated in big leather chairs on a dais, and there were bright lights and TV cameras pointing at us every time we scratched our noses.

I happened to sit next to General Kutyna. Just before the meeting started, he leans over and says, "Co-pilot to pilot: comb your hair."

I say, "Pilot to co-pilot: can I borrow your comb?"

The first thing we had to learn was the crazy acronyms that NASA uses all over the place: "SRMs" are the solid rocket motors, which make up most of the "SRBs," the solid rocket boosters. The "SSMEs" are the space shuttle main engines; they burn "LH" (liquid hydrogen) and "LOX" (liquid oxygen), which are stored in the "ET," the external tank. Everything's got letters.

And not just the big things: practically every valve has an acronym, so they said, "We'll give you a dictionary for the acronyms—it's really very simple." Simple, sure, but the dictionary is a great, big, fat book that you've gotta keep looking through for things like "HPFTP" (high-pressure fuel turbopump) and "HPOTP" (high-pressure oxygen turbopump).

Then we learned about "bullets"—little black circles in front of phrases that were supposed to summarize things. There was one after another of these little goddamn bullets in our briefing books and on the slides.

It turned out that apart from Mr. Rogers and Mr. Acheson, who were lawyers, and Mr. Hotz, who was an editor, we all had degrees in science: General Kutyna had a degree from MIT; Mr. Armstrong, Mr. Covert, Mr. Rummel, and Mr. Sutter

STS 51-L CARGO ELEMENTS

- TRACKING AND DATA RELAY SATELLITE-B/INERTIAL UPPER STAGE

- SPARTAN-HALLEY/MISSION PECULIAR SUPPORT STRUCTURE

- CREW COMPARTMENT
    - TISP - TEACHER IN SPACE PROGRAM
    - CHAMP - COMET HALLEY ACTIVE MONITORING PROGRAM
    - FDE - FLUID DYNAMICS EXPERIMENT
    - STUDENT EXPERIMENTS
    - RME - RADIATION MONITORING EXPERIMENT
    - PPE - PHASE PARTITIONING EXPERIMENT

Figure 6. An example of "bullets."

were all aeronautical engineers, while Dr. Ride, Mr. Walker, Mr. Wheelon, and I were all physicists. Most of us seemed to have done some preliminary work on our own. We kept asking questions that were much more technical than some of the big cheeses were prepared for.

When one of them couldn't answer a question, Mr. Rogers would reassure him that we understood he wasn't expecting such detailed questions, and that we were satisfied, for the time being at least, by the perpetual answer, "We'll get that information to you later."

The main thing I learned at that meeting was how inefficient a public inquiry is: most of the time, other people are asking questions you already know the answer to—or are not interested in—and you get so fogged out that you're hardly listening when important points are being passed over.

What a contrast to JPL, where I had been filled with all sorts of information very fast. On Wednesday we have a "get-together" in Mr. Rogers' office—that takes two hours—and then we've got the rest of the day to do what? Nothing. And that night? Nothing. The next day, we have the public meeting—"We'll get back to you on that"—which equals nothing! Although it *looked* like we were doing something every day in Washington, we were, in reality, sitting around doing nothing most of the time.

That night I gave myself something to do: I wrote out the kinds of questions I thought we should ask during our investigation, and what topics we should study. My plan was to find out what the rest of the commission wanted to do, so we could divide up the work and get going.

The next day, Friday, we had our first real meeting. By this time we had an office—we met in the Old Executive Office Building—and there was even a guy there to transcribe every word we said.

Mr. Rogers was delayed for some reason, so while we waited for him, General Kutyna offered to tell us what an accident investigation is like. We thought that was a good idea, so he got up and explained to us how the air force had proceeded with its investigation of an unmanned Titan rocket which had failed.

I was pleased to see that the system he described—what the questions were, and the way they went about finding the answers—was very much like what I had laid out the night before, except that it was much more methodical than I had envisioned. General Kutyna warned us that sometimes it looks like the cause is obvious, but when you investigate more carefully you have to change your mind. They had very few clues, and changed their minds three times in the case of the Titan.

I'm all excited. I want to do this kind of investigation, and figure we can get started right away—all we have to do is decide who will do what.

But Mr. Rogers, who came in partway through General Kutyna's presentation, says, "Yes, your investigation was a great success, General, but we won't be able to use your methods here because we can't get as much information as you had."

Perhaps Mr. Rogers, who is not a technical man, did not realize how patently false that was. The Titan, being an unmanned rocket, didn't have anywhere near the number of check gadgets the shuttle did. We had television pictures showing a flame coming out the side of a booster rocket a few seconds before the explosion; all we could see in General Kutyna's pictures of the Titan was a lousy dot in the sky—just a little, tiny flash—and he was able to figure stuff out from that.

Mr. Rogers says, "I have arranged for us to go to Florida next Thursday. We'll get a briefing there from NASA officials, and they'll take us on a tour of the Kennedy Space Center."

I get this picture of the czarina coming to a Potemkin village: everything is all arranged; they show us how the rocket looks and how they put it together. It's not the way to find out how things *really* are.

Then Mr. Armstrong says, "We can't expect to do a technical investigation like General Kutyna did." This bothered me a lot, because the only things I pictured myself doing were technical! I didn't know exactly what he meant: perhaps he was saying that all the technical lab work would be done by NASA.

I began suggesting things I could do.

While I'm in the middle of my list, a secretary comes in with a letter for Mr. Rogers to sign. In the interim, when I've just been shut up and I'm waiting to come back, various other commission members offer to work with me. Then Mr. Rogers looks up again to continue the meeting, but he calls on somebody else—as if he's absentminded and forgot I'd been interrupted. So I have to get the floor again, but when I start my stuff again, another "accident" happens.

In fact, Mr. Rogers brought the meeting to a close while I was in midstream! He repeated his worry that we'll never really figure out what happened to the shuttle.

This was extremely discouraging. It's hard to understand now, because NASA has been taking at least two years to put the shuttle back on track. But at the time, I thought it would be a matter of days.

I went over to Mr. Rogers and said, "We're going to Florida next Thursday. That means we've got nothing to do for *five days:* what'll I do for five days?"

"Well, what would you have done if you hadn't been on the commission?"

"I was going to go to Boston to consult, but I canceled it in order to work 100 percent."

"Well, why don't you go to Boston for the five days?"

I couldn't take that. I thought, "I'm dead already! The god-damn thing isn't working right." I went back to my hotel, devastated.

Then I thought of Bill Graham, and called him up. "Listen, Bill," I said. "You got me into this; now you've gotta save me: I'm completely depressed; I can't stand it."

He says, "What's the matter?"

"I want to *do* something! I want to go around and talk to some engineers!"

He says, "Sure! Why not? I'll arrange a trip for you. You can go wherever you want: you could go to Johnson, you could go to Marshall, or you could go to Kennedy . . ."

I thought I wouldn't go to Kennedy, because it would look like I'm rushing to find out everything ahead of the others. Sally Ride worked at Johnson, and had offered to work with me, so I said, "I'll go to Johnson."

"Fine," he says. "I'll tell David Acheson. He's a personal friend of Rogers, and he's a friend of mine. I'm sure everything will be okay."

Half an hour later, Acheson calls me: "I think it's a great

idea," he says, "and I told Mr. Rogers so, but he says no. I just don't know why I can't convince him."

Meanwhile, Graham thought of a compromise: I would stay in Washington, and he would get people to come to his office at NASA, right across the street from my hotel. I would get the kind of briefing I wanted, but I wouldn't be running around.

Then Mr. Rogers calls me: he's against Graham's compromise. "We're all going to Florida next Thursday," he says.

I say, "If the idea is that we sit and listen to briefings, it won't work with me. I can work much more efficiently if I talk to engineers directly."

"We have to proceed in an orderly manner."

"We've had several meetings by now, but we still haven't been assigned anything to do!"

Rogers says, "Well, do you want me to bother all the other commissioners and call a special meeting for Monday, so we can make such assignments?"

"Well, yes!" I figured our job was to work, and we *should* be bothered—you know what I mean?

So he changes the subject, naturally. He says, "I understand you don't like the hotel you're in. Let me put you in a good hotel."

"No, thank you; everything is fine with my hotel."

Pretty soon he tries again, so I say, "Mr. Rogers, my personal comfort is not what I'm concerned with. I'm trying to get to work. I want to *do* something!"

Finally, Rogers says it's okay to go across the street to talk to people at NASA.

I was obviously quite a pain in the ass for Mr. Rogers. Later, Graham tried to explain it to me. "Suppose you, as a technical person, were given the job as chairman of a committee to look into some legal question. Your commission is mostly lawyers, and one of them keeps saying, 'I can work more effectively if I talk directly to other lawyers.' I assume you'd want to get your bearings first, before letting anybody rush off investigating on his own."

Much later, I appreciated that there were lots of problems which Mr. Rogers had to address. For example, any piece of information any of us received had to be entered into the record and made available to the other commissioners, so a central library had to be set up. Things like that took time.

On Saturday morning I went to NASA. Graham brought in guys to tell me all about the shuttle. Although they were pretty high up in NASA, the guys were technical.

The first guy told me all about the solid rocket boosters— the propellant, the motor, the whole thing except the seals. He said, "The seals expert will be here this afternoon."

The next guy told me all about the engine. The basic operation was more or less straightforward, but then there were all kinds of controls, with backing and hauling from pipes, heating from this and that, with high-pressure hydrogen pushing a little propeller which turns something else, which pumps oxygen through a vent valve—that kind of stuff.

It was interesting, and I did my best to understand it, but after a while I told the fella, "That's as much as I'm going to take, now, on the engine."

"But there are many problems with the engines that you should hear about," he says.

I was hot on the trail of the booster rocket, so I said, "I'll have to put off the main engines till later, when I have more time."

Then a guy came in to tell me about the orbiter. I felt terrible, because he had come in on a Saturday to see me, and it didn't look like the orbiter had anything to do with the accident. I was having enough trouble understanding the rest of the shuttle—there's only a certain amount of information per cubic inch a brain can hold—so I let him tell me some of the stuff, but soon I had to tell him that it was getting too detailed, so we just had a pleasant conversation.

In the afternoon, the seals expert came in—his name was Mr. Weeks—and gave me what amounted to a continuation of my JPL briefing, with still more details.

There's putty and other things, but the ultimate seal is supposed to be two rubber rings, called O-rings, which are approximately a quarter of an inch thick and lie on a circle 12 feet in diameter—that's something like 37 feet long.

When the seals were originally designed by the Morton Thiokol Company, it was expected that pressure from the burning propellant would squash the O-rings. But because the joint is stronger than the wall (it's three times thicker), the wall bows outward, causing the joint to bend a little—enough to lift the rubber O-rings off the seal area. Mr. Weeks told me this phenomenon is called "joint rotation," and it was discovered very early, before they ever flew the shuttle.

The pieces of rubber in the joints are called O-rings, but they're not used like normal O-rings are. In ordinary circumstances, such as sealing oil in the motor of an automobile,

Figure 7. Joint rotation is caused by pressure from inside the rocket pushing the walls out farther than the joints. A gap opens, and hot gas flows past one or both of the O-rings.

there are sliding parts and rotating shafts, but the gaps are always the same. An O-ring just sits there, in a fixed position.

But in the case of the shuttle, the gap *expands* as the pressure builds up in the rocket. And to maintain the seal, the rubber has to expand *fast* enough to close the gap—and during a launch, the gap opens in a fraction of a second. Thus the resilience of the rubber became a very essential part of the design.

When the Thiokol engineers were discovering these problems, they went to the Parker Seal Company, which manufactures the rubber, to ask for advice. The Parker Seal Company

Figure 8. Thiokol attempted to cure the joint-rotation problem with shims.

told Thiokol that O-rings are not meant to be used that way, so they could give no advice.

Although it was known from nearly the beginning that the joint was not working as it was designed to, Thiokol kept struggling with the device. They made a number of makeshift improvements. One was to put shims in to keep the joint tight, but the joint still leaked. Mr. Weeks showed me pictures of leaks on previous flights—what the engineers called "blowby," a blackening behind an O-ring where hot gas leaked through,

Figure 9. Two examples of O-ring erosion. Such erosion would occur unpredictably along 2 or 3 inches of the 37-foot O-ring.

Figure 10. The correlation between temperature and O-ring incidents.

and what they called "erosion," where an O-ring had burned a little bit. There was a chart showing all the flights, and how serious the blowby and erosion were on each one. We went through the whole history up to *the* flight, 51-L.

> ## Recommendations
>
> - The lack of a good secondary seal in the field joint is most critical and ways to reduce joint rotation should be incorporated as soon as possible to reduce criticality
>
> - The flow conditions in the joint areas during ignition and motor operation need to be established through cold flow modeling to eliminate O-ring erosion
>
> - QM-5 static test should be used to qualify a second source of the only flight certified joint filler material (asbestos-filled vacuum putty) to protect the flight program schedule
>
> - VLS-1 should use the only flight certified joint filler material (Randolph asbestos-filled vacuum putty) in all joints
>
> - Additional hot and cold subscale tests need to be conducted to improve analytical modeling of O-ring erosion problem and for establishing margins of safety for eroded O-rings
>
> - Analysis of existing data indicates that it is safe to continue flying existing design as long as all joints are leak checked with a 200 psig stabilization pressure, are free of contamination in the seal areas and meet O-ring squeeze requirements
>
> - Efforts needs to continue at an accelerated pace to eliminate SRM seal erosion

Figure 11. The self-contradictory recommendations of the seals report are underlined.

I said, "Where does it say they were ever discussing the problem—how it's going along, or whether there's some progress?"

The only place was in the "flight readiness reviews"—between flights there was no discussion of the seals problem!

We looked at the summary of the report. Everything was behind little bullets, as usual. The top line says:

· The lack of a good secondary seal in the field joint is most critical and ways to reduce joint rotation should be incorporated as soon as possible to reduce criticality

And then, near the bottom, it says:

   · Analysis of existing data indicates that it is safe to con-
    tinue flying existing design as long as all joints are leak
    checked* with a 200 psig stabilization . . .

I was struck by the contradiction: "If it's 'most critical,' how could it be 'safe to continue flying'? What's the *logic* of this?"

Mr. Weeks says, "Yes, I see what you mean! Well, let's see: it says here, 'Analysis of existing data . . .'"

We went back through the report and found the analysis. It was some kind of computer model with various assumptions that were not necessarily right. You know the danger of computers, it's called GIGO: garbage in, garbage out! The analysis concluded that a little unpredictable leakage here and there could be tolerated, even though it wasn't part of the original design.

If *all* the seals had leaked, it would have been obvious even to NASA that the problem was serious. But only a few of the seals leaked on only some of the flights. So NASA had developed a peculiar kind of attitude: if one of the seals leaks a little and the flight is successful, the problem isn't so serious. Try playing Russian roulette that way: you pull the trigger and the gun doesn't go off, so it must be safe to pull the trigger again . . .

Mr. Weeks said there was a rumor that the history of the seals problem was being leaked to the newspapers. That bothered him a little bit, because it made NASA look like it was trying to keep things secret.

I told him I was entirely satisfied with the people Graham

---

* Later in our investigation we discovered that it was this leak check which was a likely cause of the dangerous bubbles in the zinc chromate putty that I had heard about at JPL.

had brought in to talk to me, and that since I had already heard about the seals problem at JPL, it wasn't any big deal.

The next day, Sunday, Bill Graham took me with his family to the National Air and Space Museum. We had an early breakfast together, and then we went across the street to the museum.

I was expecting to see big crowds there, but I had forgotten that Graham was such a big shot. We had the whole place to ourselves for a while.

We did see Sally Ride there. She was in a display case, in an astronaut's suit, holding a helmet and everything. The wax model looked exactly like her.

At the museum there was a special theater with a movie about NASA and its achievements. The movie was wonderful. I had not fully appreciated the enormous number of people who were working on the shuttle, and all the effort that had gone into making it. And you know how a movie is: they can make it dramatic. It was so dramatic that I almost began to cry. I could see that the accident was a terrible blow. To think that so many people were working so hard to make it go— and then it busts—made me even more determined to help straighten out the problems of the shuttle as quickly as possible, to get all those people back on track. After seeing this movie I was very changed, from my semi anti-NASA attitude to a very strong pro-NASA attitude.

That afternoon, I got a telephone call from General Kutyna.

"Professor Feynman?" he says. "I have some urgent news for you. Uh, just a minute."

I hear some military-type band music in the background.

The music stops, and General Kutyna says, "Excuse me, Professor; I'm at an Air Force Band concert, and they just played the national anthem."

I could picture him in his uniform, standing at attention while the band is playing the "Star Spangled Banner," saluting with one hand and holding the telephone with the other. "What's the news, General?"

"Well, the first thing is, Rogers told me to tell you not to go over to NASA."

I didn't pay any attention to that, because I had already gone over to NASA the day before.

He continued, "The other thing is, we're going to have a special meeting tomorrow afternoon to hear from a guy whose story came out in the *New York Times* today."

I laughed inside: so we're going to have a special meeting on Monday, anyway!

Then he says, "I was working on my carburetor this morning, and I was thinking: the shuttle took off when the temperature was 28 or 29 degrees. The coldest temperature previous to that was 53 degrees. You're a professor; *what, sir, is the effect of cold on the O-rings?*"

"Oh!" I said. "It makes them stiff. Yes, of course!"

That's all he had to tell me. It was a clue for which I got a lot of credit later, but it was his observation. A professor of theoretical physics always has to be told what to look for. He just uses his knowledge to explain the observations of the experimenters!

On Monday morning General Kutyna and I went over to Graham's office and asked him if he had any information on the effects of temperature on the O-rings. He didn't have it on hand, but said he would get it to us as soon as possible.

Graham did, however, have some interesting photographs to show us. They showed a flame growing from the right-hand solid rocket booster a few seconds before the explosion. It was hard to tell exactly where the flame was coming out, but there was a model of the shuttle right there in the office. I put the model on the floor and walked around it until it looked exactly like the picture—in size, and in orientation.

I noticed that on each booster rocket there's a little hole— called the leak test port—where you can put pressure in to test the seals. It's *between* the two O-rings, so if it's not closed right and if the first O-ring fails, the gas would go out through the hole, and it would be a catastrophe. It was just about where the flame was. Of course, it was still a question whether the flame was coming out of the leak test port or a larger flame was coming out farther around, and we were seeing only the tip of it.

That afternoon we had our emergency closed meeting to hear from the guy whose story was in the *New York Times*. His name was Mr. Cook. He was in the budget department of NASA when he was asked to look into a possible seals problem and to estimate the costs needed to rectify it.

By talking to the engineers, he found out that the seals had been a big problem for a long time. So he reported that it would cost so-and-so much to fix it—a lot of money. From the point of view of the press and some of the commissioners, Mr. Cook's story sounded like a big exposé, as if NASA was hiding the seals problem from us.

I had to sit through this big, unnecessary excitement, wondering if every time there was an article in the newspaper, would we have to have a special meeting? We would never get anywhere that way!

But later, during that same meeting, some very interesting things happened. First, we saw some pictures which showed puffs of smoke coming out of a field joint just after ignition, before the shuttle even got off the pad. The smoke was coming out of the same place—possibly the leak test port—where the flame appeared later. There wasn't much question, now. It was all fitting together.

Then something happened that was completely unexpected. An engineer from the Thiokol Company, a Mr. McDonald, wanted to tell us something. He had come to our meeting on his own, uninvited. Mr. McDonald reported that the Thiokol engineers had come to the conclusion that low temperatures had something to do with the seals problem, and they were very, very worried about it. On the night before the launch, during the flight readiness review, they told NASA the shuttle shouldn't fly if the temperature was below 53 degrees—the previous lowest temperature—and on that morning it was 29.

Mr. McDonald said NASA was "appalled" by that statement. The man in charge of the meeting, a Mr. Mulloy, argued that the evidence was "incomplete"—some flights with erosion and blowby had occurred at *higher* than 53 degrees—so Thiokol should reconsider its opposition to flying.

Thiokol reversed itself, but McDonald refused to go along, saying, "If something goes wrong with this flight, I wouldn't want to stand up in front of a board of inquiry and say that I went ahead and told them to go ahead and fly this thing outside what it was qualified to."

Figure 12. Progression of a flame, possibly from the leak test port area. (© NASA.)

That was so astonishing that Mr. Rogers had to ask, "Did I understand you correctly, that you said . . . ," and he repeated the story. And McDonald says, "Yes, sir."

The whole commission was shocked, because this was the first time any of us had heard *this* story: not only was there a failure in the seals, but there may have been a failure in management, too.

Mr. Rogers decided that we should look carefully into Mr.

Figure 13. An incorrectly sealed leak test port could provide an escape route for a flame which burns past the primary O-ring.

McDonald's story, and get more details before we made it public. But to keep the public informed, we would have an open meeting the following day, Tuesday, in which Mr. Cook would testify.

I thought, "This is going to be like an act: we're going to say the same things tomorrow as we did today, and we won't learn anything new."

Figure 14. Puffs of black "smoke" (fine, unburned particles) were seen escaping from the same place where the flame was observed. (© NASA.)

As we were leaving, Bill Graham came over with a stack of papers for me.

"Geez! That's fast!" I said. "I only asked you for the information this morning!" Graham was always very cooperative.

The paper on top says, "Professor Feynman of the Presidential Commission wants to know about the effects over time of temperature on the resiliency of the O-rings . . ."—it's a memorandum addressed to a subordinate.

Under that memo is another memo: "Professor Feynman of the Presidential Commission wants to know . . ."—from that subordinate to *his* subordinate, and so on down the line.

There's a paper with some numbers on it from the poor bastard at the bottom, and then there's a series of submission papers which explain that the answer is being sent up to the next level.

So here's this stack of papers, just like a sandwich, and in the middle is the answer—to the wrong question! The answer was: "You squeeze the rubber for two hours at a certain temperature and pressure, and then see how long it takes to creep back"—over *hours*. I wanted to know how fast the rubber responds in *milliseconds* during a launch. So the information was of no use.

I went back to my hotel. I'm feeling lousy and I'm eating dinner; I look at the table, and there's a glass of ice water. I say to myself, "Damn it, *I* can find out about that rubber *without* having NASA send notes back and forth: I just have to *try* it! All I have to do is get a sample of the rubber."

I think, "I could do this tomorrow while we're all sittin' around, listening to this Cook crap we heard today. We always get ice water in those meetings; that's something I can do to save time."

Then I think, "No, that would be gauche."

But then I think of Luis Alvarez, the physicist. He's a guy I admire for his gutsiness and sense of humor, and I think, "If Alvarez was on this commission, he would do it, and that's good enough for me."

There are stories of physicists—great heroes—who have gotten information one, two, three—just like that—where everybody else is trying to do it in a complicated way. For example, after ultraviolet rays and X-rays had been discovered, there was a new type, called N-rays, discovered by Prosper-André Blondlot, in France. It was hard to detect the N-rays: other scientists had difficulty repeating Blondlot's experiments, so someone asked the great American physicist R. W. Wood to go to Blondlot's laboratory.

Blondlot gave a public lecture and demonstration. N-rays were bent by aluminum, so he had all kinds of lenses lined up, followed by a big disk with an aluminum prism in the middle. As the aluminum prism slowly turned, the N-rays came up this way and bent that way, and Blondlot's assistant reported their intensity—different numbers for different angles.

N-rays were affected by light, so Blondlot turned out the lights to make his readings more sensitive. His assistant continued to report their intensity.

When the lights came back on, there's R. W. Wood in the front row, holding the prism high in the air, balanced on the tips of his fingers, for all to see! So that was the end of the N-ray.

I think, "Exactly! I've got to get a sample of the rubber." I call Bill Graham.

It's impossible to get: it's kept somewhere down at Kennedy.

But then Graham remembers that the model of the field joint we're going to use in our meeting tomorrow has two samples of the rubber in it. He says, "We could meet in my office before the meeting and see if we can get the rubber out."

The next morning I get up early and go out in front of my hotel. It's eight in the morning and it's snowing. I find a taxi and say to the driver, "I'd like to go to a hardware store."

"A hardware store, sir?"

"Yeah. I gotta get some tools."

"Sir, there's no hardware stores around here; the Capitol is over there, the White House is over there—wait a minute: I think I remember passing one the other day."

He found the hardware store, and it turned out it didn't open till 8:30—it was about 8:15—so I waited outside, in my suitcoat and tie, a costume I had assumed since I came to Washington in order to move among the natives without being too conspicuous.

The suitcoats that the natives wear inside their buildings (which are well heated) are sufficient for walking from one building to another—or from a building to a taxi if the buildings are too far apart. (All the taxis are heated.) But the natives seem to have a strange fear of the cold: they put overcoats on top of their suitcoats if they wish to step outside. I hadn't bought an overcoat yet, so I was still rather conspicuous standing outside the hardware store in the snow.

At 8:30 I went in and bought a couple of screwdrivers, some pliers, and the smallest C-clamp I could find. Then I went to NASA.

On the way to Graham's office, I thought maybe the clamp was too big. I didn't have much time, so I ran down to the medical department of NASA. (I knew where it was, because I had been going there for blood tests ordered by my cardiologist, who was trying to treat me by telephone.) I asked for a medical clamp like they put on tubes.

They didn't have any. But the guy says, "Well, let's see if your C-clamp fits inside a glass!" It fitted very easily.

I went up to Graham's office.

The rubber came out of the model easily with just a pair of pliers. So there I was with the rubber sample in my hand. Although I knew it would be more dramatic and honest to do the experiment for the first time in the public meeting, I did something that I'm a little bit ashamed of. I cheated. I couldn't resist. I tried it. So, following the example of having a closed

Figure 15. The field-joint model from which Feynman got the O-ring sample.

meeting before an open meeting, I discovered it worked before I did it in the open meeting. Then I put the rubber back into the model so Graham could take it to the meeting.

I go to the meeting, all ready, with pliers in one pocket and a C-clamp in the other. I sit down next to General Kutyna.

At the previous meeting, there was ice water for everybody. This time, there's no ice water. I get up and go over to somebody who looks like he's in charge, and I say, "I'd like a glass of ice water, please."

He says, "Certainly! Certainly!"

Five minutes later, the guards close the doors, the meeting starts, and I haven't got my ice water.

I gesture over to the guy I just talked to. He comes over and says, "Don't worry, it's coming!"

The meeting is going along, and now Mr. Mulloy begins to tell us about the seals. (Apparently, NASA wants to tell us about the seals before Mr. Cook does.) The model starts to go around, and each commissioner looks at it a little bit.

Meanwhile, no ice water!

Mr. Mulloy explains how the seals are supposed to work—in the usual NASA way: he uses funny words and acronyms, and it's hard for anybody else to understand.

In order to set things up while I'm waiting for the ice water, I start out: "During a launch, there are vibrations which cause the rocket joints to move a little bit—is that correct?"

"That is correct, sir."

"And inside the joints, these so-called O-rings are supposed to expand to make a seal—is that right?"

"Yes, sir. In static conditions they should be in direct contact with the tang and clevis* and squeezed twenty-thousandths of an inch."

"Why don't we take the O-rings out?"

"Because then you would have hot gas expanding through the joint . . ."

"Now, in order for the seal to work correctly, the O-rings must be made of rubber—not something like lead, which, when you squash it, it stays."

"Yes, sir."

"Now, if the O-ring weren't resilient for a second or two, would that be enough to be a very dangerous situation?"

"Yes, sir."

That led us right up to the question of cold temperature and the resilience of the rubber. I wanted to prove that Mr. Mulloy must have known that temperature had an effect, although—according to Mr. McDonald—he claimed that the evidence was "incomplete." But still, no ice water! So I had to stop, and somebody else started asking questions.

The model comes around to General Kutyna, and then to me. The clamp and pliers come out of my pocket, I take the model apart, I've got the O-ring pieces in my hand, but I still haven't got any ice water! I turn around again and signal the guy I've been bothering about it, and he signals back, "Don't worry, you'll get it!"

Pretty soon I see a young woman, way down in front, bringing in a tray with glasses on it. She gives a glass of ice water to Mr. Rogers, she gives a glass of ice water to Mr. Armstrong, she works her way back and forth along the rows of the dais,

* The tang is the male part of the joint; the clevis is the female part (see Figure 13).

Figure 15A. The O-ring ice-water demonstration. (© MARILYNN K. YEE, NYT PICTURES.)

giving ice water to everybody! The poor woman had gotten everything together—jug, glasses, ice, tray, the whole thing—so that everybody could have ice water.

So finally, when I get my ice water, I don't drink it! I squeeze the rubber in the C-clamp, and put them in the glass of ice water.

After a few minutes, I'm ready to show the results of my little experiment. I reach for the little button that activates my microphone.

General Kutyna, who's caught on to what I'm doing, quickly leans over to me and says, "Co-pilot to pilot: not now."

Pretty soon, I'm reaching for my microphone again.

"Not now!" He points in our briefing book—with all the charts and slides Mr. Mulloy is going through—and says, "When he comes to this slide, here, that's the right time to do it."

Finally Mr. Mulloy comes to the place, I press the button for my microphone, and I say, "I took this rubber from the model and put it in a clamp in ice water for a while."

I take the clamp out, hold it up in the air, and loosen it as I talk: "I discovered that when you undo the clamp, the rubber doesn't spring back. In other words, for more than a few seconds, there is no resilience in this particular material when it is at a temperature of 32 degrees. I believe that has some significance for our problem."

Before Mr. Mulloy could say anything, Mr. Rogers says, "That is a matter we will consider, of course, at length in the session that we will hold on the weather, and I think it is an important point which I'm sure Mr. Mulloy acknowledges and will comment on in a further session."

During the lunch break, reporters came up to me and

asked questions like, "Were you talking about the O-ring, or the putty?" and "Would you explain to us what an O-ring is, exactly?" So I was rather depressed that I wasn't able to make my point. But that night, all the news shows caught on to the significance of the experiment, and the next day, the newspaper articles explained everything perfectly.

CHECK SIX!

My cousin Frances educated me about the press. She had been the AP White House correspondent during the Nixon and Ford administrations, and was now working for CNN. Frances would tell me stories of guys running out back doors because they're afraid of the press. From her I got the idea that the press isn't doing anything evil; the reporters are simply trying to help people know what's going on, and it doesn't do any harm to be courteous to them.

I found out that they're really quite friendly, if you give them a chance. So I wasn't afraid of the press, and I would always answer their questions.

Reporters would explain to me that I could say, "Not for attribution." But I didn't want any hocus-pocus. I didn't want it to sound like I'm leaking something. So whenever I talked to the press, I was straight. As a result of this, my name was in the newspaper every day, all over the place!

It seemed like I was always the one answering the reporters' questions. Often the rest of the commissioners would be anxious to go off to lunch, and I'd still be there, answering questions. But I figured, "What's the point of having a public meeting if you run away when they ask you what a word meant?"

When we'd finally get to our lunch, Mr. Rogers would remind us to be careful not to talk to the press. I would say something like, "Well, I was just telling them about the O-rings."

He would say, "That's okay. You've been doing all right, Dr. Feynman; I have no problem with that." So I never did figure out, exactly, what he meant by "not talking to the press."

Being on the commission was rather tense work, so I enjoyed having dinner once in a while with Frances and Chuck, my sister's son, who was working for the *Washington Post*. Because Mr. Rogers kept talking about leaks, we made sure we never said a *word* about anything I was doing. If CNN needed to find out something from me, they'd have to send a different reporter. The same went for the *Post*.

I told Mr. Rogers about my relatives working for the press: "We've agreed not to talk about my work. Do you think there's any problem?"

He smiled and said, "It's perfectly all right. I have a cousin in the press, too. There's no problem at all."

On Wednesday the commission had nothing to do, so General Kutyna invited me over to the Pentagon to educate me on the relationship between the air force and NASA.

It was the first time I had ever been in the Pentagon. There were all these guys in uniform who would take orders—not like in civilian life. He says to one of them, "I'd like to use the briefing room . . ."

"Yes, sir!"

". . . and we'll need to see slides number such-and-such and so-and-so."

"Yes, sir! Yes, sir!"

We've got all these guys working for us while General Kutyna gives me a big presentation in this special briefing room. The slides are shown from the back on a transparent wall. It was really fancy.

General Kutyna would say things like, "Senator So-and-so is in NASA's pocket," and I would say, half-joking, "Don't give me these side remarks, General; you're filling my head! But don't worry, I'll forget it all." I wanted to be naive: I'd find out what happened to the shuttle first; I'd worry about the big political pressures later.

Somewhere in his presentation, General Kutyna observed that everybody on the commission has some weakness because of their connections: he, having worked very closely with NASA personnel in his former position as Air Force Space Shuttle Program manager, finds it difficult, if not impossible, to drive home some of the tougher questions on NASA management. Sally Ride still has a job with NASA, so she can't just say everything she wants. Mr. Covert had worked on the engines, and had been a consultant to NASA, and so on.

I said, "I'm associated with Caltech, but I don't consider that a weakness!"

"Well," he says, "that's right. You're invincible—as far as we can see. But in the air force we have a rule: check six."

He explained, "A guy is flying along, looking in all directions, and feeling very safe. Another guy flies up behind him (at 'six o'clock'—'twelve o'clock' is directly in front), and shoots. Most airplanes are shot down that way. Thinking that you're safe is very dangerous! Somewhere, there's a weakness you've got to find. You must always check six o'clock."

An underling comes in. There's some mumbling about somebody else needing the briefing room now. General Kutyna says, "Tell them I'll be finished in ten minutes."

"Yes, sir!"

Finally, we go out. There, in the hall, are TEN GENERALS waiting to use the room—and I had been sitting in there, getting this personal briefing. I felt great.

For the rest of the day, I wrote a letter home. I began to worry about "check six" when I described Mr. Rogers' reaction to my visiting Frances and Chuck. I wrote,

> ... I was pleased by Rogers' reaction, but now as I write this I have second thoughts. It was too easy—after he explicitly talked about the importance of no leaks etc. at earlier meetings. Am I being set up? (SEE, DARLING, WASHINGTON PARANOIA IS SETTING IN.) ... I think it is possible that there are things in this somebody might be trying to keep me from finding out and might try to discredit me if I get too close. . . . So, reluctantly, I will have to not visit Frances and Chuck any more. Well, I'll ask Fran first if that is too paranoid. Rogers seemed so agreeable and reassuring. It was so easy, yet I am probably a thorn in his side. . . .
>
> Tomorrow at 6:15 am we go by special airplane (two planes) to Kennedy Space Center to be "briefed." No doubt we shall wander about, being shown everything—gee whiz—but no time to get into technical details with any-

body. Well, it won't work. If I am not satisfied by Friday, I
will stay over Sat & Sun, or if they don't work then, Monday
& Tuesday. I am determined to do the job of finding out what
happened—let the chips fall!

   My guess is that I will be allowed to do this, overwhelmed
with data and details . . . , so they have time to soften up
dangerous witnesses etc. But it won't work because (1) I do
technical information exchange and understanding much
faster than they imagine, and (2) I already smell certain rats
that I will not forget, because I just love the smell of rats, for
it is the spoor of exciting adventure.

   I feel like a bull in a china shop. The best thing is to put
the bull out to work on the plow. A better metaphor will
be an ox in a china shop, because the china is the bull, of
course.*

   So, much as I would rather be home and doing something
else, I am having a wonderful time.

   Love,

   Richard

The press was reporting rumors that NASA was under great
political pressure to launch the shuttle, and there were various theories as to where the pressure was coming from. It was
a great big world of mystery to me, with tremendous forces. I
would investigate it, all right, and if I protected myself, nothing would happen. But I hadda watch out.

---

* The thing Feynman was going to break up was the baloney (the
"bull——") about how good everything was at NASA.

GUMSHOES

Finally, early on Thursday morning, we get to Florida. The original idea was that we would go around the Kennedy Space Center at Cape Canaveral and see everything on a guided tour. But because information was coming out in the newspapers so fast, we had a public meeting first.

First, we saw some detailed pictures of the smoke coming out of the shuttle while it was still on the launch pad. There are cameras all over the place watching the launch—something like a hundred of them. Where the smoke came out, there were two cameras looking straight at it—but both failed, curiously. Nevertheless, from other cameras we could see four or five puffs of black smoke coming out from a field joint. This smoke was not burning material; it was simply carbon and mucky stuff that was pushed out because of pressure inside the rocket.

The puffs stopped after a few seconds: the seal got plugged up somehow, temporarily, only to break open again a minute later.

There was some discussion about how much matter came

Figure 16. Detailed picture, taken from the launch pad, of the "smoke." (© NASA.)

out in the smoke. The puffs of smoke were about six feet long, and a few feet thick. The amount of matter depends on how fine the particles are, and there could always be a big piece of glop inside the smoke cloud, so it's hard to judge. And because the pictures were taken from the side, it was possible there was more smoke farther around the rocket.

To establish a minimum, I assumed a particle size that would produce as much smoke as possible out of a given amount of material. It came out surprisingly small—approximately one cubic inch: if you have a cubic inch of stuff, you can get that much smoke.

We asked for pictures from other launches. We found out later that there had never been any puffs of smoke on any previous flights.

We also heard about the low temperatures before the launch from a man named Charlie Stevenson, who was in charge of the ice crew. He said the temperature had gone down to 22 degrees during the night, but his crew got readings as low as 8 degrees at some places on the launch pad, and they couldn't understand why.

During the lunch break, a reporter from a local TV station asked me what I thought about the low temperature readings. I said it seemed to me that the liquid hydrogen and oxygen had chilled the 22-degree air even further as it flowed down the big fuel tank onto the rocket booster. For some reason, the reporter thought I had just told him some important, secret information, so he didn't use my name in his report that evening. Instead, he said, "This explanation comes from a Nobel Prize winner, so it must be right."

In the afternoon, the telemetering people gave us all kinds of information on the last moments of the shuttle. Hundreds of things had been measured, all of which indicated that everything was working as well as it could under the circumstances: the pressure in the hydrogen tank suddenly fell a few seconds after the flame had been observed; the gyros which steer the shuttle were working perfectly until one had to work harder than the other because there were side forces from the flame shooting out of the side of the booster rocket; the main engines even shut themselves down when the hydrogen tank exploded, because there was a pressure drop in the fuel lines.

That meeting lasted until 7:30 in the evening, so we postponed the tour until Friday and went straight to a dinner set up by Mr. Rogers.

At the dinner I happened to be seated next to Al Keel, who had joined the commission on Monday as its executive officer to help Mr. Rogers organize and run our work. He came to us from the White House—from something called the OMB*— and had a good reputation for doing a fine job at this and that. Mr. Rogers kept saying how lucky we were to get somebody with such high qualifications.

One thing that impressed me, though, was that Dr. Keel had a Ph.D. in aerospace, and had done some post-doc work at Berkeley. When he introduced himself on Monday, he joked that the last "honest work" he had done for a living was some aerodynamics work for the shuttle program ten or twelve years ago. So I felt very comfortable with him.

Well, I haven't been talking to Dr. Keel for more than five minutes, when he tells me he's never been so insulted in his

* The Office of Management and Budget.

life, that he didn't take this job to be so insulted, and that he doesn't want to talk to me anymore!

Now, I have a way of not remembering things when I do something dumb or annoying to people, so I forget what I said that put him out. Whatever it was, I thought I was joking, so I was very surprised by his reaction. I had undoubtedly said some boorish, brash, damn-fool thing, which I therefore can't remember!

Then there was a rather tense period of five or ten minutes, with me apologizing and trying to get a conversation going again. We finally got to talking again, somewhat. We were not big friends, but at least there was peace.

On Friday morning, we had another public meeting, this time to hear people from Thiokol and NASA talk about the night before the launch. Everything came out so slowly: the witness doesn't really want to tell you everything, so you have to get the answers out by asking exactly the right questions.

Other guys on the commission were completely awake—Mr. Sutter, for instance. "Exactly what were your quality criteria for acceptance under such-and-such and so-and-so?"—he'd ask specific questions like that, and it would turn out they didn't have any such criteria. Mr. Covert and Mr. Walker were the same way. Everybody was asking good questions, but I was fogged out most of the time, feeling a little bit behind.

Then this business of Thiokol changing its position came up. Mr. Rogers and Dr. Ride were asking two Thiokol managers, Mr. Mason and Mr. Lund, how many people were against the launch, even at the last moment.

"We didn't poll everyone," says Mr. Mason.

"Was there a substantial number against the launch, or just one or two?"

"There were, I would say, probably five or six in engineering who at that point would have said it is not as conservative to go with that temperature, and we don't know. The issue was we didn't know for sure that it would work."

"So it was evenly divided?"

"That's a very estimated number."

It struck me that the Thiokol managers were waffling. But I only knew how to ask simpleminded questions. So I said, "Could you tell me, sirs, the names of your four best seals experts, in order of ability?"

"Roger Boisjoly and Arnie Thompson are one and two. Then there's Jack Kapp and, uh . . . Jerry Burns."

I turned to Mr. Boisjoly, who was right there, at the meeting. "Mr. Boisjoly, were you in agreement that it was okay to fly?"

He says, "No, I was not."

I ask Mr. Thompson, who was also there.

"No, I was not."

I say, "Mr. Kapp?"

Mr. Lund says, "He is not here. I talked to him after the meeting, and he said, 'I would have made that decision, given the information we had.'"

"And the fourth man?"

"Jerry Burns. I don't know what his position was."

"So," I said, "of the four, we have one 'don't know,' one 'very likely yes,' and the two who were mentioned right away as being the *best* seal experts, *both said no.*" So this "evenly split" stuff was a lot of crap. The guys who knew the *most* about the seals—what were *they* saying?

Late in the afternoon, we were shown around the Kennedy Space Center. It was interesting; it wasn't as bad as I had predicted. The other commissioners asked a lot of important questions. We didn't have time to see the booster-rocket assembly, but near the end we were going to see the wreckage that had been recovered so far. I was pretty tired of this group stuff, so I excused myself from the rest of the tour.

I ran down to Charlie Stevenson's place to see more pictures of the launch. I also found out more about the unusually low temperature readings. The guys were very cooperative, and wanted me to work with them. I had been waiting for *ten days* to run around in one of these places, and here I was, *at last!*

At dinner that night, I said to Mr. Rogers, "I was thinking of staying here over the weekend."

"Well, Dr. Feynman," he said, "I'd prefer you come back to Washington with us tonight. But of course, you're free to do whatever you want."

"Well, then," I said, "I'll stay."

On Saturday I talked to the guy who had actually taken the temperature readings the morning of the launch—a nice fella named B. K. Davis. Next to each temperature he had written the exact time he had measured it, and then took a picture of it. You could see large gaps between the times as he climbed up and down the big launch tower. He measured the temperature of the air, the rocket, the ground, the ice, and even a puddle of slush with antifreeze in it. He did a very complete job.

NASA had a theoretical calculation of how the temperatures should vary around the launch pad: they should have been more uniform, and higher. Somebody thought that heat radiating to the clear sky had something to do with it. But then someone else noticed that BK's reading for the slush was much lower than the photograph indicated: at 8 degrees, the slush—even with antifreeze in it—should have been frozen solid.

Then we looked at the device the ice crew used for measuring the temperatures. I got the instruction manual out, and found that you're supposed to put the instrument out in the environment for at least 20 minutes before using it. Mr. Davis said he had taken it out of the box—at 70 degrees—and began making measurements right away. Therefore we had to find out whether the errors were reproducible. In other words, could the circumstances be duplicated?

On Monday I called up the company that made the device, and talked to one of their technical guys: "Hi, my name is Dick Feynman," I said. "I'm on the commission investigating the *Challenger* accident, and I have some questions about your infrared scanning gun . . ."

"May I call you right back?" he says.

"Sure."

After a little while he calls me back: "I'm sorry, but it's proprietary information. I can't discuss it with you."

By this time I realized what the real difficulty was: the company was *scared green* that we were going to blame the accident on their instrument. I said, "Sir, your scanning gun has nothing to do with the accident. It was used by the people here in a way that's contrary to the procedures in your instruction manual, and I'm trying to figure out if we can reproduce the errors and determine what the temperatures really were that morning. To do this, I need to know more about your instrument."

The guy finally came around, and became quite cooperative. With his help, I advised the ice-crew guys on an experiment. They cooled a room down to about 40 degrees, and put a big block of ice in it—with ice, you can be sure the surface temperature is 32 degrees. Then they brought in the scanning gun from a room which was 70 degrees inside, and made measurements of the ice block every 30 seconds. They were able to measure how far off the instrument was as a function of time.

Mr. Davis had written his measurements so carefully that it was very easy to fix all the numbers. And then, remarkably, the recalculated temperatures were close to what was expected according to the theoretical model. It looked very sensible.

The next time I talked to a reporter, I straightened everything out about the temperatures, and informed him that the earlier theory expounded by the Nobel Prize winner was wrong.

I wrote a report for the other commissioners on the temperature problem, and sent it to Dr. Keel.

Then I investigated something we were looking into as a possible contributing cause of the accident: when the booster rockets hit the ocean, they became out of round a little bit from the impact. At Kennedy they're taken apart, and the sections—four for each rocket—are sent by rail to Thiokol in Utah, where they are packed with new propellant. Then they're put back on a train to Florida. During transport, the sections (which are hauled on their side) get squashed a little bit—the softish propellant is very heavy. The total amount of squashing is only a fraction of an inch, but when you put the rocket sections back together, a small gap is enough to let hot gases through: the O-rings are only a quarter of an inch thick, and compressed only two-hundredths of an inch!

I thought I'd do some calculations. NASA gave me all the numbers on how far out of round the sections can get, so I tried to figure out how much the resulting squeeze was, and where it was located—maybe the minimum squeeze was where the leak occurred. The numbers were measurements taken along three diameters, every 60 degrees. But three matching diameters won't guarantee that things will fit; six diameters, or any other number of diameters, won't do, either.

For example, you can make a figure something like a triangle with rounded corners, in which three diameters, 60 degrees apart, have the same length.

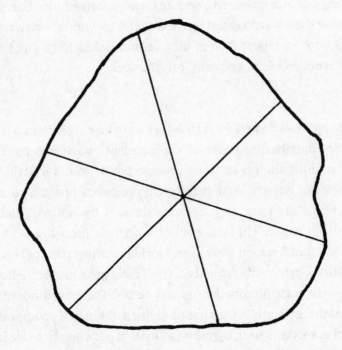

Figure 17. This figure has all its diameters the same length—yet it is obviously not round!

I remembered seeing such a trick at a museum when I was
a kid. There was a gear rack that moved back and forth perfectly smoothly, while underneath it were some noncircular,
funny-looking, crazy-shaped gears turning on shafts that
wobbled. It looked impossible, but the reason it worked was
that the gears were shapes whose diameters were always the
same.

So the numbers NASA gave me were useless.

During that weekend, just as I had predicted in my letter
home, I kept getting notes from the commission headquarters in Washington: "Check the temperature readings, check
the pictures, check this, check that . . ."—there was quite
a list. But as the instructions came in, I had done most of
them already.

One note had to do with a mysterious piece of paper. Someone at Kennedy had reportedly written "Let's go for it" while
assembling one of the solid booster rockets. Such language
appeared to show a certain recklessness. My mission: find that
piece of paper.

Well, by this time I understood how much paper there was
in NASA. I was sure it was a trick to make me get lost, so I did
nothing about it.

Instead, I pursued something surreptitiously.

It was rumored that the reason NASA tried to make the
shuttle fly on January 28th, in spite of the cold, was that the
president was going to give his State of the Union address that
night. According to the theory, the White House had it all
cooked up so that during the State of the Union address, the
teacher, Mrs. McAuliffe, would talk to the president and Con-

gress from space. It was gonna be great: the president would say, "Hello! How are you doing?" And she would say, "Fine"— something very dramatic.

Since it sounded logical, I began by supposing it was very likely possible. But was there any evidence? This kind of thing I didn't know how to investigate. I could only think of this: it's very hard to get through to the president; I also can't just call up an astronaut and talk to her—if she's in space. Therefore, switching the signals down from the shuttle over to the president while he's talking to Congress must be a complicated business.

To find out whether anybody had set up to do that, I went down to the lowest levels and asked guys at the bottom some technical questions.

They showed me the antennas, they told me about the frequencies, they showed me the big radio system and the computer system; they showed me all the ways they did things.

I said, "If you had to send a transmission somewhere else— to Marshall, say—how would you do it?"

They said, "Oh, we're just a relay station. Everything is automatically sent over to Houston, and they switch everything out from there. We don't do any switching here."

So I didn't find any evidence—at least at Kennedy. But the guys there were so nice to me, and everything was so pleasant, that I feel bad. I don't like to cheat people. It was a little sneaky, what I was doing. Nevertheless, I thought I'd better do the same thing when I got to Houston.

On Monday, Mr. Hotz came down to Florida to work with me. (He told me later that he had been sent down with specific instructions to see what I was doing, and to keep me from "going wild.") Mr. Hotz brought a list of things to look into: "There are a lot of things on this list," he said, "so I'd be happy to split the work with you." Some things he said he could do more easily, and the rest of the things I had already done—except for that piece of paper which said "Let's go for it." Mr. Hotz hinted around that it might have come from the diary of someone in the booster-rocket assembly. That wasn't enough of a clue for me; I just wasn't gonna do it. Instead, I went to see a Mr. Lamberth, who had said he wanted to talk to me.

Mr. Lamberth was way up in the works, a big cheese in charge of assembling the solid-rocket boosters. He wanted to tell me about some problems he had. "The workers used to have much better discipline," he explained, "but nowadays they're not like they used to be." He gave me a couple of examples.

The first incident had to do with taking the booster rockets apart after they had been recovered from the sea. The rocket sections are held together by 180 pins—each about an inch and a half in diameter and two inches long—all the way around.

There was some kind of procedure for taking sections apart, in which the workers were supposed to pull the rocket up a certain distance. They had gotten to paying attention only to the amount of *force* they were applying—about 11,000 pounds. That was a better method, from a physical standpoint, because the idea is to take the load off the pins.

One time the force gauge wasn't working right. The workers kept putting more force on, wondering why they weren't reaching 11,000 pounds, when all of a sudden one of the pins broke.

Mr. Lamberth reprimanded the workers for not following procedures. It reminded me of when I tried to make things work better at my aunt's hotel: your method is better than the regular way, but then you have a little accident . . .*

The second story Mr. Lamberth told me had to do with putting the rocket sections together. The regular procedure was to stack one section on top of the other and match the upper section to the lower one.

If a section needed to be reshaped a little bit, the procedure was to first pick up the section with a crane and let it hang sideways a few days. It's rather simpleminded.

If they couldn't make a section round enough by the hanging method, there was another procedure: use the "rounding machine"—a rod with a hydraulic press on one end and a nut on the other—and increase the pressure.

Mr. Lamberth told me the pressure shouldn't exceed 1200 pounds per square inch (psi). One time, a section wasn't round enough at 1200 psi, so the workers took a wrench and began turning the nut on the other end. When they finally got the section round enough, the pressure was up to 1350. "This is another example of the lack of discipline among the workers," Mr. Lamberth said.

I had wanted to talk with the assembly workers anyway (I love that kind of thing), so I arranged to see them the next day at 2:30 in the afternoon.

At 2:30 I walk into this room, and there's a long table with thirty or forty people—they're all sitting there with morose faces, very serious, ready to talk to The Commissioner.

---

* The reference is to Feynman's method of slicing string beans, recounted in *"Surely You're Joking, Mr. Feynman!"*

I was terrified. I hadn't realized my terrible power. I could see they were worried. They must have been told I was investigating the errors they had made!

So right away I said, "I had nothin' to do, so I thought I'd come over and talk to the guys who put the rockets together. I didn't want everybody to stop working just 'cause I wanna find out something for my own curiosity; I only wanted to talk with the workers . . ."

Most of the people got up and left. Six or seven guys stayed—the crew who actually put the rocket sections together, their foreman, and some boss who was higher up in the system.

Well, these guys were still a little bit scared. They didn't really want to open up. The first thing I think to say is, "I have a question: when you measure the three diameters and all the diameters match, do the sections really fit together? It seems to me that you could have some bumps on one side and some flat areas directly across, so the three diameters would match, but the sections wouldn't fit."

"Yes, yes!" they say. "We get bumps like that. We call them nipples."

The only woman there said, "It's got nothing to do with me!"—and everybody laughed.

"We get nipples all the time," they continued. "We've been tryin' to tell the supervisor about it, but we never get anywhere!"

We were talking details, and that works wonders. I would ask questions based on what could happen theoretically, but to them it looked like I was a regular guy who knew about their technical problems. They loosened up very rapidly, and told me all kinds of ideas they had to improve things.

For example, when they use the rounding machine, they have to put a rod through holes exactly opposite each other. There are 180 holes, so they have to make sure the other end of the rod goes through the hole 90 holes away. Now, it turns out you have to climb up into an awkward place to count the holes. It's very slow and very difficult.

They thought it would be very helpful if there were four paint marks, 90 degrees apart, put on at the factory. That way, they would never have to count more than 22 holes to the nearest mark. For example, if they put the rod through a hole which is 9 holes clockwise from a paint mark, then the other end of the rod would go through the hole which is 9 holes clockwise from the opposite mark.

The foreman, Mr. Fichtel, said he wrote a memo with this suggestion to his superiors two years ago, but nothing had happened yet. When he asked why, he was told the suggestion was too expensive.

"Too expensive to paint *four little lines?*" I said in disbelief.

They all laughed. "It's not the paint; it's the paperwork," Mr. Fichtel said. "They would have to revise all the manuals."

The assembly workers had other observations and suggestions. They were concerned that if two rocket sections scrape as they're being put together, metal filings could get into the rubber seals and damage them. They even had some suggestions for redesigning the seal. Those suggestions weren't very good, but the point is, the workers were *thinking!* I got the impression that they were *not* undisciplined; they were very interested in what they were doing, but they weren't being given much encouragement. Nobody was paying much attention to them. It was remarkable that their morale was as high as it was under the circumstances.

Then the workers began to talk to the boss who had stayed. "We're disappointed by something," one of them said. "When the commission was going to see the booster-rocket assembly, the demonstration was going to be done by the managers. Why wouldn't you let *us* do it?"

"We were afraid you'd be frightened by the commissioners and you wouldn't want to do it."

"No, no," said the workmen. "We think we do a good job, and we wanted to show what we do."

After that meeting, the boss took me to the cafeteria. As we were eating—the workmen weren't with us anymore—he said, "I was surprised they were so concerned about that."

Later, I talked to Mr. Fichtel about this incident of increasing the pressure past 1200. He showed me the notes he made as he went along: they weren't the formal papers that are stamped; they were part of an informal but carefully written diary.

I said, "I hear the pressure got up to 1350."

"Yes," he said, "we had tightened the nut at the other end."

"Was that the regular procedure?"

"Oh, yes," he said, "it's in the book."

He opens up the manual and shows me the procedure. It says, "Build up the pressure on the hydraulic jack. If this is insufficient to obtain desired roundness, then very carefully tighten nut on other end to get to the desired roundness"— it said so in black and white! It didn't say that tightening the nut would increase the pressure past 1200 psi; the people who wrote the manual probably weren't quite aware of that.

Mr. Fichtel had written in his diary, "We very carefully tightened the nut"—exactly the same language as the instructions.

I said, "Mr. Lamberth told me he admonished you about going above 1200."

"He never admonished me about that—why should he?"

We figured out what probably happened. Mr. Lamberth's admonishment went down through the levels until somebody in middle management realized that Mr. Fichtel had gone by the book, and that the error was in the manual. But instead of telling Mr. Lamberth about the error, they simply threw away the admonishment, and just kept quiet.

Over lunch, Mr. Fichtel told me about the inspection procedures. "There's a sheet for each procedure, like this one for the rounding procedure," he said. "On it there are boxes for stamps—one from the supervisor, one from quality control, one from the manufacturer, and for the bigger jobs, one from NASA."

He continued, "We make the measurements, go through one course of rounding, and then make the measurements again. If they don't match well enough, we repeat the steps. Finally, when the diameter differences are small enough, we go for it."

I woke up. "What do you mean, 'go for it'?" I said. "It sounds sort of cavalier . . ."

"No, no," he says. "That's just the lingo we use when we mean that all the conditions are satisfied, and we're ready to move to the next phase of the operation."

"Do you ever write that down—that 'go for it'?"

"Yes, sometimes."

"Let's see if we can find a place where you wrote it."

Mr. Fichtel looked through his diary, and found an example. The expression was completely natural to him—it wasn't reckless or cavalier; it was just his way of speaking.

On Monday and Tuesday, while I was running around down at Kennedy, Mr. Rogers was in Washington appearing before a Senate committee. Congress was considering whether it should have its own investigation.

Senator Hollings, from South Carolina, was giving Mr. Rogers a hard time: "Secretary Rogers," he says, "I'm anxious that you have an adequate staff thayah. How many *investigators* does yo' commission have?"

Mr. Rogers says, "We don't have investigators in the police sense. We're reading documents, understanding what they mean, organizing hearings, talking to witnesses—that sort of thing. We'll have an adequate staff, I assure you."

"Well, that's the point," Senator Hollings says. "From my experience in investigating cases, I'd want four or five investigators steeped in science and space technology going around down there at Canaveral talking to everybody, eating lunch with them. You'd be amazed, if you eat in the restaurants around there for two or three weeks, what you'll find out. You can't just sit and read what's given to you."

"We're not just going to sit and read," Mr. Rogers says defensively. "We've gotten a lot of people in a room and asked them questions all at the same time, rather than have a gumshoe walking around, talking to people one at a time."

"I understand," says Senator Hollings. "Yet I'm concerned about yo' product if you don't have some gumshoes. That's the trouble with presidential commissions; I've been on 'em: they go on what's *fed* to 'em, and they don't look behind it. Then we end up with investigative reporters, people writing books, and everything else. People are *still* investigating the Warren Commission Report around this town."*

Mr. Rogers calmly says, "I appreciate your comments, Senator. You'll be interested to know that one of our commission members—he's a Nobel laureate—is down there in Florida today, investigating in the way you'd like him to investigate."

(Mr. Rogers didn't know it, but I was actually eating lunch with some engineers when he said that!)

Senator Hollings says, "I'm not questioning the competence of the Nobel laureate; I've been reading with great interest what he said. There's no question about the competence of the commission itself. It's just that when you investigate a case, you need investigators. You have already brought to the public's attention a lot of very interesting facts, so I think you haven't been negligent in any fashion."

So I saved Mr. Rogers a little bit. He saw that he had an answer for Mr. Hollings by the *good luck* that I stayed in Florida anyway, against his wishes!

* The Warren Report was issued in 1964 by the Warren Commission, headed by retired Supreme Court Chief Justice Earl Warren, which investigated the assassination of President John F. Kennedy.

FANTASTIC FIGURES

On Tuesday afternoon I flew back to Washington, and went to the next meeting of the commission, on Wednesday. It was another public meeting. A manager of the Thiokol Company named Mr. Lund was testifying. On the night before the launch, Mr. Mulloy had told him to put on his "management hat" instead of his "engineering hat," so he changed his opposition to launch and overruled his own engineers. I was asking him some harsh questions when suddenly I had this feeling of the Inquisition.

Mr. Rogers had pointed out to us that we ought to be careful with these people, whose careers depend on us. He said, "We have all the advantages: we're sitting up here; they're sitting down there. They have to answer our questions; we don't have to answer their questions." Suddenly, all this came back to me and I felt terrible, and I couldn't do it the next day. I went back to California for a few days, to recover.

While I was in Pasadena, I went over to JPL and met with Jerry Solomon and Meemong Lee. They were studying the flame which appeared a few seconds before the main fuel tank exploded, and were able to bring out all kinds of details. (JPL has good enhancers of TV pictures from all their experience with planetary missions.) Later, I took the enhancements over to Charlie Stevenson and his crew at Kennedy to expedite things.

Somewhere along the line, somebody from the staff brought me something to sign: it said that my expenses were so-and-so much, but they weren't—they were more. I said, "This is not the amount I actually spent."

The guy said, "I know that, sir; you're only allowed a maximum of $75 a day for the hotel and food."

"Then why did you guys set me up in a hotel which costs $80 or $90 a night, and then you give me only $75 a day?"

"Yes, I agree; it's too bad, but that's the way it goes!"

I thought of Mr. Rogers' offer to put me in a "good hotel." What did he mean by that—that it would cost me *more?*

If you're asked to contribute months of time and effort to the government (and you lose money you would have made consulting for a company), the government ought to appreciate it a little more than to be cheap about paying you back. I'm not trying to make money off the government, but I'm not wanting to *lose* money, either! I said, "I'm not going to sign this."

Mr. Rogers came over and promised he would straighten it out, so I signed the paper.

I really think Mr. Rogers tried to fix it, but he was unable to. I thought of fighting this one to the end, but then I realized it's impossible: if I had been paid for my actual expenses, then of course all the other commissioners would have to be paid, too. That would be all right, but it would also mean that this commission was the only commission to be paid its actual expenses—and pretty soon, word would get out.

They have a saying in New York: "You can't fight City Hall," meaning "It's impossible." But this time, it was a hell of a lot bigger than City Hall: the $75 a day rule is a law of the United States! It might have been fun to fight it to the end, but I guess I was tired—I'm not as young as I used to be—so I just gave up.

Somebody told me they heard commissioners make $1000 a day, but the truth is, our government doesn't even pay their costs.

At the beginning of March, about a month after the commission started, we finally split up into working groups: the Pre-Launch Activities group was headed by Mr. Acheson; Mr. Sutter was in charge of the Design, Development, and Production panel; General Kutyna was leader of the Accident Analysis group; and Dr. Ride was in charge of the Mission Planning and Operations group.

I spent most of my time in Kutyna's group. I was in Ride's group, too, but I ended up not doing very much for her.

General Kutyna's group went to Marshall Space Flight Center in Huntsville, Alabama, to do its work. The first thing that happened there was, a man named Ullian came in to tell us something. As range safety officer at Kennedy, Mr. Ullian had to decide whether to put destruct charges on the shuttle. (If a rocket goes out of control, the destruct charges enable it to be blown up into small bits. That's much less perilous than a rocket flying around loose, ready to explode when it hits the ground.)

Every unmanned rocket has these charges. Mr. Ullian told us that 5 out of 127 rockets that he looked at had failed—a rate of about 4 percent. He took that 4 percent and divided it by 4, because he assumed a manned flight would be safer than an unmanned one. He came out with about a 1 percent chance of failure, and that was enough to warrant the destruct charges.

But NASA told Mr. Ullian that the probability of failure was more like 1 in 10^5.

I tried to make sense out of that number. "Did you say 1 in 10^5?"

"That's right; 1 in 100,000."

"That means you could fly the shuttle *every day* for an average of *300 years* between accidents—every day, one flight, for 300 years—which is obviously crazy!"

"Yes, I know," said Mr. Ullian. "I moved my number up to 1 in 1000 to answer all of NASA's claims—that they were much more careful with manned flights, that the typical rocket isn't a valid comparison, et cetera—and put the destruct charges on anyway."

But then a new problem came up: the Jupiter probe, *Galileo*, was going to use a power supply that runs on heat generated by radioactivity. If the shuttle carrying *Galileo* failed, radioactivity could be spread over a large area. So the argument continued: NASA kept saying 1 in 100,000 and Mr. Ullian kept saying 1 in 1000, at best.

Mr. Ullian also told us about the problems he had in trying to talk to the man in charge, Mr. Kingsbury: he could get appointments with underlings, but he never could get through to Kingsbury and find out how NASA got its figure of 1 in 100,000. The details of the story I can't remember exactly, but I thought Mr. Ullian was doing everything sensibly.

Our panel supervised the tests that NASA was doing to discover the properties of the seals—how much pressure the putty could take, and so on—in order to find out exactly what had happened. General Kutyna didn't want to jump to conclusions, so we went over and over things, checking all the evidence and seeing how well everything fitted together.

There was an awful lot of detailed discussion about exactly what happened in the last few seconds of the flight, but I didn't pay much attention to any of it. It was as though a train had crashed because the track had a gap in it, and we were analyzing which cars broke apart first, which cars broke apart second, and why some car turned over on its side. I figured once the train goes off the track, it doesn't make any difference—it's done. I became bored.

So I made up a game for myself: "Imagine that something else had failed—the main engines, for instance—and we were making the same kind of intensive investigation as we are now: would we discover the same slipping safety criteria and lack of communication?"

I thought I would do my standard thing—find out from the engineers how the engine works, what all the dangers are, what problems they've had, and everything else—and then, when I'm all loaded up so I know what I'm talking about, I'd confront whoever was claiming the probability of failure was 1 in 100,000.

I asked to talk to a couple of engineers about the engines. The guy says, "Okay, I'll fix it up. Is nine tomorrow morning okay?"

This time there were three engineers, their boss, Mr. Lovingood, and a few assistants—about eight or nine people.

Everybody had big, thick notebooks, full of papers, all nicely organized. On the front they said:

REPORT ON MATERIAL GIVEN TO COMMISSIONER
RICHARD P. FEYNMAN ON MARCH WA-WA,* 1986.

I said, "Geez! You guys must have worked hard all night!"

"No, it's not so much work; we just put in the regular papers that we use all the time."

I said, "I just wanted to talk to a few engineers. There are so many problems to work on, I can't expect you all to stay here and talk to me."

But this time, everybody stayed.

Mr. Lovingood got up and began to explain everything to me in the usual NASA way, with charts and graphs which matched the information in my big book—all with bullets, of course.

I won't bother you with all the details, but I wanted to understand everything about the engine. So I kept asking my usual dumb-sounding questions.

After a while, Mr. Lovingood says, "Dr. Feynman, we've been going for two hours, now. There are 123 pages, and we've only covered 20 so far."

My first reaction was to say, "Well, it isn't really going to take such a long time. I'm always a little slow at the beginning; it takes me a while to catch on. We'll be able to go much faster near the end."

But then I had a second thought. I said, "In order to speed

---

* Feynman's way of saying, "whatever it was."

things up, I'll tell you what I'm doing, so you'll know where I'm aiming. I want to know whether there's the same lack of communication between the engineers and the management who are working on the engine as we found in the case of the booster rockets."

Mr. Lovingood says, "I don't think so. As a matter of fact, although I'm now a manager, I was trained as an engineer."

"All right," I said. "Here's a piece of paper each. Please write on your paper the answer to this question: what do you think is the probability that a flight would be uncompleted due to a failure in this engine?"

They write down their answers and hand in their papers. One guy wrote "99-^{44}/$_{100}$% pure" (copying the Ivory soap slogan), meaning about 1 in 200. Another guy wrote something very technical and highly quantitative in the standard statistical way, carefully defining everything, that I had to translate—which also meant about 1 in 200. The third guy wrote, simply, "1 in 300."

Mr. Lovingood's paper, however, said,

Cannot quantify. Reliability is judged from:
- past experience
- quality control in manufacturing
- engineering judgment

"Well," I said, "I've got four answers, and one of them weaseled." I turned to Mr. Lovingood: "I think you weaseled."

"I don't think I weaseled."

"You didn't tell me *what* your confidence was, sir; you told me *how* you determined it. What I want to know is: after you determined it, what *was* it?"

He says, "100 percent"—the engineers' jaws drop, my jaw drops; I look at him, everybody looks at him—"uh, uh, minus epsilon!"

So I say, "Well, yes; that's fine. Now, the only problem is, WHAT IS EPSILON?"

He says, "10^{-5}." It was the same number that Mr. Ullian had told us about: 1 in 100,000.

I showed Mr. Lovingood the other answers and said, "You'll be interested to know that there *is* a difference between engineers and management here—a factor of more than 300."

He says, "Sir, I'll be glad to send you the document that contains this estimate, so you can understand it."*

I said, "Thank you very much. Now, let's get back to the engine." So we continued and, just like I guessed, we went faster near the end. I had to understand how the engine worked—the precise shape of the turbine blades, exactly how they turned, and so on—so I could understand its problems.

---

* Later, Mr. Lovingood sent me that report. It said things like "The probability of mission success is necessarily very close to 1.0"—does that mean it *is* close to 1.0, or it *ought to be* close to 1.0?—and "Historically, this high degree of mission success has given rise to a difference in philosophy between unmanned and manned space flight programs; i.e., numerical probability versus engineering judgment." As far as I can tell, "engineering judgment" means they're just going to make up numbers! The probability of an engine-blade failure was given as a universal constant, as if all the blades were exactly the same, under the same conditions. The whole paper was quantifying everything. Just about every nut and bolt was in there: "The chance that a HPHTP pipe will burst is 10^{-7}." You can't estimate things like that; a probability of 1 in 10,000,000 is almost impossible to estimate. It was clear that the numbers for each part of the engine were chosen so that when you add everything together you get 1 in 100,000.

After lunch, the engineers told me all the problems of the engines: blades cracking in the oxygen pump, blades cracking in the hydrogen pump, casings getting blisters and cracks, and so on. They looked for these things with periscopes and special instruments when the shuttle came down after each flight.

There was a problem called "subsynchronous whirl," in which the shaft gets bent into a slightly parabolic shape at high speed. The wear on the bearings was so terrible—all the noise and the vibration—that it seemed hopeless. But they had found a way to get rid of it. There were about a dozen very serious problems; about half of them were fixed.

Most airplanes are designed "from the bottom up," with parts that have already been extensively tested. The shuttle, however, was designed "from the top down"—to save time. But whenever a problem was discovered, a lot of redesigning was required in order to fix it.

Mr. Lovingood isn't saying much now, but different engineers, depending on which problem it is, are telling me all this stuff, just like I could have found out if I went down to the engineers at Thiokol. I gained a great deal of respect for them. They were all very straight, and everything was great. We went all the way down to the end of the book. We made it.

Then I said, "What about this high-frequency vibration where some engines get it and others don't?"*

---

* I had heard about this from Bill Graham. He said that when he was first on the job as head of NASA, he was looking through some reports and noticed a little bullet: "·4,000 cycle vibration is within our data base." He thought that was a funny-looking phrase, so he began asking questions. When he got all the way through, he discovered it was a rather serious mat-

There's a quick motion, and a little stack of papers appears. It's all put together nicely; it fits nicely into my book. It's all about the 4000-cycle vibration!

Maybe I'm a little dull, but I tried my best not to accuse anybody of anything. I just let them show me what they showed me, and acted like I didn't see their trick. I'm not the kind of investigator you see on TV, who jumps up and accuses the corrupt organization of withholding information. But I was fully aware that they hadn't told me about the problem until I asked about it. I usually acted quite naive—which I was, for the most part.

At any rate, the engineers all leaped forward. They got all excited and began to describe the problem to me. I'm sure they were delighted, because technical people love to discuss technical problems with technical people who might have an opinion or a suggestion that could be useful. And of course, they were very anxious to cure it.

They kept referring to the problem by some complicated name—a "pressure-induced vorticity oscillatory wa-wa," or something.

I said, "Oh, you mean a whistle!"

"Yes," they said; "it exhibits the characteristics of a whistle."

They thought the whistle could be coming from a place where the gas rushed through a pipe at high speed and split into three smaller pipes—where there were two partitions. They explained how far they had gotten in figuring out the problem.

---

ter: some of the engines would vibrate so much that they couldn't be used. He used it as an example of how difficult it is to get information unless you go down and check on it yourself.

across the board and hence high inflation that offsets the wage gains. In practice, unions do not seem to take account of these effects, probably because the rank and file will accept moderate demands only when the bargaining is centralized so that everyone can see that others are not getting more.

In addition to definite settlements, many contracts contain conditional clauses, stipulating that if event X occurs then Y will automatically also happen. The triggering event X can be a certain level of inflation, a certain level of negotiated wage increase or wage drift for workers in other unions, changes in the income tax or some more complex construction. Thus in the 1983 bargaining round, private functionaries and their employers agreed that if the wage increases obtained by other unions contributed to an inflation in excess of the government's goal of 4 per cent, either party could call for renegotiation. In a striking display of the art of having it both ways, the functionaries also demanded and got the right to renegotiate if other workers were to get an increase in their real wage as a result of an inflation rate *below* 4 per cent. 'The agreement contained protecting clauses for almost any conceivable change in the environment'.[21] The event Y that is triggered off can be a straightforward wage increase or, as in these examples, a right to renegotiate the agreement.

Often, agreements dump problems onto the future. The conditional clauses that trigger renegotiating rather than any specific outcome are one example. A constant headache are the so-called overhangs, agreed-upon wage increases that do not take effect until after the expiration of the contract period. In the next bargaining round the parties then have to decide whether the negotiated wage increase will come on top of the overhang from the preceding period or whether the overhang will be counted as part of the increase. If the employers do not concede to a claim made by the union, the latter can save face by obtaining a promise to pursue the matter in later negotiations. When a framework for wage drift is decided centrally, the implementation is left to plant-level bargaining. The framework being a guideline rather than a set of explicit instructions, it will, in fact, not bind the local bargaining. In practice, the suggested average turns into a floor. If agreements are silent, vague or ambiguous on such points, they are so deliberately, not by accident. Ambiguity is intentionally used to achieve agreement.

---

[21] Elvander (1988), p. 105.

The government enters multiply into the collective bargaining process. First, governments of various political persuasions have tried to achieve 'combined settlements', by offering tax rebates in return for moderate wage claims.[22] Second, Labour governments have a special relationship with LO that, depending on circumstances, can make it easier or more difficult to impose moderation. On the one hand, there is the 'Nixon–China' effect. Only a politician with unimpeachable hard-line credentials could 'give up' Taiwan. Similarly, a socialist government that asks for moderation in the national interest is less suspect of being the extended arm of business. On the other hand, of course, the socialist party depends on the vote and support of blue-collar workers. Third, the government plays an important role as employer in the public sector. This can also affect bargaining in the private sector, if unions anticipate that unemployment caused by high wage claims will be absorbed by the public sector.[23] Finally, the government can enter into the final stage of bargaining as mediator and arbitrator. Arbitration occurs only at the demand of the parties. In theory, the arbitrators will only try to find a compromise between the parties, and not take account of the wider economic interests of the country. In practice, the government is rarely able to pull its punches and abstain from using the arbitration mechanism to further these interests. Needless to say, this danger of role confusion is especially large in the public sector.[24]

The political system affects bargaining in still another way, since unions often have a choice between collective bargaining and legislation to promote their claims. In the 1964 bargaining round, the union claims included, in addition to wage demands, measures concerning layoffs, dismissals and reemployment. 'The bargaining over the security measures was conducted under the threat that LO might turn to legislative measures. This might give a less favourable solution, and also reduce the value of these issues as bargaining chips in the wage negotiations'.[25] The value of this threat depends, obviously, on the cost to LO of using its political clout. In principle, the 'Swedish model' is defined by a hands-off attitude of the political authorities. Labour and capital are supposed to solve their problems without interference by the state.[26] In practice, the close links between LO and the Social Democratic governments have ensured unions a

---

[22] Contrary to a claim that is sometimes made, the government does not use welfare policy as a carrot for the unions. There may be an overall correlation between wage moderation and a highly developed welfare state, but the causal mechanism is not that of a simple quid pro quo.

[23] Flanagan (1987), pp. 160–1.   [24] Sjölund (1987), pp. 22–3.

[25] de Geer (1986), p. 190.   [26] Elvander (1988), ch. 1, and passim.

privileged access to the political arena. Nevertheless, even socialist politicians are reluctant to be seen as too closely linked with the unions; also, they do not want to be responsible for excessively costly measures. Two years later, SAF decided to call LO's bluff in a similar situation, when LO demanded better conditions for sickness pay and added that a proposal for legislation had already been written up. SAF assessed, however, that politicians might be less than enthusiastic over the reform, which promised to be quite costly.

The final element in this thumb-nail description of the Swedish system concerns the offensive and defensive weapons at the disposal of the parties.[27] On the offensive side, the threat of legislation has just been mentioned. The key offensive weapons, however, are strikes and lock-outs. Strikes are not legal in local bargaining, nor, as a rule, in the sectoral negotiations that implement central agreements. Other things being equal, each party naturally prefers to use its weapons in a way that hurts the other party maximally and itself as little as possible. The refusal to work overtime, for instance, hurts workers relatively little but is often very damaging to firms. When unions in the public sector pick a subset of workers to strike, they choose strategically important groups such as doctors or customs officers. When public-sector employers declare lock-out, they often choose teachers as the target, presumably because the short-term damage caused by the closing of schools is deemed small. In fact, the state can even benefit, through lower wage payments. On the defensive side, the strike funds of both parties are an important determinant of bargaining power, as is membership size on the union side. Strike funds determine the credibility of threats, while the size of the membership determines their effectiveness. A brief summary of the LO–SAF negotiations over the past thirty years is presented in Table 4.1.[28]

Labour–capital bargaining

The topic of this section is bargaining between organized labour and organized capital and the problems of collective action that arise out of such

[27] The discussion of 'normative' weapons is postponed until Chapter 6.

[28] From Calmfors and Forslund (1988). A similar, more detailed survey of Norwegian collective bargaining from 1961 through 1986 is found in Norges Offentlige Utredninger (1988), pp. 182–201. The Norwegian and Swedish collective bargaining systems, while similar in most respects, also differ in some features. The role of compulsory arbitration is, for instance, much greater in Norway. A comparative study of the two systems might yield valuable insights into which institutional features affect the outcome of bargaining (and how they do so).

Table 4.1. *Wage contracts for blue-collar workers*

Year	Contract
1960–1	Two-year central agreement
1962–3	Two-year central agreement
1964–5	Two-year central agreement
1966–8	Three-year central agreement; earnings development guarantee
1969–70	Two-year central agreement; earnings development guarantee
1971–3	Three-year central agreement; earnings development guarantee
1974	One-year central agreement; earnings development guarantee; agreement on wage restraint in exchange for elimination of fiscal drag and increased payroll taxes
1975–6	Two-year central agreement; earnings development guarantee; agreement on wage restraint in exchange for elimination of fiscal drag and increased payroll taxes
1977	One-year central agreement; automatic compensation of consumer price inflation above threshold; earnings development guarantee
1978–9	Two-year central agreement; right to new negotiations without peace obligation if consumer price inflation above thresholds; earnings development guarantee
1980	One-year central agreement; earnings development guarantee; price freeze to facilitate wage negotiations; failed attempt on part of government to exchange tax reductions for negotiated wage increases
1981–2	Two-year central agreement; earnings development guarantee; automatic compensation if consumer price inflation above threshold
1983	One-year central agreement on general frame; central agreement did not encompass the engineering industry; industry negotiations without peace obligation; earnings development guarantee
1984	No central agreement; industry bargaining; engineering and steel industries key sectors; most contracts of one-year duration; earning development guarantees; tax scale adjustment and temporary freezing of profits to meet union demands; temporary price freeze
1985	One-year central agreement on frame; industry negotiations without peace obligation; earnings development guarantee; tax rebate to facilitate central agreement; freezing of profits in 'renewal funds'; price freeze to affect negotiations in engineering industry
1986–8	Two-year central agreement; earnings development guarantee; right to new negotiations without peace obligation if consumer price inflation above threshold; temporary price freeze when unions abstained from demanding compensation for price increases
1988	No central agreement; industry bargaining; engineering industry key sector

bargaining. Before the parties can bargain, however, they have to solve another collective action problem, namely how to organize themselves. Claus Offe and Helmut Wiesenthal argue that there is an asymmetry between workers and captialists in their ability to organize, partly because of